SHAKESPEARE, LOVE AND SERVICE

Peter Laslett's comment, in *The World We Have Lost*, that in the early modern period, "every relationship could be seen as a love-relationship" presents the governing idea of this book. In an analysis that includes Shakespeare's sonnets and a wide range of his plays from *The Comedy of Errors* to *The Winter's Tale*, David Schalkwyk looks at the ways in which the personal, affective relations of love are informed by the social, structural interactions of service. Showing that service is not a "class" concept but rather that it determined the fundamental conditions of identity across the whole society, the book explores the interpenetration of structure and affect in relationships as varied as monarch and subject, aristocrat and personal servant, master and slave, husband and wife, and lover and beloved in light of differences of rank, gender, and sexual identity.

DAVID SCHALKWYK is professor of English and deputy dean of the Faculty of Humanities at the University of Cape Town and was head of the English Department from 2000 to 2003. He received a Solmson Research Fellowship at the Humanities Institute of the University of Wisconsin–Madison (1999) and a Mandela UCT-Harvard Fellowship at the Du Bois Institute for African and African-American Studies at Harvard University (2005). His books include a translation of Karel Schoeman's novel, *'n Ander Land* (as *Another Country*, 1991), *Speech and Performance in Shakespeare's Sonnets and Plays* (Cambridge, 2002), and *Literature and the Touch of the Real* (2004). He has published many articles on topics ranging from Shakespeare and literary philosophy to South African prison writing. He has recently been awarded an A rating as an internationally recognized researcher by the National Research Foundation of South Africa.

SHAKESPEARE, LOVE AND SERVICE

DAVID SCHALKWYK

University of Cape Town

CAMBRIDGE
UNIVERSITY PRESS

CAMBRIDGE UNIVERSITY PRESS

Cambridge, New York, Melbourne, Madrid, Cape Town, Singapore, São Paulo, Delhi, Dubai, Tokyo

Cambridge University Press
The Edinburgh Building, Cambridge CB2 8RU, UK

Published in the United States of America by Cambridge University Press, New York

www.cambridge.org
Information on this title: www.cambridge.org/9780521886390

First published 2008
Reprinted 2010

Printed in the United Kingdom at the University Press, Cambridge

A catalog record for this publication is available from the British Library.

Library of Congress Cataloging in Publication Data

Schalkwyk, David.
Shakespeare, love and service / David Schalkwyk.
p.   cm.
Includes bibliographical references and index.
ISBN-13: 978-0-521-88639-0 (hardback)
1. Shakespeare, William, 1564–1616 – Criticism and interpretation.   2. Shakespeare, William,
1564–1616 – Philosophy.   3. Love in literature.   4. Interpersonal relations in literature.   5. Master
and servant in literature.   6. Social structure in literature.   7. Sex role in literature.   8. Gender
identity in literature.   I. Title.
PR3069.L6S36   2008
822.3′3–dc22   2007043540

ISBN 978-0-521-88639-0 hardback

For my students, and to Robert Weimann

Contents

Acknowledgments

This book emerged out of an earlier project on the performative dimensions in Shakespeare's sonnets and plays, published as *Speech and Performance in Shakespeare's Sonnets and Plays*. Throughout my work on performatives and their social and personal situations, I was struck by the fact that a great majority of the relationships with which I was dealing grappled with the affective entanglements of love, but they also almost invariably did so from relationships of mastery and service. Love and service seemed to inform a large number of the relationships represented across Shakespeare's oeuvre. I then encountered Peter Laslett's declaration that in the early modern world, every relationship of service could be considered a relationship of love, and this project was born.

As I began my investigations, which took me into social history, contemporary conduct books, and the history and philosophy of love in its various forms of *eros, nomos, philia*, and *agapē*, I discovered an urgent interest in the early modern dimensions of service pursued by scholars who, despite their own pressing research projects and my embarrassing ignorance, afforded me unstinting help, encouragement, and stimulating engagement. I am especially indebted to two of them, David Evett and Michael Neill, whose generosity has in every way been boundless and which I cannot hope to repay. Others whose careful reading and responses to various aspects of my text and with whom conversations helped shape this book include Debbie Aarons, Anston Bosman, Stephen Curtis, Tony Dawson, Heather Dubrow, Stephen Greenblatt, Richard Hillman, Jacques Lezra, Lynne Magnusson, Lesley Marx, John Parker, Catherine Robson, Rocelle le Roux, Paul Yachnin, Stephen Watson, and Susanne Wofford. Tom Bishop, Lars Engle, and Ewan Fernie responded immediately as friends and critics to cries for help and of

The text of Shakespeare's sonnets used in this book is the facsimile of the 1609 Quarto reproduced in *Shakespeare's Sonnets*, ed. Stephen Booth (New Haven, CT, and London: Yale University Press, 1978). Quotations from the plays are from *The Oxford Shakespeare*, ed. Stanley Wells and Gary Taylor (Oxford: Oxford University Press, 1987).

despondency. Ruth Morse has been an indispensable guide. Sarah Stanton of Cambridge University Press has shown patience and encouragement beyond the call of duty, and I thank the two anonymous readers of the Press for the thoroughness and helpfulness of their comments. Finally, although he has not read a word of this book, I wish to record my debt to Robert Weimann. The spirit of his work over the past two decades informs everything I have written here, and although he will doubtless disagree with me on some, if not many, points, this project could not have been written in its present shape without his example.

Earlier versions of parts of Chapters 2 and 5 appeared in *Shakespeare in Southern Africa* 17 (2006), of Chapter 2 in *Shakespeare International Yearbook* 5 (2005), and of Chapter 4 in *Shakespeare Quarterly* 56.1 (2005).

I was given time and financial support to complete this book by the University of Cape Town, the National Research Foundation of South Africa, and an indispensable Mandela UCT-Harvard Fellowship at the W. E. B. Du Bois Institute for African and African-American Studies at Harvard University. My thanks to Lisa Gregory and to Henry Louis Gates of the institute for their help and hospitality. Christina, Andrew, and James have again offered encouragement, support, and love.

Introduction

This book examines the interaction of two concepts. Both of them are messy. One is ostensibly a universal aspect of the human condition, the other a historically specific form of social organisation. Both are central to Shakespeare's work. Love, as the ordinary person exposed to the culture of the West in the twenty-first century would understand it, is the driving force in more than half his plays, his complete sonnet cycle, and, arguably, all of his nondramatic poems. Service is the informing condition of everything he wrote. If we put love and service together, every symbolic act that Shakespeare committed to paper or through performance may be said to be "about" this interaction. Shakespeare's mimetic art depends in the deepest sense of the word on the conjunctive play of love and service.

This fact involves two almost insurmountable difficulties for a scholarly monograph. First, it demands a principle of selection that cannot be determined by the concepts themselves, severally or jointly. Second, it presents a difficulty that is now the defining parameter of early modern scholarship: how do we relate a concept now so distant from Western, twentieth-century forms of social and personal life as to be barely recognisable to one that we instantly claim as our own?

CONCEPTS

Before I answer that question, let me tackle the messiness of the concepts. Scientific or scholarly argument depends upon the organisation of concepts in a rational format such that the concepts themselves do not move or slide out of place. A recent study of an issue not unrelated to my own sets out to find a "common denominator" to explain why certain attitudes to concepts and their referents in early modern Europe – beggary and theatrical players – were systematically conjoined.[1] The author assumes that beggars

---

[1] Pugliatti, *Beggary*, 2.

I

and players were related in a series of criminal statutes because the concepts pertaining to each are united by a common factor or core meaning, or that their apparent differences may be reduced to a set of attitudes that discerned the same essential ingredients in each. I do not wish to criticise such an approach so much as point out the difference of its method from my own. Each has its virtues. In my attempts to trace the patterns of love and service in both Shakespeare's work and its context, I have found two things. First, that although the two concepts are inextricably imbricated both in literary texts and in their conditions of production, neither of the concepts can be reduced to the other in any universal or consistent way. This is to say, love cannot be shown to be the same as service, nor can service be said to be "really" love, even though, in almost every instance of their embodiment or representation, they can be shown to be coterminous in some way. Nor is there any set of sufficient or necessary conditions that can be shown to join the concepts through a common denominator. Both concepts are constituted by what Wittgenstein called "family resemblances": each is made up of different strands that overlap each other in different places and for varying lengths, their concurrence being constituted by multiple and varying conjunctions, like the fibres of a rope.[2] No unifying fibre runs along the whole length, joining them via a common core.

Wittgenstein's metaphor of the conceptual relations as the fibres that constitute a rope has synchronic and diachronic aspects. The continuity of the rope suggests a certain degree of historical connection: the strands continue from one point to another, in the ways that the words "love" or "service" are used in the twenty-first century, the sixteenth, the fourteenth, or in Greek in 300 B.C. The fact that neither the strands nor their precise points of overlap coincide at each of these diachronic points indicates that continuity is not so much disrupted as constituted by differences. The respective family resemblances that make up the relationships within and between the two concepts will not be the same at each point in time. This is rendered especially complex (or messy) by the fact that each diachronic point is likely to be marked by a *variety* of related uses of the same word. It is not merely a matter of figuring out what "love" meant in Plato's time and then relating that to what it meant when Petrarch was writing his *Canzoniere*, and then to what it meant when Shakespeare wrote sonnet 116, and, finally, what it means in a twenty-first-century sitcom; or what "service" meant to Aristotle, and then to Pope Gregory, and subsequently to Lord Hunsdon, or to George Bush, or what the relationship between these

---

[2] Wittgenstein, *Books*, 17 passim.

two terms (if any) might have been at each point. The words would have meant different things at each time because they would have *used* differently, although it would doubtlessly be possible to relate such uses to each other in some way. This is why I claim that these are two *messy* concepts, but they may be no messier than any other concept used in the hurly-burly of human life. Wittgenstein remarks that concepts have the indefiniteness of human life because it is in the messy interactions of human life that they receive and pursue their vivacity: in varieties of practice, use, and abuse – not in any ideal system or structure.[3] This book is an attempt to make some sense of that messiness in the work of one poet and dramatist who self-consciously represented himself as a lover and bowed to the necessity of being a servant.

SERVICE: THE WORLD WE HAVE LOST

Until the recent proliferation of books and articles on master-servant relations in Shakespeare's England, the topic was almost completely ignored. Even twenty years after the great theoretical and political turn in Shakespeare studies of the 1980s, the only sustained work on what is now beginning to be recognized as the *predominant* form of social organization and personal experience in early modern England – service – was largely confined to two critics. Mark Thornton Burnett led the way with *Masters and Servants in English Renaissance Drama and Culture,* a compendious, scholarly account of the master-servant relations chiefly in the non-Shakespearean canon and popular literature. Drawing directly on the prevailing currents of the new historicism and cultural materialism and an impressive array of primary archival material, Burnett's monograph appeared a full decade after the new, politically conscious forms of critical writing had been established. Michael Neill followed shortly with a rich and perceptive series of essays – more questioning of prevailing modes of historicism – in which he established the centrality of master-servant relations to Shakespeare's great tragedies, *King Lear, Othello,* and *Hamlet* and in imaginative literature and social experience more generally.[4] Then, simultaneously in 2005, three critics who had earlier published discretely, even tentatively, on the topic released significant monographs on service in Shakespeare's plays: David Evett, with *The Discourses of Service in Shakespeare's England*; Judith Weil, with *Service and Dependency in Shakespeare's*

---

[3] Wittgenstein, *Psychology 2*, 652: "If a concept depends upon a pattern of life, then there must be some indefiniteness in it."

[4] Neill, *History*, "*Servile Ministers*", "His Master's Ass", and "A Woman's Service".

Plays; and Linda Anderson with *Shakespeare's Servants*. In the same year, the *Shakespeare International Yearbook*, with Neill as its guest editor, devoted its annual special section to "Shakespeare and the bonds of service". In a single year, the master-servant relation in Shakespeare's dramatic works had come of age – it was finally recognized as a major issue in its own right.

Critics and theorists may have overlooked the lived textures of these relations either because they seemed too obvious to deserve commentary or because an overriding concern with relations of power had obscured the possibility of affective interactions between masters and servants. In Shakespeare especially, master-servant relationships assume intimate, multifaceted, affective, and playful forms that cannot be reduced to mere relations of power and subordination or resentful resistance. In his recent study, Evett takes issue with the exclusive materialist interest in power, exploitation, and group politics by focusing on Shakespeare's representation of the individual subject's phenomenological experience of service as an act of will. He argues that a received theoretical and ideological inclination to discount personal aspects of what appear to be merely economic or legal forms of exploitation has rendered the human textures of Shakespeare's dramatic and poetic relationships critically uninteresting or even politically questionable.[5] The new recognition of the multilayered human quality of service has thus exposed a degree of theoretically induced myopia in prevailing assumptions and critical practice.

The need to find a place in our critical discourse for affect, ethics, and agency does not mean that we should abandon our search for the historical conditions of Shakespeare's texts, still less that we should ignore their embodiment of material conditions of existence and asymmetrical forms of power. Yet we do need to rethink the terms of our enquiry. The investigation of service in Shakespeare's England requires the recovery of what Laslett memorably calls "the world we have lost".[6] There is an otherness to the social and conceptual relations of that world that is in danger of being obliterated by our own historically and culturally conditioned experiences and professional preoccupations, despite the fact that historicism has been the major driving force of our discipline for at least twenty years. These are the questions: how do we best engage in that recuperation? What sets the "sociological imagination" in literary studies apart from what Laslett calls "statistical awareness", or rather, how may the two be combined to

---

[5] Interest in affect is growing, however, even if it tends to be confined to the recovery of the historical strangeness of the affective psychology of the early modern period. See Paster, *Body*, and Rowe et al., *Passions*.

[6] Laslett, *World*.

overcome the sense of acute alienation from and uncertainty about the *human* world of the past that he records from his position as a social historian (*World*, 88)?[7] Despite Laslett's scepticism about the capacity of literary texts to represent that world, the affective and imaginative scope of such texts as embodiments of what Raymond Williams calls the "structures of feeling" of a period invites us to inhabit them *as if* they were part of our lives. They demand a combination of historical imagination and present engagement.[8]

There is a paradoxical tendency to judge writers who are historically different from us from the perspectives of present political values. All too often, the question directed at such texts is whether they are genuinely subversive or not. This tendency is paradoxical because it insists in being ahistorical in the name of history. The text is expected to have leapt beyond its historical constraints to conform to our settled ideas of political progressiveness, in anticipation of unreasonable presentist demands.[9] Service and its strange connection with love in early modern England – and even more peculiarly in Shakespeare – needs to be taken on its own terms to be fully and critically appreciated. The otherness of the interaction between service and love marks our distance from Shakespeare and his world. We stand at a double remove from both concepts. Service has either been alienated by its reduction in a post-capitalist world to the faux choices of the hamburger emporium or the empty smile at the bank counter (as in the "service industry"), or it has come to be seen as the abstract embodiment of economic exploitation and abuse of power.

LOVE: THE WORD WE HAVE LOST

Love has not fared much better. Reduced to the mawkish sentimentality of popular journalism or appropriated by apolitical readings of Shakespeare in the middle of the twentieth century, love – the word and the concept – has all but disappeared from current critical discourse. When I asked a colleague why this should be so, he answered: "Because love is not a critical concept." He is right. The word is impossibly general and vague. It's messy.

---

[7] "The historical observer in an enquiry of this sort can only feel himself to be in the position of a scientist in his bathyscope, miles beneath the surface of the sea, concentrating his gaze for a moment or two on the few strange creatures who happen to stray out of the total darkness into the beam of light" (Laslett, *World*, 76).

[8] Williams, *Marxism*, 128 passim.

[9] For the current debate between "presentists" and "historicists", see Hawkes, *Present*; Fernie, "Presentism"; Grady and Hawkes, *Presentist Shakespeares*; and the current round-table discussion on presentism in the SHAKSPER discussion group: www.shaksper.net.

We are more comfortable with concepts such as power and desire, which, now thoroughly theorized, have promised to strip love of its obfuscating murkiness and mawkishness. They have enabled us to shift our attention from a relatively naïve and commonsense interest in feeling and morality to the structural conditions which allow such feelings to be manipulated in relations of power and subjection.

"Desire" and "power" thus promise entry into the history and politics of sexual relations that "love" positively debars. Their critical keenness gives them the capacity to reveal the structural reality underlying talk of love. We need to take care when we perform reductions of one concept to another, however. Such transformations, whereby one argues that "love is not love"[10] – it is actually desire, a formation of power, an ideological obfuscation of real relations, and so on – run the risk of simplifying or distorting the concept as it does its work in complex interactions, such as those in Shakespeare's poetry and plays.[11] Such reductions may be analytically illuminating, but when they attain a certain level of generality and supplant the original concept, they lose more than they gain. Using a method committed to an historical understanding of texts, we have replaced words that Shakespeare uses with special frequency with ones that he does not use particularly often, the theoretical inflections of which he would have found strange.

It is important to see why in recent years we have tended to shun "love" in favour of "desire" or "eros".[12] Apart from the critical softness of the concept, love has been tainted by its association with the uncritical sentiments of popular culture and, more specifically, by its idealist employment by Shakespearean critics writing before the 1980s: as a way of rising above the

---

[10] Marotti, "Love is not Love".

[11] But see Rose, *Expense of Spirit*, who made this point twenty years ago: "'Love is not love,' writes a recent critic.... Yet to assume that political power is more real – more worthy of analysis – than sexual love and marriage is to ignore the equivalence given to an analogy and to overlook the mixed, complex, and overlapping nature of public and private experience ... whatever else it may be, love, definitely, is love" (11).

[12] There are plenty of works on "eroticism", "desire", or "sexuality", but virtually nothing on love. Where love is used, it is soon transformed into desire and used as no more than an elegant variation. See, for example, Catherine Belsey, "Love in Venice" in *Shakespeare and Gender*, which promises a discussion of love in the title but soon replaces the word with "desire" in the body of the text, and Dympna Callaghan, who, in "The Ideology of Romantic Love", argues that romantic love is a signal instance of ideological misrecognition. Love in Shakespeare as a general topic or rubric has tended to be displaced by the concept of *gender*, as in *Shakespeare and Gender*, and it reappears in the title of many recent books as "eroticism". Exceptions to this trend, and perhaps sign of a revival of the concept of love, are Maurice Charney, *Shakespeare on Love and Lust*, and Alan Bloom, *Shakespeare on Love and Friendship*. See also Mary Beth Rose, *Expense*, who declares in her 1988 book that "whatever else it may be, love, definitely, is love" (11).

trammelling conditions of social, political, and economic relations.[13] Yet this is no reason for more historically or materialistically inclined critics to abandon or shun the word or to substitute for its range of meanings other concepts that are related to but not identical to it. I explore ways in which love is indeed connected to social concerns – to the inequalities of political or economic power – to show that it offers no transcendental escape from these concerns. I also want to show, however, that love is concerned not just with the absences and inequities of desire. It also seeks the pleasures of intimacy, engages in the delights of reciprocity, and finds both pleasure and pain in living for another.[14]

In Shakespeare's time, this combination of reciprocity and subordination in love was part of a set of relationships that extended from the most menial master and servant to monarch and subject, including the most powerful figures within the peerage: service. One of the methodological strengths of combining love and service as the double lenses of analysis lies in the way the concepts complement each other in the weight that they give to what, with due care, we might call the public and the private, or the personal and the structural. Whereas love pulls us in the direction of individualized affect, service reminds us of the historical and social networks in which affect is shaped and has to find expression. Each negotiation happens at the intersection of these concepts. This reminds us, in the wake of sonnet 129, that the negotiations between power and powerlessness, desire and lack, involve not just "spirit" in the physical sense of the word but also its ramifying moral, affective, and volitional aspects.[15] The sonnet reminds us that "waste" is as much a bodily place as a lamentable diminution of humane resources, "heaven" and "hell" conditions in which the physical, moral, and spiritual cannot be separated from each other.[16]

One of the apparent advantages of reducing love to desire lies in the considerable narrowing and thus simplification of these relations in the reduced concept. Following Theodore Leinwand's exemplary discussion of affect in a different context, we need to see love not as a single state but as a complex of interwoven orientations to the self and the world, embodied in forms of action rather than confined to the inscrutability of an interior affect. Leinwand calls attention to Wittgenstein's argument that "a complex

---

[13] See, for example, John Russell Brown, *Shakespeare and His Comedies*, published in 1957, 2nd ed. 1962, and reprinted in 1964, 1968, and 1970, which treats love as a central, transcendent theme of the romantic comedies, and Alexander Legatt, *Shakespeare's Comedy of Love*.

[14] In doing so, I'm following the footsteps of Evett's pathbreaking study of service in Shakespeare.

[15] Evett, in *Discourses*, is a pioneering text in this respect.

[16] See Fernie, *Spiritual Shakespeares*.

emotion . . . is less an irrecoverable, private inner, state than it is a response deeply implicated in the social world, 'a pattern which recurs, with different variations, in the weave of our life'".[17] The "weave of our life" means for Wittgenstein the ways in which words are connected through the relational practices of social life. "Love" is not merely a value produced within an abstract system of differences but is constituted out of its changing, lived relations with concepts such as desire and friendship, as well as tenderness and anger, indignation and generosity, want and repletion, satisfaction and resentment, pleasure and pain, exultation and grief. To trace and recover the strands of this text is an enormous task, even in the manifold of a single speech, a couple of lines of dialogue, or a telling silence. The advantage of working with literary texts, especially drama, is that they have the capacity to mobilise the same weave of life and language that constitutes the lived world from which they draw their material.

It takes an effort of the imagination to recover and inhabit the relationship between love and service in Shakespeare's work. It requires the capacity to recover not only the original resonances of these concepts individually but also the ways in which peculiar modes of social organization and personal intimacy made them work together and sound off each other. Love and service informed Shakespeare's daily life in both his personal and professional relations; they characterized the realities and fantasies of the people around him; and they were passed on in differently inflected forms by literary, performative, and imaginary conditions that formed the traditions from which he drew both his imaginative and his social life. Being part of existence as it was lived and represented at a particular time and place, they share the indeterminacy – the play – of life itself. As the vehicles of meaning in a complexly transforming world they are inhabited, used, resisted, and changed in ways that are critical in their own terms rather than matching the fantasies or demands of historically specific political value.

My investigation of service in Shakespeare's plays is organised by conceptual affinities and differences as they are worked out in the dramatic contexts of interaction. It assumes that the practices that underlay the use of concepts such as service in both Shakespeare's society and his imaginative work maintain a connection with us via the historical continuity of language. It also examines the way in which, in both present and historical use, the concept of service is intertwined with other concepts with which it bears a family resemblance through common forms of social and linguistic practice. Exploring in the concept of service the simultaneous product of

---

[17] Leinwand, *Theatre*, 3.

situated social practice and the *longue durée* of language as an inherited and changing system of relationships, I trace the ways in which its use in Shakespeare demonstrates its cognate affinities with other concepts with which it is intertwined in the same forms of social practice: love, of course, but also friendship and loyalty, resentment and hatred, humility and ambition.[18]

PLAYING THE SERVANT

I remarked in my opening paragraph that both the universal presence of love and service as conjoined concepts in Shakespeare's work and the messiness of the concepts make a principle of selection both imperative and difficult. In their examination of service, others have chosen dependency (Weil), personal volition (Evett), or material relations of exploitation (Burnett) to drive their respective arguments. I have turned to the concept or condition that informs Shakespeare's representation of love and service at every point: the fact that he was in multiple ways himself a servant and that the theatre through which he represented love and service depended upon the embodiment of players who were also servants.

The most significant servants on the early modern English stage were thus the players themselves. Defined as vagabonds unless they could display the livery of a master of noble birth by the 1572 Vagabond Act and earlier statutes, those who played the parts of servant or master on the stage found it difficult to discard the stigma of the "common player".[19] In an age when to be called someone's "man" indicated servility and dependency, the theatre companies would have proclaimed their subordinate status in the public nature of their names if not their liveries: the Lord Admiral's Men, the Lord Chamberlain's Men and, after James's accession, the Queen's Men and the King's Men. Technically members of the noble or royal household, players who had previously been classified alongside sturdy beggars or vagabonds – "masterless men" – because of their doubly unsettling and unsettled habit of "strolling" and "personation", now found themselves split across two arenas of service. They could be expected to provide entertainment for their master or even "swell a scene or two" by displaying themselves in his livery as part of his retinue, but at the same time they were increasingly beholden to the demands of a commercial theatre which imaginatively abrogated the hierarchical system upon which traditional service depended.[20] The

---

[18] See Engle, *Pragmatism*, chapter 1.   [19] Pugliatti, *Beggary*, 2 and passim.

[20] I am indebted to Don Hedrick, who has drawn my attention to the change in the meaning of "entertainment" at this point, from the feudal notion of accepting service to the modern concept of giving pleasure through performance.

Prologue's ingratiating solicitation of the audience of *Henry V* through the levelling appellation "Pardon, gentles all" places the Lord Chamberlain's man at the service of all who have paid, whether it be a penny or more, sitting on the stage or standing in the yard. The general shift from feudal bonds of service to cash relations in the society as a whole informed the theatre too, in the tension between an older relation of service to a patron and the newer commercial form of service to a paying audience. Even as the older bonds were being questioned on the stage by characters such as Iago and Bosola, new relations of dependency were being developed with a more unpredictable set of paying "masters".[21] These relations in tension exemplify the bond between master and servant as it is performed in Shakespeare's plays. Combining the ordinary, inherently histrionic dimensions of the roles of everyday life with the self-reflexive staging of such roles by the servants of the theatre, they allowed a degree of play (in both the ludic and flexible senses) in social and personal relationships that is both externally constrained and open to appropriation and adaptation by individual agents or actors.

The actor representing service on Shakespeare's stage thus looks in two directions and at two kinds of bond: as a liveried being, he embodies his enabling relationship to the master by whose grace his personations are permitted; as a member of a commercial theatre dependent on a paying audience, he enacts service in a more modern, market sense.[22] The performance of service on Shakespeare's stage is thus complicated and enriched by the fact that when the player personated either servant or master, he continued to embody himself as servant. For even when actors as professionals had managed to transform themselves from itinerant beggars to legitimate servants and, finally, in some cases, to masters and gentlemen in their own right, they continued to be excoriated as mere beggars and vagabonds who had illegitimately transformed themselves into creatures beyond their proper station. Meredith Skura writes that "disgust about the city player's wealth never did counteract the old image of the strolling player as less than a servant – as a beggar, always ready to humiliate himself in public to earn

---

[21] Gurr, *Shakespearean Stage*; Skura, *Playing*; Weimann, *Author's Pen*; and Pugliatti, *Beggary*. This development should not be seen as the mere replacement of one type of service with another. As Ingram observes: "Patronage, and the stability that accompanied it, must . . . have come increasingly to be seen by players operating out of London as the key to survival at about mid-century. As a result, the quest for patronage burgeoned, as local players sought to protect their livelihoods" (*Playing*, 85).

[22] Ingram, however, reminds us that the players were not considered to have been offering a "service" in the modern sense of the word because they offered nothing tangible ("Economics of Playing", 319).

a penny and 'grovelling on the stage'".[23] In her study of the coincidence of
beggar and player in the proscriptions of vagabondage on the Continent
and in England, Paola Pugliatti argues that what brought them together
was their common practice of "(mis)representation and unregulated self-
transformation" (*Beggary*, 41). The wearing of livery was an indubitable
sign of one's fixed station within a regulated social order. Shapeless beggar
and protean player alike could therefore be "fixed" in a position of service
which, as we see in Chapter 1, was hemmed about with a plethora of expectations and commands, the overriding of which was a theoretical demand
of total obedience to the point at which autonomous subjectivity might be
entirely repressed.

The players' social condition of being (doubly) servants in the play of
the world infused the world of the play with a form of dynamism peculiar
to its theatrical representational space that was also a nexus of various social
interactions. The multivocal nature of the theatre did not merely allow it
to express the voices of a range of otherwise silent or overlooked servants:
the stage and its environs were themselves the sites of contested representations of service, in the split between representing player and represented
character but also through their respective relations to different sections of
the audience. Robert Weimann continues to offer the best account of such
doubled representation on the early modern stage, by which the actor's
"self-resembling show" is placed in productive tension or in direct conflict
with the character he is personating. This double character of the player
informs Shakespeare's representation of servants at every level; it infuses the
embodiment of the servant's role on stage with a degree of self-reflexivity
that disallows a direct, mimetic reading of the performative nature of service.[24] It means that the player's real status as servant is always potentially
available to inform or disrupt his imitation of the master-servant relationship or even the representation of relations between members of the
aristocracy.

The analysis of the representation of servants or service can consequently
never remain at the level of character – of what the character knows or
appears to know. Harry Berger has used the question of what a character
knows to offer compelling analyses of a nonpsychological "unconscious"
in the form of the limits and capacities of language.[25] Yet even the broader
forms of discourse analysis that show through the strategies of verbal interaction how "addressor and addressee are shaped as subjects within [their]
interactions", such as is pursued in Lynne Magnusson's pioneering work,

---

[23] *Actor*, 40.   [24] Weimann, *Popular Tradition* and "Bifold Authority".   [25] Berger, *Trifles*.

can on its own not reveal the dynamics of theatrical representation in Shakespeare's performance of service.[26] The broader playing context of such interactions needs to be added to the immediate, mimetic exchange to take into account that what is said by any character to another may be charged with the self-expressive voice of the player as real servant. Although it is not apparent from the text of the plays, every performance would thus have been an example of service both in action and reaction: of the player-servant who, embodying actions conventionally expected of servants, subverts settled magisterial relationships with his histrionic impertinence or conservatively endorses or extends settled conditions of mastery.

MASTERY AND SERVICE IN SHAKESPEARE'S THEATRE

I have been writing as if the status of players as servants was homogenous, but recent work in theatre history shows that in addition to the honorific status that "allowed them to 'masquerade as members of the gentlemanly profession of serving men'", the material organisation of labour within the theatre meant that it was itself shaped by relations of service and mastership that informed social life and commercial enterprise and industry in the London that it represented in fiction.[27] Although theatre companies were themselves not recognised as guilds, many of their members were free members of official guilds, such as the Bricklayers', or Grocers', or Dyer's corporations.[28] Boy actors were apprenticed to the theatre companies by being attached to a master who belonged to one of these guilds; sometimes they were bought for a few pounds and indentured for periods as long as nine years.[29] Those who played the roles of women were thus in the position of some of the most tightly bonded and lowliest servants in England. Scott McMillin casts new light on the possible ways in which boy actors might have been trained by a senior actor in an analysis of "restricted" and "wide-ranging" roles for boy actors,[30] and Natasha Korda reminds us of the roles that women played, at all levels except as players, in sustaining the material enterprise of the theatre. "The visible and vocal presence of such

---

[26] Magnusson, *Dialogue*, 4.
[27] See Ingram, *Playing*, 15: "The other community – the network of social, and hence economic, inter-dependencies that formed among the men who performed these early Elizabethan entertainments – has only recently come into focus as a subject worthy of study its own terms."
[28] The guilds to which, respectively, Ben Jonson, John Hemminges, and Phillip Henslowe belonged. Korda states: "We know that many of the theatre people were themselves members of the clothing guilds; their wives and children would have gained the right to work in these guilds through marriage or patrimony, rather than through formal apprenticeship" ("Labours Lost", 205).
[29] See McMillin, "Sharer", Skura; *Actor*; Gurr, *Stage*.   [30] McMillin, "Sharer".

commercial activity [i.e., of women] in the theatres", she writes, "makes it difficult to conceive of the theatre as a 'world apart' from the market. For the relationship between the market and the theatre was not simply one of two abstract ideas, but incorporated innumerable material acts of exchange between and among male players and women workers" (219).

Korda's intervention is welcome, both because it focuses on the materiality of the theatre as a set of practices and social relationships beyond the text of the play and because it restores women to that sustaining context. However, her conception of both labour and market exchange gives insufficient weight to *service* as its fundamental personal and economic condition. Women would have been engaged not merely in commercial relations of exchange or isolated artisanal labour; their place of service would have retained older, decisive aspects of the family as Laslett defines it. Even amongst the adults in the company, ties of service and the deference of hierarchy prevailed in the social and professional distinctions between the contracted actors; the more elevated, wealthy, and powerful sharers; and finally, the all-powerful entrepreneurs such as Philip Henslowe who, as owners of theatres, controlled those who worked as actors and playwrights through strictly determined bonds of service. The stage may have made great things familiar, but it was not itself an egalitarian place. Historically, playing companies had moved from being a rabble of itinerant "beggars" to a more elevated position within a noble retinue, but even as they moved from the profession of neo-feudal "serving-man" into the market economy, they inhabited the social distinctions and unequal practices of master-servant relations of the society that provided their living. William Ingram observes that "we know less than we would like to know about how stage players, the abstract and brief chronicles of the time, were themselves affected" by the economic changes introduced by the market economy – "we should try to understand . . . how the stage player, as free entrepreneur, was caught up in the clash of these attitudes, finding himself both used and abused, and how these circumstances shaped his sense of himself and his calling".[31]

Within the ideology of service represented especially by Protestant writers such as William Gouge and John Dod and Robert Cleaver, who are discussed in the next chapter, service is amenable to performance in the way that an actor can personate a person or position that is at odds both with his real station and his inner condition. Gouge and Cleaver make much of the distinction between mere service apparent to the eye and real devotion, the former covering both a subtle form of parasitic dependency in which

---

[31] Ingram, *Playing*, 45.

one serves to enrich oneself, and the latter a more destructive, Judas-like
hypocrisy in which the outward show of proper service hides not merely
an unwilling but a positively treacherous heart.[32] The actor is the peculiar
exemplum of the "eye-service" excoriated by these moralists. At least part
of his service comes from the body rather than the heart, and his work as
servant involves putting on the habits of the master. On his back, the livery
of service is continually, if temporarily, replaced by the sumptuary effects
of a variety of different stations. Shakespeare's plays especially engage in the
overtly self-reflexive display of this double relationship, and even the nontheatrical mode of his sonnets is informed by an indelible sense of being
"subdu'd / To what it workes in, like the Dyers hand" (sonnet 111.6–7).
The actor thus represents a more ominous sense of playing, especially of
concern to the moralists, predicated upon a gap between the epistemology
and ontology of service, in which the "outward show" of service fails to
match the "inner man". A source of considerable anxiety among masters,
we are told, this always possible gap is the obverse of the idea that a good
servant constitutes the master's "other self".[33]

The unreliable servant is a player, able to assume the gestures of obedience
and compliance while undermining the master from within. This analogy
has another aspect, however. If Hamlet can find the player monstrous
because he can produce the signs of passion without the affective motions
that, according to contemporary psychology, would normally move the
body to such transformation, the player may reflect in caricature the eradication of subjectivity that obedience requires in the most conservative
tracts on service. The player is the incarnation of the servant as the furthest
reaches of ideology would have him: all gesture, outward show, the inward
man reduced to nothing by being in every sense his master's man. I develop
this idea and its dire implications for the master in my discussion of *Othello*
in Chapter 6.

In brief, then, the representation of service of Shakespeare's stage is
complicated by its embodiment of the player on three levels: (1) the player
himself as servant, symbolized by his livery as part of the retinue of a member
of the nobility or, subsequently, of the royal household; (2) the player as
master or servant (or both) within the material relations of the theatre itself;
and (3) the player as embodiment either of the "eye-service" that threatens
master-servant relations at their core or its repressing corollary, the person
reduced to mere performance, robbed of any independent subjectivity.

---

[32] Gouge, *Dvties*, 593; Dod and Cleaver, *Household*, sig. Aa2v.
[33] A classic study of the problem of interiority is Maus, *Inwardness*.

LOVE AND SERVICE

Peter Laslett's comment, in *The World We Have Lost*, that in the early modern period "every relationship could be seen as a love-relationship" (5) presents the governing idea of this book. His qualification signals the need for a change of habitual ways of seeing to enable us to recognize "circles of affection" (5) as a structural part of the organization of society which, as he demonstrates, was based wholly on relations of service. I propose to demonstrate the interaction of love and service in Shakespeare's work in light of the complication of their representation in a theatre which embodied the conjunction of neo-feudal relations, where love played a central role, and those of an incipient market economy, in which its personally affective ties appear to have been weakened. I argue that the representation of love is informed as much by the self-conscious performativity of the player as it is in the mimesis of service. Any of Shakespeare's texts might have been grist to a mill fed with a mixture of service and love. The texts I have chosen are united by their embodiment of the performative dimensions of these two concepts as they are taken up by Shakespeare's theatre and its own ties of service and love. As the framing matrix for this book, the conceptual affinities of love, service, and performance reveal deep continuities across all of Shakespeare's texts. However, they also span a variable range of personal and social conditions that cannot be reduced to any single thematic thread or ideological vision. I have organised chapters to develop contrasts and similarities between pairs of plays and, when appropriate, between the plays and the sonnets, where the interplay of love and service finds its most intense expression.

CHAPTER I

"Thou serv'st me, and I'll love thee"

Love and Service in Shakespeare's World

> For more than 500 years, the law of master and servant fixed the bound-
> aries of "free labor" in Britain and throughout the British Empire.
> Compounded of statutory enactments, judicial doctrines, and social
> practice, it defined and controlled employment relations for almost
> a quarter of the world's population in more than 100 colonial and
> postcolonial jurisdictions.[1]

The "law of master and servant" to which Douglas Hay and Paul Craven
refer was enacted a year before Shakespeare's birth. The Statute of Artificers
of 1562/3 consolidated and replaced all previous forms of legislation in
England that had sought to regulate labour relations by fixing maximum
wages, determining the conditions of employment as essentially a set of
reciprocal, if unequal, relations between masters and servants, and laying
down forms of legal censure and punishment for those who broke contracts
or transgressed the bonds of the Statute.

From the perspective of modern assumptions regarding freedom of contract, Hay and Craven's qualification of the phrase "free labor" with scare
quotes is apposite. The servants covered by the Statute of Artificers were no
slaves or bondsmen. However, nor could their choice regarding the place,
time, and conditions of employment or, in many cases, the person of their
masters, be regarded as entirely or even largely unconstrained: "Freedom
to choose one's employer did not imply freedom to remain unemployed: if
the master and servant acts did not themselves compel engagement and the
whip of hunger did not suffice, then . . . the law about vagrancy took up the
burden" (33). We shall see in due course how Tudor vagrancy laws informed
the status of Shakespeare and his fellow players, who are the most significant
servants in this book. Hay and Craven present the Statute and its successors
as an unequal exercise of power by the landowning elite that entrenched
existing relations of ownership and power against forces that we now call

[1] Hay and Craven, *Masters*, 1.

16

"the market". "Everywhere", they continue, "the policy of master and servant reflected its medieval genesis in the plague years: it was predicated upon labor shortages, and in particular on defeating the tendency of the market to bid up wages" (33). The success of this policy may be measured by the fact that in the face of chronic inflation during Shakespeare's years, real wages declined, "reaching their lowest point in the early decades of the seventeenth century (by which time they were half those of a century earlier)".[2]

Hay and Craven trace the ways in which the legal framework of master-servant relations, which grew out of the social and economic conditions of medieval and early modern England, continued to determine employer-employee relations as relationships between masters and servants for almost a quarter of the world's population well into the twentieth century – in the Indian subcontinent, the Caribbean, and Africa.[3] Well after the terms of the Elizabethan Statute had been transformed by the requirements of modern economic relations and enlightenment notions of human rights in colonies such as Canada, New Zealand, and Australia, master-servant relations were required by law, incorporated into the economy, and formed the basis for a network of residual *personal* relationships in the more racially inflected colonies of Asia and Africa. The terms through which Shakespeare would have forged his sense of personal and social identity remained in effect longest, not only residually but also actively, in apartheid South Africa, where the Master and Servants Act of 1926 and the Native Services Act of 1932 continued to determine economic and political relationships between white employers and black employees well into the last quarter of the twentieth century. Although Shakespeare might have been puzzled by the racial character of these acts, he would have been familiar with their broad conceptual and legal determinations.

This introduction to master-servant relationships in Shakespeare via the backward-looking perspective of their residual forms in post-colonial experience both situates my own "place in the story" and highlights the complex fact of affective relations in master-servant relationships within a context in which they have tended to be overlooked, even now when the prevalence and importance of service itself have come to be recognized after years of neglect. As a white South African, growing up during the height

[2] Wrightson, *English Society*, 133. This has to be read in the context of changing demographics. Wages were initially set in the fourteenth century to counteract the effects of an acute shortage of labour following the Black Death; by the sixteenth century, population growth may well have reduced wages as a result of "market forces".
[3] See Deakin and Wilson, *Labour Market*, 24: "It was not until the 1870s that criminal sanctions were removed from the law of the individual service relationship [in Britain]."

of apartheid, I was defined legally, socially, and certainly in my initial years of childhood and adolescence, psychologically, as a "master". My parents had three or four domestic servants who, except for the hours of rest, were always present in the house, and who slept and ate and conducted their lives on the property, if not under the same roof, as they might have done both in Shakespeare's experience and in other white households in South Africa. Later, when I took my first employment on a diamond mine, my relationship with the black labourers over whom I exercised charge was defined by law as that between master and servant. Black South Africans habitually referred to all white men as "master", whether they worked for them or not, and the workers who laboured under me were no exception.

I do not intend to investigate the peculiar way in which race overlay, in a neo-colonial setting, the relationships of domination and subservience inherited from the legal, social, and personal forms of existence in early modern England. What I wish to take from those formative experiences is a certain kind of psychological habitus, of which not only domination but also dependence, and even affection, were an integral part. "She's one of the family" – said by a white South African "madam" of her domestic servant – may in many cases be dismissible as a sentimental obfuscation of real relations of exploitation.[4] But the preservation, in late-twentieth-century South Africa, of the grounding framework of Elizabethan master-servant relations is striking. Peter Laslett argues that one of the central aspects of that world now lost to "us" (whoever that "us" may include or exclude) is the conception of servants as an integral part of the family:[5]

It will be noticed that the roles that we have allotted to all the members of the capacious "family" of the master-baker of London in the year 1619 are, emotionally, highly symbolic and highly satisfying. We may feel that in a whole society organized like this, in spite of the subordination, the exploitation and the obliteration of those who were young, or female, or in service, everyone belonged in a group, a family group. Everyone had his or her circle of affection: every relationship could be seen as a love-relationship. . . . But with us, the social world is such that no sentiment of the familial kind is likely to attach itself to work relationships.[6]

I would not wish to claim that the "family" of parents, siblings, and servants in which I grew up matched Laslett's seventeenth-century baker in the

---

4 See Cock, *Maids*, for an account of the relationship between domestic servants and their employees in the Eastern Cape in South Africa. Cock's empirical research reveals that whereas many white employers, especially women, regarded their "maids" as part of the family, none of their servants saw themselves in this way.
5 See Evett, *Service*, who points out that "the root of the word *family* is the word for servant" (23).
6 Laslett, *World*, 5.

general intensity or mutuality of its affective relationships, but there was no doubt that, together with the obedience and respect that were expected of child and servant alike, our "family" was infused with a variety of ties of affection. Female domestic servants charged with the care of their master's children, often from birth until they left the household, developed close ties over years of surrogate parenting, sometimes reciprocated, sometimes not.[7] They were undoubtedly part of my formative experience as a child.

My own part in this story of masters and servants thus prompts me to ensure that the growing story of service in early modern England does not overlook its deeply affective aspects, however fraught with problems they may be. I wish to afford full recognition, through close readings of Shakespeare's sonnets and plays, to Laslett's claim that "every relationship could be seen as a love relationship" (*World*, 5) by giving due weight to the ways in which affective bonds may inform and transform relations of bondage within material conditions of exploitation or subjugation. I want to give equal weight to love and service as they are embodied and expressed performatively – in the practices of daily life, through the transformative speech acts of language as a whole and staged through the self-conscious representations of Shakespeare's theatre.

SERVICE IN SHAKESPEARE'S WORLD

Service was such a prevalent condition in early modern England that for a long time its very obviousness rendered it invisible to literary scholars.[8] It was the dominant condition that tied people to each other and the framework that structured the ways in which they lived such relationships. "From apprentices learning a trade to the officials of the great noble households during the period," Burnett writes, "servants were perhaps the most distinctive socio-economic feature of sixteenth and seventeenth-century society".[9] Historians estimate that "servants . . . constituted around 60 percent of the population aged fifteen to twenty-four" and that "most youths in early modern England were servants".[10] Most of the population would therefore have been in service at least at some point, and for many that condition would have been permanent.

---

[7] See Joubert, *Poppie*.
[8] See Laslett, *World*: "[I]t could be said that service was practically a universal characteristic of pre-industrial English society" (16).
[9] Burnett, *Masters*, 1.
[10] Kussmaul, *Husbandry*, 3. See also Laslett, *World*, 13–16 and 64–5; Evett, "Surprising confrontations", 67–78; and *Discourses*.

The most important aspect of service in medieval and early modern England, systematically overlooked in a class-obsessed post-Marxist environment, is the fact that it transcended class barriers.[11] P. J. P. Goldberg writes of the "essentially classless nature of service" that "it appears unhelpful to identify servants as a 'class'", since "they may be more usefully be described in life-cycle terms".[12] In early modern England, people as socially separate as humble agricultural labourers and the children of the aristocracy would have been servants, and even powerful earls and dukes would have counted themselves as servants to the crown. Francis Bacon comments that "Men in Great Place are thrice seruants: Seruants of the Soueraigne or State: Seruants of Fame; and Seruants of Businesse. So as they haue no Freedom".[13] In many cases one could be master and servant at once, owing allegiance to a sovereign, or working as a servant in the household of a greater member of the aristocracy, while simultaneously holding sway oneself over a retinue of stewards, ushers, grooms, scullery maids, and husbandmen.[14] Much of the complexity of the relations of intimacy, authority, and service that Kate Mertes traces in the late medieval and early modern household stems from the fact that servants were part of the family.[15] Keith Wrightson notes that whereas such relationships were ruled by undoubted hierarchies of power, they were also "shot through with ambiguities and inconsistencies, if not outright contradictions. Familial relationships were hierarchical but also reciprocal. Authority was besieged with obligations of love and care".[16]

The family is thus generally regarded by social historians as the primary site of service, comprehending what we would now consider relations involving industry or commerce.[17] In addition to the bonds of obedience imposed upon daughters and wives, servants within the household from the most menial scullery maid through the dependent craftsman or spinster and husbandman to the gentleman usher or steward were members of the

---

[11] For a discussion, see Barry and Brooks, *The Middling Sort*, Introduction, and Wrightson, "Sorts of People".

[12] Goldberg, *Women, Work and Life Cycle*, 177 and 158.

[13] Bacon, "Of Great Place", *Essays*.

[14] See Gouge, *Dvties*, 5: "We must distinguish betwixt the seuerall places wherein men are: for euen they who are superiours to some, are inferiours to others: as he that said, *I haue vnder me, and am vnder authoritie*. The master that hath seruants under him, may be vnder the authoritie of a Magistrate."

[15] Mertes, *Household*.   [16] Wrightson, "Politics of the Parish", 11.

[17] Amussen argues that the family is the social and practical centre of early modern notions of order, although she does indicate signal disparities between the relationships that constitute the family and broader social ties (*Ordered Society*). See also Laslett, *World*, chapter 1, especially: "This . . . was not simply a world without factories, without firms . . . every activity was limited to what could be organized within the family, and within the lifetime of its head" (8).

political and affective structure of the patriarchal family. They were sub-servient to its head in a sense that cannot be captured by the modern notion of the nuclear family or the workplace relationship between employee and employer. The interconnection of service and familial bonds means that service was assumed to comprehend love – in the reciprocal "obligations of duty and care" that bound together both members of a broadly conceived, domestic economy and also the greater family of the commonwealth, with its mutual obligation of subjects to love their monarch and the monarch in turn to love his or her subjects.[18] Elizabeth's canny representation of herself as the spouse of her people mobilizes a trope that was ready at hand. It built equally upon the love of God that proposed Christ as the bridegroom of His church and the bonds of love that were ideally supposed to tie the lowliest household and the most powerful political institutions in a single, complex image of devotion and obedience.[19] A range of cognate concepts shade into each other here, combining notions of service and love, enforced subordination and chosen intimacy: "bind", "bond", "bound", "bounden", and, of course, "bondage".

Two concepts of service: occupational service

The variety and prevalence of service require some careful conceptual dis-tinctions, for service is a multivalent term covering a number of differ-ent but related conditions. First, there is the condition most familiar in a post-industrial society, in which service is an *occupation*. Predominantly economic, but with social and political ramifications, such a condition was tied to employment, mostly for a limited period. The servant worked for a master or mistress, in jobs ranging from domestic or personal service through crafts and cottage industries. These included weaving or brewing, sowing or harvesting, milking and tending animals, or trade and hospitality, in (ideally) mutually beneficial relationships through which the master or mistress received assistance in return for board, lodging, and wages (which were usually low). Crucially, service was the primary training ground for skills that would enable servants to set up independently as master or mis-tress themselves when their terms of service ended. It was also the primary preparation for marriage, which usually afforded a degree of independence

---

[18] See Evett, "We owe thee much": "the real foundation of a workable commonwealth is service itself" (11), and Michael Neill, *History*: "In this construction society consisted of an unbroken chain of service that stretched from the humblest peasant to the monarch who owed service only to God" (22). See also Amussen, *Society*, 3 passim.

[19] See Gouge, *Dvties*, who uses the image of the Church as the bride of Christ extensively.

for the couple (Goldberg, *Women*, 185). Such occupational forms of service were temporary, usually contracted for no more than a year, although by the early sixteenth century, contracts might be longer, and some servants remained in the same household for several years.[20]

Both women and men entered this form of service contract, starting in their early teens and ending in their mid- to late twenties, when they would be in a position to achieve independence through marriage.[21] Men were more likely than women to remain in service into their forties, often as menservants to households of the nobility or gentry (Goldberg, *Women*, 174 passim). The children of aristocrats were commonly put into service in other noble households, at least temporarily, although this practice changed as "in the course of four centuries after the Reformation, the educational role of the household would shrink and that of the school would expand" (Houlbrooke, *Family*, 33). Stefano Guazzo writes that a good master first has to have learnt to be a good servant by subordinating his will to another.[22]

The most formalized form of occupational service-in-training was apprenticeship, which was much more strictly controlled than other forms of service. The term was usually for seven years; it involved a payment to the master by the family of the apprentice for board, lodging, and training, and no wages were paid. Only citizens or freemen could act as masters of apprentices. Many children of the gentry were indentured as apprentices to men of lower rank than their fathers.[23]

---

[20] Houlbrooke, *Family*, 171 passim.

[21] See Houlbrooke, *Family*: "By late adolescence, a substantial proportion of young people, perhaps most of them, had left home finally or for a long period ... Service, apprenticeship and higher education were necessary paths to advancement. . . . Adolescents of both sexes went to work in other people's household, but the opportunities for members of each sex depended upon the character of the local economy. Farmers and husbandmen generally needed more young men than young women. . . . Domestic service offered increasing opportunities for girls as household staffs of the nobility and gentry, predominantly male in the fifteenth century, became predominantly female by the end of the seventeenth century" (171–2).

[22] Guazzo, *Conuersation*, 168:

> ANNIB The maner is set downe, if that he set service before commanunding, that is if he learne to serue before he begin to command.
> GUAZ I am of that minde, for I think it a matter impossible, that he should know how to play the maister wel, who neuer had maister.

[23] Mertes, *Household*, 68: "[H]ousehold service provided a convenient, honourable living for landless younger sons of the upper ranks of society, and an education for gently born children". See also I. M., *Health*:

> Euen the Dukes sonne preferred Page to the Prince, the Earles seconde sonne attendant upon the Duke, the Knights seconde sonne the Earles Seruant, the Esquires sonne to weare the Knightes lyuerie, and the Gentlemans sonne the Esquires seruingman: Yea, I know at this day, Gentlemen younger brothers, that weares their elder brothers Blew coate and Badge, attending him with as reuerend regard and duetifull obedience, as if he were their Prince or Soueraigne. (sig. B3)

Such occupational forms of service were part of a life cycle: they were temporary, occupational, and provided training to enable servants ultimately to leave his or her service to take up crafts, trades, or occupations in which they would themselves assume their cyclical position as master or mistress to their own servants, who often included kinsfolk or known locals. It is this service of which Goldberg writes when he declares "that service cannot be dismissed as a purely domestic and non-economic function, a form of disguised unemployment" (*Women*, 193). The cyclical nature of such service means that at some point in their lives, masters and mistresses would themselves have been servants so, as Goldberg suggests, it is possible that many of them would have some sympathy for those placed in their charge (183). The stipulation of annual contracts of service in the Statute of Labourers of 1351 protected employers rather than servants. The shortage of labour after the Black Death in the mid-fourteenth century meant, however, that servants were likely to benefit from shorter contracts because that would have enabled them to seek more beneficial conditions and higher wages in a seller's market.

Two concepts of service: hierarchical services

Cyclical, occupational forms of service, transformed by changing demography and economic conditions and activity from the late Middle Ages to the early modern period, occurred within a much broader *political* notion of service not tied either to specific occupational training or to a changing life cycle. It formed the fundamental, hierarchically organised structure of medieval and early modern society: the "Golden chain" of which Guazzo writes, informed by rank but not divided by social status or class (*Conuersation*, 167). All people would have acknowledged a master in the ranks above them and would have been acknowledged as a master in those below, even if there was no link of employment of occupation between them.[24] These more amorphous relationships, written in manner and dress rather than in public records, are most difficult to detect through the statistical, archival

---

[24] The interaction of hierarchical and occupational relations of service are expressed by Simon Daines:

> For it were absurd to think, that Gentlemen in those places that may befit their rank and fortune, though subject to their masters call, should be tied to the obsequious termes of every pedantique Groome. As first, he that waits voluntarily, and at his own expense: then Secretaries in their several ranks; then such as serve in the places of Gentleman, as Ushers and the like. Then Clarks to men eminent, and of quality; and Clarks appertaining to Offices, Factors, and Apprentices (especially about *London*) men perhaps (as is usuall in that kind) better derived than their Masters. In this respect, I say, the servant ought to consider the relation, or respect to be had, according to his Masters rank, his own person, and the nature of his service. (*Orthoepia Anglicana*, 86)

analysis favoured by social historians. They are, however, the very stuff of literary representation and central to Shakespeare's work.

Although these two forms of service – occupational and hierarchical – are conceptually distinct, they are related through the interaction of political conditions and economic forces which changed as the early modern period was subjected to the growth of the market economy. Goldberg's figures for York indicate that those who employed most servants in the early sixteenth century tended to be the civic elite – wealthy freemen who kept servants as much as an expression and display of their householder status as for the material labour they might perform (162–3), and Houlbrooke comments that "servants tended to move from poorer households to richer ones" (*Family*, 173). The "decline of the aristocracy" during the course of the sixteenth century, and the changes in social mobility linked to rising inflation and mercantile activity, however, began to put pressure on the acceptance of nonoccupational or hierarchical relations of service (Stone, *Aristocracy*, chapter 4; Wrightson, *Earthly Necessities*, chapter 7).

HISTORICISING SHAKESPEARE'S REPRESENTATION OF SERVICE

How do we give substance to Laslett's claim that every relationship of service in Shakespeare's time could be seen as a relationship of love? Shakespeare's contemporaries appear to be more mimetically engaged with the rebelliousness of the apprentice or the sexual intrigues of domestic, middle-class life. When Burnett wants to illustrate the instabilities of servile relationships in the period, he turns to Marston, Jonson, Greene, and Dekker, whereas service in the noble household is almost exclusively represented in his study by Middleton, Rowley, Webster, and Munday. Neill also ranges more broadly across the work of Middleton, Massinger, and the anonymous author of *Arden of Faversham* to trace early modern anxieties about the "social insecurities" of service (*History*, 79). In the context of this scholarship, Shakespeare appears not to be especially representative or mimetic of these aspects of Elizabethan and Jacobean social and political life. It may thus be more difficult to read Shakespeare historically than we have been assuming. There may be a greater degree of disjunction, or a more complex, mediated relationship between his texts and those usually used to anchor them to their conditions of production or circulation. This difficulty is especially well reflected by the ways in which his work represents and refracts his critical engagement with the lost world of *affective* service that Laslett recalls. Shakespeare's critical perspective is always internal to a world in which freedom from service was almost unimaginable. No matter how critical Shakespeare may be of particular embodiments of master-servant relations, his work does not envisage a world beyond or free of them, even if he does envisage a world of free mutuality within such conditions.

The chief issue regarding Shakespeare's relation to both the early modern world of service and its reflection in the contemporary discursive literature lies in the singularities of form or genre and its own material conditions of production. Bruce Robbins writes of a different genre and a later period that

[f]or the purposes of the novel as for the literary tradition that precedes it, the field of objects I call 'servants' refers less to an occupational group defined, outside of slavery, as non-kin paid to perform menial work in the house than to the conjunction of that group with a certain body of aesthetic functions, a repertory of gags and tags, expedients for pointing a moral or moving a plot, that cling to it with uncanny fidelity.[25]

Robbins's observation of the aesthetic function and tradition that cling to the servant in fictional representation reminds us that the servant embodied on the Elizabethan stage looks in two directions: sideways at his or her counterparts in contemporary society and also backward at stock types in classical Greek and Roman theatre, just as Dickens, Thackeray, and Fielding drew the vitality of their servant's roles from the Renaissance stage.[26] And that double relation is further mediated by the peculiar engagement of the dramatist or poet in the world of service. Shakespeare's representations of master-servant relations differ from Webster's, which in turn diverge from those of Middleton or Jonson. Independently of the dramatist, however, the very staging of servants as theatrical characters changes the figure of the servant as a representation drawn from beyond the stage. It also reshapes the way in which masters and servants watching the plays might have regarded themselves and their respective relationships. The representation of service, being itself a highly mediated performance of its subject matter, has an effect on its practice. One of the abiding anxieties expressed in the Puritan, anti-theatrical tracts concerns precisely this danger (or opportunity, depending on one's perspective), that the embodiment of the servant in fiction will deleteriously affect the servant in his or her relations to their masters in reality.[27] We need to be attentive to the semi-mimetic indirections of Shakespeare's texts as vehicles of performance as well as the possible *disjunction* between Shakespeare's theatre and certain kinds of

---

[25] Robbins, *Hand*, 41.   [26] See especially Evett, *Service*, chapter 4.
[27] See Pollard, *Shakespeare's Theater*, 70, 193, and 322.

nonimaginative literature if we want to understand fully the role of the servant in his plays.

There are thus two pitfalls that threaten the use of archival material to provide a summary, framing context of the representational substance of Shakespeare's texts. One is the formally attractive but misleading temptation to derive from a small selection of texts by people who had local, vested interests in the ideology of service, the historical totality of what was not merely thought and felt about the subject but also of what *could have been* thought and felt. The other is the related problem of form. The exercise tends to reduce the manifold and peculiarity of Shakespeare's own *performative* relation to the conditions and concepts of love and service by confining them within a reconstructed, monological setting generically much less dynamic than Shakespeare's. The performative relation of the theatre to the world from which it draws its imaginative resources is in tension with the differently interested discourses or genres of didactic literature. The effects or meanings of the one cannot be extrapolated directly from the other. The "body of aesthetic functions" that Robbins mentions make Shakespeare's texts irreducible to either the moralizing ideology of service or the broad sociological and economic trends constructed by historians from the archives. Some of these problems may be illuminated by examining briefly the core space of service in late medieval and early modern England, the household and its transformation by economic and social change.

FAMILIAL SUPPORT VERSUS CASH NEXUS

Wrightson shows that the household was the predominant unit of social relationship in the period, although we should bear in mind that households varied depending on whether they were urban or rural, those of a cottager, a master of a trade, or a member of the landed gentry (*Earthly Necessities*, 27 passim). He concludes his discussion of the social and economic changes as they affected familial and servile relations between the early sixteenth and the mid-seventeenth centuries by indicating the growing vulnerability of households to economic change over which they had little control:

A commonwealth based upon household had become one in which a substantial segment of the population was no longer able to sustain a household without periodic public assistance, and in which a further substantial minority could establish an independent household at all. There can be no more graphic illustration of the social transition unleashed in the sixteenth century by demographic growth and inflation. (*Earthly Necessities*, 226)

This decline is critical for master-servant relations because the establishment of an independent household was the means by which married couples attained the positions of master and mistress over others, and servants found work, sustenance, shelter, and training. Wrightson's conclusion appears to underwrite the argument that the rise of a mercantile economy gave rise to two related things inimical to at least the conservative ideology of service exemplified by its ideological spokesmen.[28] The palpable ambition of servants such as Shakespeare's Malvolio, Edmund and Iago, who refuse to acknowledge the hierarchical constraints of service, may be read as embodied reflections of a general historical movement, whereby settled familial relations of service were replaced with the more impersonal relations of the "cash nexus", in a move from feudalism to capitalism, which is generally assumed to have threatened the very foundation of service as an institution.[29]

Social historians and literary scholars of service suggest that the hierarchical but supportive relations in the Elizabethan and Jacobean family household had, by the end of the sixteenth century, succumbed to a variety of social and economic pressures. Having gradually replaced a residual, feudal system exemplified by the retainer band, they were themselves transformed by simultaneously emergent forms of commodification, in the form of temporary wage contracts rather than more settled familial relations, which threatened the established nexus of household service and therefore the "ideology of service" itself.[30] Neill writes of this crisis point (exemplified by the two different attitudes to service in *King Lear*) as a *demystification* of the old, feudal ideology of service in the form of a "sharp historical divide" (*History*, 45).[31] "In this world of progressively demystifying relationships", he adds, "most household service was coming to seem like a form of wage-slavery, more and more difficult to reconcile – whatever Kent would have us think – with honour or gentility" (33).

---

[28] William Gouge, John Dod, and Robert Cleaver, Thomas Fosset, Walter Darrell, and the intriguing I. M., for example.

[29] See Neill, *History*, 33 passim; Evett, *Discourses*, 29 passim; Burnett, *Masters*, 171ff; and Lamb, "Homoerotics".

[30] See Lamb, "Homoerotics", and Burnett, "*King Lear*".

[31] I. M.'s complaints about the decline of hospitality, liberality, and consequently the bonds of friendship between the householder and his gentleman servant certainly underscore Neill's claim. Yet whereas I. M.'s essay is instructive for the picture it presents of the phenomenology of service from the perspective of a single individual, it cannot be taken at face value as a factual picture of a general historical change.

The *locus classicus* of the perception of this change in general politicoeconomic terms is Marx and Engels's *Manifesto of the Communist Party*:

The bourgeoisie, wherever it has got the upper hand, has put an end to all feudal, patriarchal, idyllic relations. It has pitilessly torn asunder the motley feudal ties that bound man to his *natural superiors*, and has left remaining no other nexus than naked self-interest, than callous cash-payment . . . the bourgeoisie has torn away from the family its sentimental veil, and has reduced the family relation to a mere money-relation.[32]

Eric Hobsbawm and E. P. Thompson endorse this nostalgia for "idyllic" feudal relations in the face of the capitalist instrumentalisation of the servant:

[T]he proletarian whose only link with his employer is a "cash nexus" must be distinguished from the "servant" or preindustrial dependent, who has a much more complex human and social relationship with his "master", and one which implies duties on both sides, though very unequal ones.[33]

In Thompson's words, this exchange "voided the body politic of old notions of duty, mutuality, and paternal care".[34]

The argument that the new, impersonal economic nexus *demystified* old relations of service needs to be treated with care. It is in danger, on one hand, of suggesting that the new impersonality is in fact the *truth* of all forms of service, no matter what their specific conditions may have been, and on the other of sentimentalizing feudal relations as a Golden Age of the proper marriage of natural hierarchy and ethical reciprocity. It is true that relations did change from 1520 to 1640, under the pressures of a growing population, inflation, and an accompanying real reduction in wages. This was "a process of commercialization" by which "a patchwork of loosely articulated, primarily agrarian, regional economies, which contained commercialized sectors, was transformed into an integrated economic system in which market relationships were the mainspring of economic life, a capitalist market economy, albeit one which retained more traditional elements" (Wrightson, *Earthly Necessities*, 331). The new process of commercialization does not, however, mean that older, more traditional relations of more settled, mutual obligation were empty or false or mere mystifications. In his study of the representation of servants in the eighteenth and nineteenth centuries, Robbins observes that "the servants of Shakespeare . . . are descried as faithful reflections of Elizabethan England, who were 'in transition from a feudal to a modern basis'. *But this transition had been going on for some time, and*

---

[32] Marx and Engels, *Manifesto* in *Selected Works*, I, 85.
[33] Hobsbawm, *Industry and Empire*, 85.   [34] Thompson, *Poverty of Theory*, 44.

it did not end with Shakespeare. An acute essay on the servants of Dickens comes to the same conclusion, but this time makes it specific to Victorian England" (*Servant's Hand*, 40; emphasis added).

Both Robbins and Wrightson, writing from the disciplines of social and literary history, thus remind us that although market relationships had indeed informed economic life, the economy that sustained them retained residual elements of an older social order of more personal relationships. We are talking about trends, different forms of practice and expectation that coexisted for decades.[35] It is striking that the *same* catalogue of abuses in master-servant relations occurs in Thomas Chaloner's translation of Gylbertus Cognatus's *Of the Office of Servavnts* published in 1534, as in the Elizabethan and Jacobean tracts published between 1580 to 1630.[36] The two forms of service relationship appear to have existed side by side, and each contained a similar potential for exploitation or reciprocity. Yeoman farmers, for example, might have employed a number of permanent servants who were afforded customary forms of protection and care, but they also took on and dismissed seasonal, temporary labour. Others, responding to a newer commercial spirit, did away with live-in servants altogether, calculating that it was more profitable to rely entirely on day labourers for whom they had no responsibilities other than the payment of cash.[37] It is therefore difficult to isolate cash wages as the defining indicator of a turn in service relationships, because wages are characteristic of service in both the early, sixteenth-century tracts and, indeed, in both the Old and New Testaments.

Although it is correct in the broadest terms, this argument tends to be too rigidly driven by the diachronic thesis of the inexorable "rise of capitalism", so that it misses local nuances and the complicated interrelation and coexistence of residual, dominant, and emergent forces by which service continued to be practiced and experienced in differentiated and attenuated forms. Indeed, Simon Deakin, Frank Wilkinson and Douglas Hay argue that the nineteenth century saw an intensification of the more brutal aspects of the master-servant regime, the earlier, reciprocal elements being abrogated in favour of employers' power. Deakin and Wilkinson argue that "the role of the master-servant law did not *diminish* as industrialization gathered pace; significant legislative innovations in the course of the eighteenth and nineteenth centuries meant that the scope, force and severity of this body of

---

[35] See the unreferenced quotation of Perry Anderson, that societies contain "a mixture of forms" and that "historical development proceeds not by leaps but by overlaps" (*Earthly Necessities*, 24).

[36] See Burnett, *Masters*; DiGangi, "Asses and Wits", 187; and Alan Beier, *Masterless Men*.

[37] See Wrightson, *Earthly Necessities*, 195ff and 186.

law *intensified* at this point" (Deakin and Wilson, *Labour Market*, 24), and Hay concludes that "in its emphasis on penal sanctions and in its relative neglect of remedies for workers, by the mid-nineteenth century the law of master and servant appeared far more significant in the creation of great social inequalities than it had a century before".[38] At the turn of the nineteenth century, for example, courts ignored "the old authorities" which we see reflected in the writings of Gouge, Fosset and Dod and Cleaver "to find that a master had no obligation to maintain a servant or to provide him or her with medical care" (Deakin and Wilson, *Labour Market*, 66). Master-servant relations were therefore not displaced by capitalism; rather their worst aspects were mobilised as an instrument of complete exploitation of workers.

The historical fact of these economic and political changes does not necessarily tell us what is happening in Shakespeare's work. Shakespeare's interest, for example, in the household as the cornerstone of English social and economic life is selective in scope and emphasis. Apart from *Twelfth Night*, none of the texts discussed in this book directly traces the dissolution of the household in the economic terms sketched by Wrightson. Meredith Skura argues that many of Shakespeare's plays, including *King Lear*, return incessantly to the affective structures of the noble household of the 1590s at the very point when player companies were moving away from the itinerant status of actor-beggars in noble households.[39] *King Lear* is often read as a representation of the dissolution of feudal relations before the onslaught of capitalist ambition and greed, but there is nothing about the ambition and greed in the play that make them peculiarly capitalist or even proto-capitalist (as I argue in Chapter 6).[40] Such households as appear in Shakespeare's work cannot therefore be assumed to be directly mimetic of the social conditions and developments around him. How seriously, as a piece of realistic theatre, do we take the depiction of Petrucchio's household and his relationship to its servants in *The Taming of the Shrew*? Are the social relations and rivalries in the household presided over by the steward Malvolio the same as those of the household which Flavius tries to save from ruin in *Timon of Athens*? What of the household relations that we glimpse darkly in the sonnets? How are they related to the confusion of public and private service in the homes and courts of Lear, Gloucester,

---

[38] Hay, "Master and Servant in England", 264.
[39] Although his own experience lay primarily on the up-to-date public stage in London, Shakespeare's players all conform to the outdated antitheatricalist's image of the player as itinerant, a proud beggar living on alms" (*Actor*, 85).
[40] Delany, "*King Lear* and the Decline of Feudalism", and Burnett, "*King Lear*".

Albany, and Cornwall, or the claustrophobic domestic space established so precariously in the military outpost in *Othello*. How are these domestic spaces to be related to the idyllic pleasures and betrayals of Belmont on the margins of mercantile Venice, the attenuated court in *The Two Gentlemen of Verona*, the domestic home beyond the street in *The Comedy of Errors*, the strange, otherworldly dislocation and radical attenuation of family and court in *The Tempest*, or the "two households" at war in *Romeo and Juliet*?

The point is not that no historical distinction should be made between the relationship defined entirely by Marx's dreaded impersonal cash nexus and the greater, but possibly more emotionally enriching (if burdened), intimacies of service, but rather that there may be a structural continuity in various forms of society in which the kinds of affective engagement that marked what we now regard as feudal, familial forms maintain their hold through personal relationships of employment. The question is what roles are allowed (or precluded) by the interaction of structural and affective possibilities in associations between employer and employee or master and servant. Is it possible that, at least for Shakespeare, the less paternalistic transformation of service through economic transactions made available a more equitable and free exchange of mutual affection, a possibility reflected in his systematic use of economic relations to represent affective ties?

When the economics of the market does fall within Shakespeare's imaginative purview, he is as inclined to be sympathetic to the idea of the "sociability of commerce" by which "market relationships could be perceived less in terms of the pursuit of private advantage and more of expressions of interdependence and trust" (Wrightson, *Earthly Necessities*, 204). Theodore Leinwand has revealed the deeply affective aspects of commercial relationships in Shakespeare and his contemporaries.[41] "Love's wealth", the chapter title of a book on the transcendence of love over commercial relations in Shakespeare's comedies, is more than a mere metaphor in Shakespeare. It conveys a perhaps idealized sense that new economic relations should continue to be informed by old affective relations of loyalty and service.[42] As dramatist and poet, he is ambivalent about the tension between the free circulation implied by cash relations and the settled ties of neo-feudal reciprocity. He is not uniformly critical of the use of economic terms as metaphors for affective relationships – on the contrary, he is alive to the conjunction of the different senses of "dear" and a man's "worth", and also to the ways in which money may allow a greater circulation of affect beyond the limits imposed by blood. *As You Like It* reveals the double-edged

---

[41] Leinwand, *Theatre, Finance*.   [42] Brown, *Comedies*, "Love's Wealth".

nature of commodification: it exposes the Old Shepherd to the insecurities of an uncertain tenure on the one hand, but on the other it affords him the possibility of freeing himself from an abusive master when the land is sold to new owners who automatically become his masters. There is, however, little sense that Shakespeare is responding directly and critically, as Jonson and Middleton do, to a dynamic of market impersonality seen to be as threatening as it is exhilarating. In his treatment of the most residual form of service – the retainer band – Shakespeare *disjoins* love from service, showing in *Much Ado about Nothing*, *Romeo and Juliet*, and *All's Well That Ends Well*, that *eros*, especially driven by the female, is the only force capable of withstanding the irrational violence of male camaraderie.

Shakespeare's representation of service, although multifaceted and complex, does not directly follow the changing contours of his social and economic environment. He writes no "citizen" plays, being apparently indifferent to the markets and workshops of London at the very moment when his fellows, Jonson, Middleton, Dekker and Heywood, found in them inexhaustible opportunities for entertainment, satire, and social complaint. His "mouldy tales" offer no direct or sustained representation of the changes that historians trace in the economic life of the period and its immediate bearing on forms of social organization and personal experience. The much noted absence of mothers in Shakespeare indicates that he ignores the figure absolutely central to the functioning of the early modern household, including the organization of its servants and the dissemination of love and even violent control and care.[43] The domestic spaces in these plays are recognizable from what we know of early modern English familial organization, but they bear a character of their own that is peculiar to Shakespeare: of strangeness and dislocation, of attenuation in some instances and an intensified, almost obsessively surrealistic focus in others, and, above all, of a peculiar, histrionic investment by the stage on which they are presented and its own forms of service.

Shakespeare is strongly attracted to the reciprocity imbedded as an ideal in affective bonds of service, but he is also aware of the degree to which its asymmetries of power (especially in emotional terms) are open to abuse. His analysis of such abuse tends to be ethical rather than structural, conceptual rather than economic. Iago's gross manipulation of his doomed master's trust has much darker, metaphysical roots than the ambitious avarice of the acquisitive subject of emergent capitalism. A character such as Edmund

---

[43] See Wall, *Staging Domesticity*.

wishes merely to occupy the centre of feudal power from his marginal position as bastard rather than destroy or transform it. Shakespeare shows only a passing interest in the changing economic or social conditions of the apprentice, but his concern with the affective turmoil of the page or the young courtier as servant-lover is almost obsessive. He is especially interested in the vulnerability that accompanies the transformation of mere service into love, but he also shows that loving service is exemplified when the servant has the courage to oppose and even disobey his or, especially, *her* master. In Paulina the "feminization" of service traced by some historians[44] is given a wholly different twist, for in *The Winter's Tale* the fearless, oppositional care of the female courtier exemplifies true service. The most dedicated kinds of service in Shakespeare take the form of critical resistance to unreasonable or wayward masters, who are never so truly served as when they are opposed. When social and political relationships break down as a result of the intransigent failure of masters to acknowledge the mutual bonds of service, the servant that persists without reward or even acknowledgement often becomes the only ethical light in an otherwise dark landscape.

THE "IDEOLOGY OF SERVICE"

Most of the tracts that now constitute the canon of the Elizabethan and Jacobean "ideology of service" were published relatively late, at the end of the sixteenth or in the first two decades of the seventeenth century. They are a later development, in tone and didactic intention, of an earlier wave of moralist writers known as the "commonwealthsmen", who "espoused the ideal of a Christian commonwealth, governed by distributive justice, in which members of each estate should enjoy an appropriate share in return for performing their duties according to their degree" (Wrightson, *Earthly Necessities*, 150). The later moralists are more attuned to the economic changes resisted by their early Tudor forebears, but their focus is also narrower. They are particularly concerned with the bounds and bonds of service – possibly because they were perceived to be threatened – as they were embodied in the hierarchies of the middling household. The most well known of them, reprinted and used even today for its advice on marriage and the family by fundamentalist Christians, is William Gouge's compendious *Of Domesticall Dvties* (1622). John Dod and Robert Cleaver's

---

[44] See Houlbrooke, *Family*, 176–7, and Goldberg, *Women*, 194 and passim, especially 202.

A Godly Forme of Household Gouernment (1598, reprinted in 1612 and 1630) also treats the family as the locus of social and spiritual relations.[45] Because these two nonconformist Puritan divines from Oxfordshire were prevented from preaching under James's reign, it is possible that their book was "targeted to known audiences, rather than broadcast to strangers".[46] Thomas Fosset's *The Seruants Dvtie* (1613) focuses exclusively on household servants rather than the family as a whole. He emphasizes especially rigorously the servant's duty of obedience by patterning the call to suffering after Christ's own bending of his will to God the Father.

All of these tracts are infused with a moralizing, even hectoring, tenor and an anxious idealizing vision that R. C. Richardson attributes to the genre's inclination towards "social engineering", inclined to shape an ideology rather than reflect a settled set of conditions and beliefs. Although their concern with the household as the crux on which social relations were formed and economic activity was organized would appear to put them in touch with the lived relations of late Tudor and early Stuart life, their Biblical exegesis leads them to draw didactic points about the nature of service and authority from Old Testament social relations that were radically different from contemporary, English economic and social conditions.

Very different in perspective and attitude is one of the few extended written accounts of service by one of its disillusioned practitioners. The author of *A Health to the Gentlemanly Profession of Seruingmen* (1598) (by I.M., or J.M., as the initial is sometimes rendered)[47] laments the passing of a golden age of service. He offers a personal picture of service that focuses specifically upon the changing economic and social landscape in the last three decades Elizabeth's reign. The author writes from the perspective of *gentleman* servant, however – the kind of figure who, like Malvolio, might have been a secretary, usher, or steward in a noble household – the decline of whose status and treatment is the lamented topic of his book. The decay of the form of service and servant to whom I.M. proposes his "health" was caused, in his view, by the general falling-off of hospitality, which led to a diminution in both the quality and quantity of servants employed in the household. Previously gentle positions, through which master and servant could maintain a relationship of intimacy and mutual respect, became filled by "untryed drosse and dregges of lesse esteeme", who were not only incapable of performing the practical duties of the senior

[45] Families are "little churches", William Perkins writes in *Christian Oeconomy* (670), whereas Dod and Cleaver call the family a "little commonwealth" in *Household Government* (sig. A^v).

[46] Bernard and McKenzie, *Cambridge History of the Book*, 31.

[47] The author may have been Gervase Markham. See Evett, *Discourses*, 223 n10.

household servant but, most important, could not provide the affective support and companionship to the master that marked service in its golden age.[48] In I.M.'s view the decline in hospitality is not a sign of the decline of the household as such but rather of the changing value placed on service and servants.

True to their social positions and religious convictions, the writers of the household conduct-books have little to say about courtly forms of service, a major preoccupation of Shakespeare's work across all genres.[49] Shakespeare's sonnets are written from the position of a servant-lover seeking more than patronage from a well-born young master; all the comedies save *The Merry Wives of Windsor* use settings in which erotic forms of service overlap with courtly or military ones; *King Lear* and *Antony and Cleopatra* combine the public allegiances of the court with the more intimate demands of the household. For a view of service in the court, one needs to turn to translations from French and Italian, such as Stefano Guazzo's *Ciuile Conuersation of M. Stephen Guazzo, translated out of French by M. Pettie* (1586) or Torquato Tasso's *The Householder's Philosophie* (1588) and Baldassare Castiglione's *The Book of the Courtier* (1528). Written as a dialogue between Guazzo and his female interlocutor, Annabella, the *Conuersation* offers an at least fictionalized voice of a woman in conversation rather than the male-dominated monologue of the expository sermon. Like its early-sixteenth-century counterparts, it is concerned with the urbane manners of courtly life rather than the practical necessities of the middling household.[50] Moving with Guazzo into the realms of the court reminds us of the "Golden chain" of service which the work focused on middling households tends to make us forget: that service was not exclusively the task of the menial (Guazzo, *Conuersation*, 167). There were many menial servants, but the demands of broader political contexts such as the civil service and the bonds of service to the monarch (including those of war) meant that, as Bacon indicates, "great men" were themselves constrained (and presumably also empowered) by their bonds of service.

---

[48] Now for the disdain of the Gentlemanly Seruingman: You have heard before of what mettall the right Seruingman was made of, of himselfe pure and right stuffe, not mixed with any dregges and drosse of lesse esteeme: But when this mixture of mingle-mangle begunne, and that he saw him selfe confronted with a crue of such clusterfysts, he beganne to waxe weerie of his profession, euen loathing to lyue in fellowshyp with such vnserviceable people, and disdaining the degree of a seruile drudge, resolueth eyther to cleare suite of that Lorde, or els to turne ouer a new leafe. (sig. Fʳ)

[49] Evett and Neill pay proper attention to this aspect of Shakespeare's focus.

[50] Cf. Guazzo's attribution of the decline of service (it seems ever to have been in decline!) to the failure of princes to maintain their courts as training grounds for good service with I. M.'s lament over the decline of manorial hospitality: "I thinke the cause of it is, for that in this place Princes seldome keepe their courts wher seruingmen chieflie learn good behauiour" (*Conuersation*, sig. Y4ᵛ).

Apart from Protestants' obsession with the wife's place as both obedient servant and dutiful mistress within its material and spiritual economies, they all but ignore women. I. M. scarcely mentions them. This silence appears to confirm the general position taken by social historians that, at least within the noble household, there was little place for women beyond the meanest menial tasks and the more elevated but confined role of waiting upon and providing companionship to its lady. Still it ignores the degree to which women played central roles in the production and reproduction of the household economy and affective spaces.[51] This narrowness of scope limits the usefulness of these tracts for gleaning the roles and subjectivities of female servants, whose voices are absent from the didactic literature and excluded from other, more permanent forms of self-expression. We shall see that Shakespeare's representation of those voices is considerably greater and more varied, although not by any means comprehensive. It ranges from the intimacy of critical companionship, through the performance, in disguise, of male service as a vehicle of female erotic devotion, to the most unexpectedly radical representation of perfect council in the shape of the "mankind witch", Paulina, in *The Winter's Tale*. Even in Shakespeare there are few female servants between the "maid that milks" and the gentle-woman's companion (the Nurse in *Romeo and Juliet* is a signal exception),[52] unless they adopt male roles of service through cross-dressing, where such service offers homosocial intimacy which may be transformed into mutual erotic attraction, such as Viola-as-Cesario finds in Duke Orsino's court.

The Protestant conduct books are also constrained by their own positions of address. Purporting to give impartial advice on the natural or God-ordained duties of service and obedience, many are themselves divided between their possible conditions as masters or servants: their own places in the middle condition – masters of some but also owing allegiance and livelihood to more powerful figures – suggests an ambivalent personal relation to the roles they seek to delineate.[53] Gouge is exceptional in dedicating his work to his parishioners. His independence may account for the relative

---

[51] "Female household members were practically nonexistent. Those we do find are invariably chamberwomen and companions to the lady of the household restricted to the private portions of the house (and often married to another servant); or laundresses, who much of the time lived outside the household" (*Household*, 57).

[52] For a classic study of the Nurse, see Barbara Everet's wonderful "The Nurse's Story".

[53] Fosset dedicates his book to "the thrice worthy and worshipful gentleman and hous-keeper Master Thomas Spenser of Clardon"; Dod and Cleaver to three gentlemen, one a Justice of the Peace (Justices of the Peace were charged with setting servants' wages): Robert Burgaine, John Dive, and Edmund Temple; T. K. offers his translation of Guazzo's *Ciuile Conuersation* to "the worshipfull and vertuous Gentleman Maister Thomas Reade Esquier"; and Walter Darrel (*A Short Discourse of the Life of Servingmen*, 1578) addresses his preface to his cousin, Marmaduke Darrel.

subtlety of his treatise and the equal weight he places upon the obligations of masters and the lack of difference between master and servant in the eyes of God.

We should therefore take the views expressed in these books from whence they come, keeping in mind their narrowness of scope, their at times self-ingratiating idealization, the possibility that their tracts are expressions of anxiety rather than representations of social fact, and their generic difference from the dramatic texts they may be employed to elucidate.

RECIPROCAL DUTIES

Despite their generic and ideological limitations, the tracts that formulate the "ideology of service" remain useful not merely as barometers for gauging the anxieties of masters and their clerical spokesmen but also for the peculiarity of their idealization of master-servant relationships. Read against the grain, with an eye to their rhetorical character and constitutive tensions, they are indicators of ideological strain. Yet their idealizing conceptions of the reciprocity of social and personal relations do highlight real aspects of not only Shakespeare's texts but also of an ethics of social relations that is extremely distant from us today. Nor is that distance always our gain. Of particular interest in the Protestant literature is the friction between its social conservatism and its relatively independent didacticism based on a recognition of the spiritual equality of all before God. Gouge explicitly defends that conservatism by denying the egalitarian, Anabaptist argument that such spiritual parity should be embodied in the abolition of master-servant relationships in the secular realm. "Politique inequality is not against a spirituall equality", he declares bluntly (593). Yet he is nevertheless engaged by the didactic need to limit the exercise of power that masters have over their servants as a result of that conservative vision, and to give an account of the ideal harmony of a social order founded upon the "natural" subjugation of servants by masters.

Gouge attempts to secure that order by resorting to a common paradox: by willingly shouldering their duties of obedience servants become the "Lord's freemen", while masters enact their roles as the "Lord's servants" (691) by obeying God's command to take proper magisterial care of their servants. The contradiction that lies at the centre of the whole edifice of Puritan social theory – in the simultaneous claim that all people are equal before God and yet that God has also ordered the world into relations of natural subordination – is turned into a means to achieve the ideals of proper care and responsibility that lay upon the shoulders of masters as servants of the Lord. Gouge ends his tract with a warning to those that abuse their servants: "Let all such masters know that they have a master" (691) – they are "but as stewards ouer fellow seruants: euery one of them therefore shall heare this charge, *giue an account of thy stewardship*" (689). To those who believe that they are free to treat their servants as they like because their power has been endorsed by both earthly and divine authority, he warns:

[L]et masters here learne to cast off all such fond conceits, and foolish hopes. Though they be higher in place, haue more wealth, and better friends then their seruants, and though men who have carnall eies may thereby be much moued to respect them, yet will not God goe an haires bredth from iustice for the whole world. . . . If the greatest that be abuse the meanest, they shall not escape. Wherefore, O masters, giue no iust cause of complaint to any seruant. (693)

The "fear and trembling" that Gouge requires from servants in their relation to their masters is here required of the masters themselves, under the general principle that "*it is the feare of God which moueth men conscionably to submit themselues to another*" (11).

Gouge thus tries to forge a system in which no person is ever wholly a master, either spiritually or politically. The account is transparently idealist, but it would be a mistake to discount it as a merely cynical ploy to maintain the status quo. Infused by a powerful sense of an ordaining divine framework in which the individual conscience is central, this idealism assumes that if every member of this chain attended to their obligation of *reciprocal* care, then all would be well:

The reason why all are bound to submit themselves one to another is, because euery one is set in his place by God, not so much for himselfe, as for the good of others. . . . Let euery one therefore high and low, rich and poore, superiour and inferiour, Magistrate and subiect, Minister and people, husband and wife, parent and childe, master and seruant, neighbours and fellowes, of all sorts in their seuerall places take notice of their dutie in this point of submission, and make conscience to put it into practice. . . . *Masters*, by doing that which is iust and equall to their seruants. . . . Euery one, by being *of like affection one towards another*, and by *seruing one another in loue*, according to the Apostles rule. Let this dutie of submission be first well learned, and then all other duties will be better performed. (6–7; emphasis added)

"Love" and its cognate, "affection", are central to the idea that the willing submission of everybody will produce a harmonious commonwealth in which no one is abused or exploited. Even as he entrenches hierarchical relationships, Gouge offers an at least spiritually egalitarian account of the communal duty to maintain "like affection one towards another" and to "serve one another in love".

The connection between love and service in the period thus has one of its roots in the theological attempt to forge an ideology which, properly internalized, would limit the power of masters while ensuring the free obedience of the servant.[54] The fault line that divides and connects these two positions contains a tension central to this study: between the duties of reciprocal care that were supposed to inform all relations between master and servant and the personal demand for *affective* equality in relations of friendship and love that, unfulfilled, could turn to resentment. Although personal ambition may well have informed (and destroyed) many relationships of service in the period (and, if we go along with Lamb and Burnett, the ideological edifice itself), Shakespeare seems to be less interested in ambition and avarice than the complexities of abjection that arise from deeper forms of personal intimacy: the need for love, friendship, and devotion; willing self-sacrifice; and the attendant anxieties and forms of resentment that arise from feelings of rejection, betrayal, and neglect. He may be atypical of both his age and the contemporary theatre in this respect. What servants demand or need in Shakespeare is acknowledgement, in Stanley Cavell's critical sense of the word.[55] His masters are frequently incapable of granting such acknowledgement or, more destructively, of recognizing their *own* need for acknowledgement by their servants. It is also frequently the mark of his servants, however, that they offer their services freely, either expecting no acknowledgement or accepting its failure.

Shakespeare's representation of the affective and structural interdependency of master and servant anticipates in a limited way Hegel's metaphysical analysis of the logic of the master-slave relation. The degree of self-consciousness that master and bondsman derive from their respective reflection through the acknowledgement of the other is asymmetrical: both figures need the other to be conscious of themselves as living beings. This is a purely logical point, to do with the semantics of the terms "master" and "servant". One cannot be a servant without having a master, and, less obviously, perhaps, one cannot be a master without having a servant. Yet whereas the servant is a mirror that reflects the master to himself, the master seems (and only seems) to be independent: he affirms himself by negating

---

[54] Evett's central, original argument is that the theology of service creates a space for free devotion and acknowledged responsibility. My argument is that the reciprocity ideally encompassed by master-servant relations is imaginatively and affectively encompassed by love.

[55] Cavell, *Knowledge*.

the servant. The master appears to exist entirely for himself, the servant wholly for the master. The consciousness of self that marks the master can come into being only through the recognition by the servant of the master, however. This is a form of self-recognition that the master *mis*recognises. In the historical and dialectical sublation of the initiating relationship, the servant ultimately has the capacity to bring home to the master his own misrecognition in an act of independent assertion and freedom:

[T]he unessential consciousness is, for the master, the object which embodies the truth of his certainty of himself. But it is evident that this object does not correspond to its notion; for, just where the master has effectively achieved lordship, he really finds that something has come about quite different from an independent consciousness. It is not an independent, but rather a dependent consciousness that he has achieved. He is thus not assured of self-existence as his truth; he finds that his truth is rather the unessential consciousness, and the fortuitous unessential action of that consciousness.

The truth of the independent consciousness is accordingly the consciousness of the bondsman. This doubtless appears in the first instance outside itself, and not as the truth of self-consciousness. But just as lordship showed its essential nature to be the reverse of what it wants to be, so, too, bondage will, when completed, pass into the opposite of what it immediately is: being a consciousness repressed within itself, it will enter into itself, and change round into real and true independence.[56]

Shakespeare's differs from Hegel (and this is the mark of their historical distance) insofar as he does not entertain the promise of the "real and true independence" of the servant that the dialectic contains. Although he recognizes the logical interdependence of master and servant, he is primarily concerned with the ethics of human relationships – of what goes on between people rather than their relationship within a system of metaphysical speculation. It might be going too far to say that the possibility of independence lies beyond the reach of Shakespeare's imagination; it certainly plays no part in either his representations of reality or the creation of his dreams. The relationships that Shakespeare's servants desire are almost without exception those of interdependence – of equality of affection and mutual acknowledgement – with their masters. (There are singular exceptions, such as Iago.) Manumission is usually a stage for a continuation of the relationship on a different plane, and such servants who do choose independence usually fall into remorse, suffering, and death. Even Ariel's freedom, probably the only true independence achieved by any servant in Shakespeare, is tinged with a sense of loss, signalled by his unexpectedly asking Prospero whether he loves him just before he is freed. There is a

---

[56] Hegel, *Phenomenology of Mind*, §§192 and 193.

continuous ethical tension in Shakespeare between the acceptance of the
bonds of service in both senses of the word – as that which binds you to
the will of another and which provides you with sustaining, affective, and
supporting links with another – and the desire for free giving that love
entails. Bonds are not necessarily forms of bondage; but if the subject of
both love and service does not think or imagine that they are the product
of his or her own will, they will come to seem bound servitude rather than
free service (see Evett, *Discourses*).

The constraints of service and the freedom of love

The reciprocal bonds between masters and servant are emphasized in all
contemporary writing on the subject. Gouge offers an ideological (in the
non-pejorative sense of the word) account of an ideal spiritual commonwealth by intimating that what actually holds the relationship of master to
servant together is love rather than power: a mutual respect and affection
of each for the other. Evett makes such voluntary reciprocity central to his
argument in *Discourses of Service*, which offers a valuable clarification of the
paradoxical phrase from the Tudor Book of Common Prayer that "service
is perfect freedom". Tracing the provenance of this phrase in the Collect
for Peace in Thomas Cranmer's translation from the *Missa pro pace*, Evett
points out that although

> the original collect called attention to servants, and to obedience, in promot-
> ing the new one from occasional to incessant use . . . Cranmer laid the empha-
> sis of repetition and of Establishment on the paradox of "perfect freedom" in
> service . . . rendering the prayer particularly relevant to any auditors who already
> think of themselves as servants in nontheological contexts. (3)

Through his own concept of "volitional primacy", Evett offers an account
of how the theological paradox may have operated in the individual and
collective psychology of servants who voluntarily subordinated their wills
to those of others, especially in the spirit of Christ's exemplary command
to all human beings to "serve one another".[57] Having pointed out that "[i]t
is on this text that Luther and other protestant theologians primarily found
their understanding of service", Evett does not, however, explicitly link the
paradox to the injunction to serve one another "by *love*". The paradox can,
however, only be lived, as Gouge indicates, when service is lived as love.[58]

---

[57] Galatians, 5:14.
[58] Striking about this collect is not so much the paradox itself – that in the service of God one is totally
free – which is grammatically and rhetorically relatively marginal to the thrust of the prayer, but

The possible relationship between the condition of bondage and the bonds of love mitigates the ideological (in the pejorative sense of "false consciousness") tenor of Cranmer's paradox, especially if the collect is taken as an instance of the characteristically Protestant concern with willing obedience:

> The third thing whereunto a seruant is called, is to serue, that is, to obey, and to be in subjection, to have no will of his own, nor power over him selfe, but wholly to resign himselfe to the will of his Master; for what is obedience, but . . . a voluntary and reasonable sacrificing of a mans owne will, voluntarily, freely, and without any constraints: and reasonably, that is, according to reason and religion, in obedience, and feare of God.[59]

The idea that the bondage of service must be freely and voluntarily turned into freedom offers a phenomenological resolution to both a logical contradiction and an ontological condition. Bondage can be turned into freedom by thinking of it and one's relation to it differently, by *imagining* it otherwise.[60] This phenomenological transformation could provide a satisfying sense of purpose and identity in particular relationships. Yet the general social character of such a practice is open to critique and demystification. Perception of "the curse of service" by a character such as Iago is as compelling a fact of that phenomenology as the "assured friendship" extolled by Richard Brathwait as the character of all master-servant relations.[61]

Evett is right to want to focus on service as something lived by individuals in the imagination and the heart rather than embodied abstractly in groups. Nevertheless, we also need a critical perspective from which the "present satisfaction" that "the conscious and voluntary subordination of one's immediate interests to those of another" might be seen to entrench exploitative relationships rather than loving attachments (Evett, 13). The

---

rather the supplication to the power of God's protection and defence on the basis of a reciprocal bond between God and his servants. God's servants are an extension of God himself – the power that such servants fear is the power, finally, of *God's* adversaries, who by extension are theirs. For a meditation on the paradox that God has pledged his service to those who serve him by protecting them from their enemies (which are also His enemies), see Wright, *Passions*: "if service be succouring, sustaining, helping, ministering necessaries, and in every thing assisting vs in best and basest offices, I may say thou lovingly serves all, who without thy service could not serve themselves, nor all the world except thy selfe. Great, no doubt, is thy love (O God without paragon in love) to men in this life . . . it seemeth thy will and power are at the command, or ready to obey the desires of thy faithful servants" (214).

[59] Fosset, *Seruants Dutie*, 22.

[60] Both the religious and social forms of phenomenological transformation are, of course, open to materialist and psychoanalytical critique. Freud famously traduces the second commandment in *Civilization and Its Discontents*, and Marx's analysis of the ideological obfuscations of religion are well known.

[61] Brathwait, *English Gentleman*, 159.

problem is to shift the aim of historical criticism somewhat: from the position that judges a writer pejoratively for failing to achieve our own (enlightened) views, to one that asks to what degree he or she succeeds in representing most powerfully and fully the lived conditions (including its contradictions but also its satisfactions) of a different system. This involves an acknowledgement of Shakespeare's difference and an attempt to inhabit in an informed and critical way the imagination of service and love as he represents them.

PERFORMING SERVICE

The dialogical nature of Guazzo's *Conuersation* suggests that the drama might be the best place to look for a more representative, certainly a more dynamic, representation of the relations between masters and servants, especially if we are interested in the hierarchical ideology of service that framed its specific, occupational relations. In contrast to the conduct books and contemporary biographies, which represent a "top-down, idealizing representation of the social order and the place of masters and servants within it", the "multivocal" nature of the drama, in the words of a historian, "has a distinctive way of pushing servants into prominence other sources conceal or deny" (Richardson, "Social Engineering", 182–3). What the theatre renders inescapable are the performative dimensions of service: many early modern commentators suggest that service was a role that had to be learned and sustained. The most striking embodiment of such performance occurs in the opening scene of *The Taming of the Shrew* in which the identities of master, servant, and subversive wife are all assumed to be amenable to role-play.

Such performative dimensions of service inform all Shakespeare's texts, including the sonnets. Throughout this study, I propose to focus on the service rather the servant, the relationship rather than the entity, dimensions shown in performance rather than settled in essence. Guazzo's turn of phrase, "I think it a matter impossible, that he should know how to play the maister wel, who never had maister" (168), indicates a more than merely metaphorical sense that being a master meant inhabiting a role that has to be learnt by first playing its complementary part. That a good master should ideally have first played the part of a servant suggests that neither of these roles was necessarily fixed or independent. One learnt mastery through service. The performative dimensions of the master-servant relationship both allowed people to play their social parts with a degree of latitude for personal adaptation and extemporizing and also opened up dimensions of anxiety and fear for many who felt that they had invested their social security and even their personal identities in what might turn out to be no more than *play*.

LOVING SERVICE

The discussion of Cranmer's paradox and the Protestant moralists indicates that the ground of all service is love. Yet this opens the question of the extent to which love should itself be qualified as an *extension* of the ideological imagination in addition to its capacity to contradict it. The combination of reciprocity and subordination in love and service alike ran from the most menial master and servant to monarch and subject, including the most powerful figures within the peerage. The God who ordains the estates of master and servant also holds His world together through His own abiding love, which in turn infuses secular being with mutually reinforcing obligations of duty and care.[62] Gouge insists on the "near bond which is betwixt master and servants" which, by both God's law and "the law of nature . . . hath tied master and seruant together by mutuall and reciprocal bond, of doing good, as well as of receiuing good" (629 and 171–2). Further, in Guazzo's dialogues the community of master and servant in love is central:

Annib. First of all I thinke it necessarie that he which doeth desire to be well serued, require in his seruaunts three speciall things, that is to say, *loue*, loyaltie, and sufficiency: & such a one that maister shall easilie come by, which shall dispose himselfe to be a good and *louing* Maister, following the commaundement of the wise man, *Loue* him whome thou nourishest, which he shalbe forced to doe, if he will thinke himselfe that seruantes (though they serue) are men, that they are dwellers with us, yea, that they are our humble friends, and which is more, our fellow seruants. (Y3ʳ; emphasis added)

I.M., too, recalls the relationship between the gentleman servant and his master as a reciprocally loving one: "For in these dayes, what greater loue could almost be found, then betwixt the Maister and the Seruant? It was in manner equall with the Husbands to the Wyfe, and the Childes to the Parent. . . . What greater goodwil, what purer loue, or more sincere affection can be found amongst any comfort of creatures then this?" (sig. C2ʳ).

---

[62] See Reynolds, *Treatise*, 81: "The Master-Wheele, or first Mover in all the Regular Motions of this Passion, is the *Love of God*, grounded on the right *knowledge* of Him; whereby the Soule being ravished with the apprehension of his infinite *Goodnesse*, is earnestly drawn and *called out*, as it were, to desire an *Vnion, Vision*, and participation of his Glory and Presence."

I.M. is looking back, in 1598, at a changed world; Annibel and Guazzo, on the other hand, engage in one of the apparently timeless, urbane dialogues of high European Humanism. How do we deal with these various invocations of love from different philosophical, personal, national, and historical positions? If these pronouncements support Laslett's claim that in early modern England "every relationship could be seen as a love relationship" (*World*, 5), what concept of love (if indeed there is only one) is being extolled in these descriptions of master-servant relationships? Is the love that Guazzo expects the courtier to have for his prince the same as the "loue . . . betwixt the Maister and the Seruant . . . equall with the Husbands to the Wyfe" that I.M nostalgically laments, the "affection" that Gouge urges between those meant to serve and those ordained to command, and the "admirable omnipotencie of love" celebrated so ecstatically by Thomas Wright?[63]

What relations of love and service are, for example, invoked in the following dialogue?

> SILVIA Servant!
> VALENTINE Mistress?
> SPEED [*to* VALENTINE] Master . . .
>   (2.4.1–3)

The kind of devotion that Silvia presumes upon when she calls her aristocratic beloved "servant" differs from the bond between Speed and Valentine signalled by the cognate appellation "master". Valentine and Speed are different sorts of servant. Yet these forms of service are linked both historically and conceptually. The service that Valentine acknowledges by responding to Silvia as "mistress" is derived from the bonds of what we might be tempted to call "real" service. The medieval tradition of erotic devotion pledged to an elevated and idealized woman by the French troubadours took its force from the devotion that the villain or vassal owed to a feudal lord, or that the lord in turn owed to his sovereign. In Irving Singer's words, "[t]he medieval world was hierarchical, predicated upon fealty and a sense of duty that bound subject to master. The troubadours . . . offer[ed] to their lady . . . the vows of service and fidelity expected of every lower link within the medieval chain".[64] Silvia invokes that devotion whenever she addresses her lover Valentine as her "servant" (something she habitually does). Is the tradition that inverts the usual hierarchies of service – making the suppliant male the servant and the mistress the master – a mere metaphor, no more

---

[63] Wright, *Passions*, 215.   [64] Singer, *Nature of Love 2*, 51.

than a literary trope for actual conditions of a hierarchically structured, patriarchal society, or are its relationships indeed a form of service? Do its habitual discourses of self-sacrifice, devotion, and the granting of mercy fuse religious, erotic, and social forms of service into a lived rather than merely fictionalised whole?

Let us approach this question by distinguishing different concepts of love and their possible relation to service.

Nomos

The classical world offered a range of distinct concepts for the single English word "love": *eros*, *agapē*, *philia*, and *nomos*. Service is embroiled to varying degrees in all of these concepts.

The conceptual affinity between service and love as forms of obedience and obliteration of the will is especially clear in Protestant moralists. *Nomos* is the Hebrew conception of love as submission of will to another – especially God – by adhering to the Law:

Loue is the fulfilling of the Law, that is, the very life of all those duties which the law requireth. It is the *bond of perfection*, which bindeth together all those duties that passe between partie and partie. (Gouge, 225)

Christ's obedient submission of his will to that of his Father in unquestioning obedience is thus a form of love, although it is distant from *eros*. Gouge's characteristic requirement that the servant should obey the master in "fear and trembling" harks back to the Old Testament conception of God's demand of loving obedience from the children of Israel. This involves, especially in Job's case, not merely the subjugation but indeed the *annihilation* of the will: "sheer, unmitigated obedience – that is what God requires of the loving soul" (Singer, *Love 1*, 250).

The demand that the servant dedicate himself or herself totally to the will of the master is thus an analogical projection of the devotion of God's people to Him onto the relationship between secular subject and monarch and master and servant. In a world in which love had become synonymous almost entirely with the pursuit of desire, we tend not to think of it as the subjection of one's will to that of another. The Hebrew demand of obedience offers a conception of love that brooks no sentimentality, allows no assertion of personal aspiration, and, above all, provides a reason (or excuse) for the subjection to power and the acceptance of suffering in the secular world.[65] The historical affinity between love and service through

---

[65] See Fosset, 16: "The second thing whereunto a seruant is called, is to suffer, what must he suffer? Al those euils and injuries which his seruice and seruitude doth bring with it. Why so? For hereunto he is called: and Christ suffered for us, leauing us an example that we should follow his steppes."

nomos thus threatens the most definitive of philosophical reductions: the Platonic and neo-Platonic definition of love as *eros*, where the will, in the form of desire, is central.

Eros

For Socrates in the *Symposium*, love is nothing other than desire. Marked by a fundamental, definitive lack, the lover desires union with the carnal object of love as an always-inadequate substitute for an ultimate, transcendental form of beauty and goodness. In this powerful idealist tradition, the body – specifically the embodied particularity of the beloved – this person, here, now – is never good enough. The carnal union that men desire with women is merely the impetus towards the dream of immortal life through children. The more elevated desire of the older man for the beauty of a boy remains earthbound, even if it raises itself by focusing on a more pristine form of beauty and (in ideal cases) less carnal aspirations of education and intellectual pleasure. Tzvetan Todorov observes that "the logic of love-desire is diabolical".[66] It is not merely doomed to failure; it constitutes itself on that very necessity. In the words of one of its most canny celebrants, "its objects are no more than a succession of substitutes for an imagined originary presence, a half-remembered 'oceanic' pleasure in the lost real, a completeness which is desire's final, unattainable object".[67] Whether desire is inherited from Plato or Lacan, its objects are desired not for themselves; they are wanted for what they always only represent or promise (impossibly).

The Platonic provenance of this tradition means that love for human beings must always be instrumental: one loves this or that person merely as a means to loving God or the Good. For Singer, as for Todorov, this is debilitating:

Modifying Platonism in this way, Christianity inherits a static view of man. It assumes that there must be a specific and determinate *completion* to human nature, a total satisfying of desires, a perfecting of what it is to be man. Never finding the ideal in the realm of experience, it posits another world in which perfect love would make a perfect man. Since that love *is* God, the finished product must be an image, or a likeness, of the divine original. (Singer, *Love 1*, 359)

Singer's argument encapsulates secular notions of love in the Middle Ages and the Renaissance, which tend to follow the Platonic ideal. The idealized beloved of the Petrarchan tradition is precisely "an image, or likeness, of the divine original", except that to one of Petrarch's personae that image

---

[66] Todorov, *Imperfect Garden*, 123.   [67] Belsey, *Desire*, 5, who is following Lacan.

is itself a form of blasphemy, a seduction away from the pure, spiritual love of God.[68] In the Renaissance, the neo-Platonic idealization of love in Ficino's writing revisits the Socratic division between earthly and heavenly Aphrodite, recognizing in the love of carnal beauty a striving for the spiritual ideal derived from Plato.[69] This is why neo-Platonists have to resort to the counter-intuitive identification of the beauty of body and soul. Whereas neo-Platonic love emphasizes reciprocity on earth, it remains true to its Platonic heritage in being transcendentally directed – its goal being the beauty of the person in the abstract, rather than the person him or herself.[70]

The question at the heart of love needs to be turned into the difference between two questions: "Whom do I love?" and "What do I love?" The object of the second question is not the person in themselves but rather the qualities that the beloved embodies or represents or promises;[71] the object in the first is the unique person in and for him or herself. In the second case, the beloved is fungible: he or she may be substituted by someone else, provided the qualities that one loves remain unchanged. In the first the qualities may change, but the love remains constant. It is marked by a fundamentally imaginative quality: what Singer calls "bestowal" and Freud terms "overvaluation". Love involves the imaginative projection or bestowal of value not reducible to the process of valuation. Valuation implies an objective measure by which the affective engagement may be judged; bestowal indicates an investment that cannot be attributed to a causal connection: "If the love is unique and irreplaceable he must also partially escape the causes of which he is the outcome; he is shrouded by a certain indeterminacy that is responsible for his difference" (Todorov, *Imperfect Garden*, 17). Freud's notion of overvaluation assumes an objective standard by which one can measure valuation in excess, but the imaginative investments of love exceed such measures. They are by nature irreducible to the causal instruments to which outraged fathers and masters, or even the lovers themselves, would like to attribute them, like "spells and medicines bought of mountebanks" (*Othello*, 1.3.61) or the qualities of being "virtuous . . . noble, / Of great estate, of fresh stainless youth. . . . And in dimension and shape of nature / A free and gracious person" (*Twelfth Night*, 1.5.225–30). Todorov shows that the most irrational and unstable aspects of desire are transformed in

---

[68] Petrarch, *Patrach's Secret.*   [69] Ficino, *Commantary.*
[70] Singer discusses the difference in emphasis in the work of Ficino and his pupil, Pico de Mirondella, in *Nature of Love* 2, 176ff.
[71] See Pascal, *Pensées* (qtd. in Todorov, p. 131), who claims that it is only the qualities of the beloved that are loved.

love into the most miraculous characteristic of human interaction: "This is the most precious feature of human love: as Descartes said, for the sake of highly imperfect beings, for the sake of highly relative value, it manages to produce the absolute. The human race therefore has the unique capacity to fabricate the infinite from the finite, the eternal from the transient, to transform a chance encounter into a life's necessity" (*Imperfect Garden*, 133–4).

The doubly insistent declaration with which Olivia brackets her catalogue of Orsino's qualities – that despite such qualities, she "cannot love him" (224 and 230) – signals a Shakespearean obsession. If Shakespeare tends to mock the forms of erotic desire that he inherits from his literary forebears, in play after play he nevertheless takes the bestowal that constitutes love very seriously, and he often aligns its irrationality and unconditionality with deep forms of service. The anti-Platonic, erotic Humanism celebrated by both Singer and Todorov runs as a defining strand through his poetry and plays: the uniqueness of the beloved in the eyes of the lover is a defining quality of love, its peculiar hell being constituted as much by lack of reciprocity as being forced to chose its love by another's eyes (*A Midsummer Night's Dream*, 1.1.140). At the same time, Shakespeare asks us to marvel at the strange duplicity of the lover's will. On one hand, love is implacably *willful*: immoderate, insistent, impervious to advice, direction, or the demand that it account for itself. On the other, this willfulness itself lies beyond the lover's control or volition. "[T]he loving subject is not one governed by his will" Todorov writes, "one cannot love because one has decided to love. On the contrary, love is the clearest example of an action that does not originate in an act of will" (136). Yet love does not escape the demands of ethics. Whereas the lover loves beyond his or her will, the lover may secure an ethical relationship to the beloved because

the relationship that he will live with that object is up to him; thus he can surmount the antithesis of submission and freedom by accepting chance, but progressively accepting responsibility for that decision. These two qualifications, however, do not diminish the force of the main point, namely, that no one can force him to love: chance and mysterious affinities decide in the place of the subject, and control over the forces operating at this moment eludes him. (Todorov, *Imperfact Garden*, 136)

Whereas in the Platonic scheme every carnal object of desire is either merely an instrument or a series of unsatisfying shadows of an unattainable pleasure, love in the Humanist sense reaches for what Todorov calls the "finality of the *you*" (132).

Philia

In his account of loving friendship or *philia*, Montaigne offers the most uncompromising statement of the "finality of the *you*" celebrated by Todorov as the quintessence of Humanist "love joy". It is the person (the *who*) rather than his qualities (the *what*) that is loved. No reason or cause can be provided for such love: "If a man urge me to tell wherefore I loved him, I feel it cannot be expressed, but by answering: Because it was he, because it was my selfe". Although this conception of *philia* follows the rule of non-fungibility that also marks the Humanist conception of *eros*, Montaigne distinguishes the two on psychological grounds: the settled stability of sovereign friendship is utterly different from the irrational changeability of erotic desire. The difference between Montaigne and the received tradition of loving-friendship therefore lies in his refusal to subscribe to the causal morality at the heart of the Aristotelain concept of *philia*. For Aristotle, it is ultimately the *virtue* of the other that leads me to bind myself to him in a community of friendship. Montaigne's friend, on the other hand, is loved unconditionally for himself: "This hath no other *Idea* than it selfe, and can have no reference but to it selfe".[72]

Todorov's claim that "what distinguishes love from other interpersonal relationships is . . . this impossibility of replacing the love object with another" (118) appears at first sight to offer a secure conceptual distinction between lover and servant. Being a mere instrument with a use-value, a servant may readily be replaced by someone who does the same work. Servants are hired for their qualities, not their persons – for what they can do, rather than for who they are. Nor does the necessary reciprocal dependency of master upon servant that I traced earlier via Hegel and the logic or grammar of the concepts apply to the lover. It is not necessarily true that if one loves, one is loved in return. Indeed, desire takes its measure from the *absence* of reciprocity. It is, on the other hand, a logical truth that if I am your friend, you must necessarily be mine. Masters and servants are therefore in this strictly logical sense closer to *philia* than to *eros*: one is always a servant to someone else; one can be a master only in relation to another who serves you.

In Shakespeare the loneliness of the lover is often mitigated by the necessary, if unequal, reciprocity of the servant-lover's relationship to the master or mistress. The nonhierarchical reciprocity of the closed community of friends is, however, the ultimate goal of the lover, especially the

---

[72] Montaigne, *Essays*, 149.

servant-lover, like the persona of the sonnets, who wishes to transform the unequal reciprocity of the master-servant relationship into the free mutual render of *eros-as-philia*. In her fine study of the discourses of friendship in the early modern period, Laurie Shannon remarks on the "rather astonishing" nature of Thomas Churchyard's statement that friendship is "a willing bondage that brings freedom forever".[73] But Churchyard is merely restating Cranmer's paradox that "service is perfect freedom" in the secular context of Montaigne's "sovereign amity": it is an inscription of friendship as an ultimate form of mutual service. If the rule of non-fungibility appears at first sight to distinguish love from service, in Shakespeare love's defining refusal of substitution is *extended* to service: love may turn bondage to freedom and the loneliness of desire can be transformed into the necessary reciprocity characteristic of *philia*.

The ambiguity of the word "friend" – companion, servant, or lover, or all three – encapsulates the possible coming together of service, erotic love, and loving friendship in Shakespeare. A further thread that ties together erotic desire, the settled enjoyment of married love, service, and male friendship is the repeated idea of the incorporation or extension of the self in and through the other. Following a long tradition of friendship literature, Montaigne writes of his friend that he "is no other but my selfe" (152). Even the most insistent tract on the necessary subservience of the servant to the master recognizes the servant as a part of the master's being, an other self: "for my seruant is to me, *alter ego*, another my selfe" (Fosset, 36). Further, Guazzo quotes the popular saying "if thou haue a trustie seruant, let him be vnto thee as thine owne Soule" with clear approval (174). Such sentiments indicate that servants are more than instruments with a mere use value. Dod and Cleaver's conception of the incorporated instrumentality of the servant echoes the often contradictory attempts to forge identities in married love and loving friendship:

Whereupon it comes to pass, that good and faithful seruants, liking and affecting their maisters, vnderstand them at a becke, and obey them at the winke of the eye, or the bent of the brow, not as a water-spaniel, but as the hand is stirred to obey the mind, so prompt and readie is the dutifull servant to obey his his louing and kind maister. (Sig. Aa3ʳ)

This extract from a Puritan treatise of 1630 is in fact a verbatim reproduction of a passage from T.K.'s 1588 translation of Torquato Tosso's *The Householders Philosophie* (sig. E2ʳ). The emphasis on mutual love, affect, and kindness in the discussion of the peculiar instrumentality of service,

---

[73] Churchyard, *A Sparke of Friendship*, sig. 6a; quoted in Shannon, *Sovereign Amity*, 38.

which emphasizes the independence of the servant's *soul* even as it makes him an extension of the master's will, originates with the earlier, Italian writer, who goes on (as Dod and Cleaver emphatically do not) to emphasise that the relationships between masters and certain kinds of servant are most appropriately those of friendship rather than servile subordination:

a liuely & seuerall instrument of action . . . some are placed in care of families and household busines, some stretch further, and extend to ciuil administration, there are some Gentlemen . . . that vse to keep a youth, who in theyr ciuill gouernment, doth serue to write and mannedge, some of their affaires, and him they call a Clerke . . . not of seruile or materiall witt, but capable of fashions, or apt to studie or contemplate, and betwixt them and their Maisters, can be properly no seruitude or signiory, but rather that kind of friendship, which by Aristotle is applied to the highest. (Sig. E2ᵛ)

The initial conception of the servant as instrument is transformed via the recognition of the imaginative incorporation of that instrumentality into the master's own subjectivity, following one of the most traditional tropes for love.

    To sum up, then, the beloved as an "other self" constitutes the never-ending desire of *eros* for a merging with the other; it is the acceptance of mutual duty in Gouge's vision of marriage as *nomos*; and it constitutes the celebrated, achieved unity of Montaigne's *philia*. I argue that the condition of service may under certain circumstances render friendship *possible*, but those circumstances tend also to be its condition of impossibility. It promises but seldom delivers the ideal forms of autonomy and equality that sovereign amity requires, and to which *eros* in Shakespeare aspires.

"FRIENDS"

In his introduction to Volume 2 of *A History of Private Life*, George Duby argues that feudalisation represented a "fragmentation of public power"[74] and that the personal and political – the two orders are indistinguishable in this context – pledge to protect a fellow against the "public" power of the "law" constituted the feudal ground for "friendship":

Commendatio was an act whereby an individual pledged himself, his very person, to the leader of the group and through the leader to all the group's members. The relation between member and leader, a very powerful emotional bond, was called 'friendship' in both Latin and the vernacular; it was the cement that held the group together. (*Private Life II*, 8)

---

[74] Ariès and Duby, *Private Life: II*, 9.

What is striking here is the conjunction of what seems to be intensely personal to modern eyes with inescapably political relationships through the conjunction of service as retainership and friendship. The idea that the services of friendship were necessary for protection against the legal reaches of the monarch in feudal life signals a concept of loving service as both an intimate and a structural part of the organization of power. Here *philia* and *nomos* come into direct conflict at the level of both love and service. The violence inherent in each, seen in the aggression involved in the formation of a community, is pitted against the other in a struggle that echoes Freud's account of the formation of the group in *Civilization and Its Discontents*. In *Much Ado about Nothing* and *Romeo and Juliet*, for example, the violent discord between retainership and *eros* marks the residual, fundamentally homocentric combination of friendship and service in the retainer band and later forms of military service.

The third volume of *A History of Private Life* traces a concept of friendship that has moved away from the mutually dependent ties of retainership and service to ideals of reciprocal equality. "Friendly relations", Orest Ranum writes, "formed the basis of emotional life":

An individual, it was believed, could be drawn into ever more intimate relations with another through the combined effect of heart, humors, and spirit. Close friendship was a form of love whose affections and passions were held in check by reason, that is, by spirit. For an individual of the early modern era there could be no true friendship without such affection of one body for another. The iconography of friendship celebrated the union of bodies and minds.[75]

If Ranum is correct that friendly relations between men formed the basis of emotional life, then we are faced with a disjunction between heterosexual relationships, especially marriage, and the intimacy of spirit and heart that marks the affective bonds of friendship between men.[76] This misogynist conception of love and friendship has a long history, running from Ficino back to Plato, and it is present in the literature of friendship from Montaigne back through Cicero to Aristotle.

The word "friend" was, however, also extended to sexual relationships between men and women in early modern English usage. There is often a pejorative rather than a celebratory quality to the use of the word in this context. It is now generally accepted that Shakespeare stands at the cusp of a major shift, at least in terms of a framing philosophy if not in the lived textures of individual relationships, towards what is now known generally as a "companionate marriage". The Protestant ideal of a loving

[75] Chartier, *Private Life: III*, 258.   [76] Sedgewick, *Between Men*.

and affectionate, if unequal, bond between husband and wife stems, in part, from its disapproval of the Catholic ideals of celibacy and monastic removal from the corporeal world.[77] It would be a mistake to assume that marital companionship and affection were impossible before the Protestant revolution. Wrightson notes that "the weight of the evidence . . . suggests that . . . there is little reason to follow Professor Stone in regarding the rise of the companionate marriage as a new phenomenon of the later seventeenth and eighteenth centuries" (*Society*, 111), and Goldberg argues that companionate marriages formed the centre of the service economy of the household from the early middle ages (*Women*, chapter 5). Wrightson warns against positing "patriarchal" and "companionate" marriages as "a typology of successive stages of family development", suggesting instead that we see them as the "poles of an enduring continuum in marital relations in a society which accepted both the primacy of male authority and the ideal of marriage as a practical and emotional partnership" (112). We should distinguish between the relatively contingent variability of the quality of emotional attachment in all relationships from particular, historically marked ideological positions on the matter. Clearly, certain beliefs that we now take for granted, such as Milton's passionate championship of divorce, are predicated on both the possibility and the desirability of men and women sharing their lives freely, unencumbered by the external, impersonal demands of the dynastic survival of the blood-line.[78]

Few of Shakespeare's married couples are happy or companionate, but there is no doubt that Shakespeare's treatment of the *promise* of marriage, in the form of heterosexual desire and its complications within a social network designed to thwart it, upholds free choice above coercion and passionate conversation above dynastic necessity. Whatever may have been written about the reactionary effects of romantic love, it is clear that in Shakespeare *eros* is a powerful enemy of *nomos* and the social bonds of

[77] The idea that "companionate marriage" was a later, Protestant development from the more politically impersonal arrangements of earlier Catholic and feudal societies is the subject of a vexed debate. We should draw a distinction between different ideological positions with regard to mutual affection and companionship in marriage and the factual question of whether marriages in general were or were not informed by mutual affection and reciprocity. Accounts of women's actual roles in the households of small tradesmen, craftsmen, and the farming classes of yeoman and husbandman indicate a much more independent and structurally indispensable role of women as both the producers and reproducers of the early modern household. See Wall, *Staging Domesticity*, Wrightson, *Earthly Necessities*, 44 passim, and Goldberg, *Women*; also Fraser, *The Weaker Vessel*, for an account of relationships in which women shared an equal, loving role in the partnership, and for more general, pioneering critical work, Newman, *Femininity* and Dusinberre, *Women*.

[78] See Milton, *Divorce* and Singer, *Love 2*, 253 ff.

philia that constitute the closed, male world of retainer service. *Romeo and Juliet* is a prime example of what Neill identifies as "the potential subversiveness of romantic love" (*History*, 24) – its tendency "even when it is profoundly conventional, [to be] at the same time the location of resistance to convention" (Belsey, *Desire*, 7). In Shakespeare's romantic heroines, desire is rewritten or recast through the inversions of gender to mean something quite different from its Platonically derived predication upon the male will to possession. There is, however, a contradiction between Shakespeare's representation of female desire, which encompasses the need for reciprocated loyalty related to forms of service in his plays – especially in his romantic comedies – and the revulsion from heterosexual forms of will in his more personally inflected sonnets. Shakespeare either avoids or satirises conventional notions of erotic service of male lover to female beloved, as in *The Two Gentlemen of Verona*, although he is irresistibly drawn to the female figure who disguises or otherwise pursues her desire for an unobtainable male in the shape of a boy or young man.

The mingling of love and service as a matter of heart, spirit, and body is thus ambiguously encompassed by the single term "friend", which could refer to a retainer or servant (see the *Henry IV* plays, *Timon of Athens*, *King Lear*, and *Antony and Cleopatra*), a close male companionship, Platonic or sexual (*Twelfth Night*, the *Henry IV* plays, *The Two Gentlemen of Verona*, *The Merchant of Venice*, *Antony and Cleopatra*, as well as the sonnets) or an intimate, heterosexual partnership that combines reciprocal erotic desire and close affection (*Twelfth Night*, *The Merchant of Venice*, *The Winter's Tale*, *Antony and Cleopatra*). Shakespeare's most direct expressions of love – as a combination of *eros*, *philia*, and *nomos* – in his sonnets are also expressions of service, torn between the yearning for complete reciprocity which must "leaue out difference" (sonnet 105.8), and the "brand" which his hand necessarily receives from "public means which public manners breeds" (sonnet 111.4).[79]

In the sonnets, love for the young man is made possible by the prior condition of service, but service in turn renders the reciprocity that love desires difficult, if not impossible, to achieve. Further, if love and service are brought together in the presentation of the player of himself upon the stage as – whatever else he may pretend to be – a *servant*, that service itself interpolates itself *between* the kind of service that the player-poet wishes to declare as a form of devotion, whether erotic or as a form of Montaigne's

[79] See Schalkwyk, *Speech and Performance*.

amité, in his relationship with the young man of the sonnets. Service and love thus take on an increasingly burdened, performative dimension in Shakespeare's negotiations between page and stage, personal duty and public show. Here the conceptual ground is complex and uneven and will have to be traversed play by play, sometimes with the sonnets as a rough guide.

CHAPTER 2

Performance and Imagination

The Taming of the Shrew and A Midsummer Night's Dream

The precept central to the Protestant ideology of service – that service is not a form of bondage but perfect freedom if perceived and experienced in the right way – ties the psychology of service to both love and theatrical performance. The imaginative bestowal of value that is the essence of love involves a similar perspectival transformation of the phenomenological world as that which finds virtue in willing obedience. Love may be regarded as the embodiment of freely given, mutual service when it is reciprocated, and as a form of asymmetrical devotion to the other who occupies the place of master or sovereign when it is not. The metaphor of being enslaved by love is thus tied to sociological conditions of mastery and service in more than merely imaginary or literary ways. Both service and love are peculiarly performative insofar as they are capable of creating their own worlds or projective valuation through imaginative or aspect-perception. One person sees beauty in the brow of Egypt; another accepts bondage as perfect freedom.

In Shakespeare, these forms of aspectual perception are profoundly related to the performance of theatrical illusion and the exercise of ideological interpellation.[1] The acceptance of service as a fulfilling kind of identity, the forging of friendship as "a willing bondage that brings freedom forever", and the willing suspension of disbelief central to aesthetic experience form different strands of a common concept.[2] "*Think* when we talk of horses", the Chorus urges his audience in *Henry V*,

> that you *see* them,
> Printing their proud hoofs i' th' receiving earth;
> For 'tis *your thoughts* that now must deck our kings,
> Carry them here and there . . .
> (*Henry V*, Prologue, 26–9; emphasis added)

The theatre needs the projective imagination of the audience to do its work, but it also works upon the imagination of the audience, transforming their

---

[1] See especially Althusser, "Ideological State Apparatuses".   [2] Churchyard, *Friendship*, sig. 6a.

perceptions of themselves, their desires, and their relationships to others and their social being.

Each of the plays in this chapter follows the generic dictates of comedy. The plays begin with bounded ways of seeing – with bonds experienced as bondage – to open up such limits to new aspects, thereby turning individually resented forms of bondage into the sustaining ties of community. In their representation of service and its concomitant forms of love and desire as essentially modes of performance they embody the possibility of such changes of aspect in an often subtle form of self-conscious or self-reflexive theatricality. This reflexivity is encapsulated by "the social quality of the actor's relation to the real world and the imaginative and spatial dimension of the character's relation to the play world", which involves "his implicit insight into and criticism of the action of the play".[3] The two comedies are thus united by their performative self-consciousness and their shared representation of the ways in which the symbolic violence of ideological interpellation is both complicit with and resisted by the specificities of love as imaginative projection, service as alternatively communal bond or solitary bondage, and playing as exuberant impertinence.

THE TAMING OF THE SHREW

The performative qualities of the theatrical dimensions of service and the self-consciousness of the player as the double embodiment of service as representing actor and represented character are nowhere more evident in Shakespeare than in *The Taming of the Shrew*. The self-conscious theatricality, not only in the Induction but also in the general positioning of character and actor in relation to a diversity of audience positions, exemplifies my argument that it is inadvisable to read the representations of Shakespearean drama as if they were mere exemplifications of contemporary prose tracts. Shakespeare's (re)staging of commonplace belief invites us to measure the closeness or discrepancy between what Susan Amussen underlines as the unstable relation between reality and ideal in the Elizabethan framework of social order. No matter how much theorists insisted on the identity of the relation between husband and wife and sovereign and subject, for example, it remained, as Amussen reminds us, no more than an analogy.[4] The embodied conditions of address on Shakespeare's stage thus underline its

---

[3] Weimann, *Popular Tradition*, 259.
[4] Amussen, *Ordered Society*, 37: "It must be understood as an analogy, however, not an equation. As an analogy it could be used in many different ways."

analogical precariousness as much as Amussen's dense historical research into the practicalities of early modern village life.

Inductions

The framing scenes of *The Taming of the Shrew* reveal *all* the players as servants; they show that service itself is constituted by "actions that a man may play" (*Hamlet*, 1.2.84). Both versions of the play, *A Shrew* and *The Shrew*, double that awareness: first by enacting the "pastime" whereby beggar is turned into lord, servant into loving wife, and presiding lord into attending servant, and then by introducing a troupe of itinerant players (real players playing at being players) eager to indulge the idiosyncratic tastes of a mad nobleman in exchange for some easy money. The play emphasises the discrepancy between the actor representing and the representing actor.[5] It also exposes the performative quality of service in a variety of forms: in the "players / That offer service" to the Lord; in the Lord's himself becoming a servant to Sly; in the elaborate catalogue of services that the serving-men ply upon the beggar (as if the sheer weight of willing service constituted the essence of rank – its abiding illusion); and in the overtly histrionic, if precarious, embodiment of the service that would have been expected of a "lady" to her "lord", where erotic desire, submissive duty, and love are combined in a complex manifold of tantalising obeisance.

Love and service are enacted as much in the erotic as the social dimensions of compliant duty. The page's desire to win the love of his master is scarcely separable from the performance he is enjoined to enact to demonstrate an aristocratic wife's love of her lord:

> LORD (*To a* SERVINGMAN) Sirrah, go you to Barthol'mew, my page,
> And see him dressed in all suits like a lady.
> That done, conduct him to the drunkard's chamber
> And call him "madam", do him obeisance.
> Tell him from me, *as he will win my love,*
> He bear himself with honourable action
> Such as he hath observed in noble ladies
> Unto their lords by them accomplishèd.
> Such duty to the drunkard let him do
> With soft low tongue and lowly courtesy,
> And say "What is 't your honour will command
> Wherein your lady and your humble wife
> May show her duty *and make known her love?*"
> (Induction 1, 98–113; emphasis added)

5 Weimann, *Popular Tradition*.

The appearance of the lord at the tavern puts one in mind of the story of Gamaliell Ratsey, which Michael Neill re-contextualises in terms of master-servant relations.[6] As the story is recalled by Andrew Gurr, the highwayman, pretending to be a gentleman, encounters a group of players at an inn, who are more than happy to abandon their settled patron for a command performance at a liminal venue.[7] That apparently true story replicates the histrionics of service displayed so adroitly in the *Shrew*'s Induction scenes. Such performance draws together the performative dimensions of rank and gender generally, but, more specifically in this case, it emphasises the theatricality of the shrew and the display of the player as servant and servant as player. Just as the servant as player exposes the artificiality of the master-servant relationship, so the shrew exposes the actions that a lady is supposed to play vis-à-vis her lord – "with soft low tongue and lowly courtesy" – as the carefully nurtured contours of an illusion.

All claims to social status from this point on, such as Petruccio's "I am a gentleman of Verona, sir" (2.1.47), are filtered through the baring of performance in the Induction, even where the parallels are not drawn explicitly, such as the echoing of the lord's sartorial exchange with his serving-man in Lucentio and Tranio's effortless exchange of clothing and status, which is couched explicitly in the language of the theatre:

> We have not yet been seen in any house,
> Nor can we be distinguished by our faces
> For man or master. Then it follows thus:
> Thou shalt be master, Tranio, in my stead;
> Keep house, and port, and servants, as I should.
>   (1.1.193–7)

Such revelation that the difference between man and master may be no more than a fashionable cloak and an easily assumable mode of speech and carriage is the work of Shakespeare's theatre as institution. It embodies and enacts Kenneth Burke's insight that "unlike real estate, the language of privilege and authority is not the private property of any person or class. The linguistic symbols of authority... are appropriable".[8] The early modern theatre derived its power not merely from its capacity to seize and put to different uses the "linguistic symbols of authority" but also to put such instability to work to entertain and give pleasure. In every instance in

[6] Neill, *History*, 13–19.   [7] Gurr, *Shakespearean Stage*, 78–80.
[8] Lentricchia, *Social Change*, 79. For a discussion of this general point in relation to Derrida and signs of class in *The Winter's Tale*, see Schalkwyk, *Literature*, chapter 4.

which we witness the player as servant enacted as a "corrupter of words", we simultaneously see the work of the servant as player.

"Self-expressive show": servant and shrew

Servants, whose first duty, after obedience, was, like women, to be silent, are astonishingly and delightfully voluble on stage, and they habitually use linguistic ambiguity to subvert their masters' commands.[9] The most celebrated instance of this occurs in Act 1, Scene 2 of *The Shrew*:

> PETRUCCIO Here, sirrah Grumio, knock, I say.
> GRUMIO Knock, sir? Whom should I knock? Is there any man has
>   rebused your worship?
> PETRUCCIO Villain, I say, knock me here soundly.
> GRUMIO Knock you here, sir? Why, sir, what am I, sir, that I
>   should knock you here, sir?
> PETRUCCIO Villain, I say, knock me at this gate,
>   And rap me well or I'll knock your knave's pate.
> GRUMIO My master is grown quarrelsome. I should knock you line,
>   And then I know after who comes by the worst.
> PETRUCCIO Will it not be?
>   Faith, sirrah, an you'll not knock, I'll ring it.
>   I'll try how you can sol-fa and sing it.
>   *He wrings him by the ears.* [GRUMIO kneels]
> GRUMIO Help, masters, help! My master is mad.
> PETRUCCIO Now knock when I bid you, sirrah villain.   (1.2.1–19)

In an article that deals with this scene as part of a broader investigation of moments in Shakespeare in which the distinction between master and subordinate is disrupted, Thomas Moisan suggests that

Shakespeare gives voice to the tensions inhabiting contemporary class relations and stages comic challenges to authority *only* to marginalize them, only to contextualize them as minor, diversionary moments in which the social subordinates are effectively reduced to the harmless, recuperable status of clowns, in which the issues of class can easily be sublimated and read as metaphors for "larger," more central, and ultimately less socially disruptive issues.[10]

---

[9] Cf. the common emblem of the servant as an ass with his mouth locked shut in Burnett, "Trusty Servant", and Gouge's observations that servants should show reverence to their masters by "sparing to speake, without just cause in their masters presence or audience.... By forbearing to reply when they obserue their masters unwilling that they should speak any more" and "by attending to that which their masters shall deliuer to them" (*Dvties*, 596).

[10] Moisan, "Comic Misprision", 278.

Moisan overlooks the self-reflexive, theatrical tenor of this scene by assuming that it is a simple reflection of "the social anxieties and antagonisms . . . by means of which class-fixation in Tudor England gets nourished and even 'mystified'" (276). The anxieties and antagonisms, even the mystification, of which he writes take on a more complex dimension if one reads the scene as the representation *by servants* of a bit of stock master-servant intercourse, leavened with the opportunity that the public stage provides for embodying the exuberant self-display of impertinent show.[11] Petruccio embodies both the master he represents and himself as servant: he is both the putter-down of high-spirited insubordination parading itself as dutiful obedience and the embodiment of such irrepressible high spirits. The enacted scene comes across less as a reflection of high-handed magisterial obduracy than as a piece of operatic comic bravura, in which the impulsive energy of the servant-actor shines through the performance of the actor-as-master.

The same is true of the role of the shrew, which, in ever flaunting its public qualities of bravura defiance and insubordination, matches that of the irrepressible servant-player. In her attempts to isolate the phenomenon of the scold from that of the wife who is less than willing to submit to her husband as "lord, king, and governor", Amussen isolates a signal characteristic: "scolds brought their rejection of women's 'quiet' and obedience out of the household and into public view" (122). The scold, in other words, turns her subversive condition into a theatrical display. Katherine's opening display of disorder is specifically declared to be "some good pastime" (1.1.68–9); she herself complains of her public display – "I pray you, sir, is it your will / To make a stale of me among these mates?" (57–8) – and in the flyting contest between Petruccio and Katherine each inhabits that pastime of all Shakespearean clowns and servants: making words "wanton", turning them inside out "like a cheverel glove" (*Twelfth Night*, 3.1.10–4).

"Ashamed to kiss?"

Petruccio's success stems from the way in which he maintains this topsy-turvy performance, outshrewing Katherine in a display of outrageous histrionics that outdoes her own words and actions. The turning point comes when he forces Katherine to abandon her habitual, contrary disposition by aligning herself with the forces of social propriety. His outlandish

---

[11] See Weimann, "Bifold Authority", "Shakespeare (De)Canonized", and "Representation and Performance".

appearance at the church inverts the rules of personal decorum and social hierarchy. His shockingly irreverent sartorial appearance takes its effect as much from its contrast with that of his "lackey" as from its intrinsic inappropriateness.[12] Here master and servant are levelled at the point at which Tudor anxieties were especially pronounced: in clothing as a natural signifier of social difference. It is the servant, not the master, who invites the greater expression of outrage: "a monster, a very monster in apparel, and not like a Christian footboy or a gentleman's lackey" (3.2.63–4).[13] More important than the clothes that Petruccio wears is the lack of distinction – the failure to observe proper place and rank – signalled by his servant, whose inappropriate display then redounds to the master's discredit. Such a lackey could not serve a Christian; this footboy could not possibly serve a gentleman. This "monstrous" page demonstrates exactly what the player enacted every time he put on the clothes and adopted the words and gestures of a station not his own, and what the shrew put on display whenever she flaunted her will in the public streets.

Petruccio's acute outsider's awareness of the social or ideological role of shame enables him both to subject his fellows to shame and to make a series of egalitarian pronouncements on the superficiality of external accoutrements.[14] The underlying fear of public embarrassment through a failure of propriety runs through the scene as a prelude to its outrageously farcical denouement. If we ignore the ironical interplay of clothing and service that lies at the dramatic centre of this scene, we are bound to miss the most delicious of its ironies. When Tranio, for example, urges Petruccio to avoid the shame of appearing in inappropriate dress by donning clothes proper to a gentleman ("put on clothes of mine"), he underscores Petruccio's point. The clothes that he urges upon Petruccio are in fact his master's – Lucentio's. He therefore doubly embodies – as pranked-up servant and pranked-up player – the ways in which clothes may be a "shame to [socially sanctioned] estate", and therefore unreliable indicators of moral and social worth. Katherine's concern about being the most severely shamed victim of Petruccio's capriciousness shows that her antagonism towards the patriarchal society stops short of genuinely rejecting its most deeply held

---

[12] The significance of dress in this scene was first drawn to my attention at the 2003 meeting of the Shakespeare Association of America, in Amanda Bailey's paper, "Livery and Its Discontents: 'Braving it' in *The Taming of the Shrew*".

[13] For a similarly monstrous sartorial transformation of a servant by an outlandish master, see Falstaff's page in *2 Henry IV*: "A had him from me Christian, and look if the fat villain have not transformed him ape" (2.2.56–7).

[14] For an extended treatment of shame in Shakespeare, see Fernie, *Shame in Shakespeare*. Lars Engle offers a fine treatment of shame in the sonnets in "Economy of Shame".

values. In the face of Petruccio's outrageousness, Katherine clings to the
very conventionality that she ostensibly rejected before her marriage.

Katherine's final subjection to Petruccio offers a clue to the politics of
the interaction of love and service. Gouge deals with the insubordination
such as that of the shrew or the disobedient servant by pointing out two
different forms of subjection:

> a *necessary* subiection: which is the subiection of order [and a] *voluntary* subiection:
> which is the subiection of duty. [The first is] that degree of inferioritie wherein God
> has placed all inferiours . . . a wife is in an inferiour degree, though she domineere
> neuer so much over her husband.
>
> The *Voluntary* subiection, is that dutifull respect which inferiours carry towards
> those whom God hath set over them: whereby they manifest a willingnesse to yeeld
> to the order which God hath established. . . . This is to make a vertue of necessity.
> (26–7)

These distinctions indicate the relationship between Cranmer's collect and
the politics of Shakespearean comedy, namely, the voluntary bending of
hearts and wills to necessity. *The Taming of the Shrew* traces a trajectory
from one condition to the other. Like all such comedy, it needs to persuade
us that voluntary subjection is indeed voluntary, that the people who have
changed have not done so merely mechanically, unwillingly, or fearfully.
However, it also needs to address the broader question of *necessary* subjection represented in the whole theological framework of the statement
that serving God is perfect freedom. We may take pleasure in the comic
process whereby the imagination forges a remedy out of the clash between
will and reality, but the question always remains about the nature or givenness of the framing or ordering necessity. It is part of the dynamic, human
realism of Shakespeare's comedy that it almost always leaves this question
undecidable – from the problematic conversion of Demetrius through the
application of the love juice in *A Midsummer Night's Dream* to the denouement of *The Tempest*, in which the voluntary acceptance of subjection is
pushed to its absolute limits.

Katherine represents just such a move from the refusal of necessary subjection to its voluntary acceptance within the framework of reciprocal service and love expressed in her notorious final speech. Yet this is qualified by
the framing irony of the play as a whole. The supposed reintegration of the
shrew into the domestic sphere does not complete a circle of inclusive social
order. Katherine's speech on wifely obedience is echoed by, but also echoes,
countless examples from contemporary, moralising tracts. When Katherine therefore addresses her controversial set piece to an audience consisting
severally of her wayward sisters, her husband, the men on stage, and the
men and women in the theatre, she appears to be reiterating the received

notion of love and service as a mutually reinforcing "dutie of submission"
to God:

> Thy husband is thy lord, thy life, thy keeper,
> Thy head, thy sovereign, one that cares for thee,
> And for thy maintenance commits his body
> To painful labour both by sea and land,
> To watch the night in storms, the day in cold,
> Whilst thou liest warm at home, secure and safe,
> And craves no other tribute at thy hands
> But love, fair looks, and true obedience,
> Too little payment for so great a debt.
> Such duty as the subject owes the prince,
> Even such a woman oweth to her husband,
> And when she is froward, peevish, sullen, sour,
> And not obedient to his honest will,
> What is she but a foul contending rebel,
> And graceless traitor to her loving lord?
>
> (5.2.150–64)

The ideological contours of this speech may be directly traced in the didactic
literature of the time. Yet those who have compared it with the similar
oration in the anonymous *The Taming of a Shrew* have noted that such
contours can take significantly different shapes.[15] Shakespeare has stripped
all the theological import from the anonymous play, which is concerned
with the framework of a metaphysical order that keeps in check eternally
threatening confusion and disorder:

> The eternal power that with his only breath,
> Shall cause this end and this beginning frame,
> Not in time, nor before time, but with time, confusd,
> For all the course of yeares, of ages, moneths,
> Of seasons temperate, of dayes and houres,
> Are tund and stopt, by measure of his hand,
> The first world was, a forme, without a forme,
> A heape confusd, a mixture all deformd,
> A gulfe of gulfes, a body bodiles,
> Where all the elements were orderlies,
> Before the great commander of the world,
> The king of Kings the glorious God of heauen,
> Who in six daies did frame his heauenly worke,
> And made all things to stand in perfit course.
> Then to his image he did make a man.
> Old *Adam* and from his side a sleepe,

---

[15] See Thompson's Introduction to *Shrew*, 28–9.

> A rib was taken, of which the Lord did make,
> The woe of man so termed by *Adam* then,
> Woman for that, by her came sinne to vs,
> And for her sin was *Adam* doomed to die,
> As *Sara* to her husband, so should we,
> Obey them, love them, keepe, and nourish them,
> If they by any meanes doo want our helpes,
> Laying our handes vnder theire feete to tread,
> If that by that we, might procure their ease,
> And for that president Ile first begin,
> And lay my hand vnder my husbands feete.[16]

As Ann Thompson points out, the speech from *A Shrew* is obsessed with cosmic order and disorder and with the natural debt that woman owes to man for her part in the Fall. Shakespeare's more secular conception focuses on the reciprocity of loving service, by extrapolating from the stock analogy that posits a set of shared obligations in the relationships between husband and wife, master and servant, sovereign and subject. *The Shrew* focuses on a chain of mutual, social relationships and debts; *A Shrew* ignores these in favour of a long-standing metaphysical debt incurred between the original man and woman against a background of primeval chaos. Received ideas of order and obligation – crucial to both servile and erotic relations – are thus inflected very differently in the two plays. Moreover, whereas the grounding of these speeches in commonplace books and didactic literature is clear, we should remember that a speech in a play is not a passage in a conduct book. This difference is much clearer in *The Shrew*, where both the direction and place of address are more complex and ambiguous and where theatricality is given more opportunity to work its effects.

Unlike a passage from a conduct book, then, the embodied context of the play makes it unclear quite what kind of work Kate's (in)famous speech on wifely obedience is performing. It is impossible to say in the abstract what kind of speech act it is. To recognize that this uncertainty is a function of its place in a play, one must take it at face value and not reduce its multivalent qualities by overtly ironising it in favour of a particular, ideologically driven interpretation or by rejecting it as a symptom of an outmoded false consciousness. This means that we take seriously, if only imaginatively, its equation of the reciprocity of love in service and service in love. This reciprocity marks its difference from the theological dogma of the equivalent speech in *A Shrew* and opens it up to ironical and critical leverage. Such leverage is much more subtle, displaced, and elusive than

---

[16] *Shrew* (1594 Quarto), scene xviii, 117–44.

may be secured by any ideological reading or correction of the play, however. To secure that leverage, we need to succumb to its seductive charms – the charms of the theatre.

As befits its role as a piece of dialogue in a play rather than a monologue in a moralist tract, Katherine's lengthy utterance works differently on its component auditors. To the men who have just discovered a new brood of shrews within their households, it signals Kate and Petruccio's difference, their apartness and private solidarity against a set of social expectations and norms, and it underlines that difference by joining Petruccio in triumph against his sorry male rivals. Yet it also reminds him of the ideals of reciprocity that Gouge emphasises in relations between husbands and wives as much as he does between servants and masters. *"Husbands must come as neare as they can to Christ in loving their wives,"* Gouge declares:

> Though their loue in *measure* cannot equall Christs loue, yet in the *manner* thereof it must be like Christs, *a preuenting, true, free, pure, exceeding, constant loue*. . . . The *end* of Christs loue . . . is noted to shew that he so loued the Church for her good and happinesse, rather than for any aduantage to himselfe . . . he loued the Church more than his owne life. (45)

To the general audience, who would have been all too familiar with its received platitudes, the speech invites a critical weighing up of its general precepts and what they know and have seen (in their daily lives and on the stage) of the real relations between husbands and wives. We cannot tell how individual members of the play's audiences might have taken it – or the play as a whole. We should always remain aware, however, of the situational complexity of its place in a theatre, which was an uneasy component of the very relations of service and (dis)order that are discovered and toyed with in the play. This means that the complexity of the player's self-embodiment as servant extends to the audience itself: there is no homogenous response, no automatic alignment of audience member to actor or character, although the power of theatrical pleasure and incorporation gives the actor an edge in incorporating a willing audience into his histrionic display and critical commentary.

"One feast, one house, one mutual happiness"?

If one compares *The Taming of the Shrew* with its ostensibly more mature cousin, *Much Ado about Nothing*, what is striking are the different ways in which the two plays deal with the necessity of social convention and expectation. Beatrice and Benedick are ultimately drawn into the society from which they have each, in various ways, alienated themselves: the private (their declaration of love for each other – their "hearts") is turned public (their "hands") and miraculously integrated into it, trumping that reticence ("A miracle! Here's our own hands against our hearts" (5.4.91)) in the form of that most public of private forms, the sonnet. Although social tensions remain, in the form of Don John and the gritty abrasiveness that lingers between Benedick and his erstwhile "sworn brother", Claudio, the music that Benedick calls for *before* the marriages are solemnised signals a certain kind of communal integration, a virtue made of necessity. *Much Ado* is thus closer to the *Two Gentlemen of Verona*'s celebration of "One feast, one house, one mutual happiness" (*Two Gentlemen of Verona*, 5.4.171) than to *The Taming of the Shrew*, where that optimistic integration is signally resisted. Social inclusiveness is shunned for a private arrangement that hovers between virtue and necessity, paradoxically forging the only space in which the reciprocity of love and service may, just may, be viable, if only through the fantasy of delight offered by the (in)subordinate servant-player.

A MIDSUMMER NIGHT'S DREAM

Apart from being a vehicle for the self-reflexive impertinence of the player-servant, *The Taming of the Shrew* represents the paradox at the heart of Cranmer's collect: service becomes perfect freedom only by thinking of it as such. The "necessary subjection" of God's order is turned into the "voluntary subjection" of the social order. Such psychological transformation is the equivalent in the political realm of service to the bestowal or projection of value central to the transformative action of love's vision, by which it "sees not with the eyes but with the mind". The bestowal of a unique value upon the beloved that is neither a product of the will nor amenable to external compulsion or argument gives love itself a peculiar kind of performative force. Love's eye does not reflect the world. Its psychology of the imagination transforms the world into an image of its own projection and evaluation. The problem lies in its difference from other, mutual forms of imaginative transformation because its singularity may leave it isolated, at odds not only with the world as a whole but also with the very person upon which it bestows its transformative vision. Todorov shows that it is precisely this aspect of love's vision, which commonly leads to its being derided as illusionary or delusional, that is its greatest strength: its capacity to transform what is intrinsically imperfect and limited into a kind of perfection that is the ground of its singular relationship.[17]

---

[17] Todorov, *Imperfect Garden*.

The wilfulness of desire

Like the language user whose free agency is both constrained by the language system that enables him or her to speak but is also given a broader, supra-personal force by appropriable convention, the lover as agent is caught between compulsion and freedom. Most frequently seen as a form of enslavement, this compulsion is what, paradoxically, underlies the capacity of *eros* to refuse the compulsion of social and political constraints. Romantic love thus carries neither an inherently conservative nor subversive bias.[18] Its capacity for performance in the non-transformative sense of the term – of going through the motions conventionally expected of it – informs its conservative tendency, whereas its performative capacity to see the world differently under its peculiar compulsion gives it the capacity to refuse conventional calls for what may be no more than conventionally accepted notions of reason or restraint.

The psychological process whereby "nothing [is] either good or bad but thinking makes it so" (*Hamlet*, 2.2.251–2) is the shaping concern of *A Midsummer Night's Dream*. This comedy gives freer rein than most to the refusal of *eros* to accommodate any compulsions other than its own – it is Shakespeare's most compelling representation of the performative force of bestowal. Such bestowal operates both in love and also the *performance* of love and duty between master and servant, a mutual process that requires the imaginative bestowal that is also fundamental to the power of theatrical illusion. The later comedy thus transforms the performative and imaginative elements of the earlier one into a more coherent aesthetic and ideological whole. The transformation of the mind's capacity for bestowal is shown to be the most compelling social necessity, "transfiguring together" the often contradictory impulses of love, service, and theatrical performance. Both *A Midsummer Night's Dream* and *The Taming of the Shrew* recognise the violence required for such transfiguring, even if their comic modes have to leave us with the illusion that it is, in the final analysis, a completely voluntary imposition.

In the famous opening scene, the urgency of Theseus's desire is checked by both the moon-huntress, goddess of chastity, representative of the supposed perversity of female power, "long withering out a young man's revenue" – and the imposition of civil order upon the recent history of military conquest. As spokesperson for that female order and one subjected to the violence of a peculiar combination of *nomos* and *eros* through war, Hippolyta represents the subjection expected of both women and servants in the

---

[18] Cf. Callaghan, "Ideology of Romantic Love".

didactic literature. Yet she also embodies a mediating flexibility that eases Theseus's discomfort by urging him to transform his experience of time phenomenologically or imaginatively. Think of it differently, and it won't seem as long, she suggests, as a mother tempers the impatience of a child. Hippolyta's advice is related to the injunction to servants to see their service as a form of freedom. Newly conquered herself, she offers Theseus a way of submitting himself willingly to Diana's restraint. Yet she also betrays her own desire to transform the enforced service of her marriage into freedom of a sort.

For Singer and Todorov, bestowal is as definitive of love as its refusal of substitution. It is what renders substitution impossible, because the peculiar valuation with which the lover imbues the beloved is not an observable phenomenon of the objective or even the social world. The lover always sees the beloved differently from the way others see him or her. The lover is *compelled* to see the beloved in this way, embodying a helpless passivity conveyed by the common phrase, "falling in love". The fact that the lover is not open to any other form of external compulsion to look with another's judgement is what makes it "hell . . . to choose love by another's eyes". The injunction to the servant to see his subjugation as a form of freedom urges a change of mind, but it has to be adopted freely and willingly. Such freedom escapes the lover, who is caught in a paradox of will-less wilfulness, a toil of evaluative bestowal that she or he has to keep giving as if it were a product of a free will, and for which she or he constantly has to take responsibility. Hamlet, like the hapless lover, does not choose to see Denmark as a prison; that is simply how things seem and feel to him. He is as impervious to the efforts of others to change his evaluation as Mark Antony is to stop himself from seeing "Helen's beauty in the brow of Egypt". Theseus, on the other hand, has the power to choose whether to piece out the imperfections of his dutiful servants with his thoughts. His *agapē*, unlike the *nomos* that he demands of his subjects, is freely bestowed or withheld without heed for the quality of their performance of love and duty nor for the individuality of the performers.[19]

The conflicts that surround the lovers in the opening scene arise from disparate imaginative evaluations that make love possible and render it

---

[19] There is, however, a complication in the account of the relationship among *eros, nomos,* and *agapē*. One of the defining qualities of love is that it refuses all substitution. Only the person upon whom value has been bestowed will do; no other can take his or her place. However, Shakespeare's early comedy takes a perverse delight in showing that although this law may not be abrogated at one level, *eros* is notoriously fickle in substituting objects for which it, for a time, refused any substitution. This is a major topic in the Renaissance tracts on desire. Desire tends to stop the moment it has what it wants. It is replaced with "satiety and loathing" (Leone Ebreo, *Love*, 53).

impervious to rational justification. The disagreement that Theseus is asked to resolve is initially presented as a conflict between rights guaranteed by rational law and the wayward, imaginative power that governs *eros*. In the face of what is to him a perversely disobedient wilfulness, Egeus demands his right to exercise his legal power over his daughter as his property:

> . . . what is mine my love shall render him,
> And she is mine, and all my right of her
> I do estate unto Demetrius.   (1.1.96–8)

The argument is in part about the grounds of judgement, but Egeus concedes that the respective social and personal "worthiness" of the two contenders – Lysander and Demetrius – plays no part in the decision. Hermia simply has to see things as her father does:

> THESEUS Demetrius is a worthy gentleman.
> HERMIA So is Lysander.
> THESEUS   In himself he is,
>   But in this kind, wanting your father's voice,
>   The other must be held the worthier.
> HERMIA I would my father looked but with my eyes.
> THESEUS Rather your eyes must with his judgement look.
>   (1.1.54–7)

Just as Egeus refuses to see Lysander with her eyes, so Hermia cannot bring herself to look "with his judgement". The force that determines her perception is not only inscrutable; it is also incorrigibly bold, even subversive. It is not the practice of "bewitchment" of which Egeus accuses Lysander, but it is certainly moved by some kind of charm, untouched by the supposedly objective qualities of empirical sight and rational debate. It is inaccessible to the contrary vision of fathers. Rather than being vulnerable to the "stealing" of its "impression" by an external cause, as Egeus suggests, this disposition is performative in the sense of being able to either "compose" or "disfigure" the beauty of what it looks upon. Despite the rhetoric of Theseus's "cool reason", Egeus's vision is not necessarily that of "judgement", as opposed to Hermia's idle "fantasy". His preference for Demetrius is founded no better upon the man's rationally considered "worthiness" than Hermia's choice of Lysander. Egeus wants to give his daughter to Demetrius because he *loves* him (see 1.1.95). His "judgement" that Demetrius is the "worthier" is no more rationally founded than Hermia's view of Lysander.

Both Egeus and Hermia are moved by an imaginative appraisal of the respective men, despite the rhetoric of "reason" and "judgement". Neither can look with the eyes of the other. The bestowal that characterises all love is redoubled in the figure of Hermia's friend, Helena, who gives it a conventional, derogatory twist before encapsulating its distinctive psychology in a succinct couplet:

> Through Athens I am thought as fair as she.
> But what of that? Demetrius thinks not so.
> He will not know what all but he do know.
> And as he errs, doting on Hermia's eyes,
> So I, admiring of his qualities.
> *Things base and vile, holding no quantity,*
> *Love can transpose to form and dignity.*
>   (1.1.227–33; emphasis added)

The phenomenology of love knows neither social nor logical compulsion. What role does "error" play in it, then? The fairy queen's infatuation with a creature that Aristotle would have doubly disqualified pushes the independent claims of bestowal to its limits. Waking to the sight and sound of a "rude mechanical" horribly "translated" into an ass, Titania resorts to the language of compulsion characteristic of all lovers:

> Mine ear is much enamoured of thy note;
> So is mine eye enthrallèd to thy shape;
> And *thy fair virtue's force perforce doth move me*
> On the first view to say, to swear, I love thee.
> BOTTOM Methinks, mistress, you should have little
>   reason for that.   (3.1.131–7; emphasis added)[20]

This is clearly a parody of the Aristotelian precept that love arises from the recognition of the virtue of the other. Yet it is not merely a parody. The "force" that Titania invokes as the cause of her admiration is the same puzzling "power" that emboldens Hermia to forget her subordinate place before the Duke and her father:

> HERMIA I do entreat your grace to pardon me.
>   I know not by what power I am made bold,
>   Nor how it may concern my modesty
>   In such a presence here to plead my thoughts,
>   But I beseech your grace that I may know
>   The worst that may befall me in this case
>   If I refuse to wed Demetrius.   (1.1.58–64)

Hermia's discourse is like that of the deferential but potentially unruly servant who risks the displeasure of the master by questioning the command.

---

[20] See, too, Lysander's hollow rationalization of his own transformation: "The will of man is by his reason swayed, / And reason says you are the worthier maid" (2.2.21–2).

Titania's is that of the master succumbing to the unruly servant, in a carnivalesque embodiment of Malvolio's shaping fantasy.[21] In name, shape, and status, Bottom thus offers a double vision of the performative power of *eros*. He is either a beguiling instance of Todorov's precept regarding the egalitarian force of love, namely, that the "idea that every human being, even a slave, might be worthy of becoming the object of love" is alien to the Aristotelian conception of loving-friendship (*Imperfect Garden*, 128),[22] or he is a confirming example of its mad capacity for (self-)debasement. In either case, the operation of compulsive bestowal is central.

One of the delights of the scene lies in the way in which the "rude mechanical" rises effortlessly to the occasion of being at the centre the queen of the fairies' court. He is utterly unselfconsciousness about contradicting the queen, but also graciously down to earth in his acceptance of the attentions of her servants. Wendy Wall reveals the roles of Puck and the fairies as domestic servants in her claim that they "signal the play's overarching interest in those aspects of domesticity – a bourgeois housewifery or menial service class – not completely reducible to aristocratic marital order".[23] Bottom's effortless adoption of the role impressed upon him by the aristocratic power of Titania's desire underlines Wall's point. The trick on Bottom redoubles the illusion played upon Sly in *The Taming of the Shrew*. Yet whereas sexual consummation with a member of the aristocracy is only tantalizingly promised in the early scene, Bottom's enforced silence and conveyance to Titania's bower presumably signals the achievement of Titania's erotic wilfulness. Titania's subjugation to the wayward force of *eros* is a deliberate form of disparagement in the eyes of her vengeful husband, who uses the love potion to restore his power over his wife and attain his own desire for the Indian boy. Political readings of this contest of will and perception are correct, but they tend to miss the fact that the power of valuation or bestowal (abused by Oberon) is transformed by its theatrical situation into something "rich and strange". Theseus's identification of lover, lunatic, and poet indicates a madness shared equally by Titania's eye, Oberon's political magic, and Shakespeare's stage. Such madness stems from an aspect of Plato's conception of love that has the potential for

---

[21] See the conventional icon of the servant with an ass's ears in Burnett, "Trusty Servant", and the play on the servant as ass in *The Comedy of Errors*.

[22] Consequently *philia* is predicated upon a causal ground distinct from or merely embodied in the person as such. Montaigne departs significantly from this *philia* tradition by insisting that the friend is not a mere instance of a moral quality or social status: love refuses *every* demand for justification: "If a man urge me to tell wherefore I loved him, I feel it cannot be expressed, but by answering: Because it was he, because it was my selfe" (*Essays*, 149).

[23] Wall, *Staging Domesticity*, 109.

political and metaphysical subversion: the "madness of love" celebrated in the *Phaedrus* is "a divine release of the soul from the yoke of custom and convention".[24]

"*Imagining some fear*"

If *A Midsummer Night's Dream* pursues the irrational logic of *eros* with a satirical view to its pretensions to rationality and virtue, it leavens that satire with a rather more serious consideration of the relationship between *nomos* and *agapē* within the space of Shakespeare's own professions of service, both on and off the stage:

> HIPPOLYTA I love not to see wretchedness o'erharged,
>   And *duty* in his *service* perishing.
> THESEUS Why, gentle sweet, you shall see no such thing.
> HIPPOLYTA He says they can do nothing in this kind.
> THESEUS The kinder we, to give them thanks for nothing.
>   Our sport shall be to take what they mistake,
>   And what *poor duty* cannot do,
>   Noble respect takes it in might, not merit.
>   [...]
>   Trust me, sweet,
>   Out of this silence yet I picked a welcome,
>   And in the modesty of *fearful duty*
>   I read as much as from the rattling tongue
>   Of saucy and audacious eloquence.
>   *Love*, therefore, and tongue-tied simplicity
>   In least speak most, to my capacity.
>   (*A Midsummer Night's Dream*, 5.1.85–105; emphasis added)

This interchange brings together the intersection of three kinds of experience and their formation within the political and personal matrix of performance as a public expression of love and duty. Hippolyta's discomfort raises the hermeneutic question of where the "prosperity" of such expression – the essential ingredients of service – lies: "in the ear / Of him that hears it" or "in the tongue / Of him that makes it" (*Love's Labour's Lost*, 5.2.847–9). This is a crucial issue for the player-poet of sonnet 23, who seeks to express on the page the forms of devotion and love that the much more exposed sphere and activity of speech threatens to destroy.[25] At stake is the

---

[24] Quoted in Singer, *Love 1*, 61.

[25] Sonnet 23 is precisely about "tongue-tied simplicity". Meredith Skura alerts us to the fact that Theseus responds more readily to the inadequacies of performance because they are an indubitable sign of love, duty, and service: more persuasive than, as he puts it, the "rattling tongue / Of saucy

conjunction of love and service as the expressive outcome of performance. In the eye of the monarch, the inadequacy of performance – expressive of a certain kind of fear and trembling and therefore of the abject *union* of love and service – is the truest confirmation of his status and power.[26] "To my capacity" at the end of Theseus's declaration might be a qualification – "in my judgement" or "in accordance with my power" – but it is also a reference to the undisputed goal of all such performances and perfomatives: they are expressions of love aimed at the Duke's political status as secular master and his gift of bestowal as *agapē*. *Agapē* is the freely endowed love of the master for the servant who displays his or her subjection in the form of *nomos*, even, or *especially*, if, that subjection is expressed inadequately. Just as the servant turns his bondage into freedom through an act of the imagination, so the master transforms its inadequate expression into real substance by accepting it as such.

Hippolyta, on the other hand, embodies not only the embarrassment of an audience at the inadequacies of the performer (her discomfort being per-haps a sign of her doubly subjected position as woman and spoil of war) but also the desire, from even a powerful member of that audience, to share in the *pleasures* of illusion – to participate in the play opened by performance rather than stand aloof as its judgemental recipient. There is therefore a double sense of service or duty at work here: the duty expressed through love and in service – Shakespeare's company would become the King's Men after all – to the monarch as the presumed and idealised audience of all plays and the service that the player performs to a (paying) audience in present-ing a fulfilling fiction. Shakespeare's sonnet 23 adds a further dimension to this already complex situation. It apotropaically negotiates a more intimate space in which there is possibly room for erotic love and, therefore, a recip-rocal relationship that transcends, or perhaps just overlooks, the inequalities of public performance. Here Todorov's distinction is crucial: the difference between *agapē* and reciprocal love that is not caught in the debilitating failures of desire lies in the fact that the former is extended promiscuously, to all servants, whereas the love that the servant-poet of the sonnets seeks should pick him out uniquely as the single, irreplaceable subject of love.

The disagreement between Hippolyta and Theseus shows that the double aspects of service as a performative role are in tension on Shakespeare's stage.

---

and audacious eloquence" (Skura, *Actor*, 32). The source of the sonnet's anxiety is precisely not that its speaker is tongue-tied, but rather that its eloquent display of love and duty stands to be rejected for the reasons Theseus offers.

[26] See Lopez, *Theatrical Convention*, for a discussion of the constant threat of failure on the early modern English stage.

The player is torn between two kinds of service: to his paying audience as a consequence of a momentary, but ever renewable, contract; and to the monarch or patron, where the play is always a means to another end: the perfect expression of love and duty. Such devotion may be more perfectly expressed the more tongue-tied it turns out to be. Common players hovered in a liminal space between being proper servants, mindful of their duty and love, as Theseus indulges them, and masterless men, beyond the boundaries of proper social order, as the act, at least by implication, excoriated them.[27] Shakespeare adds a further dimension to this tension. Love and duty as perfect expressions of the servant seeking the charitable indulgence of the master are overlaid in the sonnets and plays with a paradoxical form of love-in-service. This takes shape in the reiterated desire to *overcome* mere desire, in the wish to turn the general, imaginative bestowal of the master's recognition of "love and duty" into the shared serving of the other that Montaigne celebrates as the highest form of loving-friendship or *philia*.

Theseus may disparage the "compact" with the imaginative projection shared by the lover, lunatic, and poet, but he celebrates his own imaginative capacity to "piece out [his servants'] imperfections with [his] thoughts".[28] If the mechanicals' performance embodies love as *nomos* – the loving subjugation to the law which is also demanded of Theseus, Hippolyta, and Hermia in respectively different ways in the opening stages of the play – it is reciprocated through the Duke's imaginative acceptance of its very inadequacy. Here Shakespeare the dramatist puts his finger on the asymmetry of bestowal that he struggles with as sonneteer. In sonnets 26, 57, and 58, Shakespeare represents the abject position of the loving servant as the willing suspension of all subjectivity: "I am to waite, though waiting so be hell, / Not blame your pleasure be it ill or well" (58.13–4). The "hell" of this position lies in the asymmetry of the will that characterises the respective positions of lover and beloved, servant and master. Caught as much as any of the lovers in the Athenian wood in the toils of desire (which lie beyond his will to the same degree as Demetrius's perception of Hermia under the influence of the love potion), Shakespeare's servant-poet can do no more than anxiously await the free bestowal of grace of the kind that Theseus embodies.

The difference between theatre and poem lies in the capacity of the former to stage the discrepancies that are for the most part suffered, but only

---

[27] For an extended discussion of the relationship between theatre and beggary in Shakespeare's England and Europe, see Pugliatti, *Beggary*.
[28] See *Henry V*, Prologue, 23.

implicitly revealed, in the sonnets. Quince and his troupe's understanding of the nature of theatrical illusion may be hopelessly naïve, but that very naïveté allows the controlling dramatist to bare the device that underlines the service of playing itself, in the divided selves of the player-servants – Snug *and* Lion, Starveling *and* Moonshine, Snout *and* Wall – who embody both the representation of pleasurable illusion and the presentation of loving service. When Bottom asks, with his characteristic mixture of enthusiasm and bombast, whether the part he is to play is that of a "lover or a tyrant", he points to the double character of the actor. To be a mere weaver and yet to be able to embody the noble position of lover or tyrant is not only to be freed, even if temporarily and in make-believe, from the dull confines of one's service, but also to have the power, as Hamlet puts it, to "show virtue her own feature, scorn her own image, and the very age and body of the time his form and pressure" (*Hamlet*, 3.223–4). That Bottom's actual practice in this case makes both the "unskilful laugh" and the "judicious grieve" should not divert us from the potential of this protean power, even in the hands of a weaver or the son of a glove-maker. Confined by the narrow choice between two stock characters, however, Bottom's question also reveals a narrowness of scope, a lack of creative and reflective range that is hardly extended by the sorry performances of Wall, Lion, and Moonshine.

The "Brief Authority" of the servant-player

It has been suggested that the mechanicals' play – superfluous to the strict demands of the plot – afforded Shakespeare a chance to poke fun at what Alvin Kernan calls the "kind of junk theatre that ordinarily made up the bill of fare at Elizabethan palaces",[29] thereby enabling him to make his own more accomplished work shine by comparison. Both the styles of delivery that Bottom considers appropriate for lovers and tyrants and the unimaginative narrowness of these types appear to belong to a theatre increasingly challenged and displaced by the realism, variety, and poetic and philosophical richness of Shakespeare's pen and stage. The mechanicals' play may be execrable and their understanding of theatrical convention nonexistent, but the parody does not run entirely against them. The aristocratic audience of "The Lamentable Tragedy of Pyramus and Thisbe" are held up to ironic scrutiny in the ostentatious superiority of their commentary, and there is something delightfully unselfconscious about "bully" Bottom's

---

[29] Kernan, *King's Playwright*, 21.

presumption to correct the Duke on a technical matter of following the script:

> THESEUS The wall methinks, being sensible, should curse again.
> BOTTOM (*to* THESEUS) No, in truth, sir, he should not.
>   "Deceiving me" is Thisbe's cue. She is to enter now, and
>   I am to spy her through the wall. You shall see, it will fall
>   pat as I told you.
>   (*Enter* FLUTE *as* THISBE)
> Yonder she comes.   (5.1.180–5)

Bottom's literal-minded correction displays the limits of royal power through the "bifold authority" of the actor.[30] This is a deliberate staging of the double movement by which the actor vacillates across the threshold between being and representation – between performance as an actual investment of nontheatrical existence, including their "socio-cultural status and interest"[31] as player-servants, and performance as representation of a pre-existing image, speech, or character. It thus is *as weaver* – breaking the illusion of his character – that Bottom amends the Duke: "You shall see, it will fall pat as I told you . . . Yonder she comes." And yet it is only *as actor* that Bottom has the authority to predict and control either speech or action. This authority is, as Shakespeare and his company knew only too well, all too "brief." It is inevitably surrendered at the end of every performance, in a customary "plea for excuses", and it is rendered particularly fragile by the precarious social and political conditions of the acting profession itself.

A Midsummer Night's Dream may be a plea for the professional theatre as a site of a changing concept of service and its relation to the declaration of loving devotion, slowly transforming that site of performance through the self-reflexive modes of performance from its residual, folk tradition into a modern, commercial one, itself informed by its own power struggles between entrepreneurial master and playing servant. Its own status, as a "tedious brief scene of . . . tragical mirth" (5.1.55–6), possibly offered as a way to "beguile / The lazy time" (5.1.40–1) of aristocratic leisure, is based upon a satirical representation of an outdated, literary representation of *eros* still residually present in aristocratic fantasy.[32] Nonetheless, the theatrically self-conscious presentation of the fragility of erotic vision and the power of the sovereign to shape such perceptions through the mercurial mediations of the errant servant reveals its artificial imposition rather natural givenness.

---

[30] Robert Weimann, "Bifold Authority".   [31] Robert Weimann, "Performance-Game", 67.
[32] See Kernan, *King's Playwright*, xvii and xix, for the suggestion that Shakespeare's company may have performed the play as court entertainment to the new king in the first year of his reign and to the royal heir the following year.

A Midsummer Night's Dream exemplifies the coming together in Shakespeare's work of love, service, and performance under the concept of the imagination and within the ambit of a broader political vision. The role of the imagination in love as *eros* was a commonplace of early modern psychological theory, although Shakespeare treats its projective capacity – its tendency to *make* a world rather than reflect it – in a much less pejorative way than his contemporaries such as Bacon. Shakespeare recognizes that imaginative projection may either "grow to something of great constancy" or end in "tragic loading" (*Othello*, 5.2.359). Equally distinctive is Shakespeare's sense of the imaginative bestowal that lies at the heart of service. That bestowal may be seen in the reciprocal interaction of love as *nomos* and *agapē*, the former being the duty that the servant owes both his secular and divine masters, while the latter may take the form exemplified by Theseus's willing indulgence of the "modesty of fearful duty" shown by his servant-players.

The double imaginative investment in service as a condition of love is what enables the phenomenological transformation of the bond of service into "perfect freedom". Transformed from a mode of perception into linguistic terms, these modes of creative bestowal become performative. Such linguistic performativity finds in the bifold representational authority of the early modern English stage a perfect medium of expression, as imaginative bestowal or projection is turned into speech act, and the figure of the Shakespearean actor as servant oscillates between two modes of being: remaining the embodiment of what he represents in fiction, he forges a new kind of service, beholden less to a quasi-feudal master than to the unstable whim of a paying audience. Confronted with the theatrical exposure of the workings of the ideological imagination, the playgoers get more than they had bargained for.

CHAPTER 3

"His man, unbound"

The Comedy of Errors and *The Tempest*

Having traced the self-consciously performative representations of love and service as a manifold of complex relations between self-expressive player and represented authority in the context of the projective imagination of "the lunatic, the lover, and the poet" (*A Midsummer Night's Dream*, 5.1.7), I complete my outline of the framing conditions of love's conjunction with service by turning to a new set of concepts. I move from questions of self-reflexive performance and imaginative bestowal to the *bounds* of service – the word conveying both its limits or boundaries and its *ties*. The plays in this chapter show that whereas servant and master are emotionally and psychologically bound and bounden to each other, the bonds of love may be experienced as the chains of slavery and the chains of slavery may be imaginatively annulled by the bonds of love.

THE COMEDY OF ERRORS

It would not have escaped the attention of Shakespeare or his audience that Ephesus, the setting of *The Comedy of Errors*, is the destination of the apostle Paul's letter which sets out with the greatest force and concision the reciprocal but hierarchical duties of husband and wife, parent and child, master and servant. Chapter 6 of the Epistle to the Ephesians is the biblical *locus classicus* of master-servant relations, and the organising text of Gouge's exegesis in *Of Domesticall Dvties*:

5 Servants, be obedient unto them that are *your* masters, according to the flesh, with fear and trembling in singleness of your hearts as unto Christ,
6 Not with service to the eye, as men pleasers, but as the servants of Christ, doing the will of God from the heart,
7 With good will serving the Lord, and not men.
8 And know ye that whatsoever good thing any man doeth, that same shall he receive of the Lord, whether *he be* bond or free.

9 And ye masters, do the same things unto them, putting away threatening: and know that even your master also is in heaven, neither is there respect of person with him. (*The Geneva Bible*, Ephesians, 6:5–9)

In this story of a pre-Christian Mediterranean, based on a Roman farce, the traditionally English eschewal of slavery in favour of free service is replaced by the bondage of human traffic.[1] The Dromio twins are bought in their infancy specifically to serve the two Antipholus brothers, and their relationships bear none of the fraught and humanising complexities of reciprocal affection of other servants in the Shakespeare canon. Yet if the play offers little psychologically interiorised representation of affiliation between servant and master, its farcical patterning does register the normative ideals of such attachment in starker outline. Ephesus represents not merely the remote, classical world of slavery and Plautine comedy. It also evokes a Christian environment in which the bondage of service and the bonds of love are inextricably, if troublesomely, intertwined.

Being bound

The word "bound", and its cognates, "bond", "bondsman", "claim", and "chain", occur some fifty times in *The Comedy of Errors*. The concept evokes a range of notions that include not only restriction or limitation but also compass, affiliation, and reciprocity. The protagonists, bound to each other across time and distance by ties of love and bondage alike, owe their lives to their being "bound" to a mast when their ship sinks; the mercantile world of travel and trade which makes this play a precursor to *The Merchant of Venice* is invoked by the repeated notion of being "bound" on a voyage; and Luciana lectures her unhappy sister on the nature of marital compliance by

---

[1] See the following uncompromising passage:

That harde and cruell seruitude, bondage, and slauery which was vsed among the Gentiles, which knew not God, is taken away by the law of grace, by that grace, mercy, loue and commiseration which Iesus Christ our Sauiour bought vs, and taught vs toward another. Yea God as hee hath created vs all alike, and called vs all alike, so hee esteemeth vs all alike. With him there is neither Iewe, nor Gentile, poore nor rich, younge nor old, master nor Seruant; but in euery Nation, in euery state, calling, or degree of men: whosoeuer feareth him and doth righteousnesse is accepted of him, and whosoeuer doth otherwise shall receiue for the euill which he hath done, GOD is no acceptor of persons. (Fosset, *The Seruants Dutie*, 46–7)

Compare Harrison's more narrowly nationalist declaration: "As for slaves and bondsmen, we have none; nay, such is the privilege of our country by the especial grace of God and bounty of our princes, that if any come hither from other realms, as soon as they set foot on land they become so free of condition as their masters, whereby all note of servile bondage is removed from them" (Harrison, *Description of England*, 119). See also Neill's comments on the relation between slavery and service in "His Master's Ass", and *Servile Ministers*.

invoking the platitude that "There's nothing situate under heaven's eye / But hath his bound in earth, in sea, in sky" (2.1.16–17). These multiple notions of being bound, which hold in productive tension the double senses of movement and restraint, complement the play's general concern with wandering, loss, and homelessness, especially in the repeated invocations of the uncanny in the Freudian sense of the word: of *Heimlichkei*, the strangeness hidden in the local and familiar, liable to be decried as magic or witchcraft.[2]

In one of the many bewildering altercations in *The Comedy of Errors*, Adriana, the wife of Antopholus of Ephesus, asks the person whom she mistakenly takes for her servant (but who is in fact Dromio of Syracuse) on what grounds her husband has been arrested: "Tell me, was he arrested on a bond?" "Not on a bond", the servant replies, "but on a stronger thing: / A chain, a chain" (4.2.49–51). The servant's pun encapsulates the play's obsessive concern with bonds and bondage – with the multiple ways in which people as social beings may be "bound" or "chained". The play on words also evokes the difference in the strength or quality of bonds. Dromio may be playing somewhat obviously on the relative strength of physical and affective bonds when he suggests that the chain that now restrains his master is a "stronger thing" than the legal bond that occasioned his arrest. Yet Antipholus has been physically chained only because of the existence of nonmaterial bonds.

Being psychological or ethically bound is embodied by various instances of actual bondage. Egeon appears in chains in the opening scene, bound to his death by an inflexible law. That physical constraint is echoed in the most literal way by the arrest of Antipholus of Ephesus for failing to honour his bond to pay for the chain, and by his being physically bound to his bondsman for their supposedly "mad" behaviour. Dromio's punning transformation of abstract bond into physical chain calls attention to the fact that for much of the play the chain destined for Adriana circulates as a signifier of multiple emotional and legal ties: from Antipholus' love for his wife, through his commercial bond with the goldsmith, to the estrangement of marital affection through extramarital wandering and the bewildering obligation that comes with the bestowal of an unexpected gift. The chain circulates much as rings do in other plays, signifying both the instability of human ties and their unavoidability.

These instances of bonds and bondage encapsulate the interweaving of love and service. The play is concerned as much with the painful demands and vagaries of affective ties as it is with those of literal slavery and bondage.

---

[2] Freud, "The Uncanny", 375.

From the irresistible compulsion to find lost brothers and wives to the painful insecurity and demands of a wife who believes that her husband's affections have been alienated and the mutual recognition of the bondsmen in the mirror of the other, it explores in a schematic rather than interiorised way the complexities of filiation and affiliation.

Estranged familiars

Let us begin with the bonds of love, which are inseparable from the ties of jealousy, fear, and the forms of estrangement that lie at the heart of what is called "home". In the world of this play, tradesmen and merchant adventurers hold centre stage. Egeon's fatal predicament is the outcome, we must surmise, of mercantile rivalry between Ephesus and Syracuse. Egeon is caught in an indissoluble bind. An alien in a hostile land, he is automatically condemned to death, and all his goods are forfeit to the state unless he can pay a fine of a thousand marks or find a local person to pay the fine for him. If his goods are forfeit, how can he pay the fine? As a stranger in enemy territory, whom can he call upon as his friend? Egeon's motive for landing on shores that are bound to his own through ties of enmity and hatred is not profit, as one would expect from a merchant, but love. He is seeking, like so many of the characters in Shakespeare's late plays, to re-establish familial bonds with his son, who has in turn felt bound to wander the Mediterranean in search of his long-lost sibling and mother. The story that Egeon tells of his enforced estrangement from his family combines affective ties with coercive bondage. His relationship with his wife unites the emotional "embracements" of married love with the "pleasing punishment that women bear" (1.1.43, 46) in the form of her double pregnancy, but both conditions are finally subsumed by a different kind of bondage and separation. Despite being mutually "bound" to the mast, their embrace is violently severed by the storm.

This pattern anticipates a different set of anxieties occasioned by marriage in the relationship of Adriana and Antipholus of Ephesus: on the one hand, Adriana's poignantly obsessive attempts to restore their marital "embracement", and, on the other, her husband's impatient desire to break away from such a bond and punish his wife – emotionally by alienating her chain and physically by inflicting a rope upon her back.[3] Like its contemporary

---

[3]
While I go to the goldsmith's house, go thou
And buy a rope's end. That will I bestow
Among my wife and her confederates
For locking me out of my doors by day.
(4.1.15–18)

play, *The Taming of the Shrew*, *The Comedy of Errors* follows early modern
Protestant treatises on marriage and the family by representing a close relationship among the liberty, bonds, and reciprocity that mark relationships
of service and those of erotic love. The conventional view that the man is
master of the household is the subject of the opening disagreement between
the shrewish Adriana and her more complaisant, but unmarried, sister. The
angry wife meets her sister's injunction to bear her husband's liberty with
patience because it is bound up in the nature of things by rejecting the
common analogy between marriage and abject service:

> ADRIANA Why should their liberty than ours be more?
> LUCIANA Because their business still lies out o' door.
> ADRIANA Look when I serve him so, he takes it ill.
> LUCIANA O, know he is the bridle of your will.
> ADRIANA There's none but asses will be bridled so.
>
> (2.1.10–14)

Asses are, as we shall see, akin to servants, and Adriana is distancing herself
as much from the human menials whom she maltreats as she does from the
beast of burden with which they are so frequently compared.

   In contrast to her unmarried sister's advice to accept unequal degrees of
liberty and restraint as part of a broad, natural order, the upstart spouse
insists, somewhat improbably, that it is her sister's *servile* attitude that keeps
her single:

> ADRIANA This servitude makes you to keep unwed.
> LUCIANA Not this, but troubles of the marriage bed.
> ADRIANA But were you wedded, you would bear some sway.
> LUCIANA Ere I learn love, I'll practise to obey.
> ADRIANA How if your husband start some otherwhere?
>
> (27–31)

This difference is never quite resolved. We do not know whether Antipholus
is habitually unfaithful. What we do see is a series of poignant attempts
by the estranged or estranging wife to reclaim bonds of affection with
her husband that have the perverse effect of alienating him. Shakespeare's
early play does not represent the intensities of fresh erotic desire so much
as rehearse the hopeless contraries of domestic bonds. Urged to defend
herself by the very sister with whom she has a fundamental disagreement
about the bonds of marriage against the Abbess's accusation that it is her
shrewish jealousy that has estranged her husband, Adriana replies ruefully,
in a poignant acknowledgement of complicity in her unhappy condition:
"She did betray me to my own reproof" (5.1.91).

The bonds of love are both liberating and uncomfortably restraining. The twins are released into the joy of recovery just as Egeon and his long-lost wife find freedom in each other's embrace. That freedom is achieved after the constant reassertion of broader social obligations and dependencies. Adriana emphasises the reciprocity of care that she enjoys with the Duke who arranged her union with her husband, and the Duke recalls the reciprocating care that is due to her husband owing to the latter's loyal, wartime service:

> DUKE (*raising* ADRIANA)
> Long since, thy husband served me in my wars,
> And I to thee engaged a prince's word,
> When thou didst make him master of thy bed,
> To do him all the grace and good I could. –
>
> (5.1.161–5)

In keeping with Adriana's conception of the mutually constituted identities of husband and wife, she believes that any good that the Duke will do him must redound to her as well.

If the Abbess is able to reaffirm her ties to her husband by substituting the language of restraint for that of freedom – "Whoever bound him, I will loose his bonds, / And gain a husband by his liberty" (5.1.340–1) –, there is no such comfort for Adriana. Her husband refuses to acknowledge her to the very end. He says nothing more to her after emphatically denying his bond to her – "And are you not my husband? / ANTIPHOLUS OF EPHESUS No, I say nay to that" (372–3) – even after the confusion has been resolved. Luciana's suggestion that a husband should live a lie so that his wife may be spared the double pain of infidelity and indifference has been wasted upon the ears of a stranger. Nor is there any indication that he would heed the plea if he had heard it himself. His last words and action to a woman involve his acknowledging and returning the courtesan's ring with "thanks for my good cheer" (394).

The marks of service

Commentators have remarked on the excessive amount of violence in *The Comedy of Errors*. Beating is not only inflicted upon the slaves and threatened against wives, but violence also infuses the language of the entire play. The Dromios are incessantly beaten by master and mistress and by mistaken master and mistress, and both draw comic attention to their punishment by making it the subject of a litany of punning complaint. To what extent are we expected to see such chastisement as a mimetic representation of actual social practice?[4]

Physical chastisement was practised in Shakespeare's time by masters and husbands, but the apologists of service took care to limit the degree of violence.[5] Furthermore, master and mistress have very different relationships with their servants in *The Comedy of Errors*. Whereas both are equally prepared to beat a recalcitrant or delinquent minion, the play suggests a strange intimacy between master and servant that is absent from the different-sex relationship. In addition to his more menial duties, Dromio often plays the fool to Antipholus, presuming upon an allowed familiarity that is common in other plays such as *King Lear*, *Twelfth Night*, *All's Well That Ends Well*, and *The Taming of the Shrew*. This is primarily a product of the theatre rather than life, a performance tradition that reflects the entertaining and satirical role of the stage(d) servant discussed in Chapter 2:

> ANTIPHOLUS OF SYRACUSE Because that I familiarly sometimes
>   Do use you for my fool, and chat with you,
>   Your sauciness will jest upon my love,
>   And make a common of my serious hours.
>   When the sun shines, let foolish gnats make sport,
>   But creep in crannies when he hides his beams.
>   If you will jest with me, know my aspect,
>   And fashion your demeanour to my looks,
>   Or I will beat this method in your sconce.[6]   (2.2.26–34)

The master's satirically inflated demand that the servant be no more than an obedient mirror to his own "aspect", is chillingly represented by Duke Ferdinand's expectation that his retainers be the public affirmation and extension his own countenance and mood[7] in John Webster's *The Duchess of Malfi*. In Webster's tragedy the retainers are easily silenced, having internalised their master's expectations. In Shakespeare's comedy, however, the servant is always allowed an impertinent riposte that calls for the master to give an account of himself and even threatens retaliation:

---

[4] See Neill, *History*, 41.   [5] See Gouge, *Dvties*, 690, and Fosset, *Dvtie*, 42–3.
[6] Cf. Guazzo, *Conuersation*, whose dialogists eschew such familiarity: "for my part I cannot sway to make my seruaunts my companions, in being to familiar with them: I like well to loue them, but not embrace them" (sig. Yiii^r).
[7] Webster, *The Duchess of Malfi*, 1.1.120–9. See Gouge: Servants should do nothing "on their owne heads without or against consent of their masters, because while the time of seruice lasteth, they are not their owne, neither ought the things which they doe, to be for themselues: both their persons and their actions are all their masters: and the will of their master must be their rule and guide (in things which are not against Gods will.)". Servants should *"labour to bring their iudgement to the bent of their masters iudgement*, and to thinke that meet and good which he doth" (635).

DROMIO OF SYRACUSE "Sconce" call you it? So you would leave
    battering, I had rather have it a head. An you use these blows
    long, I must get a sconce for my head, and ensconce it too, or
    else I shall seek my wit in my shoulders. But I pray, sir, why
    am I beaten?
ANTIPHOLUS OF SYRACUSE Dost thou not know?
DROMIO OF SYRACUSE Nothing, sir, but that I am beaten.

                                       (2.2.35–41)

Such "self-expressive display" would have spoken to powerful feelings and
ready experiences among the servants and apprentices in the audience.
Yet it would also have echoed to the masters and mistresses present the
injunctions in the ideological literature not to beat servants without cause,
if at all. Here are Dod and Cleaver:

The end in correcting must not be to wrecke and reuenge thine anger, or malice, or
to reuenge thy selfe for any iniurie done. . . . For the matters that deserue correction,
this is a rule, that there must be no rebuking, much lesse chastising, but where
there is a fault . . . by patience one must heare what the offender can say in his
defence, and not disdaine to heare him modestly alledging for himselfe: and when
his defence is made, by equitie to allow, or disallow the same . . . this patience will
also keepe thee from immoderate Anger, a thing dangerous in a correcter. (sig
Dr–D4r)

In keeping with the peculiar contradiction that besets all Puritan texts on
the duties of masters and servants to each other, a master's failure to observe
this advice gives the servant no reason to leave his service. The duty to serve
in "fear and trembling" is, with certain qualifications, total, even if masters
may in time be taken to task by God for their impatience and inhumanity.[8]
Yet the representation of service on the stage circumvents Gouge's logic
that servants should not complain about being maltreated because they
are inevitably biased and so cannot be judges in their own cause.[9] The
theatrical embodiment of master-servant relations via the frisson of the
self-expressive impertinence of the player, rather than the individualised
isolation of reading a conduct book or ideological tract, makes room for a

---

[8] See also Fosset, 18–19: "To which Seruants I say thus: that albeit their maisters doe not well to
deale hardly and euilly with them, neither can they be excused for so doing, yet if the malice and
peruersenes of their maisters be such, they notwithstanding being seruants must not shake off the
yoake, set themselues at liberty, and depart when they list, first because they haue not power of their
owne selues, they couenanted with their maisters, tyed and bound themselues to serue them so long,
and in such sort."

[9] Gouge, 613: "Seruants may not be their owne Iudges whether their correction be iust or vniust: for
men are so prone to sooth themselues and to extenuate the euill actions which they doe, as if they be
not corrected till they thinke it iust, they would neuer be corrected."

more egalitarian, public judgement under conditions in which master and servant respond as common playgoers. The possibility, and likelihood, that different members of the audience would respond differently to the satirical wit of the player-servant as servant shows that the relationship between self-resembling show and audience cannot be conceived in too homogenous a way: such self-expressive impertinence would in all likelihood have *divided* the audience members, depending on their own positions as masters or servants.

Lost at home

In *The Comedy of Errors*, the settled sense of what Evett evokes as a consequence of service is destabilised by the superficially conventional, farcical device of mistaken identity. Shakespeare's doubling of the twins in his source is more than the theatrical pyrotechnics of an apprentice playwright: it is a representation of what happens when the consistency that allows human beings to be bound to each other, the world, and a sense of individual self is disrupted. The question of identity, especially that of the masters, is anything but settled, and such instability concerns their being *bound* to the servant or slave who bears their marks.

In *The Comedy of Errors* identity is relational, expressed largely through material bonds of love and service rather than the representation of interiority. Such dependency is conveyed most poignantly in the longing that Antipholus and Adriana express, in almost identical terms, about their natural ties in love to another whose loss entails their own dissolution. "He that commends me to mine own content", Antipholus of Syracuse laments in response to the Merchant's conventional farewell, "commends me to the thing I cannot get":

> I to the world am like a drop of water
> That in the ocean seeks another drop,
> Who, falling there to find his fellow forth,
> Unseen, inquisitive, confounds himself.
> So I, to find a mother and a brother,
> In quest of them, unhappy, lose myself.
> (1.2.33–40)

The severing and coming together of twins, parents, and spouses anticipates the abiding sense in the rest of Shakespeare's work of the difficulty, if not the impossibility, of achieving one's "own content" without the ties that bind the self to others. Adriana is even more painfully aware of her spiritual dependency upon her husband:

> How comes it now, my husband, O how comes it
> That thou art then estrangèd from thyself? –
> Thy "self" I call it, being strange to me
> That, undividable, incorporate,
> Am better than thy dear self's better part.
> Ah, do not tear away thyself from me;
> For know, my love, as easy mayst thou fall
> A drop of water in the breaking gulf,
> And take unmingled thence that drop again
> Without addition or diminishing,
> As take from me thyself, and not me too.
>
> (2.2.122–32)

The striking recurrence of the image of a drop of water exemplifies both the possible loss of personal identity through others and the incorrigible constitution of the self through its inseparability from society. Adriana's heartfelt plea to her husband that in leaving or neglecting her he wounds both of them recalls the poet-lover's anguished sense of painful division in the sonnets which hurts precisely because of its violent rending, the *tearing*, of each constituent self. Adriana intensifies that notion of painful unity by reflecting on the fact that the moral stain of her husband's imagined actions soils her as much as it does him:

> I am possessed with an adulterate blot;
> My blood is mingled with the crime of lust.
> For if we two be one, and thou play false,
> I do digest the poison of thy flesh,
> Being strumpeted by thy contagion.
> Keep then fair league and truce with thy true bed,
> I live unstained, thou undishonourèd.
>
> (2.2.143–9)

Adriana uses the image of the drop of water to stake a claim against her reduction to "nothing". Insisting upon the spiritual, legal, and religious bonds, she reminds her husband that he cannot separate himself from her. Her plea is made both more poignant and grotesquely comic by the fact that she addresses it to a *stranger* who knows nothing of what she is talking about, even if he might be struck by an uncanny duplication of his own feelings about loss of self through the alienation of those he loves.

From the perspective of the audience, it is apparent how little it takes to maintain and disrupt the sense of self. The man who is indeed a stranger to her bespeaks in the most palpable form Adriana's deepest fears about the estrangement of her husband's affections. Yet his readiness to play the role that she expects from him indicates the possibility of shaping a process of performative reciprocity. In contrast to the public encounter in the street, Adriana emphasises the personal communality of a private dinner ("let no creature enter") and appropriates the most readily available discourse of privacy and interiority in her promise to "shrive" his misdemeanours as "a thousand idle pranks" (2.2.210, 207).

When we turn to the identity of the servant, however, even this bare sense of reciprocal interiority is absent. Here all turns on the rigidity of names in tension with the flexibility of performance. The Dromios remain slaves, whatever forms of alteration they are forced to undergo. Both the consistency of such servile identity and their fantastical transformation are encapsulated by vision of the bondsman as an *ape*, the epitome of mimicry and changeability:

> LUCIANA Why prat'st thou to thyself, and answer'st not?
>   Dromio, thou drone, thou snail, thou slug, thou sot.
> DROMIO OF SYRACUSE (*to* ANTIPHOLUS) I am transformèd,
>   master, am not I?
> ANTIPHOLUS OF SYRACUSE I think thou art in mind, and so am I.
> DROMIO OF SYRACUSE Nay, master, both in mind and in my shape.
> ANTIPHOLUS OF SYRACUSE Thou hast thine own form.
> DROMIO OF SYRACUSE No, I am an ape.
> LUCIANA If thou art changed to aught, 'tis to an ass.
> DROMIO OF SYRACUSE (*to* ANTIPHOLUS)
>   'Tis true she rides me, and I long for grass.
>   'Tis so, I am an ass; else it could never be
>   But I should know her as well as she knows me.   (2.2.196–205)

In this extension of the bestialisation of servants, the slave is confirmed in his identity (knowing and being known, even by strangers) after some initial resistance (against being turned into a drone, a slug, a snail, an ape, an ass, and in the brief longing for freedom: "I long for grass") by the litany of bestial insults and his accustomed role of being "ridden" and "marked". The identity of the servant is shaped by the reduction of the individuality of the proper name to the generic performance encompassed by a common substantive. Whatever he does, he is "marked", both physically and symbolically: he shifts from being Dromio of Syracuse to a generic Dromio, before being reduced to servant, slave, and ass. Like the player, he bears all these transformations in the the figure of the ape.

The dislocation of identity occurs because the Syracusans are transported as aliens to a strange and hostile shore, but it is the Syracusan master-servant pair's initiation into *normal* life that proves to be most bewildering. Precisely because they are taken for well-known locals and treated as if their lives, identities, and actions are consistent with all that makes human beings feel at home with each other and the world, the Syracusans reveal the deep *Heimlichkeit* or uncanniness of the ordinary or the home. That home is the heart of both erotic relations and those of service, each exposed though the displacement and confusion of identities to be a place of occluded darkness.

Antipholus of Syracuse is bewildered and reassured in equal measure by behaviour that he would in any other circumstances take for granted:

> ANTIPHOLUS OF SYRACUSE There's not a man I meet but doth
>   salute me
>   As if I were their well-acquainted friend,
>   And everyone doth call me by my name.
>   Some tender money to me, some invite me,
>   Some other give me thanks for kindnesses.
>   Some offer me commodities to buy.
>   Even now a tailor called me in his shop,
>   And showed me silks that he had bought for me,
>   And therewithal took measure of my body.   (4.3.1–9)

This is a marvellously evocative and detailed catalogue of the performative events that constitute the self within a network of social relationships, given a telling specificity by a speaker who is accustomed to mastering it over others. However much he may be convinced that those plying their services are "Lapland sorcerers" set to deceive him, the attentions of so many respectful friends, tailors, and merchants – all in place to *serve* him – are uncanny and disconcerting precisely because they are so normal for a person of his status and station. This chain of communal attentions takes more than the measure of his body – they measure and confirm his rank and status. They underwrite his magisterial identity while simultaneously dislocating it with their very familiarity. Such attentions constitute links in a communal chain that make up further, legal and ethical bonds which are generically true while being specifically mistaken. Antipholus of Ephesus finds himself legally bound for a chain that he has never received, arrested because the goldsmith from whom he ordered it is himself bound for a sum of money to a merchant, who is himself "bound to sea" (4.1.33), and subject to a plea for dutiful intimacy by a women who is a stranger to him.

That chain and the trust that are bound up in the transaction for it signify a more general set of obligations, ties, and relationships that fall variously under the notion of love, erotic and nonerotic. The chain itself is commissioned as an ultimately alienable sign of Antipholus's affection for his wife, but she would readily forgo the gift if she could secure his real love in the place of its unreliable signifier: "Sister, you know he promised me a chain. / Would that alone o' love he would detain, / So he would keep fair quarter with his bed" (2.1.105–7). Initiated as a token of his affection, it circulates as the sign of estrangement. Materially, it also signals affective ties without which the masculine marketplace could not work. "Belike you thought our love would last too long", Antipholus of Ephesus declares angrily to Angelo the Goldsmith, "If it were chained together, and therefore came not" (4.1.25–6).

The master-slave dialectic revisited

The anxiety of being chained too long in love is not confined to the erotic or mercantile relationships of the play. It is most striking in the chaining together of master to servant. For whatever confusions may be released by mistaken identities regarding the two sets of twins, their respective relationships as master and servant remain undisturbed. Each Dromio slots perfectly into the space left vacant by the other; each is subjected to a set of *generic* actions and attitudes that confirm the servile status of both. The tie that binds servant to master is never in question. What matters in this play is not individual subjectivity but rather generic identity as a place-holder in a system.[10]

In the arrest and incarceration of Dromio and Antipholus of Ephesus by the citizens of their own city, on the grounds that their strange behaviour is a sign of their shared madness, we see the opposite picture of that bewildering reassurance of normal relationships noted by Antipholus in 4.3.1–9. Just as the alien territory paradoxically disconcerts through its habitual patterns of behaviour, so the familiarity of home is violently disrupted by the collective judgement of the citizens of Ephesus that behaviour which seems perfectly normal to Antipholus and Dromio is in fact a sign of insanity.

Unlike *Twelfth Night*, in which casting into outer darkness is reserved for a single reprobate for his transgression of the bounds of service, master and servant are here tied together in a common condition of bondage

---

[10] This is also true of Sebastian in *Twelfth Night*, who slots effortlessly into the space vacated by his sister.

and social alienation which also confirms their strange intimacy. "Master, I am here entered in a bond for you" (5.1.120), Dromio of Ephesus says to Antipholus.[11] His master angrily denies this bond, but the two of them will soon not only be literally "bound together" (5.1.249), it will be the master who unbinds the servant, gnawing through their mutual bonds with his teeth. This is an interpretive crux for anyone trying to ascertain the play's final take on the subservience and abuse of service. Evett reminds us that it is a custom in classical comedy for slaves to be freed at the end in recognition of their services (*Discourses*, 60). In the Elizabethan play, their release is ambiguous at best. Evett regards Dromio of Ephesus's response to the question of his relationship to his master as a confirmation of his continuing servitude:

> EGEON (*to* ANTIPHOLUS) Is not your name, sir, called Antipholus?
>   And is not that your bondman Dromio?
> DROMIO OF EPHESUS Within this hour I was his bondman, sir,
>   But he, I thank him, gnawed in two my cords.
>   Now am I Dromio, and his man, unbound.   (5.1.287–91)

The dialogue between father and son, master and servant, is not simply about servitude or about simple servitude. Desperate to loose his own fatal bondage which confirms him as an unrecognised alien, friendless and solitary, Egeon eagerly seeks to re-establish a bond with the person whom he thinks he recognises as his son. This involves establishing the tie that binds son and father to a common bondsman. A desperate move to establish a saving identity as a member of a family and confirming community by someone who is used to being an independent master in his own house, it acknowledges the dependence of the master's identity upon the servant's recognition. It is thus the servant – the person characteristically not addressed personally – who responds to the question of the master's identity.

Dromio's reply reiterates the theatrical, self-expressive show of wit by the irrepressible servant as player and player as servant. This double role affords him the agency to confirm an identity that reinflects his relationship to his master in a subtly different way. After incessant, violent abuse, veiled threats, and hints of abscondment, Dromio of Ephesus finally suggests that the master's willing reduction of himself to a beast to free them both ("gnawing with my teeth my bonds in sunder" (5.1.250)), has subtly changed the quality of that relationship but not abrogated it. "Within this hour I was his bondman, sir", he states, "But . . . I thank him . . . / Now I am Dromio,

---

[11] Because members of the aristocracy could not be prosecuted for debt, it was common for them to press their senior servants to stand surety for them. See Engle, *Market*, 85–6.

and his man, unbound" (289–91). "Dromio, and his man, unbound" – in a play in which the subjectivity of the servant always threatens to be reduced either to the common condition of the slave or to the wordless endurance of the beast of burden, Dromio's free affirmation of his personal name is as significant as his replacement of the epithet that signifies bondage with one that speaks, to some degree, of choice. His utterance confirms a status that would be paradoxical if Evett had not so carefully prepared us for its possibility: not the manumission of the slave but the declaration by the slave that he is both "unbound" *and* his master's "man".

If the slave in Plautus's *Menaechmi* is freed at the end, Shakespeare does not release his bondsmen except through their final recognition of themselves in each other. This underlines the fact that a condition beyond service in Elizabethan society is unimaginable. It also affirms, however, mutual reflection of servants to each other. There is nowhere for Dromio to go other than into the service of another master. Freed from Shylock's service, Launcelot Gobbo in *The Merchant of Venice* can move only to a different, more indulgent master in Bassanio. This asymmetry between early modern forms of service and classical slavery marks the fundamental, conceptual difference between the two conditions. In the final lines of *The Comedy of Errors*, the servant's voice displaces, if only briefly, that of the master. In his declaration of their joint empathetic identification with Egeon's condition, Dromio of Ephesus speaks for the mutual bonds that tie master and man together. He also expresses through an imaginative form of recognition and acknowledgement completely absent from masters, the recognition of a common condition when he responds sympathetically to Egeon's plea:

> EGEON I am sure you both of you remember me.
> DROMIO OF EPHESUS Ourselves we do remember, sir, by you;
> For lately we were bound as you are now. (292–4)

The Comedy of Errors incarnates through theatrical embodiment the estranged doubleness underlying the sonnet sequences to or about *both* the young aristocrat and the dark woman. In the dark anxieties of the sonnets clustered around number 94, Shakespeare's poet grapples with the impenetrability and inscrutability of the beloved that are staged in the scenes of mistaken identity in *The Comedy of Errors*. Adriana, Luciana, and Antipholus of Syracuse are united by their serial attempts to pierce another who is both familiar and strange, both present and withdrawn, a denizen of the home and an utter stranger. Such forms of address in both the plays and the sonnets, where the effect is less apparent, are primarily performative rather than descriptive. Adriana pleading for love from a man who is her husband in body but not in spirit encapsulates the sonnets' painful disjunction of the inscrutable beloved – "Thy looks with me, thy heart in other place" (sonnet 93) – even as they appeal against that disjunction.[12] In his entreaties to Luciana to accept his passionate devotion, Antipholus of Syracuse embodies the displacement of affect that underlies her sister's relationship with her husband.

Shakespeare's repeated excoriation of "painting" in the sonnets to the young man may be read as an attempt to avoid the duplication that renders constancy and reciprocity impossible. The displacement of the other is the basis of what Joel Fineman calls Shakespeare's "perjured eye" in the sonnets to the dark woman.[13] Although such displacement is most apparent in the difference between what the poet's eye sees and what his heart feels with regard to his mistress, that threatening disjunction lies as much at the heart of the anxieties of the poems to the young man. The theatrical device of the twins disarms the anxieties and uncertainties that inform the sonnets, because dramatic irony and the conventional ending allow the uncertainties to be kept in place and controlled. Yet what may be resolved in a fairly straightforward way on stage when characters finally come to see the split persona as two different people remains as an ethical and emotional tearing of the eye and heart of the poet in the sonnets.

Brotherly love

I began with Paul's letter to the Ephesians. Marjorie Garber reminds us that another biblical epistle might also encompass the play's conception of love and service, brotherhood and marriage:[14]

1 Let brotherly love continue.
2 Be not forgetful to lodge strangers: for thereby some have received Angels into their houses unawares.

---

12 Luciana's plea to her brother-in-law to observe the "office" of a husband consists of twenty-eight lines of rhyming quatrains, or two sonnets joined by four lines of mutually rhyming couplets (3.2.1–28). It is a halting, preparatory exercise for arguments and feelings that will find much more flexibly powerful expression in real sonnet form. In addition to words and phrases that anticipate the sonnets to the young man ("Shall love, in building, grow so ruinous?"), her appeal dwells on the ideal of fidelity that so painfully informs the servant-poet's respective attempts to negotiate love with the unreliable aristocratic friend and the promiscuous dark woman. Sonnet 93's self-defensive declaration to "live, supposing thou art true, / Like a deceiued husband" joins the more well-known, ironic celebration of mutual dishonesty of sonnet 138, "When my loue swears that she is made of truth, / I do beleeue her though I know she lyes", in Luciana's heartfelt, pragmatic attempt to shield her sister from the pain and shame of her husband's infidelity and indifference: "'Tis double wrong to truant with your bed, / And let her read it in thy looks at board." Antipholus's declaration of devotion to Luciana is also a sonnet.
13 Fineman, *Shakespeare's Perjured Eye*.   14 Garber, *Shakespeare after All*, 174.

3 Remember them that are in bonds, as though ye were bound with them: and them that are in affliction, as if ye were also *afflicted* in the body.
4 Marriage *is* honorable among all, and the bed undefiled: but whoremongers and adulterers God will judge . . .
17 Obey them that have the oversight of you, and submit yourselves: for they watch for your souls, as they that must give accounts, that they may do it with joy, and not with grief: for that is unprofitable for you. (Hebrews, 13:1–17)

If it promises no restoration of marital embracement for Antipholus of Ephesus and Adriana, the play does end with the restoration of magisterial relations. But they are complicated by the double embodiment of the servant twins, who oscillate between the role of classic slave and the self-expressive impertinence of theatrical show.[15] Unlike other plays, in which the servant's role is overshadowed by often self-satisfied aristocratic posturing, the bondman twins are given the last word. They express a mutual discovery of self through the shared recognition of filial likeness or kind:

> DROMIO OF EPHESUS Methinks you are my glass and not
>   my brother.
>   I see by you I am a sweet-faced youth.   (420–1)

"Sweet-faced youth": Nothing that has been said by anybody in the play has offered *this* perspective on the pair of slaves. On the contrary, the verbal mirror that master and mistress have held up to their "men" has projected the opposite image: drudges, drones, slugs, asses and apes. The mirroring of the twins to and in each other asks us to imagine the possibility of Caliban recognising himself in Ferdinand and Ferdinand seeing his own image in the "salvage and deformed slave". "Methinks you are my glass": this is both the fantasy of the servant-poet who yearns to be accepted as the "glass" of his own "sweet-faced youth" and the more profound outcome of the concept of human identity underlying the comedy's farcical twinning. It encapsulates in the embodied possibilities of the theatre the inverse of Antipholus of Syracuse's sense of the dissolution of his identity without the affirmation of others to whom he is bound: "I to the world am like a drop of water / That in the ocean seeks another drop, / Who, falling there to find his fellow forth, / Unseen, inquisitive, confounds himself" (1.2.35–8). The bonds that tie us to others may be felt as a kind of bondage – a kind of domestic darkness – but they are absolutely constitutive of our sense of ourselves and of the continuities that constitute human identity. These bonds are encompassed, as Stanley Cavell has argued and this closing

---

[15] See the double sense of "fool" as "idiot" and "player" in the closing couplet of sonnet 57: "So true a foole is loue, that in your Will, / (Though you doe any thing) he thinks no ill".

scene exemplifies, by the mutual recognition that comes with reciprocal acknowledgement.[16]

The Dromio brothers are servants or bondsmen, so whatever social difference the minute of their respective births might make is not great. Nevertheless, if through their own reflections upon and of each other in this moment of re-birth the play can transform the vision of the audience to recognise or acknowledge the slaves as "sweet faced youths", then their egalitarian refusal to accept the imposition of social difference through the accident of birth offers a powerful concluding image to a story in which the humanity of servant or bondsman is always in question:

> DROMIO OF EPHESUS Will you walk in to see their gossiping?
> DROMIO OF SYRACUSE Not I, sir, you are my elder.
> DROMIO OF EPHESUS That's a question. How shall we try it?
> DROMIO OF SYRACUSE We'll draw cuts for the senior. Till
>   then, lead thou first.
> DROMIO OF EPHESUS Nay, then thus:
>   We came into the world like brother and brother,
>   And now let's go hand in hand, not one before another.
> (*Exeunt to the priory*)   (422–30)

In an aristocratic world, their egalitarian gesture would be barely thinkable, since the first-born, even by the blink of an eye, would be master, automatically relegating the younger brother to the status of supplicant servant, and possibly to a lifetime of burning resentment. Within the context of the theological tracts on service, the two young bondsmen exemplify a generosity of spirit that belies the intensity of the pejorative use of the epithet "slave" as a term of intense abuse. It also recalls, especially in the biblical echo "we came into the world", Paul's insistence that "GOD is no respecter of persons".[17] In their recognition of self through the mirror of the other without difference – drop for drop – the twin brothers offer a possible way out of Hegel's master-slave dialectic. They point beyond its definition of each dependency as a necessary condition of misrecognition and enslavement to the bo(u)nds of power.

THE TEMPEST

The last non-collaborative play that Shakespeare wrote encapsulates the bounds of service represented in the earlier comedies and the imaginary projection characteristic of love with an even more intense, though less

---

[16] Cavell, *Disowning Knowledge.*   [17] Fosset, *The Seruants Dutie,* 47.

obvious, self-consciousness about the work of the theatre. Magic reappears as the force that integrates the violence of ideological projection, theatrical illusion, and the imaginary forms of bestowal that characterise service and love as the conjoined interface of social and personal life. *The Tempest* involves the recovery of a dynasty through love, which means that the clash between the politically sanctioned wills of fathers and the peculiar imaginative projections of *eros* needs to be reconciled on two fronts. Two people unaware of the existence of each other need to be made to fall in love, and all possible blocks to their marriage need to be eradicated, including the putatively contrary will of the other father. Surrounding this love plot (which from one perspective is no more than politics by another name) are the now well-known paraphernalia of service and slavery, without which the main purpose of harnassing Eros to power cannot be achieved.

Many have noted that *The Tempest* represents its protagonist as a dramatist and director whose will to power is embodied by the actor-servants who set up and enact his desires. Daniel Vitkus notes that the self-reflexive theatricality of the play should be read as a reflection of the bonds of service *within* the material labour relations of Shakespeare's theatre itself.[18] The labour performed by Ariel, and the relationship of service that it involves with Prospero, is analogous to the often exploitative labour relations between theatrical entrepreneurs such as Philip Henslowe and the players, dramatists, and apprentices whom he controlled through his canny manipulation of the debts, loans, contracts, and services and, of course, to Shakespeare himself as one of the ultimate "masters" within his company of players. The significance of the master-servant relations between Prospero and his bondsman and slave, Ariel and Caliban, may thus be sought much closer to home than the far-flung reaches of the Mediterranean or the stormy shores of Bermuda. They also reside in the labour conditions, still wholly informed by the relations of master and servant, that made the work of the theatre itself possible. This is a valuable complication of my own desire to read service through the performativity of the stage, because it reminds us that the theatre as an economy reflected the service relationships, exploitative or otherwise, of the society in which it sought its commercial existence. To the two aspects of service in the theatre already mentioned – the players as the residual retainers of a pre-eminent aristocrat or sovereign, and their new, freer cash relationship to a paying audience – we need to add a third: a differentiated hierarchy of relations that divided the lowest, apprentice

---

[18] Vitkus, "Meaner Ministers".

boy actors from hired hands and dramatists contracted to a company, those players and dramatists from independent sharers in the company, and finally entrepreneurs such as Henslowe who wielded immense power across the board. The self-reflexive show of impertinent service traced in *The Taming of the Shrew, A Midsummer Night's Dream,* and *The Comedy of Errors* is thus complicated in *The Tempest* by being subsumed within the hierarchy of mastery that constituted the social politics of the theatre itself.

By shifting love and service from the medium in which characters move to their stereotypical embodiment in a simplified and reduced representation of both family and state (or family *as* state), Shakespeare focuses much more sharply than before on the ideological (and therefore historical) *formation* of these concepts. In other words, the overt theatricality of *The Tempest* bares the devices through which imaginative violence works to shape self-perception more starkly than in the other plays discussed so far. In his other work, Shakespeare seldom calls the institution of service itself into question. It is a given – the unquestioned framework in terms of which individual actions are judged. This is not the case in *The Tempest.* His late play asks questions from its opening lines about natural and arbitrary authority in its dialogical presentation of the *historical* narratives of how servants came to be subordinated and masters occupied their positions of power. It does this by splitting itself in two: into Shakespeare's play on one hand, and on the other, the performative excesses within Prospero's play that signal his project as the projections and manipulations of the master's will.[19] The tension between these two plays reveals further the dark intricacies, but also the affective intimacies, that bind servant and master.

Masters

"Master" is the third word of *The Tempest.* It introduces in the starkest terms hierarchical relationships under pressure. The master referred to here – the shipmaster – remains in absolute authority over his ship under conditions of extreme danger. His impatient response to the invocation of royal authority – "What care these roarers for the name of a king?" – anticipates a number of key issues in the play as a whole: the questioning of merely nominal legitimacy, made especially acute by the disruptive context of New World discovery and loss; the indifference of the natural world to human constructions of power; and the shipmaster's own relativised competence

---

[19] See Barker and Hulme, "Nymphs and Reapers".

vis-à-vis that natural world.[20] There is also a possible deictic reference to the "roarers" who pack the theatre in search of pleasure and entertainment. More of such roarers later.

The shipmaster's name most nearly matches nature: his mastery is the mastery of natural or acquired competence. There are compelling practical reasons for him to enjoy supreme command of the ship. In the context of such *motivated* mastery, all other claims to mastery and impositions of service are opened to question because they are arbitrary, not motivated. By withdrawing to private study, Prospero himself fails in the first of his obligations as a ruler: to serve his people. He acts like a shipmaster who locks himself in his cabin during a storm to study the theory of navigation.

Shortly after the self-incriminating narrative of his deposition, Prospero encounters the first direct challenge to his mastery over the new world. First, Ariel forces him to give reasons why he should be forced to continue to obey his commands. Ariel's service is given a history, and although Prospero forces Ariel to rehearse it in the master's favour, the very fact that it is forced to be recounted opens it up to questioning. Ariel is properly speaking a bondsman – someone who has freely given up his freedom to a master. Both the conflict between servant and master and its resolution lie in the imprint of contestable memory. Ariel reminds Prospero of their contract; Prospero recalls with undue impatience the bond of gratitude that ties the spirit to his command and his naked power to return his servant to his arboreal prison. This indenture is onerous but finite. Ariel can look forward to release at some future date, provided he fulfils his side of the bargain. His service is therefore conditional and to a degree rational. It is informed by the discourse "of late Elizabethan household service . . . characterized by relatively impermanent bonds between master and servant", rather than slavery or serfdom (Evett, *Discourses*, 33).[21]

Almost at once the exchange between Prospero and Ariel is echoed by the notorious encounter between Prospero and Caliban. The conversation (if we can call it that) moves once again (and unusually) into the "dark backward and abyss of time" (*The Tempest*, 1.2.50) to uncover the historical conditions that have given rise not to a bond of service but rather to the bondage of slavery. The contours of the argument are too well known – especially

---

[20] Perhaps the most complex and mystifying lies in the fact that in the world of the play the second is not a self-evident truth: its major representative of discursive relations of authority and power – Prospero – is also someone who has limited but impressive power over nature. Indeed, these waves are roaring in *his* name.

[21] See Southern, *Middle Ages*, 97 passim, for an account of serfdom as a condition related to freedom and restraint.

in post-colonial analysis – to be rehearsed at any length here.[22] I want to draw attention to two related things: this relationship allegorises contested or disloyal service in a general sense, but its contestation is given a distinctly local habitation and historical urgency in the form of Shakespeare's personal knowledge of contemporary encounters with the New World. The New World enters and transforms the parameters of a distinctly traditional anxiety about service in the Old. Caliban may at one level be read as little more than the monstrous face of insubordination and rebellion that simmers beneath all accounts of traditional service, but the colonial inflections of the play give it a new shape. Shakespeare gives both a disturbing new purchase to a traditional challenge to the rigid givenness of master-servant relations and also presents prescient grounds for the rationalising of the enslavement of indigenous peoples through the abrogation of earlier expectations of reciprocity. In the colonial dislocation from home traditional bonds of serice are called into question, whereas in relation to indigenous populations such bonds are replaced by bondage.

The crucial move here is the removal of the servant from the traditionally nurturing environment of the family. Once Caliban is characterised as that upon which nurture will not stick and as a danger to the sanctity of family relations and their security, the path is opened to his alienation from the inclusive circle of the family and a naturalised condition of enslavement:

> PROSPERO   Thou most lying slave,
>   Whom stripes may move, not kindness!
> [...]   Abhorrèd slave,
>   Which any print of goodness wilt not take,
>   Being capable of all ill! But thy vile race,
>   Though thou didst learn, had that in 't which good natures
>   Could not abide to be with; therefore wast thou
>   Deservedly confined into this rock,
>   Who hadst deserved more than a prison.   (1.2.344–64)

Removing Caliban from the family on the grounds of his abhorrent nature legitimises the use of pure force – power rather than authority – to impose his bondage – "cramps, / Side-stitches that shall pen thy breath up . . . [pinches] / As thick as honeycomb, each pinch more stinging / Than bees that made 'em" (1.2.327–32). Such naked coercion is contrasted to the ethical bond that is at least invoked between Prospero and his "tricksy spirit" (5.1.230). Whereas Shakespeare usually uses the appellation "slave"

---

[22] Critical literature and debate on this topic is now legion. For representative voices, see Kermode, 'Introduction'. Lamming, *Exile*; Hulme, *Colonial Encounters*; Skura, "Discourse and the Individual"; Brown, "This Thing of Darkness"; and Fuchs, "Conquering Islands".

as a metaphorical insult against free servants who show signs of insubordination or rebellion, Caliban is depicted as a "natural" slave – someone whose insurrection wastes itself as a pathetic servility to the commonest of real-world subordinates, fools and drunkards. The fool and drunkard in question embody in farcical caricature the dislocation of traditional ideological bonds of authority in the disruptive spaces of the New World, where subordinates argued that shipwrecks abrogated the traditional authority of master over subject.[23] Nor is this crisis of authority confined to lower servants such as Stephano and Trinculo. It takes a more dangerous form in the usurping actions and fantasies of the aristocratic brothers, whose resentment at being someone else's "men" is even more intense than the commoners' laughable utopian fantasies which retain the repressive forms of bonded servility of the old.[24]

Montaigne uses the different forms of social organisation revealed by the New World to put critical pressure on the assumptions of the superiority of Old-World practice. It is well known that the utopia that the old courtier Gonzalo entertains on the island reflects the French essayist's account in "Of Cannibals" almost exactly:

> GONZALO (*to* ALONSO) Had I plantation of this isle, my lord –
> ANTONIO (*to* SEBASTIAN) He'd sow 't with nettle-seed.
> SEBASTIAN   Or docks, or mallows.
> GONZALO And were the king on 't, what would I do?
> SEBASTIAN (*to* ANTONIO) Scape being drunk, for want of wine.
> GONZALO I' th' commonwealth I would by contraries
>   Execute all things. For no kind of traffic
>   Would I admit, no name of magistrate;
>   Letters should not be known; riches, poverty,
>   And use of service, none; contract, succession,
>   Bourn, bound of land, tilth, vineyard, none;
>   No use of metal, corn, or wine, or oil;
>   No occupation, all men idle, all;
>   And women too – but innocent and pure;
>   No sovereignty –
> SEBASTIAN (*to* ANTONIO) Yet he would be king on 't.
> ANTONIO The latter end of his commonwealth forgets the beginning.
> GONZALO (*to* ALONSO) All things in common nature should produce
>   Without sweat or endeavour. Treason, felony,
>   Sword, pike, knife, gun, or need of any engine,

---

[23] See Strachey, "A True Repertory". For a classic account of the significance of the report for *The Tempest*, see Greenblatt, *Shakespearean Negotiations*, chapter 5.

[24] See the terms of Antonio's enticement of Sebastian to murder his brother: "My brother's servants / Were then my fellows; now they are my men" (2.1.278–9).

> Would I not have; but nature should bring forth
> Of it own kind all foison, all abundance,
> To feed my innocent people.
> SEBASTIAN (*to* ANTONIO) No marrying 'mong his subjects?
> ANTONIO None, man, all idle: whores and knaves.
> GONZALO (*to* ALONSO) I would with such perfection govern, sir,
> T' excel the Golden Age.   (2.1.149–74)

A full quotation shows the dialogical situation of the speech, a complication not present in Montaigne's essay.[25] The basic characteristic of Gonzalo's utopian plantation is the absence of two conditions that were fundamental to early modern European *polis*: labour and the authority to control it in the form of the law of master-service relations. "Use of service, none . . . ." Significantly, the eradication of service also implies the dissolution of conventional sexual bonds and hierachies – there will be no marriage (including the obedience by wife of husband that it implies), but all his subjects would nevertheless remain "innocent and pure".

This vision is entertained by the play's *exemplary* servant: the only person who embodies the ideal qualities of the servant as courtier. "The good old lord Gonzalo", as Prospero calls him (5.1.15), is loyal, courageous, and dedicated, having intervened to save his old master from certain death. At the same time, he is pragmatic enough to adapt to the demands of the new regime, tempted by none of the dangerous changes of allegiance to the given order that, for example, marks Camillo in *The Winter's Tale*. Through Gonzalo's utopian vision Shakespeare unusually imagines a world without service, which includes one in which wife is not subordinated to her husband under the reigning concept of service. The fact that it is a fantasy of the play's pre-eminent servant gives it undoubted weight. On the other hand, its unrealistic projections and logical contradictions are exposed by the cynically compelling interjections of Antonio and Sebastian. They represent a peculiarly interested or biased perspective on service: expecting it of subordinates but refusing it for themselves, they exemplify the abuse of master-service relations that gives rise to the dream of a servantless world in the first place. The parody of master-servant relations in the subplot of *The Tempest* supports the two lords' cynicism, however, by showing that freedom from law, labour, and authority produces nothing but felony, idleness, treachery, and dissension rather than innocence and abundance. Shakespeare has read his Montaigne, and he is having none of it. Or rather, he is canny enough to want to use the dreams of the New World to convey

[25] Montaigne, "Of Cannibals", in *Essays*.

the attractiveness of the fantasy, while showing that in reality it is irredeemably flawed. The doubleness of such a perspective is conveyed by the dialogical interference of views and voices, through which the right view is crossed with the wrong voice and vice versa. We tend to open ourselves to the fantasy precisely because Gonzalo is its spokesman, but we recognise in Sebastian and Antonio a hard-headed realism that questions the dream while not endorsing the system it is supposed to displace.

Loving service

If the island prompts the dream of a world in which service has no place, what stands in the place of that dream, in its real personal and political relationships? Shakespeare's exposure to the realities of the New-World ventures, especially in the form of the erosion, under conditions of material hardship and social disruption, of traditional, voluntary acceptance of master-servant hierarchies, leads him unusually to represent such relationships almost wholly as the products or effects of coercion. Gone are the ethical dimensions of a reciprocal, if unequal bond, such as Enobarbus discovers and which leads Eros to take his own life instead of his master's in *Antony and Cleopatra*, or which induce selfless devotion in Flavius (*Timon of Athens*) and Adam (*As You Like It*). They are replaced by a relentlessly material and conditional relationship of "profit" and bondage. The double structure of the play – its self-consciousness self-reflexivity as theatre or show – exposes and puts on display the processes by which its representational stereotypes are made to stick or minds bent to an imposed reality.[26] The depiction of Prospero's narrative silence – apparent from his lack of any narrative riposte in historical terms to the substance of Caliban's claim to have been dispossessed of his kingdom – calls into question the ideological grounds used to justify the latter's bondage.

Yet this is not quite the whole story. If love is violently disjoined from service in the representative, "tottering" state on the island, love and service are as powerfully *conjoined* in the forging of a new dynastic family, in the erotic relationship between Ferdinand and Miranda. Here love is depicted not merely as willing service but as voluntary, mutual enslavement to each other.[27] This returns us to the fundamental process at the

---

[26] To use such terms is in one sense problematic, for it suggests that *The Tempest* is fully a colonial play, whereas its references to the new colonies is at best glancing or analogous. See especially Skura, "Discourse and the Individual".

[27] Evett devotes a chapter to the discussion of Miranda and Ferdinand's love as an exemplum of the volitional primacy that is at the centre of his treatment of service (chapter 9). I am much indebted to his argument.

heart of *The Tempest* (indeed, of all Shakespearean comedy and romance) and the single factor that, more than anything else, unites love's vision with service as an ideological condition: the imaginative (and possibly imaginary) transformation of bondage into bonds, of constraint into freedom by thinking of the condition differently. We have seen that the collect in the Book of Common Prayer transformed by Cranmer into the shibboleth of service posits a reciprocal relationship between God and those who serve him as part of the idea that freedom (*real* freedom) is to be found only in the total commitment to His service. The service of God necessarily involves a commitment to serve one's neighbour, exemplified by Christ's washing his disciples' feet. The problem arises when that duty is inflected by already established, self-interested hierarchical relationships in the secular world.

What does *The Tempest* offer? By reducing servile relationships to two types and investigating the historical origins of those relationships via a contest of memory and narrative, it exposes the enabling conditions of relationships that would otherwise be taken for granted. Yet the central, erotic relationship towards which both the play as a whole and Prospero's own staged scenarios move offer a curious perspective on this problem. As Evett argues, the love between Ferdinand and Miranda is convincingly cast as a perfect example and vindication of the idea that willing service is the experience of perfect freedom. Ferdinand, who thinks himself no less than the king of Milan, declares that he is completely happy to be reduced not just to Prospero's servant but also to the condition of abject slavery (the condition, in fact, of Caliban), provided that he can remain in Miranda's presence:

> My spirits, as in a dream, are all bound up.
> My father's loss, the weakness which I feel,
> The wreck of all my friends, nor this man's threats
> To whom I am subdued, are but light to me,
> Might I but through my prison once a day
> Behold this maid. All corners else o' th' earth
> Let liberty make use of; space enough
> Have I in such a prison.   (1.2.489–96)

The parallel between Ferdinand and Caliban should be clear in production, where each of them enters under a burden of logs. Miranda reciprocates Ferdinand's feelings totally. She offers to share his burden, and they pledge their freely given love to each other precisely in terms of a willing service which, given the circumstances, renders materially concrete the literary vows of servile devotion in a whole tradition of love literature:

> FERDINAND I am in my condition
>   A prince, Miranda, I do think a king –
>   I would not so – and would no more endure
>   This wooden slavery than to suffer
>   The flesh-fly blow my mouth. Hear my soul speak.
>   The very instant that I saw you did
>   My heart fly to your service; there resides
>   To make me slave to it. And for your sake
>   Am I this patient log-man.
> MIRANDA   Do you love me?
> FERDINAND O heaven, O earth, bear witness to this sound,
>   And crown what I profess with kind event
>   If I speak true! If hollowly, invert
>   What best is boded me to mischief! I,
>   Beyond all limit of what else i' th' world,
>   Do love, prize, honour you.
>   [. . .]
> MIRANDA I am your wife, if you will marry me.
>   If not, I'll die your maid. To be your fellow
>   You may deny me, but I'll be your servant
>   Whether you will or no.
> FERDINAND (kneeling)   My mistress, dearest;
>   And I thus humble ever.
> MIRANDA My husband then?
> FERDINAND Ay, with a heart as willing
>   As bondage e'er of freedom. Here's my hand.
>   (3.1.59–73, 83–9)

Paradoxes are multiplied in this mutual gift. From a condition of literal enslavement and spiritual thraldom to the god of love, Ferdinand gives his hand to Miranda in a voluntary act both unconditional and unconditioned. Ferdinand's love for Miranda turns his imprisonment and slavery into a condition that he is able not merely to endure but also joyfully to embrace. Furthermore, the couple's love for each other enables them to dedicate themselves in perfectly reciprocal service to each other. So concerned is Shakespeare to underscore the intersubjective phenomenology of this transformation of service into freedom – or perhaps, more accurately, the discovery of freedom *through* service – that he makes Ferdinand declare his willingness to marry Miranda through the paradoxical truism of bondage's desire for freedom. Bound by both his love for Miranda and the chains of her father, Ferdinand can declare his acceptance of his condition by resorting to a naturalised urge for freedom that contradicts the received idea that servants should be satisfied with their condition. With this vow in the name of freedom, Ferdinand binds himself forever, transforming constraining bondage into sustaining bond.[28]

This paradox of Ferdinand's acceptance of the bonds of love and the bondage of slavery as mutually entailed conditions of freedom via an appeal to the natural desire of bondage for freedom would be relatively straightforward if the play did not infuse it with its own peculiar brand of dramatic irony – if we did not know and could not see, then and there, that Miranda and Ferdinand's declarations of devotion to each other are presided over by a stage-managing father who has set the scene so that the free choices of the lovers proceed according to a grander – not to say darker – purpose. What difference does this knowledge make?

It forms part of this curious play's relentless baring of the institutions of social order and their interpellation of lived experience. We should not make the mistake of discounting the freely given love of Miranda and Ferdinand by suggesting that it is manipulated in some straightforward way by the mage – by subsuming it to the manipulations of power or the false consciousness of ideology. Prospero has no power to make Ferdinand love Miranda or to make her reciprocate that gift. The lack of this particular power may account for not a little of his irascible nervousness. He does have the power to prevent the match which they innocently believe is in *their* power to settle, but as master-figures as varied as Theseus in *A Midsummer Night's Dream* and the King in *All's Well That Ends Well* discover, forcing them love each other is beyond even his capacity.[29]

What is striking about Prospero's purpose is the fact that he should want the dynastic marriage to be concluded in mutual love rather than be enforced by the necessities of power. In contrast with what appears to be Claribel's coerced political union in Tunis, Prospero wants the marriage of Milan and Naples to be informed by love experienced as reciprocal service. Does the fact that things go according to his plan trammel the freedom in service that their love entails? I do not know how to answer this question in any simple way. I do know that it complicates any straightforward notion of the relationship between freedom and service, love and grace. Is it better that the dynastic marriage that finally secures Prospero's darker political purposes is, from the point of view of the partners, their chosen destiny

---

[28] See Todorov, *Perfect Garden*, 136: "[T]he loving subject is not one governed by his will. One cannot love because one has decided to love. On the contrary, love is the clearest example of an action that does not originate in an act of will."

[29] See my argument to this effect in "Love and Service in *Shrew* and *All's Well*".

rather than subject to the enforcements of the service and slavery of Ariel and Caliban or the constraints suffered by poor Claribel?[30] I suspect that it is. In his comedies, Shakespeare seeks to harmonise personal agency, in its phenomenological transformation of structural constraint into freedom, with the broader political realities of that constraint. *The Tempest* comprehends the violence of enforced marriage by focussing on *indirection*. Prospero's power as art rather than force enables the reconciliation of necessity and choice, service and love, in the interests of a larger political purpose. Some might find that even more disturbing than the use of naked coercion.

ACKNOWLEDGEMENT

Shakespeare's sense of the possibilities of the theatre ensures that we remain aware of the vertiginous paradox of the central, Protestant theology of service in the early modern period, that once one has internalised the condition of service as a willing condition, it becomes perfect freedom. This is what Gouge is talking about when he draws a distinction between "a "*necessary* subiection: which is the subiection of order" and "*voluntary* subiection: which is the subiection of duty" (26). Wives and servants are necessarily subjected to the God-given order of obeying and serving husbands and masters, however they may actually behave in practice. It is the work of nurture, of ideological indoctrination or interpellation, to make that subjection one of *choice* – to induce people to accept in mind and body the overarching reality of necessary subjection. One could also say that the process constitutes the basic structure of Shakespearean comedy.[31] In the context of the kind of loving reciprocity in which Ferdinand and Miranda dedicate themselves in service to one another, the paradox of freedom in service is at least apparently resolved (and can there be any resolution to these issues except in appearance?) As we see the adored mistress casting aside the one-sided devotion of the desiring lover by taking up his burden – as we see her dragging Ferdinand's logs across the stage and speaking the words of his love-song – it seems that the ideal of loving friendship that Montaigne, following a long tradition, reserved for men is enacted magically before us by a woman.[32] Nor should we underestimate the extraordinary freshness of Miranda's action, which replicates the slavish gestures of Caliban and

---

[30] Compare Marvell's notion of destiny being a choice in the closing lines of "Upon Appleton House".
[31] See Krieger, *Shakespearean Comedy*, which offers a Marxist reading of this comic structure.
[32] Montaigne, "Of Friendship", in *Essays*.

Ferdinand as an act of free generosity.[33] Miranda's act of willing servility completes Katherine's voluntary placing of her hand beneath her husband's foot at the end of *The Taming of the Shrew*. For although it rejects courtly devotion in service of the beloved that at least at one level marks Bianca's relationship to her suitors in the early comedy, it also transforms what seems to be Katherine's aligning of "voluntary" and "necessary" subjection into an act of reciprocity that embodies the potential egalitarianism in the Protestant ideal of companionate marriage.

If we turn from the mutual enactment of erotic service as a form of grace to the bondage of Caliban and Ariel, matters become more intricate. Miranda and Ferdinand would not dream of wanting to free themselves from their service to each other: Gonzalo's fantasy would make no sense to them, unless we take that utopian contradiction, in which the absence of marriage nevertheless encompasses sexual relationships of "innocence" and "purity", as a transformation enacted by loving service. Servant-spirit and native-slave, on the other hand, desire manumission above all else. Caliban's attempts to find such freedom in the company of the drunkard and fool from the Old World appear to confirm him as a natural slave, incapable of either nurture or freedom. He chillingly anticipates the stereotype through which service would be turned into slavery in the new colonies. Yet in a curious echo of the ending of *The Comedy of Errors* in which master and man reaffirm their bonds, the three sorry conspirators are finally redistributed to their proper masters. "Two of these fellows you / Must know and own", Prospero declares in a gesture that re-establishes the solidarity of masters vis-à-vis servants, "This thing of darkness I / Acknowledge mine" (5.1.277–9). What a world of difference there is in the mode of Prospero's acknowledgement of his servant from Antipholus of Syracuse's declaration: "I am your master, Dromio" (*The Comedy of Errors*, 5.1.414)! It is a commonplace that the master's statement does not merely lay a claim of ownership and power; it *owns up* to an affinity, a bond, that ties the master to the supposed "thing of darkness" from which he has wished to distance himself and his daughter. This darkness is akin to the *Heimlichkeit* that lies in the familiar in *The Comedy of Errors*.[34]

Early in the play, Prospero gives his daughter an *instrumental* reason for why Caliban is indispensable: "We cannot miss him. He does make our fire, / Fetch in our wood, and serves in offices / That profit us" (1.2.313–15). On multiple levels, however, the play shows that his relation to his slave

---

[33] But compare Prospero's comment: "Poor worm, thou art infected. / This visitation shows it" (3.1.32).

[34] The twin brothers in *The Comedy of Errors* are embodiments of such *Heimlichkeit*: they are both self and other, familiar and strange.

is not merely instrumental. It also hints at why he cannot admit those reasons to his daughter or himself. Like so many of the servants in the plays and sonnets, Caliban is part of his master's being.[35] That Prospero remains constrained to regard that aspect as a representation of his own *darkness* is a complex twist to the scene of Antipholus, bound to his slave in a gloomy prison, chewing through their mutual bonds to set them both free. Incapable or unwilling to declare that he is, unbound, his master's "man", Caliban instead mutters about seeking for grace. He does not know that Prospero, having broken his staff and drowned his books, is no longer capable of subjecting him to the tortures of enforced subjugation, and we do not see or know what grace might mean for Caliban, if it is extended at all, by his newly disinvested master. We do not even know whether Caliban is taken back to Italy or whether, no longer "profitable", he is merely abandoned to his island – its lonely and pointless master.

Matters are different between master and the bond-servant Ariel. If we are liable to be taken aback by the intensity of Prospero's dismissal of Ariel's early claim to freedom, there is a telling moment at the end of the play when Prospero is invited to recognise his own humanity (and that of his enemies) in the glass of his nonhuman servant.

The Tempest is curiously a play without friendships. Such friends as it does contain are mere parodies of the noble relationship celebrated by Aristotle, Cicero, and Montaigne. Its friends are devoid of virtue in the classical sense, being either evil (Antonio and Sebastian) or fools and drunkards (Stephano and Trinculo). Neither pair would be worthy foundations of a classically conceived civil society. Nor is there any friendship developed, as there is in *Twelfth Night*, *Antony and Cleopatra*, and *The Winter's Tale*, between master and servant. There is, however, a moment (and it is no more than a moment) when the question of love between servant and master *is* raised. In the midst of an acknowledgement of obeisance to Prospero's command, Ariel asks, suddenly and unexpectedly: "Do you love me, master?" (4.1.48). There are two remarkable things about this question. First, the phrase "Do you love me?" occurs only *twice* in all of Shakespeare. *Both* are in *The Tempest*.[36] This is an amazing fact, considering the almost obsessive concern with love (and that question especially) throughout the canon and

---

[35] Cf.: "For my seruant is to me, *alter ego*, another my selfe" (Fosset, *Seruants Dutie*, 36) and "if thou haue a trustie seruant, let him be vnto thee as thine owne Soule" (Guazzo, *Conuersation*, 174).

[36] See the online Shakespeare Concordance at: http://www.it.usyd.edu.au/~matty/Shakespeare/test.html. It's familiar form – "Dost thou love me?" – occurs only once: it is addressed by Juliet to Romeo in *Romeo and Juliet*, 2.1.132.

the apparent indifference of *The Tempest* to the question. It is first posed by Miranda in the decisive instant before she and Ferdinand pledge loving service to one another. The question is decisive because, as in *Romeo and Juliet*, it overrules everything else: once Ferdinand has said "yes", the world itself is reduced to an epiphenomenon of their service of and for each other.

Prospero stages his elaborate masque against Eros for the loving couple to bring the demands of the world back to their consciousness. It is precisely at the point before the masque, when Ariel is acquiescing in the command to bestow the "vanity of [Prospero's] art . . . upon the eyes of this young couple" (40–1), that the servant makes Miranda's question his own by testing his irascible master. One could play the scene in two ways. Prospero could answer quickly and somewhat impatiently, eager to hurry on to more important business. His response is *textually* perfunctory:

> PROSPERO Dearly, my delicate Ariel. Do not approach
> Till thou dost hear me call.   (4.1.49–50)

On the other hand, the question could come as a shock, as an unexpected intrusion of the demands of affective reciprocity into the everyday business of command and obedience. Prospero could register surprise – he could be momentarily disconcerted by the challenge, forced to consider the place of love between master and servant at the very moment when he is using the servant to create a particular vision of *eros* dominated by politics or instrumentality. His answer, when it comes, might therefore be more considered, with due weight given to "dearly" and the possessive "my". In other words, whereas many have fixed the crisis in this scene at the point at which Prospero's masque falters when he remembers Caliban's plot, Ariel's question might be read as a more subtle moment of crisis for the magisterial magician. To acknowledge love for the servant would signal the recognition that he is bound up in the other. It would project a pang of real loss for the master in the anticipated manumission. It would also turn the servant from profitable instrument into a fully other self, thereby registering an implicit acknowledgement of his servant as both possible subject and object of love.

All of these are aspects of the recognition or acknowledgement of humanity, both of the self and the other, to which Stanley Cavell has called our attention. This brief crisis of affect between Prospero and Ariel prepares the ground for another crisis, when the servant's pity for Prospero's enemies provokes the recognition in his master of *their* humanity. His acknowledgement of that commonality is signalled especially strongly by the fact that Ariel, although humane, is himself not of human kind:

> Your charm so strongly works 'em
> That if you now beheld them your affections
> Would become tender.
> PROSPERO   Dost thou think so, spirit?
> ARIEL Mine would, sir, were I human.
> PROSPERO   And mine shall.
> Hast thou, which art but air, a touch, a feeling
> Of their afflictions, and shall not myself,
> One of their kind, that relish all as sharply
> Passion as they, be kindlier moved than thou art?   (5.1.17–24)

"Kindlier moved": this encapsulates the crisis of service as it is conceptualised by Renaissance moralists. Are masters and servants of the same *kind*? Is the affect that binds or moves each in the ambit of the other a mere exercise of power, or is it a sign of a shared condition before God and embodied by and in God? And what happens when the settled notions of service move beyond the known world, to encompass the monstrous, the strange, or the other, especially when such monstrosity shows itself in the possible absence of master-servant relations or in wholly different possibilities of erotic love?

Naked service

Michael Neill observes that *The Tempest* stages the decisive role of clothing as the sign of social difference, especially as it reflects the hierarchical divide between master and servant.[37] *The Winter's Tale* offers a similar perspective by showing the ease with which such signs may be appropriated and circulated, despite all efforts to curtail their grafting effects. Livery, which initially referred to the provisions and lodging by which masters sustained their servants, came to refer metonymically to the sumptuary badge of status and ownership: the "liveried man was not merely clothed in his master's identity but absorbed into his social body, to be fed as his own body was fed" (Neill, *History*, 23). Neill argues that Caliban's nakedness, and his lack of interest in the glittering array that traps his fellow conspirators, confirm his "otherness". In the world that lies beyond Caliban, "costume is what effectively determines the legibility, the visibility, in effect the *reality* of bodies" (411). Caliban's lack of interest in sumptuary show ("trash", he calls it (4.1.224)) could be seen as a confirmation of the reality of bodies rather than

---

[37] Neill, *History*, chapter 15.

the "frippery" of costume, which always requires a certain kind of magic to sustain its show. To put it slightly differently, the play's incessant alternation of masqueing and unmasking draws attention to the ways in which the player's livery (in the sense of sustenance) derives not only from his mercurial ability to *shift* his clothing but also from the capacity of the stage to expose the semiotic mechanism that invests mere pieces of cloth with magical significance. Caliban may be awestruck by the figure of Prospero as he finally appears in his full regalia as the Duke of Milan ("How fine my master is!" (5.1.265)), but his earlier rejection of the clothes on Prospero's "line" should have distanced the *audience* from an unquestioning acceptance of the intrinsic value of apparel. The player has it both ways. Able to break out of the confining livery of the servant, Prospero's shape-shifting trades on the continuing signification of costume as political *reality*.

What, then, does the figure of Prospero signify when he finally appears in the liminal space between player and audience in the epilogue? Whose servant is he?

> PROSPERO Now my charms are all o'erthrown,
> And what strength I have's mine own,
> Which is most faint. Now 'tis true
> I must be here confined by you
> Or sent to Naples. Let me not,
> Since I have my dukedom got,
> And pardoned the deceiver, dwell
> In this bare island by your spell;
> But release me from my bands
> With the help of your good hands.
> Gentle breath of yours my sails
> Must fill, or else my project fails,
> Which was to please.   (Epilogue, 1–12)

Despite the theological import of the player-servant's final lines, which remind the audience of their godlike power and their own need of the grace of God, the service that the player invokes seems to be entirely conditional. It depends upon satisfaction – on a reciprocity that can be invoked only on condition that the audience has received its money's worth. Unlike Antonio's bond for Bassanio or Kent's dedication to his king, such service is instrumental in the way that Prospero would like to think that Caliban is instrumental and, as he possibly comes to see, Ariel is not. The language of grace appears to be a subterfuge here: an unusual cover-up in this most uncovering of plays of the hard-headed realities of the new, commercial theatre. Servants of the king Shakespeare and his company may have been, and therefore technically part of his family. Yet face to face with the paying audience, stripped of their costume, their staffs broken, the service that they render looks forward more to the bank teller or the fast-food server than back towards Enobarbus or Adam, Ferdinand or Kent.

And yet. The Catholic language of pardon and indulgence in Prospero's plea continues to invoke, across a great distance of memory and ritual, a common condition – a communality of reciprocal obligation that breaks free from the isolation of the Protestant subject in its unique relation to a master and God. Prospero's plea ends with a request for the saving breath of communal prayer:

> Now I want
> Spirits to enforce, art to enchant;
> And my ending is despair
> Unless I be relieved by prayer,
> Which pierces so, that it assaults
> Mercy itself, and frees all faults.
> As you from crimes would pardoned be,
> Let your indulgence set me free.
>
> 						(13–20)

The "indulgence" that the player-duke seeks here from all the members of his audience affirms a common condition of mutual service and even affection: between player and play-goer, whose ends are finally conditioned by the reciprocal rituals of performance.[38]

---

[38] For a recent discussion of the theological residue of Catholicism in Shakespeare, see Hunt, *Shakespeare's Religious Allusiveness.*

CHAPTER 4

"More than a steward"
The Sonnets, *Twelfth Night*, and *Timon of Athens*

In *Twelfth Night*, the spaces of domestic service seen in *The Taming of the Shrew*, and in a displaced and etiolated way in *The Tempest*, are expanded by the intensely personal affects of *philia* and *eros*. I ask in this chapter what it is about intimate forms of service within the household that allowed it to be transformed into the classically informed relation of friendship, and what kind of conceptual and affective space might Shakespeare forge for the conjunction of erotic devotion and loving friendship – not merely between men but also between men and women. In the latter case, the *staged* embodiment of Viola as both desiring woman and gentleman servant transforms the formal, imaginative constraints of Montaigne's essays.

THE SONNETS

The sonnets present a paradox in their quest for the reciprocities of love within the conditions of social inequality that are intrinsic to relations of service. The servant-poet who begins the sonnets as a project of pure service – as a commission to persuade a recalcitrant aristocratic youth to bend to the necessities of his social and familial position – finds himself caught in the toils of service of a different kind and expectation. There is a decisive moment in sonnet 10 when the argument is informed by a new, personal urgency in the plea: "Make thee an other selfe *for loue of me*" (emphasis added). It turns the contemplation of erotic service from the abstract instrumentality of procreation to sustain the continuity of an aristocratic household into a personal demand for reciprocal love or friendship (or both) that seeks to transcend differences of rank and status. The word "friend" thus tolls with an insistent ambiguity throughout these poems, simultaneously direct, suggestive, and opaque as it shadows the early modern connotations of "companion", "lover", and "servant".

I have argued elsewhere that the key sonnet in the sequence to the fair friend is sonnet 23, with its actorly plea for mutuality outside the public glare of the stage:[1]

> AS an vnperfect actor on the stage,
> Who with his feare is put besides his part,
> Or some fierce thing repleat with too much rage,
> Whose strengths abondance weakens his owne heart;
> So I for feare of trust, forget to say,
> The perfect ceremony of loues right . . .

The acute self-consciousness of being no more than a "common player" seems to infuse all the sonnets directed to the well-bred young man. This is not the anxiety or shame of being a servant, for service was in itself no stigma and could afford its carriers a secure sense of place and dignity. What is conveyed in Shakespeare's sonnets is the disgrace that continued to attend the player no matter how much money he made or how far he rose in social status and the consequent inappropriate nature of his love in the form of *eros* or *philia* (rather than *nomos*) for his master.

Sonnet 23 cannily excuses its tongue-tied speaker by invoking the stage fright suffered by the actor as no more than an analogy, but the sense of the vulnerability of loving service declared and staged in the public gaze is carried as a subliminal anxiety throughout the subsequence. Love is not merely a set of mutual, private feelings: it demands a "perfect ceremony" as its "right/rite", which may be marred by an excess of feeling. Its "abundance" may weaken its very seat. Meredith Skura quotes Otto Fenichel's remark that "stage fright is the specific fright of the exhibitionist: shame. Unconsciously, it is the shame of an inferiority" (Skura, *Actor*, 241 n75). Fenichel and Skura both offer psychoanalytical causes for this sense of shame, but in the case of the speaker in the sonnets it has a perfectly adequate social explanation. His plea for "trust" is a request to withdraw, not to a space of complete privacy, but at least to one appropriate to the poet rather than the player: "O let my books be then the eloquence, / And domb presagers of my speaking brest, / Who pleade for loue, and look for recompence, / More then that tonge that more hath more exprest".

The constitutive tensions of the sonnets to the young man arise from the poet's consciousness of his social inferiority, on the one hand, and his desire for an intimate, affective relationship, on the other. The initiating condition of service is transformed into a demand for free mutuality that seeks to transcend the social hierarchy that made them possible in the first

[1] Schalkwyk, *Speech*,

place, before the relationship is finally abandoned in a chilling admonition that as the servant of Nature the indifferent master will in due course have to submit to her reckoning.

Five of Shakespeare's sonnets are especially germane to this narrative. Three of them – 26, 57, and 58 – mobilise strategies of politeness and declarations of erotic devotion that tease out the intricate relationships and differences between abjection and the demand for reciprocal affection and respect. Sonnet 26 is the least complex:

> Lord of my loue, to whome in vassalage
> Thy merrit hath my dutie strongly knit;
> To thee I send this written ambassage
> To witnesse duty, not to shew my wit.

There is little to suggest that the servant-poet seeks a greater intimacy than the hyperbolic declaration of duty and service to a patron. The invocation of vassalage recalls the older, feudal relations of mutual dependence, infused with a newer senses of general subordination (*OED*, 1500), that exceed the specificity of feudal tenancy (*OED*, 1563). It also conveys later notions of baseness and slavery (*OED*, 1589) from which older expectations of reciprocity have all but disappeared.[2] The poem's invocation of the transformative power of fortune (cf. Malvolio's "'Tis but fortune, all is fortune" (*Twelfth Night*, 2.5.22)), alludes to later opportunities for social mobility. It masks and declares its modern fantasies and demands through a residual language of duty and service that cannot be dismissed as merely metaphorical or archaic.[3]

The sonnet's appeal to his lord's "soules thought (all naked)" to "put apparell on my tattered louing" (8 and 11) alludes to the materiality of sumptuary difference and the gift of livery at the same time as it seeks to transcend social difference through the inclusiveness of naked, spiritual reciprocity. Although the poet declares that he "dare not boast" of his love before being gracefully "proved" by his master, the poem is itself a declaration of affective intimacy that crosses the line between public boastfulness and private restraint.[4] I draw further parallels between the sonnets' servant-poet and *Twelfth Night*'s steward, Malvolio, at the end of this section. For the moment let me merely register the obsequious ambition of both characters,

---

[2] See Neill, "Servile Ministers".

[3] See Elton, *England*, 1–17, for an account of the shift in reciprocal relations of service from feudalism proper to "bastard feudalism" (7) as early as the fourteenth century.

[4] Lynne Magnusson demonstrates how such strategies of politeness express both passive subjection and active resistance through the rhetoric of "negative politeness, which works in such a way as to simultaneously do and undo the speech actions it undertakes" (*Dialogue*, 50).

their desire for "some good conceit" from master or mistress to endorse their material and erotic fantasies, and their initial awareness that the display of their veiled desires would provoke public disgrace. Sonnets 124 and 125, however, eschew the power and status that are the actual objects of Malvolio's erotic ambition. They call instead for a free and loving reciprocity that eschews the politics of "policy" and "difference".

Sonnet 57 pushes the concept of vassalage used in 26 even farther away from feudal ideals of reciprocity towards a commonplace, early modern conception of the household servant as abject menial:

> Being your slaue, what should I doe but tend,
> Vpon the houres, and times of your desire?
> I haue no precious time at al to spend;
> Nor seruices to doe til you require.
> Nor dare I chide the world without end houre,
> Whilst I (my soueraine) watch the clock for you,
> Nor thinke the bitternesse of absence sowre,
> VVhen you haue bid your seruant once adieue.
> Nor dare I question with my iealious thought,
> VVhere you may be, or your affaires suppose,
> But like a sad slaue stay and thinke of nought
> Saue where you are, how happy you make those.
>   So true a foole is loue, that in your Will,
>   (Though you doe any thing) he thinkes no ill.

Subservient, silent, uncomplaining, and undemanding, the emblematic servant is figured with large ass's ears and a locked, pig's snout to convey his abject readiness to obey and his dedication to silence: "Nor dare I chide . . . nor think . . . Nor dare I question . . . where you may be . . . or your affaires suppose",[5] the servant-poet declares, in apparent acceptance of his subordination to his master's will. Yet the very acknowledgement of the routines of service signals an affective relation closer to the stereotype of friendship than abject slavery. One of the defining characteristics of friends is that they "thinke the bitterness of absence sowre". Nevertheless, the "dutie" invoked in sonnet 26 is represented in 57 as a singularly *un*reciprocated form of "service" – not because paternalistic obligations of material provision are lacking but because the socially unacceptable affects of *eros* and *philia* speak through the poem's attestation of *nomos* or loving obedience.

---

[5] See Burnett, "Trusty Servant".

This tension between erotic love or friendship and menial service is even
more apparent in the next sonnet:

> That God forbid, that made me first your slaue,
> I should in thought controule your times of pleasure,
> Or at your hand th'account of houres to craue,
> Being your vassail bound to staie your leisure.
> Oh let me suffer (being at your beck)
> Th' imprison'd absence of your libertie,
> And patience tame, to sufferance bide each check,
> Without accusing you of iniury.
> Be where you list, your charter is so strong,
> That you your selfe may priuiledge your time
> To what you will, to you it doth belong,
> Your selfe to pardon of selfe-doing crime.
> > I am to waite, though waiting so be hell,
> > Not blame your pleasure be it ill or well.

The common editorial practice of lowering the Quarto's upper-case "God"
negates the force of the opening speech act by turning it from a resentful
acknowledgement of a divinely sanctioned social obligation into a merely
overblown cliché about Cupid's thrall.[6] We may not want to take "that
made me first your slaue" entirely literally, but we do need to acknowledge
the religious and political overtones of broader, political subordination.
The hierarchical obligations between bound "vassal" and "leisured" lord
suggested in sonnets 57 and 58 invoke commonplace strictures placed upon
lower servants in Elizabethan England. We obscure that condition if, reducing God to Cupid, we see the poem as a mere exercise in the histrionics
of infatuation. Mere infatuation cannot account for the complex, contradictory registers of weakness, resentment, and felt subordination that
are invoked through the discourse of service. It would, however, also be
wrong to allow a political reading of the sonnet's speech acts to obliterate
its expression of erotic devotion. The poem clearly asks to be read as one
party's retort in a lover's tiff – "God forbid that *I* should take you to task
for indulging in your pleasure!"[7] Furthermore, its attempt to achieve an
ethical platform for reproach assumes a degree of intimacy and daring not
commensurate with slavery, although it may accord with certain kinds of

---

[6] The opening line echoes Galatians 6:14: "But God forbid that I shulde rejoice, but in the crosse of
our Lord" (Booth, *Shakespeare's Sonnets*, 233).
[7] See Vendler, *Sonnets*, 277.

service. Sonnets 57 and 58 thus add an erotic dimension to the invocation of love, duty, and service absent (save in retrospect) from sonnet 26.[8]

Taken together, these three sonnets indicate that love in Shakespeare's sonnets cannot be reduced to personal intensity, a variation on a received trope, or the displaced locus of political ambition.[9] It is an amalgam of all three. The sonnets declare ardent erotic attachment even as they acknowledge the burden of a political condition.

Shakespeare's incisiveness comes from his unerring interest in the nuances and shifts of the *conceptual* relations between love and service. These sonnets represent the *logical* compatibility or incompatibility of a particular notion of love and the social obligations of service in personal circumstances of patronage and the forms of rivalry that attend it. The intertwining of love and service in Shakespeare's work situates their conceptual relationship more firmly in lived historical reality than in the attenuated, literary discourse of courtly devotion. It also disaggregates them, however, insofar as love (rather than mere desire) is shown to be incommensurable with a kind of subjection in which service slides through perceived vassalage towards slavery. The subservience affirmed and simultaneously contested in these sonnets thus encompasses more than the social powerlessness demanded of real servants by the moralists. By giving the political expectations of service an erotic charge, Shakespeare empties out the subjectivity of the subordinate, transforming him into the hollow instrument of the master's desire: "But like a sad slaue stay and thinke of nought / Saue where you are, how happy you make those" (57, 11–12). At the same time, however, the sonnets present a speaking voice that contests the very negation of subjectivity that they explicitly proclaim. By representing the speaker in the third person, the couplet of sonnet 57 allows him to split his subordinated and speaking selves into two parts: a silent object-for-another on the one hand, and an active, protesting subject on the other. This tension is encapsulated by the shift in the speaking voice from the expected "you"

---

[8] Shakespeare is tracing a path between a concept of erotic love that took its informing metaphors from the feudal ideals of social and political service in the twelfth century in France – the *'fin' Amours* of the troubadours – and a different medieval conception of love as an ennobling exercise in reciprocity (see Singer, *Love 2*, 1–128). What is especially distinctive about Shakespeare's sonnets is the relative absence of the troubadour notion of service in the poems to and about the woman and the complex struggle between the ideals of service and reciprocity in the poems concerning the young man. In the latter, the erotic metaphors of service and idealisation that are derived from the medieval French literary tradition are embodied and lived through in the actual condition of service of the player-poet vis-à-vis his well-born patron.

[9] See Marotti, "'Love is not love'".

and "I" to the distanced third-person "he": "So true a foole is loue, that in your Will, / (Though you doe any thing) *he* thinkes no ill." The conceptual division between affection and desire is widened by the ambiguity of "in your Will", which nominates the poet as both the embodiment of willing love (the fool love inhabiting the poet, Will) and abject instrument of the master's (Will?) desire. By implication, the couplet *dis*joins "will" or desire on the one hand and "love" or affection on the other. At the same time, it affirms a degree of affinity between them that cannot be transcended by the demands (or will) of the poet-lover as servant. Personifying himself as love itself, the speaker is forced to acknowledge that this role encapsulates the part of the fool, partly because he allows the loving relationship to be determined by his socially determined servility.

For the servant-poet of the sonnets, service is thus emphatically not its own reward. This is not quite so in the plays, however. For the gentle steward Flavius in *Timon of Athens* and at least initially for the doubly loving figure of Viola/Cesario in *Twelfth Night*, service is more oblation than mutual render. The tension between these two conceptions of giving is the constitutive paradox of sonnet 125. Montaigne tries to avoid this conceptual tension in his essay on friendship by reducing the difference between friends to such complete mutuality that they transcend the logic of the gift itself. They are as conjoined as the right and left hands of a single person:

> For even as the friendship I beare unto my selfe, admits of no accrease, by any succour I give my selfe in any time of need, whatsoever the Stoickes alleage; and as I acknowledge no thanks unto my selfe, so the union of such friends, being truly perfect, makes them lose the feeling of such duties and hate, and expell from one another these words of division, and difference; benefit, good deed, duty, obligation, acknowledgement, prayer, thanks, and their like. All things being by effect common between them ... being no other than one soule in two bodies, according to the fit definition of *Aristotle*, they can neither lend or give ought to each other. (150–1)

This argument is impeccable at one level. It transcends the debilitating economy of giving – encapsulated by the asymmetry or difference that a gift always involves by demanding its return – by reducing the difference between friends to nothing. It has both a social and logical dimension. Classically, friendship requires equality of social rank or station. There can be no friendship between master and servant because its fundamental logical and ethical requirements of autonomy and mutuality cannot be fulfilled in such relationships. The question posed by the sonnets and *Twelfth Night* is one of logical precedence: is likeness required as a condition of friendship, or does friendship create likeness?[10] We shall see through *Twelfth Night* that despite his insistence on the lossless economy of friendship, even Montaigne is forced to admit the cost of friendship and the grievance that exists as the condition of its possibility.

TWELFTH NIGHT

Twelfth Night is as much a study of master-servant relations and the possibilities and travesties of friendship as it is a comedy of romantic love. Every instance of desire in the play is intertwined with the circumstances of service within the early modern noble household.[11] Viola's status as Orsino's servant is simultaneously the condition of possibility and impossibility of her love for him and Olivia's erotic desire for her as Cesario; Orsino embodies courtly infatuation as a form of service in his dotage on Olivia; Malvolio exemplifies, Shakespeare-like, the servant's fantasy of social elevation though erotic conquest; Antonio's homoerotic affection for Sebastian restates courtly devotion to the beloved as a form of service; and even Sir Toby follows the pattern of reciprocating service when he marries his niece's servant "in recompense" (5.1.353) for her gulling of Malvolio. To the essentially unequal relationships of *eros*-in-service, the play adds the requirements of mutuality and equality in the classical conception of friendship or *philia*. I discuss three issues here: first, the degree to which service *makes possible* the intimacies of both friendship and erotic love; second, the way in which the embodied figure of Viola/Cesario on stage questions a tradition of friendship literature that declares women intrinsically incapable of such solidarity; and finally, I show how the inequities that remain within even intimate relations of service mean that service is finally the condition of *impossibility* of love or friendship.

Service as the condition of (im)possibility of love

In both the sonnets and *Twelfth Night*, the favours of service create the conditions for the development of personal affection and erotic desire – for love not merely as the loyal bond of duty towards a superior but also as

---

[10] See Aristotle, *Ethics*, Book Eight, and Montaigne, "Of Friendship," in *Essays*. For a discussion of friendship in *Hamlet*, see Neill, "Friendship and Service". Also Shannon, *Amity*, Chapter 1.

[11] For accounts of the place and role of the household in early modern England, see Laslett and Wall, *Household and Family*; Stone, *Family, Sex and Marriage*; Fletcher and Stevenson, *Order*; Laslett, *World*; Amussen, *Ordered Society*; Friedman, *House and Household*; Wall, *Staging Domesticity*; and Wrightson, *English Society*.

sonnet 125's fantasy of "mutuall render".[12] The circumstances of service in which Viola finds herself in relation to Orsino – especially in the familiarity of a homosocial relationship uncontaminated by heterosexual tensions – prepares the ground for a kind of intimacy that would not be possible if she were acting as herself – as a woman. Such homosocial possibilities of intimacy through service are embodied in the relationship between Sebastian and Antonio. Yet if both relationships represent master-servant relations as the conditions of possibility of love, their respective outcomes offer different views on successful transformation of such associations into affairs of affective reciprocity. In Shakespeare's sonnets, service also prevents true reciprocity in the unfolding of erotic affection: service is the condition of possibility for love, but it is also its condition of impossibility. Service appears to be founded upon a lack of equality or likeness that is generally regarded to be inimical to friendship. Shakespeare claims that whereas such inequality may make love possible, because the reciprocity that is part of its discourse offers a path out of the isolation of unrequited desire, *eros* shares with *philia* the fundamental requirement of spiritual autonomy and equality.

That service is both natural and precarious is evident from the initial scenes of the play. Service as a youth (or eunuch)[13] in an aristocratic household strikes Viola as the most obvious solution to her predicament. The speed with which she captures her new master's favour also indicates the possible capriciousness of such preference, however. Orsino's favouritism renders her vulnerable to court gossip and envy. Despite Valentine's quick denial that the Duke might be "inconstant . . . in his favours" (1.4.5–6), his comment that she is "like to be much advanc'd" if the Duke "continue[s] these favours towards [her]" (1.4.1–3) raises a general concern about reciprocal reward and incipient rivalry among the courtiers. Such rivalry is a major feature of Olivia's household, where Viola would initially have attempted to find a place alongside Maria as one of the countess's serving companions. In one respect, Viola's position echoes Malvolio's. Each is a servant of roughly similar social rank (although the nature of their service or profession is very different) who wants to turn public service into

---

[12] Neill writes of the demystification of the traditional notions of reciprocity in relations of service in the period: "In this world of progressively demystified relationships, most household service was coming to seem like a form of wage-slavery, more and more difficult to reconcile . . . with honor or gentility" (*History*, 33). I.M.'s *Health* deplores the slow decline of service as fewer members of the gentry consider it an appropriate profession. This decline is noted by a number of historians and critics, including Neill, *History*, Burnett, *Masters and Servants*; Friedman, *House and Household*; and Mertes, *Household*.

[13] See Elam, "The Fertile Eunuch".

reciprocated personal attachment.[14] Although each is strictly speaking a "gentleman", Shakespeare's treatment of Malvolio underlines the declining status of the "gentleman-steward" in the late sixteenth century, so deplored and lamented by I.M, but it also suggests that Malvolio's ambitions would have been proscribed by seventeenth-century social mores.[15] The play undoubtedly panders to both ruling-class, patriarchal anxieties and the realities of interservant rivalry within aristocratic households in an apparently conservative way. However, Malvolio is thwarted for reasons of both gender and social politics and personal, affective and moral inadequacy. Perceived through the lens of Milton's passionate insistence upon equality and the continuity of affection in marriage, he is no more than a "*kind of Puritan*". Being "full of self-love", he cannot begin to comprehend the autonomy and mutuality-in-*eros* demanded by radical Protestantism. Mary Ellen Lamb's claim that Malvolio's ambitious individualism "will eventually succeed in emptying out the ideology of service at the heart of other employer-servant relationships in the early modern culture" is undermined by two facts: first, there was no single "ideology of service", and second, many of its diverse elements survived in the social fabric of Victorian England and beyond.[16]

Erotic relationships are not merely a politically dangerous aberration of those of service. Shakespeare shows that they may be made possible by them and that the mutual dependencies and reciprocities at the core of master-servant relationships provide a conceptual model for rethinking erotic and friendly relationships. Viola's subjection of her will to Orsino's desire enables an intimacy that encompasses more than the mere social advancement of a favoured servant or "pitifull thriuor" like Malvolio

---

[14] Stewards, who occupied critical positions of authority and trust in extended late medieval and Elizabethan households could be drawn from a variety of social ranks: from yeoman, through the lesser gentry, to, in some cases, the upper gentry. Malvolio's invocation of his rank as a gentleman to underwrite his pledge of gratitude for the procurement of "a candle, and pen, ink, and paper" during his imprisonment suggests that he may be typical of the "servingmen" to whom I.M. proposes the "health" in his nostalgic treatise (see 4.2.74–6).

[15] See Lamb, "Heterosexual Erotics". Maria's triumph over Malvolio has a strong component of gender rivalry, and her marriage to Sir Toby is a signal triumph of social mobility in a context in which the mere fact of service in a noble household elevated the social position of the servant: "[Servants] could legitimately raise their status, and their standards of comfort and elegance, higher than that of their relatives outside the household" (Mertes, *Household*, 69). At the same time, Mertes notes that "female household members were practically nonexistent. Those we do find are invariably chamberwomen and companions to the lady of the household of women servants in noble household, restricted to the private portions of the house (and often married to another servant); or laundresses, who much of the time lived outside the household" (Mertes, *Household*, 57).

[16] See Robins, *Servant's Hand*, Hay, "Master and Servant" and Deakin, *Labour Market*, and the discussion in Chapter 1 above.

(sonnet 125). Like the poet of the sonnets, Viola "tend[s] / Vpon the houres, and times" of her aristocratic master's "desire," having "no precious time at al to spend; / Nor seruices to doe til [he] require[s]" (sonnet 57.2–4). Her complete attentiveness to his will provokes promises of material reward and, ultimately, of manumission. What *she* really wants, however, is a transformation of the conditions of her service from page to wife:

> Prosper well in this
> And thou shalt live as freely as thy lord,
> To call his fortunes thine.
> VIOLA   I'll do my best
> To woo your lady – (*aside*) yet a barful strife –
> Whoe'er I woo, myself would be his wife.
>
> (1.4. 37–41)

The question is whether the subservience at the heart of the initiating relationship will or should be carried over into the subsequent marital one. Does Cesario's role as servant model Viola's subsequent role as a wife?[17] What is at stake in the triangular relationship of Viola/Orsino/Olivia is the difference between love and desire as they are interlaced with the bonds of service. The "golden service" (4.3.8) that Orsino receives from Cesario is the enabling condition for the redirection of the circuit of his desire from Olivia to Viola. That desire is finally displaced, however, and comes to rest on a person whom he discovers he already *loves*. Indeed, the play shows us the qualitative difference between Orsino's *desire* for Olivia and his *love* for Cesario, something of which the character is himself deeply unaware, although it is a continuous source of delight to the audience. Viola can therefore develop a kind and degree of intimacy with Orsino as the male servant Cesario that would be impossible for her in the figure of a woman. There are three reasons for this: first, because there was little space in aristocratic households for women as servants except in utterly menial positions or as the companions of its aristocratic lady (as Maria is to Olivia);[18] second, because marriage to Viola would at first sight have involved disparagement to the Duke, who had set his sights on a countess; and third, even if Orsino might have recognized in the female figure of Viola a desirable love-object, this would not have resulted in the kind of or degree of intimacy that he enjoys with Cesario through service as the foundation for *philia*. The possibility of that intimacy is where the unconventional core

---

[17] Malcomson, "What You Will". See also Wall, *Staging Domesticity*: "*Twelfth Night* is unusual only in foregrounding the absolute reducibility of the vocabulary of loyal service to that of desire" (180).

[18] See footnote 15 above.

of *Twelfth Night* resides, for it reconfigures the traditional platitudes and stereotypes of erotic service that are encompassed by Orsino's imagination of heterosexual love in the form of his "fancy's queen" into something approaching the early modern ideal of friendship between men.

The commonplace of that ideal is the prejudice that whereas women *desire*, men *love*. The concept of service, so central to the poems concerning the young friend, is all but absent from the sonnets traditionally thought to be addressed to the dark woman. This is no accident: the sonnets are consumed by heterosexual lust as a perverse, self-imposed form of slavery, but they negotiate the affective relations between men as if the *nomos* of servant duty could be converted into the free reciprocity of *philia*, *eros*, or both. However intimate a relationship Viola establishes with Orsino as confidant and wooer by proxy – "I have unclasped / To thee the book even of my secret soul" (1.4.113–14), he declares in a moment of intimacy early on – her double role as male servant and female lover requires her to suppress her own subjectivity, in an echo of sonnet 26. Viola is one of the few cross-dressed heroines in Shakespeare who is trapped by her disguise rather than freed by it. The very condition that allows her intimate access to her beloved's "secret soul" prevents her from revealing her own. Magnusson argues that the self-denial characteristic of servants in the period is part of a set of transpersonal discourses that inform a range of early modern genres. Viola-as-Cesario is thus caught in the discourse and the relations of power characteristic of master-servant relationships, but she is also trapped by the ways in which gender is inscribed in those discourses. As an intimate servant, she has access to the man she loves, but that very role prevents her from occupying the subject position of an *actively* desiring woman.[19] This trap is, however, also the enabling condition for Shakespeare's representation of a wholly unconventional combination of *eros* and *philia* as it may be embodied in a woman. Both its fiction of maleness and its condition of service makes the marriage of *eros* and *philia* possible.

Eros *and* philia

There is a moment of crisis in the representation of Cesario as subservient youth and Viola as assertive woman when, expected to acquiesce in the

---

[19] Viola fulfils Coeffeteau's non-Platonic definition of self-denying love: "Loue then is no other thing, but, To will good to some one, not for our owne priuate interest, but for the loue of himselfe; procuring with all our power what we think may bee profitable for him, or may giue him content" (*Passions*, 103–4).

superior pronouncements of the older man on the unreliability of women, she finds herself contradicting her master in a spontaneous effort to assert her own female integrity in love. Because Orsino's pronouncements against women are grounded in his own overbearing experience, she can contest her superior's declarations in neither of her available personae. The presumed youthful inexperience of her male persona lacks the authority of age or experience to attest to the constancy of female devotion: there is no language available to her to do so with any authority. However, if she exposed herself as the living embodiment of female devotion she would lose the very thing she seeks. She therefore has to displace herself as a sister whose actions exemplify faithfulness as a female stereotype of patient endurance but whose "history" of unrequited constancy can be no more than a "blank" (2.4.109) because it lies in the undecided future of the unfolding performance. The sister that Viola invents combines mourning and constancy, love and silence in a memorial figure of grief and grievance:

> She pined in thought,
> And with a green and yellow melancholy
> She sat like patience on a monument,
> Smiling at grief. (2.4.112–15)

"And was not this love indeed?" she demands, coming as close as she ever does to making this claim on her own behalf. The concepts of loving friendship and erotic devotion are given a more than imaginary unity by their simultaneous embodiment in the doubly gendered figure of Viola as both mourning sister and actively loving brother. As a male servant, Viola has to conceal her love "like a worm i' th' bud" (111), but her position of male service makes possible a condition of friendly intimacy with her master that would normally be impossible for a woman. As Viola's intimacy with Orsino begins to approach the faithfulness of *philia*, it lays the foundation for the kind of mutuality and equality to which the poet of the sonnets aspires. In *Twelfth Night*, this possibility is represented as an unconventional union of *eros* and *philia*, by which the woman behind the mask is able to embody both erotic desire and close friendship. Even as Viola yearns silently for a beloved who is oblivious of her love, *in the figure of Cesario* she can live the mutuality of loving friendship with her master. This exemplifies the conceptual difference between friendship and erotic desire. One may love someone without being loved in return and one may be loved without knowing it, but one cannot be someone's friend without that person also being your friend. It makes perfect sense to say, "I love her, but she does not love me", but not, "I'm her friend, but she's not mine".[20] Lovers may yearn singly; friends always come in pairs. To claim the title of friend is thus always to proclaim a necessary mutuality.

The possibilities of an erotic, heterosexual friendship between master and servant in the relationship between Orsino and Viola are modulated in the relationship between Viola's brother Sebastian and Antonio, where service is also sought as a means to conjoin of *eros* and *philia*. Although there is clearly a difference of rank between Sebastian and his rescuer, their language reflects a considerable degree of equality and intimacy. The two men are introduced at the point at which Sebastian, after an interval of some weeks or months, reveals his gentle birth to the unsuspecting sea captain: "You must know of me then Antonio, my name is Sebastian, which I call'd Roderigo. My father was that Sebastian of Messaline whom I know you have heard of" (2.1.13–15).[21] "Knowing of me" means knowing Antonio's social status, the new awareness of which threatens to destroy the "likeness" between the men, and therefore the grounds for friendship. Faced with what is in effect a rebuttal from Sebastian (masked as inconsolable grief at his sister's supposed death), the desperate Antonio resorts to a discourse of relation and obligation ready at hand. He begs to be allowed to be his companion's servant, *literally speaking*, even as he presumes upon the younger man's established love in making the request:

> ANTONIO If you will not murder me for your love, let me be your
>   servant.
> SEBASTIAN If you will not undo what you have done – that is kill
>   him, whom you have recovered – desire it not.   (31–3)

His demand stems from the necessary mutuality that is entailed by the concepts of friendship and service. Sebastian's acknowledgement of Antonio as either friend or servant would necessarily create a mutual bond between them. If he cannot continue to be his friend, service will allow Antonio to prolong intimate contact with Sebastian, and perhaps even gain some affective hold on him, through its conventional protocols of reciprocal love and care. As the condition of possibility of love, service now reverses the usual progression: Antonio moves from friend to putative servant, in contrast with the other characters like the servant-poet of the sonnets, who

[20] This is a logical or conceptual point, a matter of definition, as Aristotle declares in the *Nichomachean Ethics*, 1155 *b* 28: "Those who wish well to others ... are merely called well-disposed, if the other does not return the well-wishing, 'reciprocal goodwill' being the definition of friendship" (*Aristotle on Friendship*, 9).
[21] My thanks to Lars Engle for drawing this to my attention.

seeks to be transformed from servant to friend, and Viola and Malvolio, both of whom wish to be transformed *through service* from servants into lovers.

Despite his strategies of negative politeness, Sebastian refuses to play the roles of either master or friend. Sebastian's language appears to convey the care of friendship, but it fails to live up to either of Montaigne's requirements. His insistence on continuing on his own seems to express a concern for the well-being of his friend rather than open rejection:

The malignancy of my fate might perhaps distemper yours, therefore I shall crave of you your leave that I may bear my evils alone. It were a bad recompense for your love to lay any of them on you. (2.1.2–7)

There is a double paradox here: first, if Sebastian regarded Antonio as a true or "sovereign" friend, as Montaigne puts it, he would let him share everything with him, including the "malignancy" of his "fate"; second, his apparently meticulous, ethical concern that Antonio's love should receive proper "recompense" (the essence of reciprocity, one might think), reduces a relationship that should know no economy to one of calculation. Sebastian's refusal to put his friend in a position to do him good by being his servant negates the central ethical imperative of true friendship. Montaigne would say that these paradoxes are illusory, because friendship between them is precluded by their social difference. Moreover, it is precisely the "malignancy" of Sebastian's "fate", which Antonio has both attenuated by rescuing him and shared, that has brought them together as friends in the first place.

It is possible to stage the final scene of *Twelfth Night* so that Antonio and Sebastian are joyfully reunited and look forward to an intimate relationship (as friends, lovers, or both) in Olivia's household. The text offers few clues to this effect, however – even fewer than *The Merchant of Venice*, for which Alan Sinfield has suggested such a scenario.[22] The only (poignantly ironical) indication of Sebastian's continued appreciation of Antonio's friendship exists in his reflection that the sea captain would have done him "golden service" (4.3.8) if he had been at hand to give him some advice about Olivia's advances.

The most fully developed form of friendship in *Twelfth Night* exists, unexpectedly, between a man and a woman, Viola and Orsino, even if the woman appears to be a man. Only in the role of man and servant ("Orsino's man" – compare "your Will" in sonnet 26) can Viola engender the intimacy

---

[22] See Sinfield, "How to Read *The Merchant of Venice*".

of *philia*. The question is whether such friendship is carried over into an erotic, heterosexual relationship. In more broadly ideological and structural terms, the question is whether *Twelfth Night*'s peculiar embodiment of friendship in a woman challenges the received, homocentric conception of *philia* exemplified, among others, by Montaigne.

Mourning and the costs of friendship

Twelfth Night opens with a triple blow of separation, mourning, and loss. Each of the twins, Sebastian and Viola, is in mourning when we first encounter them, stricken by the belief that the other is dead. That double grief is multiplied by Olivia, herself grieving for the loss of a brother. Jacques Derrida notes the conceptual imbrication of friendship and grief – both in the English sense of mourning and also in the French sense of bearing a *grievance*, "in which accusation mingles with mourning to cry out from an infinite wound".[23] Moreover, even in Montaigne's idealizing paean, friendship is implicitly conditioned by loss. The friendship of which Montaigne speaks is being grieved for at the moment of writing: it is something lost, celebrated in a state of mourning after the event, and for all its perfection, it is predicated upon a fundamental feeling of inadequacy and grievance:

> For, this perfect amity I speak of, is indivisible; each man doth so wholly give him-selfe unto his friend, that he hath nothing left him to divide else-where: moreover, *he is grieved* that he is [not] double, triple, or quadruple, and hath not many soules, or sundry wils, that he might confer them all upon this subject. (151; emphasis added)

Even in "perfect amity", each man "is grieved". The indivisibility presumed as the essence of "sovereign friendship" and which precludes the economy of the gift – with its necessary implications of division, difference, obligation, and gratitude – involves a grievance which rests upon a residual and unfulfilable desire: to give "in overplus", multiplying *sundry* wills rather than settling for a united soul, paradoxically to fulfil the ideal of a single, indivisible, will. Perfect friendship thus involves the primal cost of a felt

---

[23] Derrida, *Friendship*, x. Also:

> *philia* begins with the possibility of survival. Surviving – that is the other name of a mourning whose possibility is never to be awaited. For one does not survive without mourning. . . . Hence surviving is at once the essence, the origin and the possibility, the condition of possibility of friendship; it is the grieved act of loving. This time of surviving thus gives the time of friendship. (14)

Cicero's *De Amicitia* opens with a discourse on the death of Scipio Africanus.

inadequacy, a primary state of being *grieved*. That sense of grief or grievance arises, paradoxically, in a treatise on kindness as both likeness and generosity, out of the desire for *otherness* – the friend wishes that he had sundry wills so that he may transfer them to the other who is part of his soul.[24]

The grief and mourning that condition friendship are expressed in Montaigne's repetition of Aristotle's paradoxical apostrophe: "O my friends, there is no friend." That cry, which calls upon friends only to say that there are no such things – perhaps that there can never be such a things – could be seen as the muted call of Shakespeare's sonnets as a whole: they presume or try to bring into being a friendship that seems always already to have failed, the "dearness" of which encompasses preciousness and cost in equal measure. Montaigne would say – along with Aristotle and Cicero – that such a friendship as the persona of the sonnets seeks is impossible from the start. It is contaminated by baser motives that are a consequence of social difference and illicit erotic desire. No dream of "leav[ing] out difference" (sonnet 105) between already unequal "friends" can be realised. When Montaigne invokes the Aristotelian paradox, then, he is not signalling the general impossibility of friendship. He is drawing a distinction between different kinds or levels of friendship: between "sovereign friendship" on the one hand, which does exist but only once every two or three thousand years, and "common or customary" friendship on the other, which cannot properly be called friendship at all. This distinction is true to Aristotle and Cicero, although it is not clear that Aristotle's apostrophe does signify what Montaigne takes it to mean.

Can women be friends? The theatre's answer

Cicero does not mention women at all in *De amicitia*. Aristotle includes them only by indirection in the *Nichomachean Ethics*, as an example of the lower form of friendship between unequal partners in marriage, and he concludes that the partners maintain their amity purely through their children. Neither excludes women directly on the grounds of their constitutional incapacity to sustain friendship. Montaigne's claims about the radical disjunction between *eros* and *philia* are, however, made in the language of Renaissance psychology, derived from Galen and exemplified in English by Thomas Wright and in French by Nicholas Coefetteau,[25] which

---

[24] It should be noted that Montaigne is in fact groping towards the recognition of the other that is central to Todorov's notion of "love-joy" in contrast to "love-desire".

[25] Wright, *Passions*, and Coefetteau, *Passions*.

imputes to women an unstable humoural temperament unsuitable for the settled constancy of friendship:

To compare the affection towards women unto it, although it proceed from our owne free choice, a man cannot, nor may it be placed in this ranke; Her fire, I confesse it . . . to be more active, more fervent, more sharpe. But it is a rash and wavering fire, wavering and diverse: the fire of an ague subject to fits and stints, and that hath but a slender hold-fast of us. In true friendship, it is a generall and universall heat, and equally tempered, a constant and settled heat, all pleasure and smoothness, that hath no pricking or stinging in it, which the more it is in lustfull love, the more is it but the raging and mad desire in following that which flies us. (147–8)

Yet Montaigne's metaphor of fire and heat indicates not so much a difference in kind as a disparity in intensity and stability. Fire and heat apply equally to *eros* and *philia*: but whereas the first is "more active . . . fervent and sharpe", the latter follows the Aristotelian ideal of reliability and endurance: it is "a constant and settled heat". These differences are radically gendered. Erotic love, with its wavering, unreliable intensity, is female; the settled evenness of friendship is male. Eros and women are unstable, whereas loving friendship is male in both its personae and quality. Women are by nature the creatures of Eros:

Seeing (to speake truly) that the ordinary sufficiency of women, cannot answer this conference and communication, the nurse of this sacred bond: nor seeme their minds strong enough to endure the pulling of a knot so hard, so fast, so durable. (147)

Montaigne's misogynist sentiment is echoed almost exactly in the self-important pronouncement of the Duke of Illyria:

> There is no woman's sides
> Can bide the beating of so strong a passion
> As love doth give my heart; no woman's heart
> So big, to hold so much. They lack retention.
> Alas, their love may be called appetite,
> No motion of the liver, but the palate,
> That suffer surfeit, cloyment, and revolt.
> But mine is all as hungry as the sea,
> And can digest as much.   (2.4.92–100)

Orsino is speaking of the female incapacity to sustain erotic passion, but his remarks may be extended to women's capacity for friendship. Whereas Orsino gives full reign to his own erotic desires, believing them to be constant and durable, Montaigne eschews their blind indulgence in his preference for friendship above desire. In Montaigne's view, Orsino would be right to insist on the insufficiency of women to form enduring relationships, but he would be wrong to think that in their pursuit of *eros* men are any better than women. *Eros* is effeminate and effeminising; it seduces men into a false belief in their retentive capacity, which only the exceptional bond of loving friendship *between men* can attain and retain. Montaigne's distinction resembles the difference discussed earlier between desire and love: the former is unstable, intense, and liable to "suffer surfeit, cloyment, and revolt", whereas the latter basks securely in the warmth of constant devotion.

The theatrical context of Orsino's utterance, however, offers a *contrary* perspective on the received truth about women not available to Montaigne's essay. The theatre's capacity to represent two genders in a single body creates an imaginary space in which a woman can live up to the demands of friendship in the figure of a man. Viola is equally friend and lover, both enduring and stung. As the double figuration of service and sexual difference s/he represents both a challenge to and an exemplification of Montaigne's conception of loving friendship. In her male persona, s/he affirms one half of the bond of loving friendship that Montaigne simultaneously celebrates and mourns. As the favoured courtier to whom he has unpacked the secrets of his soul she overlays the erotic intensity of her desire as a woman ("a rash and wavering fire") with the "constant and settled heat" of her friendship with the Duke. The boy/girl figure of Cesario/Viola thus proclaims without saying it the blind untruth of Orsino's (and by implication, Montaigne's) complacency. Whatever erotic desire the young woman Viola may feel for Orsino, *in the male figure of Cesario*, she consistently performs the bonds of (male) friendship. The ambiguously gendered figure of Viola/Cesario thus exemplifies the embodied dialogism of the stage to encapsulate the possibility of female friendship while simultaneously reconciling *philia* and *eros* in that figure. One of *Twelfth Night*'s most obvious contradictions of the received denigration of female "retention" is the fact that Viola is the play's exemplary figure of constancy of affection, not the aristocratic man who indulges in that claim on his own behalf and that of his sex in general.

Friends and enemies

Shakespeare's sonnet 144 entertains the anxious thought that a fiend may well lurk within the friend:

> And whether that my angel be turned fiend
> Suspect I may, yet not directly tell;
> But being both from me, both to each friend,
> I guess one angel in another's hell.   (8–12)

Twelfth Night does the opposite: it troubles the commonsense distinction between friend and enemy by seeking the friend within the foe or the other.[26] From the early antagonism between Orsino and Olivia, encapsulated by Orsino's alienation from women as a whole, through the inimical friendship of Toby and Andrew and the household servants and their steward, to the complicated relationship between Antonio and Sebastian in enemy territory, *Twelfth Night* transforms enemy into friend and finds the friend in the process of defining the enemy. Combining the figures of man and woman, Viola/Cesario unites the opposites of friend and enemy in gender terms. Sebastian as the enemy figure of Cesario[27] is transformed into a fiend when he appears to deny his friend: "his life I gave him . . . pure for his love . . . and [he] grew a twenty years' removèd thing / While one would wink" (5.1.76–86). The confusion of friend and enemy is especially pronounced in the decisive moment when, thwarted by beloved and f(r)iend alike (as he thinks), Orsino declares that his "thoughts are ripe in mischief" (5.1.115–30):

> ORSINO Why should I not, had I the heart to do it,
>   Like to th' Egyptian thief, at point of death
>   Kill what I love
>   [. . .]
>   But this your minion, whom I know you love,
>   And whom, by heaven I swear, I tender dearly,
>   Him will I tear out of that cruel eye
>   Where he sits crownèd in his master's spite.
>   [. . .]
> VIOLA And I most jocund, apt, and willingly
>   To do you rest a thousand deaths would die.

Orsino's sudden, terrifying determination to kill what he loves is marked by the eruption of a deeply suppressed emotion, as if he has always been straining against the knowledge that affinity and distance, love and hatred, are separated by a hair's breadth. More strikingly, Orsino's declaration of newly realized enmity paradoxically releases Viola from mourning into joy. As Orsino's perceived enemy or fiend – sitting "crownèd in his master's spite" – Viola/Cesario is released to declare herself her master's friend *and* lover. Orsino's posturing threat breaks the silence to which she has patiently constrained herself. The "thousand deaths" that she would take upon herself are proclaimed in an equally histrionic mode as the reiterative tests of

---

[26] For a deconstruction of the opposition friend-enemy, see Derrida, *Friendship*.
[27] As Orsino's favourite personal servant and friend, Cesario would necessarily be Antonio's enemy insofar as he is "on base and ground enough / Orsino's enemy" (5.1.70–1).

love: the equivalent of Montaigne's desire to multiply his will and soul, so that he might bestow them *all* repeatedly upon his friend. Cesario/Viola's declaration, "And I . . . To do you rest a thousand deaths would die" attests both to a total, self-obliterating "loving friendship" and also to the passionate, erotic heat of shared sexual pleasure, blissfully repeated in a thousand "little deaths".[28]

In contrast to the sonnets' struggle against time, Viola abandons herself to it, hoping that her devotion to her master, the fundamental truth of her sex and blood, and the "whirligig of time" (5.1.364) will reward her desires and complete her love. Unlike the sonnets' poet, she can assume that the inherent quality of her birth will allow time to rescue her (2.2.38–9). Because *Twelfth Night* obeys its generic expectations, this trust is justified. The Duke's requital of her devotion is couched in the language and gesture of manumission: he offers himself as a reciprocating reward for services performed, even if he does not withdraw the title of master with the gift of his hand:

> Your master quits you, and for your service done him
> So much against the mettle of your sex,
> So far beneath your soft and tender breeding,
> And since you called me master for so long,
> Here is my hand. You shall from this time be
> Your master's mistress. (5.1.310–5)

The reciprocity of erotic affection – signalled by the use of "you" and "your" – is thus expressed as a consequence of, or at least as an expression of, the reciprocity between master and servant, who are now also friends and lovers. It is impossible to account for the quality of Viola's feelings for her master by dividing them among "real" sexual desire, friendship, and the devotion of a servant. Her erotic devotion is deeply informed by her internalized commitment to service: Orsino's affection for her cannot be divorced from the intimacy of friendship which allowed him to "unclasp . . . the book even of [his] secret soul" (1.4.14–15).

The much-noted fact that Viola/Cesario is not restored to the trappings of her former sexual identity at the end of the play both exemplifies and complicates the play's imagination of friendship as a heterosexual, erotic relationship "where a man might wholly be engaged" (Montaigne, 147). Orsino prolongs Viola's identity as Cesario presumably to maintain her identity as the embodiment of *philia*, or possibly *philia-in-eros*. However, his promise in the closing moments that once her customary garments have

---

[28] My thanks to John Kerrigan for drawing this to my attention.

been found, she will be his "fancy's queen" (5.1.384) offers the disturbing prospect of Viola being (re)turned to the figure that Olivia had so resolutely and correctly resisted. This fantasy is the conventional notion of love as courtly service in which the male role is fancifully inverted in abject servitude to the adored woman but which actually preserves male ascendancy and control. The newly reinforced, hierarchical distance between the duke and his servant – or the duke as fantasized servant – signalled by Orsino's use of the third person and the reinvocation of his self-indulgent "fancy" from the opening lines of the play, threatens to reinstate the difference between men and women upon which the exclusion of the latter from the realm of friendship was based.

At least until its closing lines, *Twelfth Night* embodies woman as both desiring lover and constant friend. This appears to be a radical departure from the literature on friendship that runs from Aristotle to Montaigne. Let us allow the French essayist a final word, however. There is a brief passage in "Of Friendship", often missed, in which Montaigne entertains the fantasy of a *truly* ideal friendship – with a woman:

> And truly, if without that, such a genuine and voluntarie acquaintance might be contracted, where not only mindes had this entire jovissance, but also bodies, a share of the alliance, and where a man might wholly be engaged: It is certain, that friendship would thereby be more compleat and full. (Montaigne, 147)

Having not only endorsed the Aristotelian and Ciceronian exclusion of women from the bonds of *philia* but also underscored it by adducing the natural, incapacitating psychology of women, Montaigne concedes that, were it possible, friendship with a woman would be "more compleat and full": it would be the (impossible) place "where a man might wholly be engaged". The impossibility of this dream is admitted to be accidental and contingent rather than universal and necessary. Montaigne merely states that there is no example (yet!) of woman attaining to it, before adding, in the 1592 revision, that in any case by the "common agreement" of the ancient schools of philosophy "she is excluded from it". However, in the posthumous 1595 edition, prepared by his "daughter in alliance", Marie de Gourney, the text goes much further. Marie, Montaigne declares with extraordinary passion, is a living example of the loving friendship that he had earlier preserved only for men:

> I have greatly pleased my selfe in publishing in sundrie places the good hope I have of *Marie de Gournay le Jars*, my daughter in alliance, and truely of me beloved with more then a fatherly love, and as one of the best parts of my being enfeofed in my home and solitariness. There is nothing in the world I esteem more then

hir . . . [H]ir minde shal one day be capable of many notable things, and amongst others, of *the perfection of this thrice-sacred amitie whereunto we read not, hir sex could yet attaine*; the sinceritie and soliditie of her demeanors are therein already sufficient. (599–600; emphasis added)[29]

Marie de Gourney is clearly exceptional, but so are friends. This late passage reiterates the major components of Montaigne's definitive discourse, almost twenty years earlier, on all-male friendship: the claim that Marie is one of the better parts of his being; the exclusiveness of his love for her; his admiration for her soul and judgment rather than her beauty; and finally, the sense that friends yearn for each other even before they have set eyes upon the other: "We were seeking each other even before we set eyes on each other . . . we embraced each other by repute."[30] Despite these intimations of amity, Montaigne poignantly and generously reserves proper, "sovereign" friendship for De Gournay as a future possibility, presumably because he wishes to allow her (even if it has passed him by in his old age) the complete engagement of the *whole* person – the union of *eros* and *philia* – about which he had permitted himself only a fleeting fantasy two decades earlier.

Montaigne's momentous concession in effect reiterates Aristotle's cry, "O my friends, there is no friend!" In this context, however, it does not complacently distinguish secondary friendship from a truly loving amity exclusive to men.[31] It expresses a fundamental dissatisfaction with that homocentric ideal; it mourns a necessary lack, a "grief at grievance", that no mere thought of the male friend can console. Furthermore, when he finds a woman who exemplifies the qualities of the complete friend to the extent that there is no one in the world that he "esteems more than her", he can do so only from a position of loss, of implicit grief and grievance that it will be with someone else whom she will share a friendship more complete than even he had had, briefly, with his soul mate, Etiénne de Boétie.

Grievance and revenge

We have seen in the three relationships – servant-poet and master-friend, Viola and Orsino, and Antonio and Sebastian – literal service, sexual desire,

---

[29] This passage, which appears only in the posthumous, 1595 edition, edited by Marie de Gournay, is contested by many Montaigne scholars, who believe that it was insterted by Gournay herself. See Gournay, *Preface*, fn. 101, and Horowitz, "Marie de Gournay", 282, ff.

[30] Cf. Screech's translation: "We were seeking each other even before we set eyes on each other . . . we embraced each other by repute" (212).

[31] Montaigne's qualification of his the exclusion of women from loving friendship is expressed in its essence in the 1580 edition of the essays.

and loving devotion coming together in tangled ways.[32] The subservience of service impinges on the quality and possibility of love, impeding the reciprocity sought by both erotic desire and caring affection. Yet it also makes it possible. The ideal of reciprocity that is part of the concept of service also holds out the promise of reciprocity in sexual love: the logic of unequal mutuality in master-servant relations suggests itself into the quite different grammar of desire, in which being unrequited threatens to be the norm. In the sonnets and the Antonio-Sebastian relationship, what seems at first to be a wholly self-deprecating position of powerlessness on the part of the servant-lover is transformed into a fatherly authority characteristic of an older man's relation to a younger. The older men gradually assert their independence and command in both the sonnets and the comedy, but in each text that independence ends as a disillusioned excoriation of the fickleness and selfishness of ungrateful youth.

Both *Twelfth Night* and the sonnets represent the grievance that friends, servants, or lovers may harbour when they feel that the respective demands of mutuality in the relationships have not been met. When love in service becomes thwarted rather than fulfilled desire, abject devotion can transform itself into vengeful retribution. This is especially evident in the general settling of scores and distribution of rewards through which Malvolio and Antonio lose as much as Sebastian and Viola gain. The spirit of carnivalesque revelry that dominates the subplot makes it easy to overlook the steward's role as spokesman for the obligations of service as a reciprocal relationship of respect and care between master and servant. Scarcely ten lines after Orsino's signal acknowledgement of his reciprocal bonds of love and service vis-à-vis Cesario, Malvolio echoes the sonnets' shift from the poetics of praise to those of blame when, as slighted senior servant, he levels a public complaint against his mistress that takes her to task for abrogating her duties of care and reciprocal responsibility.

Malvolio's letter to Olivia, read out in public, ignores the proscriptions rehearsed by sonnets 57 and 58 regarding the denial of a servant's right to "accuse" the master or mistress "of injury" (58.8). Acknowledging the fact

---

[32] The relationship between Sebastian and the Countess is a compressed version of the affinity that we have witnessed at greater length between Viola and the Duke as master and servant. Sebastian takes the Countess's initial invitation as exactly the sort of gentlemanly household service that his sister sought initially, and then, in the blink of an eye, he succumbs to his new mistress's erotic interest. His telescoped fate is thus an actualization of Mavolio's prolonged but thwarted fantasy. A move from household servant to erotic partner in one instance is established as the compressed pattern in another, but the relationship between Sebastian and Olivia exemplifies none of the depth or commitment of Viola's with Orsino, nor its integrity as a form of erotically charged *philia*. See Jardine, *Reading Shakespeare Historically*, chapter 4.

that he "leave[s] [his] duty a little unthought of," the steward nonetheless presumes upon his right to "speak out of [his] injury" (5.1.299). The letter is shockingly direct. It observes none of the protocols of politeness and indirection conventionally expected of such interchanges. Olivia's steward presumes upon a public right to shame his mistress for her inappropriate treatment of him, in direct contrast to the poet-servant's concession to his master-friend that "your charter is so strong, / That you your selfe may priuiledge your time / To what you will, to you it doth belong, / Your selfe to pardon of selfe-doing crime" (58.9–12). The opening oath of his letter inverts the initiating "that God forbid" of sonnet 58: "By the Lord, Madam," he writes, "you wrong me, and the world shall know it." Noting that "I yet have the benefit of my senses as well as your Ladyship," he goes on to promise to "do myself much right, or you much shame" (5.1.292–8). Olivia's steward expresses, in the most public terms, the duties that could be expected of magisterial relationships. It is especially significant that he should in the end reject all protocols of duty, service, and social distinction by speaking from a position of undiluted grievance: "I'll be revenged on the whole pack of you!" (365).

Within the context of the comedy, Malvolio's complaint against his mistress is unjustified. His abominable treatment arises from a commonplace rivalry among servants and others within the aristocratic household.[33] Even if the charge does not ultimately hit its mark, the mistaken context nevertheless permits an unrestrained, public expression of blame and complaint that would have resonated with the fantasies of those members of the audience in various conditions of servile resentment. Despite its comic spirit, *Twelfth Night* thus represents the aggrieved, public expression by a professed servant who feels that his service to a master has not been properly reciprocated. This occurs in the play on not one but two separate occasions. Malvolio's unconstrained invective is anticipated by Antonio. Like his counterpart in the sonnets, the servant-lover inveighs against a similarly duplicitous, self-centred and "ingrateful boy" to whom he had wastefully devoted his life and love: "A wreck past hope he was. / His life I gave him, and did thereto add / My love without retention, or restraint, / All his in dedication" (5.1.73–6). Like Malvolio's letter, Antonio's complaint is a powerfully independent expression of *moral* outrage at the perceived failure of the well born to reciprocate love and service. Like that letter, its failure to hit its intended mark does not detract from its rhetorical force or aptness. Viola may not be

[33] See Friedman, *Household*, 38ff, for an account of the rivalry that beset an exemplary noble household: "while ceremonial occasions were designed to present an image of order and control, behind the scenes relationships were rife with faction and intrigue" (38).

guilty as charged, but she provides a virtual target for the expression of real
feelings of outrage about the "self-doing crime" (sonnet 58.12) of careless,
youthful nobility. The charge against Viola is indeed applicable to Sebastian
who, despite his appreciation of Antonio's "golden service," does grow "a
twenty years' removed thing / While one would wink" (83–1). The generic
requirements of comedy require the accusation to be circuited harmlessly
through the sister, but that does not detract from the performative intensity and appropriateness of the charge as such. Despite its conventional
romantic ending, *Twelfth Night* is constructed and builds upon grievance:
the originary grievance of friendship to which Derrida alerts us and the
fundamental grievance of service in the face of apparently careless masters.

Nature's debt

The sonnets' conceptual analysis of love in its relation to service departs
from the conflation of love and service in at least certain key relationships
in *Twelfth Night*. The abject devotion expressed in sonnet 26 and repeated
ironically in sonnets 57 and 58 is ultimately declared to be incompatible
with the reciprocity that is the essence of love. The very aspects that make
love possible in conditions of service are finally declared to thwart it. The
later sonnets to the master offer a more hard-headed view of service as
self-seeking "policy" (sonnet 124.9), characteristic of the jaundiced perspectives of an Iago or an Edmund. Sonnet 120 returns to the question of
reciprocity through the ethics of forgiveness, but it does so in a peculiarly
ambivalent way:

> THat you were once vnkind be-friends mee now,
> And for that sorrow, which I then didde feele,
> Needes must I vnder my transgression bow,
> Vnlesse my Nerues were brasse or hammered steele.
> For if you were by my vnkindnesse shaken
> As I by yours, y'haue past a hell of Time,
> And I a tyrant haue no leasure taken
> To waigh how once I suffered in your crime.
> O that our night of wo might haue remembred
> My deepest sence, how hard true sorrow hits,
> And soone to you, as you to me then tendred
> The humble salue, which wounded bosomes fits!
>   But that your trespasse now becomes a fee,
>   Mine ransoms yours, and yours must ransome mee.

Unlike the earlier sonnets, this poem contains none of the protocols of
politeness that signal service bowing to necessity. The poet's pose of denying
any subjectivity independent of his master-beloved's "Will" is abandoned

for a new self-possession that speaks with a secure sense of familiar equality. The speaker acknowledges necessity as he did before, but now it is a different kind of compulsion. It is accepted voluntarily, as a form of ethical reciprocity. He allows himself to be judged as an act of his own will. He does not await judgement as the God-ordained condition of his being.

At first sight, the poem seems to be built upon an inexorable logic of mutual empathy and forgiveness in which the other is treated as an imagined extension of the speaking self. The sonnet heaps blame, however, even as it pleads for mutual exoneration. If it says, "I know, from my own experience, how you are feeling," it also implies, "I hope you now know just how badly you made me suffer". Although it does not indulge in the unservantlike outrage of a Malvolio or Antonio, it nevertheless contains something more discomfiting: a secure assumption that reciprocity obeys the logic of the double-entry ledger. An earlier moral failing is reckoned a credit that cancels the new ethical debt. The young aristocrat now bears the burden of a necessity that arises from a "mutuall render" posited as given: "Mine ransom's yours, and yours must ransom mee" (14). This tone and attitude are a considerable distance from servile abjectness of sonnet 26. However, the language that replaces both the earlier abjectness and the more equitable notions of quittance developed in *Twelfth Night* is nonetheless not a mutual expression that arises from the free gift of the self. Ransom is what is transacted in war, between enemies. That the poet now speaks as an equal and that this poem is ostensibly an acceptance of an apology does not necessarily signal the reciprocity of *love*, even if the sonneteer does break free of the bonds of service.

The sonnet confirms the peculiar Shakespearean paradox whereby service is simultaneously the condition of possibility and impossibility of love. The sonnets generally echo Viola's growing intimacy with Orsino by showing that service enables the developing intimacy between master and servant. Nevertheless, the continued hierarchical nature of such reciprocity renders mutual love impossible. Whereas reciprocity is entirely compatible with the unequal demands of service, there are ethical dimensions to the concept of love as Shakespeare develops it – in the double demand for *equality* of obligation and *freedom* of render – that make love and service incompatible. The things that hold them together also wrench them apart. This is apparent from the beginning, in the concept of duty invoked so insistently in sonnet 26. Because it entails restraint or compulsion, duty is incompatible with true friendship, love, or hospitality.[34] These should be given freely, not out of any consideration of obligation or decorum. This has the paradoxical

---

[34] See Montaigne, "Of Friendship", and Derrida, "Passions".

outcome that some kinds of love transcend the demands of reciprocity, which is too closely tied to the duty of service, even if service can be used to inform desire with the expectation of mutual render.

In sonnet 126, the last poem addressed to the young man, the quest for free mutual render is abandoned, as the poet switches allegiances to a new mistress. The poem expresses the steward's revenge:

> O Thou my louely Boy who in thy power,
> Doest hould times fickle glasse, his fickle,hower:
> Who hast by wayning growne, and therein shou'st,
> Thy louers withering, as thy sweet selfe grow'st.
> If Nature (soueraine misteres ouer wrack)
> As thou goest onwards still will plucke thee backe,
> She keepes thee to this purpose, that her skill.
> May time disgrace,and wretched mynuit kill.
> Yet feare her O thou minnion of her pleasure,
> She may detaine,but not still keepe her tresure!
> Her Audite (though delayd) answer'd must be,
> And her Quietus is to render thee.

Opening with a securely independent rhetoric of condescending familiarity, the sonnet records a dramatic switch of allegiance and a chillingly restrained withdrawal of all that has up to now been given in service to the young man: the promise to cancel his debt to time by offering everlasting beauty and infinite life in "these blacke lines" (sonnet 63.13). The poet transforms himself from the rival of desiring Nature in sonnet 20 into her newly entertained bookkeeper. In that position, he endorses everything that he had formerly promised to oppose as the young man's "slaue." In his new office as Nature's steward, he abandons his previous service, through which he sought to "repair" rather than "ruinate" the "beauteous roof" (sonnet 10.7) of aristocratic settlement. He now chillingly underwrites Nature's inevitable "Audite:" the "Quietus" through which she – Shylock-like – will call in her certain bond against his beautiful, careless master.

This spirit of revenge and grievance takes us to *Timon of Athens*.

TIMON OF ATHENS

Setting the gritty, unfinished, and uneven *Timon of Athens* (probably written in collaboration with Thomas Middleton)[35] beside the polished perfection of *Twelfth Night*, with the sonnets as a bridge between them, reveals a darker

---

[35] For an account of such collaboration, see Vickers, *Shakespeare, Co-Author*.

vision of the interactions of love, duty, reciprocity, and sacrifice. Both plays represent the tension between conspicuous hospitality and consumption and the bitter realities of waste and loss in a noble household. However, *Twelfth Night*'s pleasurable fantasy of erotic yearning and fulfilment is absent from the *Timon*, which has little place for women except as stereotyped entertainers and camp followers. That does not mean that the devotion embodied by Viola is entirely absent from the tragedy. Her place is taken by the household steward – indeed by servants as a class – who is differentiated from his counterpart, Malvolio, in *Twelfth Night* by his singular lack of ambition and judgemental self-importance.

Viola traces the trajectory that the servant-lover of the sonnets desires – starting in service, developing reciprocity through friendship, and ending, through the union of *eros*, *nomos*, and *philia*, in a relationship in which, in Montaigne's words, the whole person is engaged. Timon's devoted steward, on the other hand, receives no reward but rather acts as the foil against which the failure of friendship and magisterial responsibility and care are judged. Unlike Malvolio and the servant-poet of the sonnets, he feels no resentment or inclination to revenge himself upon his careless master. Flavius represents servant devotion as a positive ethical force: his is the service of agency, or volitional primacy (to use Evett's phrase) in which the desire for reciprocity makes no demand other than to be allowed to bestow the gift of his "golden service" upon his master without any further condition. Flavius achieves the greatest autonomy at the point at which his material fortunes are lowest. No longer a servant, he gives away his money to his fellow-servants and decides to seek out his master to rededicate himself to him as an act of free will.

"Pitiful thrivers"

Evett makes the absence of expectation of reciprocity central to his argument that for many servants, service was its own reward: the fear and trembling in which servants were expected to obey and serve their masters, like the similar, fearful devotion that every person owes to God, is not the result of a bargain or contract. Protestant theology insists that one owes God one's love without the promise or expectation of anything in return. To what degree, then, can the divine expectation of service beyond the economy of reciprocal reward be expected in earthly relationships, in which political demand, religious injunction, and personal expectation are difficult to disentangle?

This question encapsulates the Evett's issue with materialism. Wishing to do justice to forms of historically specific, lived experience, and representation without reducing them to mere instances of ideological mis-recognition or false consciousness, one is nevertheless obliged to recognize the degree to which the formation of such experience and self-consciousness may well be the product of repressive and self-serving forms of political organization. Modern criticism has found it easy to recognize struggles of power and expressions of resentment in master-servant relations, but much more difficult to comprehend the personal and ethical intensities of self-denial and devotion. Shakespeare's sonnets and *Twelfth Night* encompass both facets of these relationships, but *Timon* presents a more intractable vision. How do we account for the utter selflessness of the servants, especially the "master steward", in this play? Does it exemplify the ethics of Evett's "volitional primacy": a willing bowing to necessity through which perfect freedom is discovered phenomenologically (or spiritually, depending on one's framework) by one's refusing to desire anything beyond one's allotted position? Or is Flavius's determination to seek out his master and regain himself through service a sign of the ways in which particular kinds of hegemonic relations shape subjective identities to support dominant forces of repression and exploitation? Mary Ellen Lamb's essay exemplifies this dilemma when she concedes, in an analysis that offers a generally materialist account of master-servant relations as instances of class and gender struggle, that the aristocratic women who manipulate and are in turn manipulated by their senior servants may actually have *loved* them (Lamb, "Heterosexual Erotics")? She does not, however, elaborate on what that might mean.

The ubiquity of service in the early modern world makes it difficult to draw a firm line between private and public space, affective affinity and political necessity. Sonnet 125 uses the language of religious and political ceremony to castigate the lack of personal reward within a system of patronage beset by intense forms of rivalry and emotional extortion. It focuses on the ledger book of exchange, paradoxically, to circumvent its double bookkeeping. To "spend" oneself in "gazing", "los[ing] all or more" in the process, is the worst of a series of bad bargains. The poem pleads for a personal space of free reciprocity that is in but not of the economy of patronage. This possibility appears, however, to be denied by the intelligencer who makes a sudden, dramatic appearance in couplet. In contrast to the pitiful thrivers of the sonnet, the majority of its servants in *Timon of Athens* are sympathetic beings, in both senses of the word. They represent a site of moral rectitude and selfless devotion within a landscape of ruling-class cupidity and hypocrisy. The exceptions to this general vision of service as the site of ethical insight and selfless love in *Timon* are the poet and the painter. "Dwellers on forme and fauor . . . pittifull thriuors in their gazing spent" (sonnet 125), they proffer services of a sort,[36] but they are wholly disaffected from the reciprocities of settled, household service. They are staged representations of the rivals against whom Shakespeare's servant-poet tries to defend himself in the sonnets: hyenas who scavenge off expediency and empty promises. In contrast to the simple reciprocities of love embodied by Timon's household servants, poet and painter represent the empty allure of deliberately postponed desire, the form of fashion, and the epitome of corrupting mimesis against which the sonnets warn (5.1.17–29).

Even the usurers' minor servants offer sympathetic commentary on Timon's predicament and damning criticism of their own masters' thankless rapacity. Timon's own steward, Flavius, exemplifies selfless devotion and generosity not only to his fallen master, but also to the abandoned servants who are left destitute by the bankruptcy of their master. He is matched by Timon's other servants, who are fully alive to the ethics of reciprocity but do not necessarily expect it for themselves. Flavius's companion servant, for example, refuses to be suborned by Lucullus when he is sent to ask his master's supposed friend for help. Patronised with a bribe to report that Lucullus is not at home, the servant flings the money back at this "disease of a friend" before turning to the audience both to voice his contempt for his superior, in a term usually reserved by masters for servants, and to express his master's anger and sorrow as if they were his own:

> *This slave*
> Unto this hour has my lord's meat in him.
> Why should it thrive and turn to nutriment,
> When he is turned to poison?
> (55–8; emphasis added)

Given the context of Timon's banquets as the sites of self-serving appetite, it is strikingly the servant who invokes the reciprocity that is supposed to inform the act of breaking bread together. His unflinching image of Timon's meat sitting in the man's bowels encapsulates the visceral poisoning of the spiritual dimensions of sharing a meal by focusing on the material grossness that will in due course also poison Timon's vision.

Equally careful stewards in the observance of their professions, both Flavius and Malvolio understand all too well the dangers of thoughtless

---

[36] See 5.1.70–3:

> PAINTER We are hither come to offer you our service.
> TIMON Most honest men. Why, how shall I requite you?
> Can you eat roots and drink cold water? No.
> POET AND PAINTER What we can do we'll do to do you service.

consumption and waste. Why, then, is Flavius a sympathetic figure but Malvolio is not? In part the reason should be sought in an ethical vision of the servant that is conservative insofar as it underscores the major precepts of the ideology of service. Yet it turns out to be radical insofar as it draws out the ethical implications of such conservative precepts. *Timon* pushes the concepts of dutiful service and boundless generosity to the point at which they turn into their opposites: Timon's reckless generosity is transformed into an equally thoughtless misanthropy, yet destitution and abandonment turn the steward's earnest but futile determination to curb his master's reckless hospitality into a peculiar kind of generosity. Flavius is a self-evidently "good" servant in his lack of self-regard or ambition and his complete devotion to his master and household. He seeks nothing more from his office than the satisfaction of service itself. In doing so, he may be thought to exemplify those "honest knaves" whom Edmund and Iago excoriate who, "doting on [their] own obsequious bondage, / Wear out [their] time much like his master's ass / For naught but provender, and when [they're] old, cashiered" (*Othello*, 1.1.45–7). He is not unaware of the dangers of wearing out his time. Like Adam in *As You Like It*, he wisely saves up for the day on which he will almost certainly be cashiered, but his private prudence is no sign of miserliness. It gives him the opportunity to share his savings with his fellow servants, carelessly abandoned by the negligent wastefulness of their master. The generosity and concern with which he takes upon himself his master's moral responsibilities can hardly be counted a "dotage" on obsequious bondage, however. Timon's irresponsibility may represent the radical failure of the "ideology of service", but the steward's moral agency represents an ethical commitment to his fellow servants that is scarcely encompassed by the political imaginations of the moralists of service.

In the desiccated moral landscape of *Timon*, the sight of the steward sharing his pension with the subordinates and fellows who remain in his charge provides a powerful corrective to both Timon and Apemantus's misanthropy. In Act 4, Scene 2, Flavius enters "with two or three servants".[37] Gradually, as they discuss their plight, the stage fills with servants, now held together only by bonds of companionship and duty that their master has abandoned. "Hear you, master steward, where's our master?" the First Servant asks, "Are we undone, cast off, nothing remaining?" (4.2.3). The aptly named "master" steward now assumes the responsibility that the

---

[37] This scene is thought to have been shared by Middleton and Shakespeare. See Vickers, *Co-Author*, 286.

self-obsessive master has forgotten. He establishes an empathetic bond with the gathering band of lower servants, first by affirming his own, unprivileged poverty, and then by encompassing them desolately as the "broken implements of a ruined house". That instrumentalising epithet is contradicted by the humanity and agency of the servants who reaffirm both their continued devotion to their forgetful master and their common bond of fellowship through the *affective* ties of service: "Yet do our hearts wear Timon's livery. / That see I by our faces" the Third Servant replies, "We are fellows still, / Serving alike in sorrow" (17–19).[38] Especially striking in a play that focuses so darkly upon the difficulties of seeing the "minds construction in the face" is the simple directness of the servant's declaration of transparent affection that arises from a shared condition. The First Servant can declare on behalf of his fellows that they wear Timon's livery in their hearts simply by what he sees in their faces. Flavius can see it too, and it prompts him to a further gesture of generosity. He offers to share the "latest" of his "wealth" with them (23):

> FLAVIUS   Good fellows all,
> The latest of my wealth I'll share amongst you.
> Wherever we shall meet, for Timon's sake
> Let's yet be fellows. Let's shake our heads and say,
> As 'twere a knell unto our master's fortunes,
> "We have seen better days."
> (*He gives them money*)
>   Let each take some.
> *Nay, put out all your hands.* Not one word more.
> Thus part we rich in sorrow, parting poor.
> (*They embrace, and the Servants part several ways*)
>   (22–9; emphasis added)

It is clear from the implicit stage direction that, in contrast to the leeches who hang upon and then drop from Timon, the abandoned and destitute servants hold back from accepting their "master steward's" gift. It is a strikingly poignant moment in an otherwise emotionally bleak play. It affirms companionship in sorrow, in contrast to Timon's self-imposed isolation. Most striking is the fact that they extend their sense of companionship to the master, for whom they continue to feel sympathy and loyalty,

---

[38] Note Gouge's insistence that the duty of service is intrinsic to the relationship; it does not depend upon the wealth of the master: "When masters are poore, meane, weake, aged, or otherwise impotent, then proud seruants are prone to despise them; which argueth a base minde, shewing that they respect their masters power more than his place: the poorest and weakest have the same authority over seruants, that the richest and strongest haue; all beare Gods image alike" (595).

despite the fact that he has abandoned them. The reality of their predicament is palpably embodied at the end of the scene when, after embracing, "they part several ways", each facing an uncertain condition of poverty and vagabondage.

The moral touchstone of the play is thus to be found in the affective bonds of service, which offer neither the ambitious fantasy of promotion nor the resentment of interminable bondage, but rather combine the continuity or constancy of devotion with the fellowship of empathy. The blindly indiscriminate nature of Timon's hatred is exposed by his failure to acknowledge the real bonds that tie him to his servants. Even at the height of his munificence towards his well-born "friends", Timon ignores the degree to which he is sustained by those who serve him.[39] His subsequent invective against all human relations and institutions is thus contradicted by the generosity with which his steward stands in for him and by his servants' willingness to interiorize his threadbare livery. Moreover, his incapacity to acknowledge the bonds of friendship in his servants rather than his peers is signalled by the curse that he pronounces upon service itself: "Bound servants, steal! / Large-handed robbers your grave masters are, / And pill by law" (*Timon*, 4.1.10–13). An isolated figure driving himself into the wilderness, like a self-afflicted Lear, Timon embodies the dissolution of the world in which "Th'unkindest beast more kinder [is] than mankind" (36). The servants' scene is a reminder of Timon's own forgetting – of his reckless unkindness towards those who have served him and depend upon him, and who continue to serve him because they "wear his livery in [their] hearts".

The curse of hospitality

The servant-polemicist I.M. attributes the decay of master-servant bonds and the deteriorating status of the gentleman-servant (who would have been exemplified in the figure of the household steward) to the decline of hospitality in the "good life" of a "proper house". The cashiering of Timon's servants, and their consequent destitution and displacement into vagabondage, is the result of an *excess* of hospitality. The crisis of hospitality, much noted by modern social historians and early modern writers, brings *Twelfth Night* and *Timon of Athens* together in preoccupation, if not in attitude, mood, or outcome.[40] If Malvolio and Flavius are united in their professional concern for the wastefulness of "riot" – conspicuous

---

[39] This is in contrast to Antony, who recognises the degree to which his identity and power have been constituted by those who serve him. See *Antony and Cleopatra*, 4.2.10–33.

[40] See Hutton, *Merry England*; Williams, *Country*; and Wrightson, *Earthly Necessities*.

consumption that cannot be maintained by the householder's estate – then the polemical "serving gentleman" reads the aristocratic open house as the outward sign of a well-ordered social life in which, although each knows his place, none of the deserving is unprovided for.[41]

> When Countrys causes did require
> Each Nobleman to keepe his house,
> Then Blewcoates had what they desire,
> Good cheare, with many a full carouse:
> But not now as it wont to be,
>   For dead is Liberalitie.
> [. . .]
> What Squire now but rackes his Rentes,
> And what he hath, who will give more?
> The giffe gaffe promise he repentes,
> The Lord hath neede, surcease therefore:
> Weepe, weepe, for now you well may see,
>   That dead is Liberalitie.

The death of "Liberalitie" means more than the loss of "Good cheare" and "many a full carouse". It attests to a cramping of spirit and community in which personal ostentation and social miserliness accompanied the racking of rents and the demise of annuities for deserving servants:

he that hath wherewith to maynteyne himselfe in very Gentlemanlike sort, with men about him for his credite, being descended of an ancient house and worthy parentage, burieth in obliuion his state and dignitie, and becomming a very seruile slaue, and thraull, to this donghyll drosse, his golde and money, leadeth his lyfe in most miserable maner. (127)

Compare Timon's steward on his master's boundless "liberalitie":

> FLAVIUS If you suspect my husbandry or falsehood,
>   Call me before th' exactest auditors
>   And set me on the proof. So the gods bless me,
>   When all our offices have been oppressed
>   With riotous feeders, when our vaults have wept
>   With drunken spilth of wine, when every room
>   Hath blazed with lights and brayed with minstrelsy,
>   I have retired me to a wasteful cock,
>   And set mine eyes at flow.
> TIMON Prithee, no more.   (2.2.152–60)

---

[41] Wrightson's comments are apposite: "This was not an idyllic traditional world. It knew conflict and self-interest well enough. But it was also a world which gave emphasis to the needs of the community as well as to those of individual households, and in which the restraining bonds of mutual obligation could powerfully influence the conduct of economic affairs" (*Earthly Necessities*, 86).

Shakespeare and Middleton's fictional steward is ultimately more interesting than the historical pronouncements of an actual gentleman servant with an axe to grind because the dialogical representation of the theatre can convey more acutely the complex dynamics of master-servant relationships under pressure. A prevalent anxiety about the trustworthiness of senior servants frames the steward's attempts to bring home to the head of the household that his proud refusal to accept the counsel of those who serve him has brought both master and those who depend upon him to ruin. At the same time, the steward's use of the first-person plural in his heartfelt description of rash expenditure means that he finds it impossible to detach his own affective investment in the "weeping" house from his master's condition. Timon's reckless consumption eats away at his steward's emotional investment in the household as a whole, the latter's sorrow being perfectly captured in the brilliant picture of the pouring spigot. The steward weeps in sympathy as the substance of the house drains away.

Timon cannot comprehend his steward's tears because he has a misguided faith in the necessary reciprocity that gifts imply: he equates hospitality with friendship and friendship with the natural reciprocity encompassed by the ethics of "guest-friendship" derived from Homeric Greece:

[T]he guest, having come under the protection of the scared hearth, and been assimilated to the family through the partaking of a meal, is bound to the host for the remainder of their lives. This bond is mutual: from henceforth each is bound to render hospitality to the other whenever required. (Percival, *Aristotle*, xvi)

Because Timon continues to believe in the inviolability of this bond, he cannot see that the tears he is questioning fall from the eyes of the only friend he has. Only in the figures of his servants does the sense of dutiful reciprocity underlying various forms of classical and feudal friendship continue to be nurtured. Flavius's servile defensiveness barely masks the censure appropriate to the friend rather than the flatterer.[42] His certainty of the precariousness of Timon's hold on those he would call his own shows itself in a rare outburst in which the servant turns the epithets usually used of disobedient or unreliable menials ("slaves and peasants") upon amoral nobility:

> FLAVIUS "Heavens," have I said, "the bounty of this lord!
> How many prodigal bits have slaves and peasants
> This night englutted! Who is not Timon's?
> What heart, head, sword, force, means, but is Lord Timon's?
> Great Timon, noble, worthy, royal Timon!
> Ah, when the means are gone that buy this praise,

---

[42] For a discussion of the literature on friend and flatterer, see Shannon, *Sovereign Amity*, 46–51.

> The breath is gone whereof this praise is made.
> Feast won, fast lost; one cloud of winter show'rs,
> These flies are couched."
> TIMON Come, sermon me no further.
> . . . Why dost thou weep? Canst thou the conscience lack
> To think I shall lack friends?   (60–73)

Representing his own opinions as reported speech ("Heavens," have I said . . .) allows Flavius to adopt a position of blame that might be thought incommensurable (if we follow writers such as Fosset and Dod and Cleaver, and Shakespeare himself in his "sad slave" sonnets) with his own menial position. Timon's initial impulse is magisterial annoyance at the temerity of his steward's "lecture", but that soon changes, once he is sure of his "fortunes", into an acknowledgement that the keeper of his household carries no blame for its dissolution: "Prithee, be not sad. / Thou art true and honest – ingenuously I speak – / No blame belongs to thee" (216–18).[43]

The servant's combination of censure, social inferiority, sadness, love, and anger at the ethical hollowness of a wayward master is expressed with special intensity in Shakespeare's sonnets, especially in the poems to the young man which "sermon" him for debasing himself to the "politic" love of parasites and flatterers who would "paint" him as he is not. Sonnet 69 is a barbed warning that making oneself common by cultivating false friends is the very thing that will destroy the "breath . . . whereof the praise is made" (*Timon*, 2.2.167). Related to *Timon*'s concern with the relationship or disjunction between monetary and moral worth and the presence of the poet and painter among his admirers, sonnet 81 takes up the recurrent thought expressed most succinctly in line 6 of sonnet 69 – "But those same toungs that giue thee so thine owne" – that praise is a parasitic transaction. It feeds off the very thing upon which it is ostensibly bestowing value:

> . . . what of thee thy Poet doth inuent,
> He robs thee of, and payes it thee againe,
> He lends thee vertue, and he stole that word,
> From thy behauiour, beautie doth he giue
> And found it in thy cheeke: he can afford
> No praise to thee, but what in thee doth liue.
>   Then thanke him not for that which he doth say,
>   Since what he owes thee, thou thy selfe doost pay,

Both poems insist that the failure of the protagonist to recognise that the economic asymmetry of the transactions involving praise denotes a bankruptcy of *moral* vision. Moral insight in each case is almost exclusively

---

[43] For a rehearsal of the fortunes of a steward who was found to have been dishonest or negligent, see Webster, *The Duchess of Malfi*, 3.2.

the preserve of the servant. Reading *Timon* and the sonnets together shows that what appears to be merely metaphorical in one carries over into the literalness of the other, and vice versa. The metaphorical, affective transactions of praise are twinned with material desire, whereas the material conditions of the relationships in the play carry a moral and affective burden.

"Men of worth"

It is a commonplace that Timon is unable to see the degree to which what he calls love and friendship are no more than a social veneer that barely covers naked cupidity: a man's "worth" is in fact reducible to his wealth or poverty. It is also a commonplace that Timon's failure lies in his incapacity to distinguish between true friendship and reckless generosity. He assumes that his stake in the hearts of those who have fed upon him is as assured as his power over his servants:

> If I would broach the vessels of my love
> And try the argument of hearts by borrowing,
> Men and men's fortunes could I frankly use
> As I can bid thee speak.   (2.2.174–7)

Much as it is tempting to separate material and moral worth, both Flavius's tears at the consumption of the estate and the steward's generosity towards the lower servants suggest that they cannot be completely divorced within the household economy of early modern England. Part of I.M.'s motive for decrying the decline of hospitality lies in his perception that miserliness of spirit and miserliness of pocket go hand in hand, and, complementarily, that ostentatious expenditure on the trappings of status attest to a wasteful selfishness that is contrary to the maintenance of the community of traditional good cheer: "Where are the great Chines of staulled Beefe? the great blacke Jackes of doble Beere, the long Haull tables fully furnished with good victuals, and the multitude of good fellowes assembling to the houses of Potentates and men of worth?" (I.M., *Health*, 50). The striking double sense of "men of worth" invokes *Timon*, suggesting that the two senses of worth (like the two meanings of "dear") are not easily kept apart.

Throughout Shakespeare's work commercial bonds are interwoven with those of affection or affiliation, so that it becomes impossible to tell where the one begins and the other ends or to tease out the literal from the supposedly metaphorical meanings in a key word or image.[44] One of the reasons for

---

[44] See Greene, "Pitiful Thrivers". For a more general account of the place of the market in Shakespeare's thought, see Engle, *Pragmatism*.

the despair that finds expression in I.M.'s conservative nostalgia is that the freer circulation of cash abrogates the affective bonds that were previously thought to tie people together. A cash relation replaces what was permanent with what is temporary, what was closely affective with emotional distance, and it encourages circulation – the displacement of one value for another in an economy of indifference – instead of the settlement of love, loyalty, and custom. It is no coincidence that the informers and murderers whom Evett incisively calls Shakespeare's "tool villains" are engaged, often ostentatiously, with cash (Evett, *Discourses*, 31). In direct contrast, when Cesario refuses Olivia's offer of cash, saying "I am no fee'd post, lady", she is rejecting the corrosion of loyalty and fleeting affinity that cash represents. Yet her own enterprise depends entirely upon the availability of ready cash after her shipwreck. She engages the captain and buys his silent service by promising to "pay [him] bounteously" (*Twelfth Night*, 1.2.48).

In short, then, the problem is not so much that a form of spiritual value is displaced, through semantic contamination, by a purely material one. Rather, a particular kind of value that takes material form – cash – drives a wedge between the material and the spiritual that could be held together in more traditional notions of a man's "worth". This is because cash, like language, does its work only where and in the manner in which it is used. I.M.'s attempt to keep apart the ideals of the "Golden days" from the corrosive effects of gold itself calls attention to the relationship between the literal and metaphorical senses of the word: "To compare the pleasures of their *Golden* dayes, when *Gold* was so smally regarded, with the miserie of this latter, nay last age, were able in my iudgement, to wring teares out of the eyes of Adamant" (146; my emphasis). When the flowing wine wrings tears from Flavius's eyes the steward is weeping for the seeping away of his master's "worth" in both senses. His tears fall in equal measure for the material waste of a great house and its demise as a centre of social and moral community. The two go together. Timon's scorn for gold at the end of the play does not recover "Golden dayes, when Gold was . . . smally regarded" but rather betrays his incapacity to see the subtlety of this imbrication and to recognize the performative dynamics of money. That failure is present at the very beginning, when he cannot see that his (ab)use of his wealth cannot guarantee reciprocal friendship. When Timon exclaims, "I am wealthy in my friends" (2.2.181), the claim to wealth hovers uncertainly between a metaphorical sense of the treasures of friendship (as the classical literature would understand it) and a belief that his friends are no more than the repositories of his assets, to be "use[d] . . . toward a supply of money" (188) when the time calls.

Keeping this in mind allows us to cast some retrospective light on the role of "riot" in *Twelfth Night*. We know (although many commentators are apt to forget it) that without the care of her steward, Olivia's "worth" is likely to be wasted by her parasitical uncle, Sir Toby Belch, and his hangers-on. Yet the play stacks the cards against its steward in favour of the wastrel knight. There are two obvious reasons for our affective engagement and distance, respectively: one is the fact that Toby and his band appear to be much less of a threat to the material security of Olivia's household than the misguided profligacy of Timon to his, including his servants. The other is that their revelry is not self-consciously staged as a means to social ends, as Timon's and his parasites' are, but rather erupts as a spontaneous *joie de vivre*. The fact that it occurs below the stairs rather than in the banqueting hall gives it a comic, carnivalesque legitimacy, as if I.M.'s "great Chines of staulled Beefe . . . the great blacke Jackes of doble Beere . . . and the multitude of good fellowes assembling" (150) could be recovered by the community of serving-men alone. It represents, in short, "the spirit of the Butterie" that had been "banyshed" (151), if I.M. is to be believed, with the demise of the profession of the serving-man and hospitality in general. Add to that our sense that Malvolio objects to the enjoyment of "cakes and ale" owing to his spiritual desiccation as much as his responsible devotion to his stewardship, and the play's infectious recreation of festive holiday, and our affective preferences are easily accounted for.

Yet it is part of the greatness of *Twelfth Night* that it doesn't banish entirely the spirit of *Timon of Athens*. (It may be part of the smallness of *Timon* that its revelry is much less expansive than *Twelfth Night*'s.) The persistent place of Feste – a humanely attenuated Apemantus, capable of being touched, unlike his Cynical counterpart, by the weaknesses of the human heart – ensures that we do not lapse entirely into sentimentality. He is more acutely aware than Malvolio of the costs of human desire. He is also attuned to the pain of such cost, even if he is impervious to the sentimentality that often accompanies it. The complex spirit of "riot" and its relation to the heart (rather than to the pocket, stomach, or eye) are apparent in the interplay of bittersweet nostalgia and reckless abandon in the great scene which pits Sir Toby against Malvolio, where "a love-song" and "a song of good life" are ironically offered as mutually exclusive choices:

> FESTE Would you have a love-song, or a song of good life?
> SIR TOBY A love song, a love-song.
> SIR ANDREW Ay, ay. I care not for good life. (2.3.34–7)

What Feste's "love-song" impresses upon Toby (and more so upon Maria, if we take our cue from Trevor Nunn's recent film) is the burden of incipient loss in the midst of festivity. If "in delay there lies no plenty", Toby calls for "present laughter" precisely to forget or dispel, under the show of "riot", the economy of dearth that barely sustains his "present mirth" (2.3.34–58). That sense of loss is sharpened by Sir Andrew Aguecheek, who has been lured through his desire to be loved into a trap: he is the food upon which "present mirth", in the form of Toby's carnivalesque body, feeds. It is easy to take Toby's red-blooded declaration as a claim to be "on the side of life" rather than death, but there is something peculiarly deathly in Toby's living – especially in its modes of friendship. Toby's contempt for mourning in his apparently sensible declaration, "What a plague means my niece to take the death of her brother thus? I am sure care's an enemy to life" (1.2.1–2), betrays a concomitant incapacity for friendship.

If cash threatens the world of settled reciprocity (it depends, of course, on reciprocity of a different kind) which is represented in an attenuated, nostalgic form in Toby Belch's dependence upon Olivia, and Maria's upon both of them, its liberating potential is encapsulated by the figure who bears the greatest resemblance to Shakespeare as servant-player (rather than as poet-lover): the Fool. In contrast to Viola's aristocratic refusal to be contaminated by a "fee", Feste allows no opportunity to pass without begging such a fee, often touching, goading, or amusing his benefactors into paying him twice or thrice over. Such ready, even promiscuous, reliance on cash from any and every source gives him an independence that other servants lack. It loosens the ties that would bind him to an affective loyalty of dependency upon any single person or household. Nominally part of Olivia's household, he circulates with ease, like the money he begs. That ease is displayed in a self-expressive, detached (im)pertinence that is the mark of the growing independence of the theatrical joint-stock company, which relied for its commercial viability upon the circulation of disposable income and the power of accumulated capital.[45] What is striking is the absence of such a player-like figure in *Timon of Athens*, and it is the absence of the independent, self-expressive bravura of the player-servant that gives *Timon* its peculiarly troubling quality. It is generally accepted that the greater proportion of the servant scenes was written by Middleton. They are certainly wrenching in their depiction of the vulnerability and moral rectitude of servants,

---

[45] See Ingram, *Playing*, and Lamb, "Heterosexual Erotics".

but they miss the opportunity for self-expressive show that is characteristic of almost all servants in Shakespeare.[46]

"*He's caught me in his eye*": *the gift of acknowledgement*

Having witnessed the singular failure to recognize reciprocal obligation in all of Timon's so-called friends, let us return to the steward, Flavius, whose ethics of service encompass a form of loving devotion that combines the intensity of *eros* and the devotion of *nomos*. One feels that for all their protestations of abjection, sonnets 26, 57, and 58 are in fact rehearsals for the demand (stated in 125) for complete reciprocity within a *Timon*-like society, in which profit and loss are distributed arbitrarily and unevenly under the cover of friendship, rather than in its true name. The "mutual render" demanded in the poem is fairly conventional, even if its combination of same-sex *eros* and *philia* is not. Conceptually and ethically, an erotic mutuality seeks to derive itself from the initiating reciprocity of obligation and care that marks master-servant relationships. In an echo of Montaigne, the bridge from one to the other is shown to rest on the performative production of equality through free choice: the "oblacion" offered in a continued gesture of service transforms itself into a demand for mutuality by being "poor but free". The dutiful, subservient reciprocity central to social theories of service is thus sublated into the free, but crucially mutual, exchange of love.

We have seen that the steward's selfless care and generosity towards those whom his master has discarded offers an ethical example against which the master himself may be judged. Flavius's own view of his relationship with Timon does not encompass such judgement, however. His generosity towards the servants who were once in his charge indicates that he is himself capable of playing the part of the master. As a servant, however, he demands nothing of the master except to be allowed to continue to serve him:

> My dearest lord ... Alas, kind lord!
> [...]
> I'll follow and enquire him out.
> I'll ever serve his mind with my best will.
> Whilst I have gold I'll be his steward still.
> (42–51)

The repeated vocatives of affection and pity attest to a deeply emotional devotion in the abandoned servant that cannot be accounted for in

---

[46] See Vickers, *Co-Author*, chapter 4.

structural or materialist terms. It goes beyond even Evett's timely corrective that service offered its own rewards. Flavius's pronouncements are the
declarations of *love*. It is not merely the office of service that provides its
own reward: it is the continued affective bond with the master that has
an erotic intensity, even if it is devoid of sexual longing. This is love of a
peculiar and difficult kind, conveyed in a language full of internal tensions,
and it cannot be reduced to any simple conception of political materiality.
Moreover, the position of selfless service is conveyed in language of the
surest agency. The servant achieves his state of greatest autonomy when
he is most destitute. Being at last his *own* man, he nevertheless seeks to
reinstate himself as his master's man. Unlike the twins of *The Comedy of
Errors* or the divergent bondsman and slave of *The Tempest*, Flavius can
now *choose* service, heedless of any expectation of reward.[47]

Contrary to the provisions of the Statute of Artificers, which granted
manumission to servants who had accumulated a fixed amount of property
or money, Flavius does not treat his savings as a means to gain independence
from his master.[48] Rather, he tries to reinstate himself as his master's man,
in a gesture reminiscent of Kent's dogged rededication to Lear. As it does
in *King Lear*, the confrontation between master and servant recalls Stanley
Cavell's transformative discussion of the ethics of acknowledgement:

> FLAVIUS   *He's caught me in his eye.* I will present
>   My honest grief unto him, and as my lord
>   Still serve him with my life. – My dearest master.
> TIMON Away! What art thou?
> FLAVIUS   Have you forgot me, sir?
> TIMON Why dost ask that? I have forgot all men;
>   Then if thou grant'st thou'rt man, I have forgot thee.
> FLAVIUS An honest poor servant of yours.
> TIMON Then I know thee not. I never had
>   Honest man about me; ay, all I kept were knaves,
>   To serve in meat to villains.
> FLAVIUS   The gods are witness,
>   Ne'er did poor steward wear a truer grief
>   For his undone lord than mine eyes for you.
>   (*Timon*, 4.3.471–82; emphasis added)

---

[47] I am here underwriting the central, powerful argument of Evett's book via a play which does not
form part of his analysis.

[48] We are not told how much money Flavius has managed to save, but it may have been enough to
have secured his independence from service in terms of the Statute of Artificers, as Adam's is in
As You Like It. The point is worth making to defend him against the argument that he is merely
ingratiating himself with his old master, although there are a number of imponderables, not least of
which is the fact that the Statute did not apply in ancient Athens.

Cavell shows that the contradictory desire for acknowledgement and the incapacity to bear that desire informs Lear's relation to both his family and his subjects.[49] Both that need and aversion are repeated here in a different key, as the servant seeks the recognition of a master who has placed himself beyond acknowledgement, but *who could himself be rescued* through the recognition (as both subject and object) of his servant. This scene therefore enacts not merely the possible affirmation of identity – a ubiquitous preoccupation in criticism and theory – but the recognition of *humanity*. What Flavius seeks above all is to be "caught in the eye" – to be acknowledged fully in the master's gaze. This is the expectation, rehearsed in sonnet 24, of recognition as the reflection of the self in the eye of the other. Instead, Timon sees him but refuses to acknowledge his ties to him. This refusal is grounded on the master's general disparagement of all humanity, including his own. More specifically it shows itself in the reduction of all servants to "knaves", good only for feeding "villains". The punning collapse of social rank in the running together of these two terms occludes the singular status or quality of the servants throughout the play, who offer repeated, embodied correctives to Timon's general cynicism.

When it comes, Timon's recognition of Flavius and his acknowledgement of his steward as a solitary instance of human goodness appears too glib (especially in the context of the extraordinarily complexity of the scenes of attempted recognition in *King Lear*), even sentimental, to be entirely convincing:

> FLAVIUS I beg of you to know me, good my lord,
>   T' accept my grief,
>   (*He offers his money*) and whilst this poor wealth lasts
>   To entertain me as your steward still.
> TIMON Had I a steward
>   So true, so just, and now so comfortable?
>   It almost turns my dangerous nature mild.
>   Let me behold thy face.
>   . . . I do proclaim
>   One honest man – mistake me not, but one,
>   No more, I pray – and he's a steward.
>   How fain would I have hated all mankind,
>   And thou redeem'st thyself!   (4.3.488–501)

Unlike Feste's emancipated beggary or Malvolio's self-regarding desire, Flavius asks to be acknowledged as more than the giver of a gift, because the very process of giving has been hollowed out by Timon's own practice. "I beg of you to know me . . . T' accept my grief". This plea to be "known" is a request to be recognized as a servant and fellow in suffering: it is a plea for his *grief for the master* to be acknowledged by the master. That grief is a gift of a kind, but it does not follow the logic of exchange. One grieves with or for others, through a shared humanity, in the solidarity of friendship. Nothing is expected in return except the acceptance of one's grief. The steward's offer of gold alongside his grief, however, seems to be an appalling lapse of judgment. It arouses the master's suspicion that his steward offers gold merely to initiate a further series of exchanges and obligations: the result of a "usuring kindness . . . as rich men deal gifts" (510). How would the steward convince his master that he offers this gift outside the economy of exchange, in a spirit that is "poor but free"?

Ken Jackson sees his response as a sign that Flavius has transcended the normal condition of gift giving, which usually places a reciprocal obligation to return the gift to the giver in some commensurate form. The steward's gesture embodies a gift that exists beyond "exchange": "Timon . . . discovers . . . a pure obligation or ethics towards the other, one not grounded in any economy of exchange but grounded on itself alone:"[50]

> FLAVIUS That which I show, heaven knows, is merely love,
>   Duty and zeal to your unmatchèd mind,
>   Care of your food and living; and, believe it,
>   My most honoured lord,
>   For any benefit that points to me,   .
>   Either in hope or present, I'd exchange
>   For this one wish: that you had power and wealth
>   To requite me by making rich yourself.

Timon may finally be sufficiently persuaded of the purity of his steward's motives to declare him a "singly honest man" and to register a self-damning surprise that such unique honesty should be embodied by a servant, but he fails to respond to him or *acknowledge* him, in the sense that Cavell has made so compelling.[51] Rather than evade the economy of exchange (as Flavius does), Timon fiercely engages it in an attempt both to avoid or negate the singularity of Flavius's gift and to transform his steward into a clone of his misanthropic self:

> TIMON Look thee, 'tis so. Thou singly honest man,
>   (*He gives* FLAVIUS *gold*)
>   Here, take. The gods, out of my misery,

---

[50] Jackson, "One Wish", 65. For the philosophical context of Jackson's argument, see Derrida, *Given Time*, and Mauss, *The Gift*.

[51] See Cavell, *Disowning Knowledge*, chapter 2.

> Has sent thee treasure. Go, live rich and happy,
> But thus conditioned: thou shalt build from men,
> Hate all, curse all, show charity to none,
> But let the famished flesh slide from the bone
> Ere thou relieve the beggar.   (507–13)

The gold that the *servant* offers the master is transformed into "something rich and strange" by both the steward's affective investment in the relationship and the role that such gold plays in the lives of abandoned servants. Yet Timon negates the servant's genuine gift of *himself* by (re)turning it into (or as) more gold. That gold is now a form of poison, like Timon's meat sitting in the guts of Lucullus. The gift is not merely rendered valueless; it constitutes a *rejection* of Falvius's love. A gift in which one has nothing invested and so has nothing to lose is no more than a simulacrum. What Flavius receives from Timon in exchange for the gift of himself – "merely love" (507) – is the curse that he subsequently bestows upon whores and killers. Timon's bestowal of gold upon his servant is in effect an act of manumission. If we look at it in the context of Cesario/Viola's "quittance" by her master, it is at once apparent that manumission is the last thing he desires. Like Viola, the steward seeks to be allowed to continue serving the master in love, not turned away into a solitary world.

Beyond reciprocity

The steward's offer puts into ethical perspective all the gifts in which Timon has been engaged before this moment. If we recall Shakespeare's representation, in sonnet 125, of a similar attempt to avoid the economy of "pitiful thrivors" echoed in the halls of Timon's villa, it is striking that Flavius does not desire even the "mutual render" that the servant-poet seeks from his master. The steward does not plead for reciprocity, he begs merely to be accepted as a servant. This curiously echoes the selfless ideal of *eros* in unrequited love but is closest to *nomos*. The master need do no more than accept the offer of service to have reciprocated – to bestow the grace or *āgape* of acknowledgement. When Timon concedes that his servant has indeed redeemed himself, that recognition does not, however, encompass an acknowledgement of his *own* humanity. By failing to acknowledge his servant – by refusing to accept his love – the master fails to redeem himself. One way in which Timon could be saved would be by acknowledging the human dynamics of service as love and love as service. The steward is thus superficially rewarded, but the reward itself is a sign that he remains unacknowledged. Like Antonio in his desire to be allowed to be Sebastian's servant, where the purse of gold serves a similar function as a gift rather than an exchange, Flavius wants no more than to be *permitted* to "stay" and "comfort" his "master". That failure of acknowledgement dooms the master.

The end of the master

What "will or testament", what "performance" (5.1.26–7), is left for the protagonist at the end of the play, once he has sent poet and painter packing, heaped gold and scorn in equal measure upon the women accompanying Alcibiades in the voice of the sonnets to the dark woman, and financed the general's sack of Athens in a speech that makes Henry V's oration before the battle of Harfleur seem benign? The answer lies in the paradoxical work of the poet. Despite the clear affinities between the subject-position that many of the sonnets adopt and those of the abject or loving servant, abjectness is not the sonnets' only stance. Just as we can hear Malvolio's voice in the sonnets, they also bear some of the accents of the later Timon.

Critics and editors have found it puzzling that Timon is able to write his own epitaph, simultaneously proclaiming his name and expressing the desire to be forgotten. Still more impossibly, he inscribes the epitaph upon a tombstone, buries himself, and manages to erect the tombstone on his own grave:

> Here lies a wretched corpse,
> Of wretched soul bereft.
> Seek not my name. A plague consume
> You wicked caitiffs left!
> Here lie I, Timon, who alive
> All living men did hate.
> Pass by and curse thy fill, but pass
> And stay not here thy gait.   (5.5.71–8)

Does some servant perform these rites in secret? Does Flavius sneak back, despite being dismissed, to perform this last, dutiful service as the consummating act of his devotion – a gift that again evades the necessity of exchange? It would be easy enough in a performance of the play to insert such a dumb-show between 5.3 and 5.4. It would certainly be in the spirit of the play's view of the redeeming virtue of loving service.

If we take the role that Shakespeare tried to carve out for the poet in a position of service seriously – as the representative of a certain kind of reciprocating love and duty, certainly, but also as the correcting voice of moral outrage that Timon's steward never quite brings himself to adopt and as the figure who promises to ensure that his beloved master will live eternally in men's eyes through the power and longevity of his verse, while simultaneously consigning his own name to oblivion – then we can see that the paradox of Timon's end is not simply the result of an improperly finished play. Here is sonnet 81, about death, forgetting, and the making of epitaphs:

> OR I shall liue your Epitaph to make,
> Or you suruiue when I in earth am rotten,
> From hence your memory death cannot take,
> Although in me each part will be forgotten.
> Your name from hence immortall life shall haue,
> Though I (once gone) to all the world must dye,
> The earth can yeeld me but a common graue,
> When you intombed in mens eyes shall lye,
> Your monument shall be my gentle verse,
> Which eyes not yet created shall ore-read,
> And toungs to be, your beeing shall rehearse,
> When all the breathers of this world are dead,
> You still shall liue (such vertue hath my Pen)
> Where breath most breaths, euen in the mouths of men.

This poem is the "gentle" counterpart of sonnet 126. Whereas the later sonnet chillingly calculates and then insists upon Nature's final reckoning, this one attempts to mitigate the inevitability of that account by suggesting that the servant-poet will pay that debt in the master's stead, twice over: by giving up his own name in the place of the master and by providing the latter's monument. The master's "being" will be "rehearsed" through the obliteration of the servant-poet – "Although in me each part will be forgotten. / Your name from hence immortall life shall haue, / Though I (once gone) to all the world must dye". This negating substitution is, as we have seen, the archetypal role of the servant, and it is repeatedly rehearsed in *Timon of Athens*. Yet as texts that have moved beyond their original contexts of address and promise, Shakespeare's sonnets attest to the opposite process: here the epitaph, which was supposed to bury his own name, serves only to pronounce it over and over again, and to induce wonder at the fecundity of his living "breath".[52]

I ended the section on *Twelfth Night* by suggesting that, contrary to the promise of "gentle verse" contained in this sonnet, Shakespeare's final poem to the young man is a sort of revenge – a curse, in the form of an anticipatory epitaph, that warns him of the debt that he owes to Nature.

---

[52] Note the repetition of that name in the Quarto running-head: "SHAKE-SPEARES SONNETS".

That Shakespeare was (inevitably) right about that debt should not detract from our sense of his rightness about the power of the steward of that death – in the name of the writer of the epitaph. It is the servant's plight always to be forgotten, to bury himself in his master's need, to be the overlooked agent of the (im)possibility of the gift. However, his place in the *story* can also, under certain circumstances, displace that of the master. Within a context in which the emergence of a market economy threatened the fabric of social relations, the view that selfless service is the only ethically admirable position may seem hopelessly conservative. There may have been more politically acute or prescient positions available to Shakespeare and Middleton, but it is difficult to see how an ethical position could have been developed that did not involve the quest for acknowledgement in service exemplified by Timon's steward. Malvolio's individualism may, as Lamb claims, threaten to "hollow out" the ideology of service. Flavius's loyalty, however, closer to Viola in intensity of affect than that of the steward in *Twelfth Night*, offers a signal reaffirmation that, in a world in which human bonds are mere simulacra, service chosen from a position of real, and not merely imagined, freedom may be the only positive form of ethical agency.

CHAPTER 5

"Office and devotion"

Henry IV Parts 1 and 2, the Sonnets, and *Antony and Cleopatra*

In the English history plays that are the subject of this chapter, the conjunction of love and erotic notions of service are severely attenuated: sexual service is now almost exclusively confined to the brothel. The relationship of companionship and service is both broadened and sharpened, however, especially in the context of warfare, rebellion, and the politics of state. This might appear to remove it from the ambit of the sonnets, but in the two parts of *Henry IV*, those poems' anxiety concerning the contaminating effects on nobility of its nonmagisterial contact with commoners is given a special place. The poet's charge that the nobly born young friend "dost common grow" is redoubled in the figure of Hall amongst the roisterers of Eastcheap, and especially in the troubled friendship between the old Vice Falstaff and his "sweet wag", the Prince of Wales.

HENRY IV PARTS 1 AND 2

The role of performance also takes on a more subtle, less overtly metatheatrical role in these plays. It is shifted to the possibilities and limitations available to masters and servants *within* the world of the play. In the figure of Falstaff the world itself becomes the medium of performance or play, as the fat knight mobilises the histrionic possibilities of war and tavern alike to evade the consistency upon which responsibility and accountability depend. The interaction of *locus* and *platea* becomes more flexible. At one level, the Eastcheap tavern is the *platea* to the *locus* of broader civil strife, commenting upon the actions and motives of the contending masters and servants of the main plot. At another level, the tavern is itself split between the *virtual* potentialities of *locus* and *platea*. In this more confined relationship, the master unconventionally undermines the ambitions of the servant, especially the servant's capacity as master. In both of these plays, and especially in the second, the master unconventionally occupies the *platea* to the servant's *locus*: Prince Hal almost always exposes the player

Falstaff to deflation and ridicule. At the same time, however, the role chosen by the apprentice king turns out to constrain his actions and relationships in ways to which his declaration of superior confidence – "I know you all . . . " – proves to be blind.

In addition to the general preoccupation with service and love as constitutive of a general political bond between members of the nobility and the ruling family, the two *Henry IV* plays offer a sustained *realistic* representation, sometimes parodic, of service as it might have touched the drawer or ostler, the apprentice or lowly steward, the minor military officer or the unfortunate conscript, not to speak of the more nebulous, ungoverned "services" of the tavern or the brothel and the more settled reciprocities of rural Gloucestershire. Nowhere else in Shakespeare do we catch such striking glimpses of service and its subversion as they might have touched contemporary life in town and country. In addition to its depiction of the precarious bonds of service between a king whose legitimacy is in question and the nobility that helped him to the throne and the ordinary lives of drawer and steward, the plays offer an exceptionally piercing account of the more directly derived forms of feudal allegiance and duty, in the form of military service. Such representations of service, always inflected with degrees of rebellion and precariousness, offer a powerful counter-variation on the grander themes of political legitimacy and discontent.

Apprenticeship and countenancing

Two scenes, from *1 Henry IV* and *2 Henry IV*, respectively, offer a perspective on affective forms of investment in service.

In the first, having shown off his own protean, player-like capacity for absorbing the discourse and manners of "a leash of drawers", Hal devises a practical joke that will expose the dull narrowness of one Francis, "an underskinker, one that never spake other English in his life than 'eight shillings and sixpence', and 'You are welcome', with this addition, 'Anon, anon, sir! Score a pint of bastard in the Half-moon!' or so" (*1 Henry IV*, 2.5.20–4). The joke appears to be harmless if somewhat puerile fun. Hal engages Francis in conversation, while Poins calls him incessantly from the next room, "so that his tale to [the prince] may be nothing but 'Anon!'" (28). It is the substance of the conversation, if such it is, that is significant. For Hall interrogates Francis on the point of his service – how long he has to serve, and by implication, how much of his indenture he still has to suffer, and most significantly, whether he is brave enough to break trust with his master and "be so valiant as to play the coward with [his] indenture,

and show it a fair pair of heels, and run from it?" (*1 Henry IV*, 2.5.40–2).
Tantalized by his royal interlocutor, the increasingly flustered and lacklustre
apprentice only half grasps Hal's riddling suggestion that servile devotion
to the landlord holds no future or reward – that failure to "rob this leather-
jerkin, crystal-button knot-pated, puke-stocking, caddis-garter, smooth-
tongue, Spanish-pouch" (65–7) – the master-landlord – will condemn him
to a life both inexorably dull and mean.[1]

The cruelty of the joke lies in the way in which Hal tortures the young
man with the suggested promise of release, for he sets up the prank so
that his immediate, servile obligations (to the calls from the customers in
the other room) clash with his self-interested conversation with a prince
who promises much but delivers little. The broader thematic or ideological
significance of the joke lies in the indifference with which the wayward royal
apprentice entices a future subject to throw off his burden of settled bonds
and then abandons him to his bondage.[2] Against Hal's easy manipulation of
his subject and the literally bewildering range and facility of his language,
we are invited with Poins to laugh at Francis's inarticulacy and pathetic
hopes for manumission or at least promotion into the service of the heir-
apparent. What is most striking is the way in which the prince shows up
the fixed or settled role of the apprentice against his own apparently more
free-ranging, histrionic ability to assume any role at whim. Both are subject
to future expectation and uncertainty, encapsulated by the repeated call,
"Anon", and their respective capacities to fulfil such expectation and control
its uncertainty in the scene in question diverge radically. Yet we shall see
when we consider the emotional and ethical options available to Hal as royal
apprentice that his options are less in his control than they appear to be.

Here is another scene, from the second play:

> (*Enter* DAVY)
> DAVY Here, sir.
> SHALLOW Davy, Davy, Davy; let me see, Davy; let me see. William
>   Cook – bid him come hither. – Sir John, you shall not be excused.
> DAVY Marry, sir, thus: those precepts cannot be served.
>   And again, sir: shall we sow the headland with wheat?
> SHALLOW With red wheat, Davy. But for William Cook; are there no
>   young pigeons?
> DAVY Yes, sir. Here is now the smith's note for shoeing and
>   plough-irons.

---

[1] The Norton Shakespeare suggests in a note that Hal imagines "this employer in the manner of an
upwardly mobile Londoner" (*Histories*, 583).

[2] Hugh Grady reads the scene as an allegory of the conflicting demands that are being made upon the
Prince himself, by the exercise of free subjectivity in the tavern and the reified role of Machiavellian
power that is expected of him as Prince of Wales. See Grady, *Machiavelli*, 165.

SHALLOW Let it be cast and paid. Sir John, you shall not be excused.
DAVY Sir, a new link to the bucket must needs be had; and, sir, do you
    mean to stop any of William's wages, about the sack he lost at
    Hinkley Fair?
SHALLOW A shall answer it. Some pigeons, Davy, a couple of
    short-legged hens, a joint of mutton, and any pretty little tiny
    kickshaws, tell William Cook.
DAVY Doth the man of war stay all night, sir?
SHALLOW Yea, Davy. I will use him well; a friend i' th' court is better
    than a penny in purse. Use his men well, Davy, for they are arrant
    knaves, and will backbite.
DAVY No worse than they are back-bitten, sir, for they have marvellous
    foul linen.
SHALLOW Well conceited, Davy. About thy business, Davy.

                             (2 *Henry IV*, 5.1.7–29)

Coming just before the death of the old king and the succession of his heir
in a time of extreme uncertainty (and expectation), this exchange mixes the
settled, day-to-day business between esquire and his dutiful steward with a
more precarious desire for social mobility. In its easy speech rhythms and
shared purview, it conveys a relationship of considerable stability within
a settled cycle of rural life. Why is it here? Incidental to the plot, the
dialogue affords us a glimpse of an established relationship that emphasizes
the reciprocity of mutual support, care, and responsibility of service in the
ideal. However, in the reference to William Cook's loss of wages, it also
reminds us of the precariousness of ordinary service. The sense of reciprocal
obligation is given depth but is also somewhat darkened by the exchange
that follows Shallow's conventional instructions to his steward about the
day-to-day running of the household, when Davy asks the justice to take
the part of his friend, William Visor, in an up-coming case:

SHALLOW There is many complaints, Davy, against that Visor.
    That Visor is an arrant knave, on my knowledge.
SHALLOW I grant your worship that he is a knave, sir; but yet God
    forbid, sir, but a knave should have some countenance at his
    friend's request. An honest man, sir, is able to speak for
    himself, when a knave is not. I have served your worship truly,
    sir, this eight years. An I cannot once or twice in a quarter bear
    out a knave against an honest man, I have little credit with
    your worship. The knave is mine honest friend, sir; therefore I
    beseech you let him be countenanced.
SHALLOW Go to; I say he shall have no wrong. Look about, Davy.

                             (34–46)

Invoking equally the bonds of friendship and service, Davy asks a favour on behalf of a friend, countering his master's objection to the questionable honesty of the man with a reminder of his own honest devotion: "I have served your lordship truly, sir, this eight years". This is what Weil underscores as "countenancing" or "accommodation": the protection or support, often beyond questions of desert, that a master or patron would afford a servant.[3] It reaches its apotheosis in Falstaff's fantasy of being given the laws of England at his "commandment", and is enacted by Hal's protecting his fat friend from the reach of the Sheriff in *1 Henry IV* 2.5 and his countenancing of the knight's claim to have killed Hotspur.

The loyal servant's calling in of debts raises moral and political questions of considerable complexity that resonate throughout the Henriad. Against Hal's truant dalliance with the selfish desires of a young city apprentice, this scene tells a tale of settled rural obligation and trust. However, it also recalls, in Shallow's anxious instructions that extensive hospitality be extended to Falstaff and his crew, the blatant self-interest of the middle-ranking Justice of the Peace.[4] This simple scene encapsulates ordinary relations of servant obedience and magisterial care, but it also points to more self-serving, less honest motives that may inform such relationships. It does so not as a bit of comic relief or mere illustration of broader political issues, but in its own right. Moral judgment is, however, carefully withheld. We can both sympathize with Davy for feeling that his loyal service to the justice entitles him to ask the occasional favour of his master on behalf of his friends and equally recognize the potential for social abuse that the accession to that request implies. It is in fact Falstaff who offers judgement on the scene, revealing his own cynical readiness to feed off the minor official's eagerness to ingratiate himself with someone who, he believes, will carry influence in court. Falstaff's contempt for Shallow is expressed as a disdain for the mindset of the justice, reduced to the mentality of a "servingman" by his closeness to his servants:

It is a wonderful thing to see the semblable coherence of his men's spirits and his. They, by observing him, do bear themselves like foolish justices; he, by conversing

---

[3] Weil, *Dependency*, 80 passim.

[4]   DAVY Doth the man of war stay all night, sir?
          SHALLOW Yea, Davy. I will use him well; a friend i' th'
                      court is better than a penny in purse. Use his men well,
                      Davy, for they are arrant knaves, and will backbite.
                                      (*2 Henry IV*, 5.1.25–8)

As a Justice of the Peace, Shallow would have been a key figure in enforcing the law covering masters and servants. The Statute stipulated Justices as the officers who set servants' wages and adjudicated complaints from masters and servants. See Hay and Craven, *Masters*, 5ff.

with them, is turned into a justice-like servingman. Their spirits are so married in conjunction, with the participation of society, that they flock together in consent like so many wild geese. If I had a suit to Master Shallow, I would humour his men with the imputation of being near their master; if to his men, I would curry with Master Shallow that no man could better command his servants. It is certain that either wise bearing or ignorant carriage is caught as men take diseases, one of another; therefore let men take heed of their company. (5.1.54–66)

Apart from the obviously ironical application of the final warning to his own relationship with the heir apparent, Falstaff offers a characteristically Janus-like observation on social institutions. On the one hand, we might recoil from his failure to recognise healthy, affective bonds of reciprocity in the closeness of master and man; on the other, precisely such affective ties render the relationship vulnerable to self-interest and exploitation. The intimate relationship that has been established over a number of years through the bond of service threatens – even in the small – the larger, structural, and impersonal concerns with impartial justice exemplified by Hal's later decision to embrace the Lord Chief Justice and reject his exploitative friend:

> You did commit me,
> For which I do commit into your hand
> Th' unstainèd sword that you have used to bear,
> With this remembrance: that you use the same
> With the like bold, just, and impartial spirit
> As you have done 'gainst me.   (5.2.111–16)

Falstaff thus bridges these two scenes, proving clear-sighted enough about the force of self-interest to be able to feed off the naïve justice but so blinded by his own relationship to Hal that he fails to anticipate the new king's rejection of the very things that he scorns in Shallow's "company". Shallow spares no expense in extending his hospitality (and his purse) to the knight in expectation that the new king will act as he does in "countenancing" his servant Davy. That is to say, he assumes that the chain of recognition of personal obligations of service and friendship will extend, unbroken, from the new king, through Falstaff, to himself, and by extension to those in his care: "a friend i' th'court is better than a penny in purse" (5.1.27).[5] Hospitality, in one context the exemplification of nostalgic comradeship, is in a newly developing one seen as an investment in the promises of a new order of selfishly personal relationships. Yet it is a venture that fails

---

[5] See Weil, *Dependency*, chapter 4, for a general discussion of the relationship between friendship and service; also, Shannon, *Amity*, for a different perspective.

precisely because, despite Hal's playful testing of the bonds of service in the scene with Francis, the new king opts for their impersonal and structural rather than their intimate and affective aspects.[6]

Possibilities of performance

These two scenes indicate that the identities in terms of which Falstaff and Shallow, Hal and Francis, Davy and Pistol, Poins and Bardolph are either fixed or mobilised are relatively specific. Prince and knight, justice and apprentice, are required to embody at once the roles with which we are now familiar – not merely master and servant, but also friend and companion, landowner and retainer, soldier and debtor. Except in its form as a purely libidinous desire for pleasure beyond the Symbolic – as Hugh Grady puts it in a reference to Lacanian psychoanalysis – subjectivity, however fluid, needs to occupy roles that are socially available, if not wholly determined.[7] Moreover, the broad matrix of master-servant relations encompassed hierarchical relations not only of varied hierarchy, dependency, and reciprocity but also more or less charged with affective investment and obligation. To offer just one example, the impersonal rejection of the claims of friendship that Henry V enacts at the close of the play may not be quite the embodiment of cold Machiavellianism and reified power presented in Grady's reading. The inauguration of modernity signalled by the Prince's "I know you not, old man" constitutes a rejection of feudal obligations of personal reciprocity as "countenancing" or "accommodation" that a society based on the impersonal preservation of equality requires if friendship with those in power is not to degenerate into the ruthless exploitation of nepotism.

It is striking that although the sonnets finally reject both the moral and material bankruptcy of patronage, they never cease to strive for the personal and affective intimacies of friendship. Hal's rejection of his old friend may be illuminated, if not entirely resolved, by viewing that friendship in terms of the tensions, sketched here and evident in the sonnets, between the structural and affective aspects of service. Entirely absent from these plays is any sense that service is the condition of possibility of Hal and Falstaff's companionship. We do not know how they met. Nor is their relationship described overtly in terms of service. Hal is clearly Falstaff's master, but he does not perform that role with any consistency. On the contrary, if anyone occupies the position of master to servants in the plays, it is Falstaff

---

[6] See especially Shannon, *Sovereign Amity*.   [7] Grady, *Machiavelli*, chapter 3.

himself, who through his abuse of his military rank corruptly presses men into military service. In the second play, he has no fewer than three personal attendants: his ensign, Pistol, a direct result of his military exploits; Bardolph, whom he claims to have "bought . . . in St Paul's" (1.2.44); and the Page, given to him by Hal as a gift: "A had him from me Christian, and look if the fat villain have not transformed him ape" (2.2.56–7).[8] In contrast to his complaint in *1 Henry IV* that he "bates" and "dwindles" (3.3.1–2), Falstaff's claim to have killed Hotspur and Hal's gracious willingness to underwrite that lie have indeed done him "grace" (5.4.150) by the time the second begins.

Falstaff's social position differs considerably between the two plays. The change may be measured by his transformed relationship to the prince. In the first, in an echo of the sonnet's anxieties about the contaminating effects of the poet's company and love, much emphasis is placed on his corrupting effect on the prince as the "devil that haunts [him] in the likeness of an old, fat man" (*1 Henry IV*, 2.5.408). In the second, their complicated but undoubted companionship is greatly attenuated. Falstaff occupies the centre stage. Hal moves, sometimes literally, into the shadows, until he reveals himself at the end "by breaking through the foul and ugly mists / Of vapours that did seem to strangle him" (1.2.180–1). Poins replaces the fat knight as a more intimate, if less engaging, friend. This discrepancy is just one of many signs that we should not read the second part of *Henry IV* as a simple sequel to the first. Even though they offer some kind of diachronic progression, the second play revisits many of the issues of the first, deepening and darkening the conceptual relationships of service, friendship, the obedience expected of the political subject, and familial obligations and affection.

Although Falstaff rarely occupies or enacts the role of an occupational servant, early in *1 Henry IV*, he does mockingly describe his "vocation" (1.2.93) as a form of servile devotion:

Marry then, sweet wag, when thou art king let not us that are squires of the night's body be called thieves of the day's beauty. Let us be "Diana's foresters", "gentlemen of the shade", "minions of the moon", and let men say we be men of good government, being governed, as the sea is, by our noble and chaste mistress the moon, under whose countenance we steal. (1.2.20–6)

In a tetralogy concerned with the alliance of linguistic and political power, Falstaff's request is a further instance of the double nature of the institution

---

[8] Weil discusses Bardolph's role as servant at some length. See *Dependency*, 81ff.

of service as a commingling of affect and structure, devotion and self-interest, abandon and control. Falstaff's "minions of the moon . . . squires of the night's body" both obey and scorn "government". This is one of the few instances in which Falstaff speaks of his own position in terms of common service. After his exploits on the field at Shrewsbury, he shamelessly flaunts his service in another, especially inapposite, sense, in the form of his military service to the king. Falstaff as knight thus becomes a parody of the title, which was instituted during the Middle Ages specifically for military service to the monarch and the protection of the weak. Like others, such as the common players, who could hide troubling subversion behind the assurance of a livery, Falstaff's service is a mask for self-interest and self-display. In the first play, Falstaff occupies the place of the player whose actions fall outside the demands of ethical responsibility because they are in effect those of the character he is playing. It is Falstaff's character or role that is called to account on stage, never the player behind the role. That is because the knight is able to shift his character, as one shifts one's shirt, moving from one to another so rapidly and with such bravura that the player behind the masks is only ever fleetingly glimpsed, never caught in the spotlight.

Whereas the Prince of Wales plays the part of the apprentice, especially in *2 Henry IV*, Falstaff cuts the figure of a master, where he is much less sympathetically presented than he is as the glamorized apprentice to the moon. He is fond enough of those who serve him, treating them indulgently as companions rather than as servile minions, and they hang onto him for his promised "countenance" as much as for his companionship. The relationships in the play thus form a chain of "countenancing" that presents the darker side of the "auncient and of long continuance . . . loue and affection" between master and servant that I.M. extols.[9] Falstaff's friends and servants hope ultimately to benefit from their knight's friendship with the heir apparent, even though he feeds off them in the meanwhile. As an obvious character of admittedly small (and undeserved) authority, Falstaff is a figure for moral judgement in the later play rather than an object of pleasure, as he is in the former. He is funnier and more attractive as the minion of the moon than he is as the captain of a company. We can understand from the structural roles of master and servant why this should be so, but it is also a function of his changing role between the plays from player-figure to figured player: from a delightfully protean creature whose essence is change to a discernible or fixed character whose mode of existence or operation is cynically to change his shape.

---

[9] *Health*, sig. C3ʳ.

In his reading of the Henriad as a representation of the tension between a Montaigne-like, unfixed subjectivity and the reifying determinations of a Machiavellian will to power, Hugh Grady sees both Hal and Falstaff as differently inflected "possibilities of self-definition under conditions of modernity".[10] Within this schema, Henry V's decision to reject his old friend represents the domination of the reifying demands of power as opposed to the carnivalesque resistance to power made possible by more fluid, unconstrained possibilities of subjectivity, released especially in the world of the tavern. Grady writes repeatedly of a "rich ensemble of possible social roles" and the "idea of the self as a social station which one can choose to serve or not" (162 and 163), but he seldom specifies such roles or conducts his analysis by specifying their "myriad potentialities" (169). He may be right to claim that Shakespeare's theatre "becomes a model for life in a world newly opened to the unfettered subjectivity created through shifting ideologies, religions, social stations, changing gender roles, and malleable sexuality" (147), but he is both vague about the moment of such "becoming" and its achievement. For in Grady's brilliantly conceived grand narrative, Shakespeare stands at the threshold of a modernity of which the defining characteristic – following the Frankfurt School – is an intensified form of reification of identity and value through power, and in which the momentary performance of counter-identity through an autonomous, unfettered kind of subjectivity will finally be marginalised as the realm of the "aesthetic" (158ff).[11] If we try to specify some of the roles available for the unfixed subjectivity that both marks the inception of the modern and is the inevitable victim of modernity's drive towards reification, we may be able to reinhabit some of Grady's most powerful insights.

The time of royal apprenticeship

Within the master-servant dyad, Prince Harry occupies a complex and uncertain position. His prank on Francis makes dramatically clear the affinity of his own position to that of the indentured labourer. As apprentice king, Hal appears to have "played the coward with his indenture, and shown it a clean pair of heels". Unlike the sorry under-skinker, however, whose

---

[10] Grady, *Machiavelli*, 162.

[11] "Henceforth, what had been ritual and sanctioned disorder for pre-Modern Europe would have to be transformed into an emerging, historically new category of autonomous, subjective art, and the London commercial theatres of Shakespeare's day were early prototypes for this development" (158–9).

fate it is to serve time, the royal apprentice promises to *redeem* time through freely chosen action:

> I'll so offend to make offence a skill,
> *Redeeming time* when men think least I will.
> (*1 Henry IV*, 1.2.186–95; emphasis added)

Time seen from the perspective of apprenticeship takes a very different form from the representation of its passage in the sonnets.[12] In contrast to the sonnets' anxious desire to arrest the wearing effects of time, the apprentice experiences time as something that has to be arduously worked through and from which release is eagerly sought. Hal's prank on Francis works because the prince fully understands the apprentice's debt to time. Hal, on the other hand, *bides his time*. He is able to take up a satirically distanced stance vis-à-vis the drawer because he has already shown his indenture a "fair pair of heels". This is not to say that he is entirely free, however. Unlike Francis, he has a choice either to abandon the responsibilities of his apprenticeship or to fulfil its lonely requirements, with their concurrent burdens, exhilarations, and dangers. They are, however, not entirely within his control.

Structure and affect

In *2 Henry IV*, Poins replaces Falstaff as Hal's chief companion and confidante. In the opening of Act 2, Scene 2, we see a prince who has come to rely on the affective bond between master and servant that Falstaff excoriates in Act 5, Scene 1:

> PRINCE HARRY Before God, I am exceeding weary.
> POINS Is 't come to that? I had thought weariness durst not have
> attached one of so high blood.
> PRINCE HARRY Faith, it does me, though it discolours the
> complexion of my greatness to acknowledge it. Doth it not
> show vilely in me to desire small beer?
> POINS Why, a prince should not be so loosely studied as to
> remember so weak a composition.
> PRINCE HARRY Belike then my appetite was not princely got;
> for, by my troth, I do now remember the poor creature small
> beer. But indeed, these humble considerations make me out
> of love with my greatness. What a disgrace is it to me to

---

[12] Cf. Knights, "Time's Subjects".

remember thy name! Or to know thy face tomorrow! Or to
take note how many pair of silk stockings thou hast –
videlicet these, and those that were thy peach-coloured ones!
Or to bear the inventory of thy shirts – as one for superfluity,
and another for use.   (2.2.1–16)

In contrast to the discordant theatricality of the conversations between
Hal and Falstaff, this interchange is marked by an unusual, even poignant,
intimacy. It is reminiscent of Portia's conversation with Nerissa in the second
scene of *The Merchant of Venice*, another exchange informed by the need
for emotional support through the hierarchies of service. In the history
play, hierarchy is reduced by the melancholic royal's need for comfort from
his common companion and his confession of his growing love for things
"base, common, and popular" (*Henry V*, 4.1.39).

Hal conveys his declining taste and company in terms that suggest the
demeaning role of the personal menial. Who else but a servant (or lover,
or both) would have such intimate knowledge of the colour and number
of shirts and stockings of another? (The rendering literal of Hal's role as
servant is enacted later in the scene, when he and Poins disguise themselves
as drawers to spy upon Falstaff.) Hal's language conveys a deep sense of self-
alienation that arises from what he at first tosses off as a mere performance.
His taste for small beer and his affinity with Poins show that his role
of knowing mastery ("I know you all") has unconsciously engendered a
different, less controllable subjectivity. His performance as renegade has
contaminated his capacity for crafted self-display and affiliation with his
own class and kin: "keeping such vile company as thou art hath, in reason,
taken from me all ostentation of sorrow" (*2 Henry IV*, 2.2.37–9). Like
the poor drawer's apprentice in whom he takes such mocking delight, the
prince is in fact trapped in his adopted role as wayward apprentice, and
even the possibilities of play or performance ("ostentation") are now beyond
his control. Despite his declared intentions, his situation forges bonds of
affection to which he dare not fully admit. Structurally it prevents him
from expressing emotional ties that he is obliged to display and which he
may well genuinely feel as the son of the ailing king. Structure and emotion
clash here, as they do in all bonds of service, whereas performance threatens
to become reality through the effects of mimetic contamination.

Hal does not recover from this self-imposed condition until the end of
the play, when he adopts an entirely different kind of performance. His lack
of agency before his final self-revelation is the consequence of his chosen
role: far from offering the freedom of untrammelled subjectivity, however,

his servile role places unexpected restrictions on forms of subjectivity that
he might have liked to inhabit, like that of the genuinely loving son:

> Thy due from me
> Is tears and heavy sorrows of the blood,
> Which nature, love, and filial tenderness
> Shall, O dear father, pay thee plenteously.
> (*2 Henry IV*, 4.3.168–71)

Far from allowing him the freedom to shift between "myriad potentialities", as Grady claims, the roles that Hal chooses preclude his being "more
[him]self" (*1 Henry IV*, 3.2.93). The adopted role as the companion of
menials prevents him from inhabiting his "natural" role as loving son.

THE DEBTS OF SERVICE AND THE REWARDS OF LOVE: FROM PEERS TO SERVANTS

Hal's contamination through his intimacy with Poins is variously expressed
in the sonnets. The player-servant-poet dwells on his own "publick meanes
which publick manners breeds" and the uncomfortable truth that his "his
name receiues a brand, / And almost thence [his] nature is subdu'd / To
what it workes in, like the Dyers hand" (sonnet 111.4–7). In contrast to the
passive sense in most of the sonnets that "th'impression . . . / Which vulgar
scandall stampt vpon my brow" may be "filled" with the "loue and pittie"
of the young man, Hal can take consolation from the fact that he will be
able to fill that impression through his own agency – through his capacity,
"anon", to exchange one stage (and role) for another, although that agency
is constricted, as I have been arguing, by the very "counterfeiting" forms
that he has adopted. Such capacity lies beyond the structural constraints of
normal relationships of service, even though characters such as Falstaff and
Shallow live upon the hope that affective ties will overcome those limits.
Hal needs to redeem the time that his father pawned through his theft
of the crown. Where the poet of the sonnets seeks to make time "stand
still", Hall needs to make it "run".[13] His apprenticeship is self-fashioned
and self-governed, precisely because the institution of monarchy into which
he would as a legitimate prince have fitted is severely compromised: the
broader bonds of service that are assured by the monarch have been violated
by Henry IV's usurpation and murder of the anointed king. This has, in
turn, compromised the bonds that would normally have existed between the

---

[13] This is dramatically conveyed by the gesture, from which he can never recover, of taking the crown
before his father has died.

former Earl of Hereford and the nobility. The latter have been transformed from peers to servants.[14]

That crucial transformation is nowhere more evident than in the opening scenes of the first play, where Worcester uses the language of chastisement to protest the king's treatment of the Percies and their supporters:

> Our house, my sovereign liege, little deserves
> The scourge of greatness to be used on it,
> And that same greatness too, which our own hands
> Have holp to make so portly.
>
> (*1 Henry IV*, 1.3.10–13)

That Henry is alive to this invocation of master-servant relationships is clear from his response, which in both descriptive epithet and performative force puts the upstart earl in his place:

> Worcester, get thee gone, for I do see
> Danger and disobedience in thine eye.
> O sir, your presence is too bold and peremptory,
> And majesty might never yet endure
> The moody frontier of a *servant* brow.
> You have good leave to leave us. When we need
> Your use and counsel we shall send for you.
>
> (14–20; emphasis added)

More than merely *naming* his former peer as his servant, he *enacts* the master's prerogative to keep his servants at his beck and call.[15] Henry's presumption of masterly behaviour is what especially rankles with the rebels, who regard themselves as the new king's *creditors* rather than his servants. They may owe him allegiance, but he owes them much more in gratitude – not only for helping him against Richard but also for protecting him against the likes of Douglas and Glendŵr. The fact that the Percies can use their prisoners to bolster their rebellion attests to the genuine fears of the king, whatever the feudal prerogatives concerning rights over prisoners might be.

Henry is trying to secure mastery over all those who threaten his state, even if, as Harry Berger has perceptively argued, that means goading his former peers into revolt.[16] That the rebels need to turn their former foes to their own cause demonstrates the historical demise of the power of

[14] See Starkey's argument in *The English Court*, that the nature of the monarchy changed from the Lancastrian kings, who were first among equals, to the Tudors, who elevated themselves above the former "peers" as being different in kind (3).

[15] We are reminded of the opening lines of sonnet 57: "Being your slaue what should I doe but tend, / Vpon the houres, and times of your desire?"

[16] Berger, *Trifles*, 148 passim.

the nobles, who were finding it increasingly difficult to call upon feudal obligations of military service in competition with the monarch's rights. It is perhaps one of the Percies' most debilitating weaknesses, and a sign of their undue dependence upon those on the periphery of Henry's rule in Scotland and Wales, that they find it difficult to levy sufficient armies under the old feudal obligations of military service.

What is most striking about the language in which these allegiances are formed or broken is the fact that the affiliations or disaffiliations of service and obligation are expressed in the language of love. Although there is a family resemblance between the word as it is used to declare and cement political allegiance on the one hand and erotic attachment on the other, it appears at first sight to mark quite distinct structural and affective affinities in its feudal, political context. If the excessive intensity and passion of erotic love give it an unstable and unreliable quality that was regarded as effeminate, the manly declaration of loving allegiance might indicate a more resolutely masculine world. Love in the latter context is closely tied to the structural allegiance and reciprocity that we now recognise in the bonds of service, and we may see in such bonds something of the character of *philia*.

It would be strange to discover that a declaration of erotic attachment was not the expression of some kind of intensely felt emotion; it does not, however, empty a declaration of love in a broader, political sense to believe that the person speaking has no affective attachment to the person to whom he is declaring his love. Like the notion of service, the word "love" in this sense stands for, or intensifies, attitudes of obligation and expectations of reciprocal duty. If the declaration of erotic service tends towards the metaphorical, attestations of political love move in the opposite direction, shifting the valences of the personal towards the realities of public service. To love someone in this context is to accept a set of socially and politically sanctioned obligations that may but need not signal any emotional attachment. One may dislike one's king or be indifferent towards him on a personal level, but still in all sincerity declare one's love for him.

The presence of a body of especially Elizabethan writing that urgently sought to conflate erotic attachment and political devotion does not detract from this conceptual point. Indeed, in the affective trajectory of his sonnets, Shakespeare seems finally to reject the marriage of service and personal devotion. The love that is celebrated in sonnet 124 is emphatically distinguished from that which is "but the childe of state":

> YF my deare loue were but the childe of state,
> It might for fortunes basterd be vnfathered,
> As subiect to times loue, or to times hate,
> Weeds among weeds, or flowers with flowers gatherd.

No it was buylded far from accident,
It suffers not in smilinge pomp,nor falls
Vnder the blow of thralled discontent,
Whereto th'inuiting time our fashion calls:
It feares not policy that Heriticke,
Which workes on leases of short numbred howers,
But all alone stands hugely pollitick,
That it nor growes with heat, nor drownes with showres.
     To this I witnes call the foles of time,
     Which die for goodnes, who haue liu'd for crime.

There are striking echoes of the Henry plays in this sonnet, although they are more allusive than direct. In the most general terms, the third-last sonnet in the sequence to the young man echoes the better-known sonnet 116 in its declaration of love's transcendence of all the accidental qualities of time. Love, which is emphatically the *poet's* love in the later poem, is in this strict sense *unnatural*: it "nor growes with heat, nor drownes with showres". The major burden of the poem is its rejection of the political vagaries depicted in the history plays: the capricious alternation of time's "loue" and "hate" in the conflicted relationship between "smiling pomp" and "enthrallèd discontent". The opening lines are allusively suggestive of the fraught, chiasmic relationships of fathers and sons in the Henriad that Berger has analysed so well – in Henry's unfathering wish that Hotspur were his son and Harry some bastard changeling; in Hotspur's transformation into "fortune's bastard" by his own father, who never escapes time's thrall; by Hal, who bides his time to steal his accumulated fame; and in Hal's own fathering and unfathering by Falstaff's strange capacity to evade time, at least for a while (Berger, *Trifles*, 251 and passim). Hal's design to "redeem time" by engaging in the very "policy" that the poem decries as "that *Heriticke* / Which works on leases of short numbred howers" is a strategy to avoid being transformed into "fortunes bastard". The perplexing "foles of time" of the couplet find at least one possible equivalent in the failed rebel leaders, who in their own eyes at least "die for goodnesse", even if in the kings' eyes they may have "lived for crime".

The most intriguing of parallels exists between Falstaff and the poetic voice of the sonnets. For all his perspicuity, Falstaff fails to see that the love between himself and the prince, which he believes is not "the child of state", will inevitably be trumped by "policy". Falstaff may indeed stand "hugely pollitick" in the play insofar as he remains unaffected by the normal course of time's love and hate, and in his subjection, from the *platea*, of political value to trenchant irony, but in the question of Hal's love (and probably his own), he is hugely mistaken.

It is difficult to believe that Shakespeare does not intend a semantic echo of "policy" in "politick", even though the two terms are strongly contrasted in the syntactical dynamics of the sonnet. Like its companion, sonnet 116, the most well-known declaration of the nature of love in English, sonnet 124 offers no real argument, merely a series of declarations. As Booth points out, those declarations are undermined by a series of internal contradictions and discordances (*Sonnets*, 419ff), and those uncertainties are underscored by the egocentric bombast of the poem. Unlike 116, 124 is not a disquisition on love in the ideal or in general: it boasts the quality of the *speaker's* love. We might also say that the Henriad gives that claim the lie by showing both the inextricable imbrication of politics (if not policy) and love and the uncertainty of knowing oneself and others in love. Does Hal love Falstaff? Does Falstaff love Hal? Does Falstaff love Mistress Quickly? Does she love him? Does Hal love his father? Does his father love him? Does Hotspur love his wife? Does Hotspur love honour and hate rhetoric? Do the rebel lords love each other? These questions are raised repeatedly throughout the plays, but it is almost impossible to come to a settled answer to any of them. Definite answers may be rendered impossible by the shifting nature of subjectivity that Grady sees as the tetralogy's anticipation of a certain strand of modernity. Love may on the one hand anticipate the concept of the subject in flux because its deeply irrational and unstable passion refuses the confining dimensions of settled identity. On the other hand, however, love that encompasses "tenderness" and the devotion traditionally attributed to *philia* requires the stabilization of the subject in flux if it is to have any purchase at all, certainly any sort of ethical purchase.

The distinction that I have drawn between love as a structural quality, closer to service than to *eros* and therefore more reliable, "masculine", and stable, is, however, undermined by the structural unpredictability of affiliations and allegiances in the overtly masculine world of these histories. Here is Henry, meditating on being "subiect to times loue, or to times hate" (sonnet 124.3):

> 'Tis not ten years gone
> Since Richard and Northumberland, great friends,
> Did feast together; and in two year after
> Were they at wars. It is but eight years since
> This Percy was the man nearest my soul,
> Who like a brother toiled in my affairs,
> And laid his love and life under my foot,
> Yea, for my sake, even to the eyes of Richard
> Gave him defiance.   (*2 Henry IV*, 3.1.53–74)

Contrasted with Henry's questionable assurance that he was merely bowing to the necessities of the state and the time ("Though then, God knows, I had no such intent, / But that necessity so bowed the state / That I and greatness were compelled to kiss" (67–9)), is his bewilderment at the fragility of men's love signified by the easy "division of our amity" (74). The language of amity that we now know so well is repeated here – in the notion not merely of "great friends" feasting with each other, but also of true friendly devotion and dedication. Yet against the conventional idea that Percy was "the man nearest his soul", Henry betrays a retrospective attitude to the friendship that belies the ideal, reciprocal equality of such amity: he shifts all too quickly from the equality of the soul to servile abjection beneath his now-royal foot: "And laid his love and life under my foot". The seeds of the division that Henry speaks of here are already apparent in the language he uses to describe their puzzling shifts of friendship. It is clear that although he regarded Percy as his bosom friend, his dedication to "policy" was already turning such personal ties into the bondage of instrumental service. Quite simply, he was using the Percies as Falstaff uses his poor conscripts – or, for that matter, as Hal uses Falstaff – by feeding upon their loss.[17]

The oscillation between time's love and hate that Henry bewails is the substance of the Henriad, which explores that shifting difference in the terms set out in sonnet 124. The accounting of debt and credit that Engle[18] analyses so well needs to be seen not solely in monetary terms but also in the ledger book of love and service. Worcester states this forcefully at the beginning of *1 Henry IV*:

> . . . bear ourselves as even as we can,
> The King will always think him in our debt,
> And think we think ourselves unsatisfied
> Till he hath found a time to pay us home.
> And see already how he doth begin
> To make us strangers to his looks of love. (1.3.279–4)

His argument is not merely that they are unsatisfied. Their precarious position stems from the king's imputed awareness of his debt to them and their attribution to him of the assumption that they believe that this debt can never be repaid. Resentment thus feeds not merely on a mutual awareness

---

[17] See Shakespeare's sonnet 146. It is precisely to avoid such instrumentality that Montaigne reserves true friendship for the private sphere, withdrawing it from public politics. See Grady, *Machiavelli*, chapter 3.
[18] Engle, *Pragmatism*, chapter 5.

of uneven reciprocity but also on the certainty that there is *structurally* no way to repay the debt. This is because the relationship has changed: friends have become servants; peers have been turned into masters. Under such circumstances, the nature of love itself changes: from the equality of loving friendship to the much more politically derived love between subject and sovereign, which for *both* parties has become either unbearable or unsustainable. This shows us that the answers to my earlier rhetorical questions need to be sensitive to the *concept* of love in question and its transformation by time and circumstance.

Berger draws our attention to Hobbes's acute identification of the nature of the interplay of love and hatred that attends such indebtedness:

> To have received from one, to whom we think ourselves equal, greater benefits than there is hope to requite, disposeth to counterfeit love; but really secret hatred. . . . For benefits oblige, and obligation is thraldom; and unrequitable obligation perpetual thraldom; which is to one's equal, hateful. But to have received benefits from one, whom we acknowledge for superior, inclines to love; because the obligation is no new depression: and cheerful acceptation, which men call *gratitude*, is such an honor done to the obliger, as taken generally for retribution.[19]

Striking about Hobbes's analysis of these political debts, which are also personal, is the close relationship between love and hatred and service and obligation within a hierarchical political and social system. Acts of love are turned into conditions of hatred in relationships of equality because they incur debts that can never be repaid. This creates a mentality of "thraldom", a psychology of perpetual service, with which love between equals is incompatible.[20]

To the headstrong Hotspur, "*time serves*" in which to erase both that debt and the resentment that it provokes:

> . . . yet time serves wherein you may redeem
> Your banished honours, and restore yourselves
> Into the good thoughts of the world again,
> Revenge the jeering and disdained contempt
> Of this proud King, who studies day and night
> To answer all the debt he owes to you
> Even with the bloody payment of your deaths.
>
> (*1 Henry IV*, 1.3.177–83)

The irony behind Hotspur's optimism, apparent to any reader or member of the audience with a modicum of historical knowledge, is the fact that

---

[19] Hobbes, *Leviathan*; qtd. in Berger, *Trifles*, 255.
[20] For a philosophical discussion of the impossibility of the gift, see Derrida, *Given Time*.

Hotspur and his family are the ones who *serve time*. Worcester silences his nephew because his own conception of the debts involved is wholly different from the young Percy's. Hotspur's marriage to the idea of honour means that dying well would redeem time and the debts that the king owes them. In this respect, Hotspur's sense of good service depends entirely on "the good thoughts of the world".

Compare sonnet 25:

> LEt those who are in fauor with their stars,
> Of publike honour and proud titles bost,
> Whilst I whome fortune of such tryumph bars
> Vnlookt for ioy in that I honour most;
> Great Princes fauorites their faire leaues spread,
> But as the Marygold at the suns eye,
> And in them-selues their pride lies buried,
> For at a frowne they in their glory die.
> The painefull warrier famosed for worth,
> After a thousand victories once foild,
> Is from the booke of honour rased quite,
> And all the rest forgot for which he toild:
>   Then happy I that loue and am beloued
>   Where I may not remoue, nor be remoued.

The final quatrain may refer to soldiers like Hotspur, whose accumulated glories are only as good as their next battle and whose conception of honour had already been made anachronistic by "villainous saltpetre / . . . which many a good tall fellow had destroyed so cowardly" (*1 Henry IV*, 1.3.59–62).[21] The sonnet as a whole, however, rehearses a familiar thought that touches our discussion more generally, viz. the difference in category and value between public love and the honour that belongs to a less politic realm. This idea appears so frequently in the sonnets as to be obsessive, and such obsession conveys a sense of too strident protestation.

I have argued elsewhere that these sonnets do not describe an achieved state so much as they indulge in quasi-performative speech acts which attempt to bring into being the quality being demanded or celebrated.[22] In the context of the *Henry* plays, it is especially striking that the poet should invoke the notion of honour as something that escapes the public realm: honour that depends on "public manners" is said to be fragile, unreliable, and illusory. In this respect, it is identical to *eros*. Only the

---

[21] See Berger for a fine discussion of Hotspur's conception of honour and especially the affinity between Hotspur and the lord he so deprecates in 1.3, in *Trifles*, chapter 13.

[22] Schalkwyk, *Speech*.

devoted honouring embodied in *philia,* both sought for and celebrated in sonnet 124, is assuredly reciprocal and stable. Honour without a public sphere does not exist, however. Honour is the gift of others; it lives only in "the mouths of men":

> When you intombed in mens eyes shall lye,
> Your monument shall be my gentle verse,
> Which eyes not yet created shall ore-read,
> And toungs to be, your beeing shall rehearse,
> When all the breathers of this world are dead,
>   You still shall liue (such vertue hath my Pen)
>   Where breath most breaths, euen in the mouths of men.
>
> (Sonnet 81)

Might we say the same of love? Certainly, in both the sonnets and the two *Henry* plays, Shakespeare aligns a certain kind of love – that which belongs to the public sphere – with honour and emphasises its proneness to "accident". There is, in contrast, a different kind of love, which involves a more steadfast "honouring" of the other in a "mutuall render" that stands above such accidents of time and circumstance. This is evident in the decisive shift in attitude from sonnet 25 to 81. Contrasted with the early sonnet's attempt to withdraw from the vagaries of the public world, the later poem reminds the person honoured of the debt that he owes the poet, in whose vocation lies the real power ("such vertue hath my Pen") to achieve Hotspur's dream of monumental honour. The glorious field of military service, Hotspur believes, will enable him to escape his servile subjection to his family's former peer, whether they emerge alive or not: "To answer all the debt he owes to you / Even with the bloody payment of your deaths". These are the actions and words of the disenchanted servant, whose new dedication carries an extraordinary erotic intensity. That intensity cannot be trumped – as Lady Percy discovers – by real erotic devotion. The debts that Hotspur means to erase on the battlefield come into direct conflict, and overwhelm, the erotic service that he owes his wife:

> For what offence have I this fortnight been
> A banished woman from my Harry's bed? . . .
> Why hast thou . . .
>   . . . given my treasures and my rights of thee
> To thick-eyed musing and curst melancholy?
>
> (2.4.32–40)

The poignant powerlessness of Kate's demands – couched not merely in personal but also the public language of mutual service – underscores sonnet

124's aversion to "publike honour and proud titles". Yet there is a curious anomaly in Hotspur's declaration, whereby the rebels are supposed to answer the debts of their king with their *own* deaths, that reflects the conjunction of sonnet 146 and Hal's sonnet-like "I know you all" speech, whereby the master repays his debt to God by feeding upon the loss of the servant.[23]

This aversion to the politic dimensions of love is especially striking in the scene of Prince John's Machiavellian treachery, when he persuades the rebels to disband their troops on the promise that their grievances will be redressed. We know from Hobbes and Machiavelli (and from Worcester, who would never have acceded to the peace) that such repayment of debt is structurally impossible: that "counterfeit love" under the "perpetual thraldom" of "unrequitable obligation" is in fact "secret hatred". So when the rebels and their enemies begin increasingly to adopt the language of "restorèd love and amity" (*2 Henry IV*, 4.1.291), we know that the thraldom of resented service and obligation cannot sustain such discourse. It is one of the most intriguing dimensions of the sonnets that they carry the "secret hatred" that is the inverse of unrequited love as a burden through the length of their narrative. Such "secret hatred" is in fact one of the major unifying strains of the whole sequence. The question is whether the servant-poet's insistence on the difference between the two systems of honour and love can be sustained. The answer may be found in the "secret hatred" that marks another couple: Hal and his friend and honour's critic, Sir John Falstaff.

The play of Hal and Falstaff

Critics who see in Falstaff the untrammelled embodiment of the carnival tend to overlook his increased self-consciousness about his rank and authority in *2 Henry IV*.[24] As much as he may be "minion of the moon" and "squire of the night's body" in the earlier play, in the second instalment Sir John combines an exploitative sense of rank with a cynical abuse of authority.[25] Engle's perceptive argument that Falstaff is all too aware of the costs of carnival, even if he is unwilling to bear them himself, is apposite.[26] However, his claim that, in contrast to Hal's efforts to store up value, Falstaff

---

[23] The speech (1.3.173–95) takes the form of twenty-three lines, ending with a couplet.

[24] See Bristol, *Carnival and Theater*; Holderness, *Shakespeare's History*, 83–95 and Grady, *Machiavelli*, 145 passim.

[25] Grady emphasizes the disjunction between the two plays: Falstaff's role as the critic of reification is more pronounced in the first than the second.

[26] Engle, *Pragmatism*, 121.

insists on putting it into circulation, does not give sufficient weight to our gathering sense of Falstaff's body as an increasingly bombastic container of waste. What Falstaff wastes ends up in his own waist:

> LORD CHIEF JUSTICE Your means are very slender, and your
> waste is great.
> FALSTAFF I would it were otherwise; I would my means were
> greater and my waist slenderer.　　(*2 Henry IV*, 1.2.128–31)

This waste does not occur – his waist does not increase – within an economy of plenty as Falstaff would make us believe. *2 Henry IV* repeatedly reveals that Falstaff's expanding waste/waist means the shrinking of someone else's means. Whereas it may be easy to ignore the costs of Falstaff's life and living in *1 Henry IV*, when they are borne by nameless servants and a faceless commonwealth, *2 Henry IV* gives that cost a local habitation and a name, not least in the poor figure of Mistress Quickly, who is reduced to pawning her plate and hangings by the knight's consumptive habits, and in the poor, bare figures of the impressed soldiers on whom he feeds. In the second play, Falstaff embodies a peculiarly ambivalent relation to the conclusion of sonnet 146: his *body* feeds upon the loss of others, whom he treats, like the careless masters who exploit their servants in I.M.'s *Health*, with exploitative contempt. They, in turn, embody the abject willingness of the besotted servant to "pine within and suffer dearth". We are constantly reminded of the size and age of Falstaff's body, of its fleshly pleasure and spiritual recklessness. Yet the body itself never ceases to signal dearth of a different sort, encapsulated by the physical and emotional narrowness of Hal and Shallow alike.

Engle offers the corrective view that the prince and Sir John are much closer to each other than is commonly supposed. What draws them together is their complementary attitudes towards the expenditure that carnival involves. Aware that "no carnival suspends settlement of outstanding debts indefinitely", Hal seeks to accumulate value, whereas Falstaff, no less aware of the costs of carnival, seeks to encourage the endless circulation of debts so that they never finally fall to him (Engle, *Pragmatism*, 123). If Hal reminds us of the precariousness of the contingency that Falstaff celebrates and embodies, Engle argues, then Falstaff prevents us from buying into Hal's attempts to forget contingency when it least suits him. Engle's critical schema has the virtue of allowing us to see the irreducibly exploitative aspects of Falstaff while recognising in his encouragement of carnivalesque circulation our own vicarious investment in that pleasure. None of us would like to be in the shoes of Mistress Quickly, Francis Feeble, or Justice Shallow, vis-à-vis the fat knight, but we can enjoy the spirit of irresponsible circulation that he engenders through those relationships via the paradoxical distancing and engaging pleasure of theatrical performance.[27] We are fooling ourselves if we fail to acknowledge how utterly unreciprocal Falstaff's relationships are. Engle's framework, which emphasises the prince and the knight's respective attitudes to a general economy, although helpful, is a bit too broad or abstract to deal with the felt results or experience of such attitudes. Reading the play with the sonnets in mind helps us to focus more precisely on those relations of affect.

The force of performance

The problem with the *Henry* plays, especially the first, is that any sustained ethical perspective will always ignore or attenuate the performative force of the plays' scenes of carnival irresponsibility. Considered as an example of Aristotelian friendship, Hal and Falstaff offer no more than a burlesque of classical ideals. They represent what friendship is *not* for that tradition. Their respective physical existence embodies in the most palpable way discrepancy rather than the identity celebrated by Aristotle, Cicero, and Montaigne:[28] the "bull's pizzle" will always underscore its incongruity with the "roast Mannigtree ox". They are vastly discrepant in rank, virtue, and temperament, and yet at some level Shakespeare asks us to recognise that they are indeed friends. They may even be said to love each other. How does he achieve this? Not by following his classical and Renaissance precursors. Writing about the relationship between Hal and Falstaff as a form of service that has shaded into dependent friendship, Weil argues that Falstaff represents the deep need by all ranks in early modern England for the "accommodation" that literally ensured protection and sustenance in an insecure social and economic world. She also suggests, however, that as a "symbolic giant" Falstaff represents much more than a mere dependant or sycophant.[29] He persists as the incorrigible "mock[er] of tendentious myths" (91), even as he embodies a great deal of tendentiousness within his girth.

The friendship between Hal and Falstaff is thus not philosophical as it is in Aristotle, or even a combination of personal experience and conceptual analysis as it is in Montaigne. It is above all dramatic or performative. It is striking that the single most feared attribute of the corrupting servant of

---

[27] Grady points out that Falstaff's meta-theatrical self-commentary contributes a great deal to the pleasure that we derive from the knight.
[28] See Shannon, *Amity*, chapter 1.   [29] Weil, *Dependency*, 91.

people in high places – their corrosive propensity for flattery – is wholly absent from Falstaff's relationship with Hal. If anything, Falstaff is instead given to mocking, deflating, and insulting his royal friend and master. Furthermore, as Shannon observes, Falstaff's impertinent remark to the Chief Justice – that it is not he who is the corrupter of the prince but rather the prince who misleads his "companion" – contains a grain of truth. Like the relationships between Beatrice and Benedick and Cleopatra and Antony, affinity is expressed through an intensely aggressive intimacy. Such aggression no doubt contributes to a certain impression of "character", but its drive is fundamentally theatrical.

The dependency that informs the relationship between the prince and his fat knight is much more symbolically telling than the naturalistically conceived need by a lower member of the aristocracy down on his luck for the protection or "countenance" of the heir-apparent to the throne. The continuing engagement of Falstaff and Hal is *staged* in a strange inversion of the relationship between *platea* and *locus*. Falstaff needs Hal and Hal needs Falstaff in the way that the players of Shakespeare's company needed each other to make a play work. We could seek psychological, or even sociological, causes for the continual propensity for deflation, embarrassment, conflict, and abuse that marks their relationship, but the chief reason lies in the rewriting of the classical rules of friendship (and the Protestant expectations of service) from a bloodless philosophical discourse or even the abstract ideals of memory, into one that is borne by performing bodies, self-reflexively aware of the theatrical forces that bring them together. Hal and Falstaff take pleasure in each other as sites of continually inventive, creative, and human performance. One of the most singular aspects of this performative dimension is the inversion of the usual division, in terms of rank and status, between the representing and the representative body. Hal most often inhabits the *platea* mode, from his early soliloquy, "I know you all" (*1 Henry IV*, 1.2.192ff), through the setting up of Falstaff on Gadshill, to the unmasking of the knight's lies and pretensions in both of the great tavern scenes in *Parts 1* and *2*.

This performative dimension of the character underscores Shannon's inclination to see Hal's role in structural rather than psychological, developmental terms.[30] Shannon argues that Hal and Falstaff's friendship plots

---

[30] The structural dimension upon which Shannon focuses is the movement in political history from one kind of relationship between private and public to another. I am adding the theatre. Seeing friendship in performative terms – as the embodied pleasure gained from interactive modes of enactment, which include conflict – complicates the classical model of friendship.

a course from a feudal to a modern conception of the relationship between public duty and private passion:

> *Henry IV* proposes that the founding moment of polity or commonwealth is the moment that friendship, as a mode of affective partisan loyalty, is exiled from a public world of law and government. This presentation of friendship accords it not the slightest trace of the civic relevance it enjoyed in Cicero and clung to in Montaigne [since it stems from the need] to make government impersonal, neutral, procedural, and bureaucratic. (*Amity*, 184)

She puts her finger on tensions that inform the notion of "corruption" in modern politics, where the concept of a "friend" in political life retains many of the feudal expectations that Falstaff expresses when, as the new king's "careful friend and true subject" (2.4.325–6), he assumes "the Laws of England are at my commandment" (5.3.135–6). Whatever delight we may feel at the companionship of the tavern scenes, the careless certainty of the knight's assumption of the bounds of friendship at this point is frightening, especially considering the language of beatitude with which he clothes the concept: "Blessed are they that have been my friends" (135). The sacralization of friendship and service alike in earlier models becomes a grotesque valorisation of nepotism. Against the feudal sense that friendship was part of public life and Montaigne's belief that friendship offers a "world elsewhere" that transcends public existence, Falstaff's notion assumes a public life (service to the commonwealth) that is no more than the domain upon which a small, *private* circle can feed without limit.

Beyond friendship

In a play in which the historical, early Lancastrian idea that the king is merely a first among equals is displaced by the Tudor conception of the king as a lonely being "elevated above even the greatest of [his] Lords", Shakespeare forges a conception of the affective relations between the monarch and his friends and servants that replaces the ideal of local reciprocity in feudal relations with a notion of service more attuned to the birth of the modern state.[31] As Shannon points out, this means that the monarch's "body private" posited by contemporary theorists is in fact subsumed wholly within the "body politic", thereby denying the ruler control over his or her affective relationships to shield him or her from personal demands. Friendship makes way for a peculiar notion of political love and service. As Elizabeth

---

[31] Starkey, *English Court*, 3.

herself put it, she was wedded to her people, bound to them in a reciprocal duty of service over which neither had any free choice.[32] In Shannon's
words: "The king's status as *res publica* (public matter or property) emphasises his serviceability to the common wealth. . . . The serviceable monarch's
full dedication was required in a sphere defined in the maxim *quod omnes
tangit* as one who touches or affects all" (149).

Let us pursue in greater detail the relationship of such "serviceability",
which Shannon presumably means in a noninstrumental sense: as a matter
of reciprocal or mutual obligation, for the good of both parties. Conceptually interesting here is the fact that whereas the monarch's relation to
others may encompass both love and service, it necessarily excludes friendship. We might say that the queen serves or loves her people, but it is
difficult to encompass a sense of her enjoying the *friendship* of her people.[33] The competing forms of "serviceability" that Shannon underlines in
the political relationship contradict Montaigne's requirement that "with
friendship there is no traffic or commerce with anything but itself" (209).
The monarch's position *beyond* friendship is the burden of the two solil-
oquies by the respective kings in *Henry IV* and *Henry V* on the loneliness
of the "head that wears the crown" (*2 Henry IV*, 3.1.31), and, according to
Shannon's argument, of the *Henriad* itself.[34]

If service, and even love, require a certain performative dimension – an
acting out of a role that is to some degree at least in the public domain –
the same is not true of friendship.[35] It is has often been observed that Hal
prepares for his succession to the throne as a series of carefully planned,
successive roles that, alive to the context of his succession, are more astute,
in Machiavellian terms, than the Machiavellian roles his father had adopted.
Bolingbroke boasts of carefully withholding himself from the public eye in
a paradox of astutely invisible stagecraft:[36]

---

[32] See Shannon, *Amity*, 128, n. 9: "Thus when Elizabeth I reportedly claimed marriage to the realm,
her language not only represented an improvisation upon gender; it aptly figured the degree of
commitment required of the ethical monarch. The relation to the realm is preemptive of other
"loves."

[33] Guazzo seems to be drawing this distinction between love and the familiarity of friendship in the
remark that he would not "make my seruants my companions, in being to familiar with them: I like
well to loue them, but not to imbrace them" (Guazzo, *Conuersation*, sig. Yiii[r]).

[34] Shannon argues that it is not the personal likeness that unites father and son in these thoughts but
rather a structural condition of monarchy itself (180).

[35] This is not to say that friendship cannot be mimicked, but such mimicry is not friendship; it is
flattery or hypocrisy. Service may well be mimicked without destroying its character. Indeed, most
forms of service could be considered such forms of performance. The fact that the commentators on
service found in this thought cause for considerable anxiety does not negate this conceptual point.

[36] See Roe, *Machiavelli*, chapter 2.

Thus did I keep my person fresh and new,
My presence like a robe pontifical –
Ne'er seen but wondered at – and so my state,
Seldom but sumptuous, showed like a feast,
And won by rareness such solemnity.

(*1 Henry IV* 3.2.55–9)

What he does not recognise is the fact that Hal's flirting with what Shannon calls *mignonnerie* – the cultivation of false friendships, which threatens to corrupt the common good – is itself a carefully plotted play, with the same intended result as Bolingbroke's charade. We need not, however, endorse Falstaff's platitude about the defiling qualities of pitch in his own travesty of Hal's father to recognise that there is something about Falstaff's company that touches the prince in more than mere play.

The "play extempore" that Falstaff and Hal stage is more than an indication of the performative qualities of their respective identities: it is a curious enactment of the *simultaneous* embodiment of representing and represented matter. Falstaff represents both the king and himself. He inhabits in a playful way the authority of the father at the same time as he directs the request for special dispensation in his own name. The speech act is thus enacted both as a command and a plea, the representing friend's request being overlaid with the force of the represented king's word. The asymmetry of the relationship is brought out when the two players switch roles, and Hal can play not his father, but himself, projected as future king, to a figure who now in effect speaks in his own, mock-pathetic voice:

Banish not him thy Harry's company,
Banish not him thy Harry's company.
Banish plump Jack, and banish all the world.
PRINCE HARRY I do; I will.   (483–6)

The shift in tense signals an abrupt relocation from the fiction of the performance to the world performed. A performative act in the present tense of the former world is turned into a promise, threat, or prediction in the not-too-distant future of the historical world. We can see through this tear or passage between the world of play and real action a glimpse of the performance that Hal will finally throw off, like a player's old costume, to reveal the concealed "robe pontifical" of unsullied kingship in his passage, as Shannon wittily remarks, from "I know you all" to "I know you not" (*Amity*, 183). But does the Prince know himself? Everyone can see that Falstaff's sentimental plea for himself asks for the world to be banished in his stead, so that he may "steal" under the "countenance" of his friend, in a travesty of both "good government" and the "world elsewhere" achieved between friends in Montaigne's essay. Yet the very performance over which he seems to have such secure command traps Harry in its own toil: when he banishes Falstaff both in play and in promise, his performative speech act is burdened by the condition that Falstaff has imposed upon it. "Banish *all the world*": "I do; I will". In the process of banishing his friends, Henry does indeed dismiss the world of companionate society. Falstaff's exile is thus the first action of a new kind of performance in which a whole domain of affective relationships is alienated.

Even the play world of the tavern thus circumscribes drastically the "myriad potentialities" that Grady perceives in the subversive instability of Montaignesque flux. We should take care not to transpose too quickly the unfixed subjectivity that becomes apparent to a writer like Montaigne as he assays his identity in the form of the essay and the world of social action, even as it is represented in the relative freedom of play. In both *Henry* plays, the parameters of variation in subjectivity are relatively constrained. As the exemplum of free-ranging and self-fashioned identity, Hal moves among the social roles of royal son, dissolute prodigal, self-mastered apprentice, and military hero, but each of those roles restricts the possibilities of fully inhabiting the others or another. The heir-apparent finds that he can never recover the affective tenderness of the loving son, no matter how much he might wish to, and his carefully laid plan to garner Hotspur's honours is thwarted by the demands of Falstaff's playing.

Falstaff himself occupies the dual roles of fallen knight and knight honourable because he is able to feed off his royal friend's lie, but the actual forms of social identity that he is able to inhabit do not go beyond those of the prince's companion and the exploiter of service in the form of small-time master of a bunch of retainers and exploitative recruiting agent. Only within the free, localised theatrical space of the tavern can different forms of identity be tried without consequence, and even within such fictions, each of its actors finds that their adopted roles place unforeseen restrictions upon others which they may like to play in the world beyond carnival.[37] The fictions of Sir John's imaginary parts are all, in the end, ruthlessly exposed by Hal's realistic deflation, and even Hal finds himself curiously restrained by the roles that he adopts vis-à-vis Falstaff, Poins, and his father's world. The ethical thrust of Montaigne's meditations, in the essays on cruelty, the otherness of the new world, sexuality, and friendship, all indicate that an

---

[37] In this respect, the tavern duplicates the world of the stage.

identity in total flux affords no purchase for community, reciprocity, or respect for others. If such flexibility threatens the reifying tendencies of power, it also threatens the very things for which carnival is supposed to stand: "freedom . . . fellowship [even] wit" (Grady, *Machiavelli*, 169).

The servant's loss

In summary, then, the celebration of unfixed subjectivity attributed to Montaigne from a post-modern perspective overlooks two related things: first, the ways in which subjectivity, however free, needs to occupy preconstituted social roles, which then restrict the possible occupation of other roles because of the performative effects and restrictions of such roles that lie beyond the power of the player; second, the fact that completely free subjectivity becomes a tyranny in itself, placing itself beyond the ethics of reciprocal relations – such as love, service, and friendship – which are the concrete sites in which the reification and abuse of power are resisted. Shannon's reading of the Henriad as a definition of the limits of friendship under the pressure of a dispensation of detached, impersonal government and a new, universal concept of political rights is spot on. That emphasis on impersonality is perfectly captured by the Lord Chief Justice's explanation that in his earlier *contretemps* with the prince, it was as the "image of the King whom I presented", and the new Henry V's concurring injunction that under the new regime "you use the same / With the like bold, just, and impartial spirit / As you have 'gainst me" (*2 Henry IV*, 5.2.78 and 114–16). The appearance of Hal and the Lord Chief Justice together in the final scene registers an emblematic displacement of one form of service by another. However, this new, impersonal notion of service, which knows no friends, is different from the "cash nexus" that commentators usually posit as the historical replacement of feudal forms of service. It retains a deep sense of reciprocal obligation at the political level and therefore retains the crucial aspect of mutual responsibility of its precursor entirely missing from proto-capitalist forms of exchange. This politics of service thus eschews both the corrosive impersonality of money and the potentially corrupting affect of personal devotion. As an alternative conception of detached mutual obligation, it exposes I.M.'s lament for the serving-man of old as a form of special pleading just as self-seeking as the expectations of Falstaff or Justice Shallow.

Sonnet 146 is unusual in Shakespeare's sequence for being its only overtly religious poem, but is it also central to the sequence's general representation of master-servant relationships? It offers, through the conventional theological contest between body and soul, a picture of the *feeding* of the master on the servant's store, a profiting from the subordinate's loss:

> Poore soule the center of my sinfull earth,
> My sinfull earth these rebbell powres that thee array,
> Why dost thou pine within and suffer dearth
> Painting thy outward walls so costlie gay?
> Why so large cost hauing so short a lease,
> Dost thou vpon thy fading mansion spend?
> Shall wormes inheritors of this excesse
> Eate vp thy charge? is this thy bodies end?
> Then soule liue thou vpon thy seruants losse,
> And let that pine to aggrauat thy store;
> Buy tearmes diuine in selling houres of drosse:
> Within be fed, without be rich no more,
>   So shalt thou feed on death, that feeds on men,
>   And death once dead, ther's no more dying then.

Sonnet 146 reckons the relationship of soul to body in the familiar language of the ledger book and the pervasive discourse of service, within an all too recognizable economy of dearth. Yet its readily recognisable echoes of the first seventeen sonnets, in which the aristocratic "lord and owner" is urged to restore his "fading mansion" through the "eternal summer" of procreation, ring hollow. The relentlessly restricted economy of the body's relation to the soul has no place for the regenerative powers that Nature (and, we might add, love) offers, despite her inevitable "Audit", through "breede", in sonnet 4. Nor, more ominously, does she seem to have any space for the quest for pure reciprocity registered through the by now familiar images of payment and loss, spending and giving, and the gaining or losing of the heart that we find in the penultimate sonnet to the young aristocrat.

The sonnet's theological argument may be unexceptional, but its use of the metaphor of master-servant relations remains disturbing. For the subject position of the servant in the rest of the sonnets to the young man, sonnet 146's solution is especially debilitating: one can lay bases for eternity, one can purchase a bond against waste and death, solely from the position of the *master*, who learns betimes that the only way to save himself is to consume the body of servant. If we take Hal's trajectory, from the opening jests about "the time of day" in *1 Henry IV* to his "redeeming time" (*1 Henry IV*, 1.2.1 and 195), through Falstaff's banishment at the end of the second play as a carefully plotted redemption, then we can see that such redemption comes from the rational, if cold-hearted, decision to follow the path of the master in sonnet 146. The costs of the eradication of the affective qualities of service are not immediately evident or palpably represented in *Henry V*, although we feel them as an abiding absence or sense of loss of "company" in the broadest sense of the term, no matter how strongly we agree with Henry's banishment of his companion as the necessary action of one whose service and love are due to the people whom he may love but who cannot be his friends.

A dream or fantasy of friendship and affection *remains*, as a condition of the performance that we have witnessed throughout the Henriad. Deeply embedded in the pleasure we take in the play's full-bodied, bravura performance of the bonds of service, love, and friendship (which are simultaneously conditions of exploitation and conflict), those bonds leave us with a profound sense of loss when they are severed.[38] Why should we be moved – as his friends clearly are, however much they have suffered beneath his selfish waist/waste – at the thought of the fat knight breathing has last, "babbl[ing] of green fields"(*Henry V*, 2.3.16–17)? Why should Falstaff not be satisfied with a pension that would allow him to live comfortably with Mistress Quickly and his retinue of servant-friends? The answer lies not simply in his expectations of much greater power and influence, nor in the loss of face that his public banishment entails.

One needs to take care not to be sentimental at this point. I have repeatedly emphasised Falstaff's indifference at best and grasping exploitation at worst in his (in)capacity as master of others. Being a master requires the acknowledgement of reciprocal duties and obligations, and kingship demands an ethical monarch if it is not to turn into tyranny. On the other hand, Montaigne insists that sovereign friendship precludes obligation and can do without virtue. "Banish not him thy Harry's company", Falstaff pleads, only half in play, and we need to give full weight to the reiterated word, "company". Weil writes that "there is something tragically lunatic about his trust in Hal's countenancing" (*Dependency*, 91). We might add that this tragic lunacy is the human condition because human beings need other people, not in the sense of their "serviceability" but simply as an irreducible desire for their "company". I am therefore taking the "countenance" in "countenancing" here in the more restricted sense of being in the presence of the other. Deprived of each others' company, "uncountenanced", both Hal and Falstaff shrink – they "fall away . . . bate . . . and dwindle". However, they do so in different ways and in different dimensions. The knight, so large in these two plays, shrinks to an unfulfilled promise and a bit of sentimental reported speech. Hal, convincing his people that he will

---

[38] See Grady's fine discussion of "proleptic mourning" in *2 Henry IV*, in *Shakespeare*, 193–200.

serve them best by waging war on "strands afar remote" (*1 Henry IV*, 1.1.4), becomes a Machiavellian colossus, but also a figure who can call himself "friend" only in disguise.[39]

The concept of "company" and its loss returns us to the theatrical quality of the relationship between Hal and Falstaff and their contact with the audience. What is lost after the *Henry IV* plays, and only partly restored in *The Merry Wives of Windsor*, is the pleasure that we derive from the larger-than-life theatricality of these characters as performers. "Banish him not thy Harry's company": the words encompass the loss of a figure such as Tarlton from the company of players and the pleasure of the audience, for whom the interaction of Hal and Falstaff as player-characters is more engrossing than their historical reality. If Falstaff's dramatic role lives on as a faint echo in Henry's deconstructive disquisition on "ceremony" (*Henry V*, 4.1.213–66), Henry's increasing exercise of service as a (particularly military) discipline that excludes all forms of affectionate bias eradicates service insofar as it involves love and friendship.[40] Here the apparently diverging forms of service encompassed by residually feudal relations and new commercialised forms of the theatre come together in the *love* that paying audiences might develop for the player-character, such as Falstaff, who moves across the *platea* into the hearts and imaginations of a more than merely paying audience.

---

[39] See *Henry V*, 4.1.90. It is especially telling that when Henry V unmasks the traitors, he betrays a peculiar intensity towards Scrope, described as having shared a particularly close friendship with him:

> But O
> What shall I say to thee, Lord Scrope, thou cruel,
> Ingrateful, savage, and inhuman creature?
> Thou that didst bear the key of all my counsels,
> That knew'st the very bottom of my soul,
> That almost mightst ha' coined me into gold
> Wouldst thou ha' practised on me for thy use.
> (*Henry IV*, 2.2.90–6)

This betrayal of friendship, which inverts the final scene of the *2 Henry IV*, is the only scene in which friendship as such is invoked in the play. Compare the Henriad, in which, as Shannon points out, "friend" and its cognates appears some seventy-seven times (Shannon, *Amity*, 166).

[40] See his execution of Bardolph, and the strangely poignant gap between Harry le Roi and Pistol's effusive emotional attachment to his old companion:

> PISTOL The King's a bawcock and a heart-of-gold,
> A lad of life, an imp of fame,
> Of parents good, of fist most valiant.
> I kiss his dirty shoe, and from heartstring
> I love the lovely bully. What is thy name?
> (*Henry IV*, 4.1.45–9)

ANTONY AND CLEOPATRA

Considering the Henriad alongside the later Roman tragedy highlights the parallels between the relationships of friendship-in-service involving Henry and Falstaff on the one hand, and Antony and Enobarbus on the other.[41] But the question of service, friendship, and love are not confined to the relationship between Antony and his right-hand man. They pervade the play at every level. Enobarbus's mysterious death of a broken heart is echoed directly by Iras, who dies at the touch of her mistress, and by Charmian, who follows Cleopatra's suicide. Servants oscillate between positions of power and subordination, loyalty and betrayal, critical commentary and silent acquiescence. Masters and mistresses themselves share this vacillation, occupying subject positions that, at least in the imagination, liken them to servants.[42] The variety of these relationships, which both conform to and break free from social models of master, servant, and friend, revisit the issue of subjectivity and agency discussed in relation to the Henriad. The political context shifts from the residually feudal relationships of English history to the rivalry between Rome and Egypt, Venus and Mars. If Eros plays a marginal role in the English plays, he takes centre stage in this one, embodied not only in the colossal pairing of the Roman general and the queen of Egypt, but also in the appellation of a minor personal servant who literally represents the sacrifice of self distilled through the loving service that Antony and Cleopatra finally, but severally, perform for each other.

Antony and Cleopatra is an exception to my earlier claim that love has disappeared from the critical vocabulary of Shakespeare critics in the past two decades. The traditionally considered alternatives, that the play either celebrates the world well lost for love or that it demonstrates the tragic consequences of obsessive infatuation, continue to inform commentary, even of critics primarily concerned with racial and gender politics. Jonathan Dollimore claims that Shakespeare's tragedy does not show "love which transcends power" but rather focuses on "the sexual infatuation which foregrounds it". He offers a timely reminder of the imbrication of desire and power in the play's central sexual relationship:[43] "Right from the outset,"

---

[41] Weil writes perceptively about both these plays in relation to friendship and service, but her approach, via the notion of "friendly flattery", is different from mine. See *Dependency*, chapter 4.

[42] David Evett usefully divides the play's depiction of master-servant relations between commodified service, characterised by instrumentality, contract, and exchange, and more selfless, affective relationships (*Discourses*, chapter 8).

[43] Dollimore, *Radical Tragedy*, 217.

he observes, "we are told that power is internal to the relationship [between Antony and Cleopatra] itself" (216). Dollimore is right; but we might ask what that relationship "itself" is. Unless we take his shift from "love" to "sexual infatuation" as a mere stylistic variation, there is a curious moralism in his claim that puts him in the company of those who have disapproved of the relationship, and especially Cleopatra's part in it, because it does not conform to a peculiar ideological view of sexuality and women.[44] Is power foregrounded by "sexual infatuation" or by "love"? Does the play offer a clear distinction between these two concepts? There are two ways of approaching this question: one by relying, as Dollimore does, on what "we are told"; the other by what the lovers do (which includes what they say), or perhaps with the ways in which their actions and service are encompassed by the concept of idleness, which is given a different inflexion by Cleopatra in contrast to Falstaff.[45] What they do and say and what we are told change and contradict each other, often radically, as the performance progresses. This makes the difference between infatuation and love and their relation power difficult to articulate with any certainty.

We are invited from the first line of the play to view *eros* in traditional ways: as a violently unstable passion that turns masters into slaves, as something that destroys masculine capacity for action and reason, and as a force that dissolves identity itself. There could hardly be a more traditional or conservative perspective. As the play progresses, however, Antony and Cleopatra inhabit the role of lovers differently, extending and changing the concept of *eros* itself. It is the more significant that this happens in relation to other roles that would not normally be related to the erotic, with the result that *eros* becomes infused with the subjectivities of soldiership, mastery, service, beggary, play, friendship, and transcendence. Nonsexual roles take on an unexpected, erotic aura. If the tavern is the space in which alternative subjectivities may be tested through play in the Henriad, Egypt itself offers such opportunities in *Antony and Cleopatra*. When Antony and Cleopatra seem to have least scope for manoeuvre, they live up to the demands of choice: they forge their identities either by inhabiting available or expected roles or changing the "bourn" of such roles to discover "new heaven, new

---

[44] The most well-known and outspoken of such critics is George Bernard Shaw: "after giving a faithful picture of a soldier broken down by debauchery & the typical wanton in whose arms such men perish, Shakespear finally strains all his huge command of rhetoric & stage pathos to give a theatrical sublimity to the wretched end of the business, & to persuade foolish spectators that the world was well lost by the twain" (Shaw, *Three Plays for Puritans*, xxx).

[45] Cf. Hawkes, *Talking Animals*, 190: "In Rome, love is a word; in Egypt, love is a deed". Like most statements about *Antony and Cleopatra*, this is half true. It is noteworthy that Hawkes calls his chapter on *King Lear* and *Antony and Cleopatra* "The language of love".

earth". Their actions occur *within* the domain of political and military struggle and constitute a move within that game. Their moves transform the terms of the game, but they do not take the game into a separate or transcendental sphere.

"Office" and "devotion" vs "idleness"

Antony and Cleopatra begins and ends with the most self-conscious of theatrical gestures. It self-referentially invokes the status of the players and the dramatist as the lowliest of servants. [46] The first fifty lines represent three things. First, the conflict between two demands of service in Antony: the "office" of empire on the one hand and effeminising "devotion" on the other. A servant-actor playing Philo, a servant, invites the audience – now in the magical, liminal position of "masters" – to consider his master, one of the triple pillars of the world, as no more than a servant, a base slave to a woman, who in this instance is played by an apprentice actor – a servant to servants. "Office" is thus unconventionally represented by the Roman servants on the *platea*, whereas "devotion" is literally embodied by the eunuchs fanning the Egyptian queen, their actions making concrete the emasculation and servility of Antony's reduction to being the mere "bellows and the fan / To cool a Gypsy's lust" (1.1.9–10). Second, the servility of erotic devotion is denied from the *locus* in Antony's claim of mutual love staged through the lovers' embrace. Such love is claimed to extend beyond the bounds of empire itself. Finally, reoccupying the *platea* position formerly taken by Philo and Demetrius, Cleopatra subverts that very claim – "excellent falsehood", she says – via her own embodiment of the uncertainties of love in service of empire and empire in the face of love.

We are thus invited by the disapproving servant, Philo, to judge the contest between two forms of service under the onslaught of uncontrolled desire. Antony is not being presented as a master who has merely reduced himself to the level of servant: what is in question are two kinds of service, two different demands upon his "office" and "devotion". The demands of the former press upon Antony almost at once with the arrival of more servants: the ambassadors from Rome. They are reinforced by Egypt's queen

---

[46] Of all Shakespeare's plays, *Antony and Cleopatra* has possibly attracted the most commentary regarding its self-conscious theatricality. See Rackin, "Shakespeare's Boy Cleopatra"; Singh, "Renaissance Anti-Theatricality"; and Loomba, *Gender*. Adelman, in *The Common Liar*, observes that this opening invitation to judge, coming in the midst of an implied disagreement which begins before the play opens, "signals the dialectical shifting of perspectives from the very beginning". A similar observation is made by John Danby in *Poets*.

herself, who taunts her lover, in Philo's vein, for being no more than an instrument of others' desires, a servant to a mere boy and a woman:

> Fulvia perchance is angry; or who knows
> If the scarce-bearded Caesar have not sent
> His powerful mandate to you: "Do this, or this,
> Take in that kingdom and enfranchise that.
> Perform 't, or else we damn thee."   (21–5)

Cleopatra's mimicry, especially its sarcastic parody of Roman master-servant relations, stings. She provokes Antony to assert his expected role as Roman master over his juvenile partner and rebellious wife, but at the same time challenges him to break free from the master-servant roles that Rome expects of him.

Antony rebuts this imputed instrumentality with a performative creation of a "world elsewhere":

> Let Rome in Tiber melt, and the wide arch
> Of the ranged empire fall. Here is my space.
> Kingdoms are clay. Our dungy earth alike
> Feeds beast as man. The nobleness of life
> Is to do thus; when such a mutual pair
> And such a twain can do 't – in which I bind
> On pain of punishment the world to weet –
> We stand up peerless.   (35–42)

For a brief moment of intensity, in which erotic and histrionic passion are united, the two bodies on the stage occupy a singular, revolutionary space in which servile devotion is eschewed for the immediacy of loving reciprocity. This moment of self-conscious theatre is as significant as Cleopatra's later projection of herself as an anticipated object of theatrical derision: "I shall see / Some squeaking Cleopatra boy my greatness / I' th' posture of a whore" (5.2.215–17). For the space that Antony's speech act heroically (or recklessly) declares its own, in contrast to the merely verbal invocation of "kingdoms" and the "ranged empire", is measured and secured before our eyes, in the embodied performance of self-reflexive mutuality. This is an embodiment as palpable as Falstaff, but to very different effect. For all the local habitation of its incarnation before our eyes, love is also claimed to be without measure, not of this earth.

Antony's unexpected recognition of Fulvia's death as a loss rather than a release brings with it a sudden revaluation of the relationship that he has just enacted with Cleopatra as an exercise not of service but rather of *idleness*:

> I must from this enchanting queen break off.
> Ten thousand harms more than the ills I know
> My idleness doth hatch.   (121–3)

What was earlier proclaimed as the "nobleness of life" is now no more than inactivity and slothfulness, the celebrated "mutual pair" sundered by the disenchanted epithet, "this enchanting queen". Antony's sudden disapproval (along with Philo) of "idleness" is not so much a "Roman thought" as a distillation of number of Elizabethan and Jacobean anxieties that rolled together a disapproval of *eros* as "love-in idleness" (*A Midsummer Night's Dream*, 2.1.168)); idleness exemplified by the vagabond, beggar, or masterless man; and the idleness of "common player", who may have worn the livery of a noble lord but nevertheless spent his time drawing those who should be at work or in church to the leisure of theatrical spectacle.[47] By combining all three forms of idleness in her histrionics, her indulgent sexuality, and the epithet "Gypsy", Cleopatra transforms it into a different form of "sweating labour". First, she exposes Antony's posturing with her own theatricality by joining her waiting-women on the *platea* in opposition to Antony's verbose histrionics on the domestic *locus*:

> ANTONY   By the fire
>   That quickens Nilus' slime, I go from hence
>   Thy soldier-servant, making peace or war
>   As thou affects.
> CLEOPATRA   Cut my lace, Charmian, come.
>   But let it be. I am quickly ill and well;
>   So Antony loves.
> ANTONY   My precious queen, forbear,
>   And give true evidence to his love, which stands
>   An honourable trial.
> CLEOPATRA   So Fulvia told me.
>   I prithee turn aside and weep for her,
>   Then bid adieu to me, and say the tears
>   Belong to Egypt. *Good now, play one scene*
>   *Of excellent dissembling, and let it look*
>   *Like perfect honour.*

---

47 See Pugliatti, *Beggary*: "Vagabondage and idleness . . . were not the only faults imputed to strolling players . . . strolling players and other 'performers' were equated to professional beggars and vagrants on account of their being idlers and of their unstable abode and feigned identity" and "John Greene . . . attributes to them 'idleness'" and "says that players . . . stand to take money of euery one that comes to see them loyter and play" (3, 5, and 118).

ANTONY   You'll heat my blood. No more.
CLEOPATRA You can do better yet; but this is meetly.
ANTONY Now by my sword –
CLEOPATRA   And target. Still he mends.
  But this is not the best. *Look, prithee, Charmian,*
  How this Herculean Roman does become
  The carriage of his chafe.   (1.3.68–95; emphasis added)

Cleopatra's purpose is primarily to undercut Antony's conventional (and spurious) assurance that as her "soldier-servant" he acts on her behalf, putting into effect *her* desires and commands. Drawing attention to her own protean performance ("I am quickly ill or well / So Antony loves"), she makes him play the role of dissembling player, alternating ridiculously between Bottom's stock figures of a "lover or a tyrant" (*A Midsummer Night's Dream*, 1.2.19). By showing up Antony's "excellent dissembling", Cleopatra reveals his blindness to his own, peculiar "idleness". That word gathers a different charge when the Roman dismisses her with the contemptuous comment, "But that your royalty / Holds idleness your subject, I should take you / For idleness itself" (92–4).

"Idleness itself" – what might that be? Cleopatra responds that it lies both "near the heart" and that it involves "sweating labour":

  'Tis sweating labour
  To bear such idleness so near the heart
  As Cleopatra this.   (94–6)

The meta-theatrical nature of this scene embroils the concepts of both service and love such that each becomes a subject of play, in the deepest sense of the word (including "sweating labour") as the play itself progresses. Antony will in due course abjure all labour or force upon being deprived of Cleopatra's idleness ("now all labour / Mars what it does; yea, very force entangles / Itself with strength" (4.15.47–9)), and Cleopatra will face the horrific, anti-theatrical thought of her own transformation by the idleness of the theatre, before she confuses *locus* and *platea* in the staging of her own death as a celebration of the "sweating labour" of idleness.

Fungibility in love and service

The play's presentation of its pattern of early modern concerns about service in the first fifty lines forms a framing context for Antony and Cleopatra's decision to refuse to be the slaves of Fortune through the performative mastery of themselves. Yet this self-expressive mastery is achieved only through the acknowledgement of a certain kind of service. The problem in *Antony and Cleopatra* is not the full acknowledgement of the other but rather the acknowledgement of oneself as living wholly for the other. If the play shows how difficult it is to know love and live by it in the heterosexual example of Antony and Cleopatra, it demonstrates how the bonds of service may often forge unconscious ties of loving dependence that the subject may not recognise until it is too late. This point may be illuminated by turning once again to the respective relation of love and service to the possibilities and necessities of substitution.

What Evett terms commodified service is service amenable to substitution, in which all that counts is the fact that the there is some place-holder in the relation; it does not matter who, in the deepest, human sense, that is. A sense of irreplaceable loss, such as Antony feels upon Cleopatra's death and such as she shares with her "girls", is the mark of relationships in which the place-holder is irreplaceable, or felt to be so. One of the sources of both Antony and Cleopatra's anxieties about the other's loyalty lies in their shared suspicion that they are merely the latest in a series of substitutes: in Cleopatra's serial affairs with Pompey and Caesar and Antony's marriages to Fulvia and Octavia. The low-key but decisive role of the concept of marriage in *Antony and Cleopatra* underscores this logic of nonsubstitution in love: Cleopatra soon realizes, after her bitter sense of betrayal, that Antony's cynical marriage to Caesar's sister will not replace her in his affections, and at the end of the play, she embraces marriage as a condition of nonfungible loyalty and devotion by sacrilising their relationship in the self-authorising, performative cry: "Husband, I come" (5.2.282).

What of service? There are plenty of examples in which the bonds between servant and master are amenable, under conditions of expediency, to fungibility. The most striking is Menas, who leaves Pompey's service, paradoxically because his master refuses what might seem to be his supreme act of service, killing the other members of the triumvirate, which would make Pompey "the lord of all the world" (2.7.58). "In me 'tis villainy", Pompey responds regretfully to Menas's equally treacherous and liberal offer, "In thee 't had been good service" (2.7.72–3). Menas's posture of extreme servility, in the rhetoric of cap-in-hand menial – "I have ever held my cap off to thy fortunes" – is taken by Pompey as the exemplum of faithful devotion – "Thou hast served me with much faith" (54–5). Once Menas has decided that Pompey has squandered his good fortune, however, that faith evaporates: "For this, I'll never follow thy palled fortunes more. / Who seeks and will not take when once 'tis offered, / Shall never find it more" (78–80). The radical distinction between the same action as performed by master and servant ("villainy" vs. "good service") shows Pompey's reduction of his servant to an instrument in which the ethics of hospitality are not fungible. He has a relationship of trust to his guests; his servant has a relationship of obedience only to him.

A subtle variation on this theme occurs in the very next scene, where, on the far-flung battlefields of Parthia, Antony's lieutenant, Vinditius, refuses to press home his advantage, because that would put his master too much in his debt.

> Caesar and Antony have ever won
> More in their officer than person . . .
> Who does i' th' wars more than his captain can
> Becomes his captain's captain . . .
> I could do more to do Antonius good,
> But 'twould offend him, and in his offence
> Should my performance perish.   (16–27)

Vinditius's cautious servility is the obverse of Menas's more ranging ambition, although both exemplify the fact that the servant is the occluded substitute and instrument of magisterial fame and power. This is not merely a statement about practical ability, it is also about the limits of ethical capacity. Servants can achieve for their masters more than their masters can because they are supposedly free of the constraints that impinge upon their masters. This perspective from below of the power relations between master and servant at their most uncompromising shows not only the dependence of master upon servant but also the self-conscious perspicuity of the servant who struggles to maintain a precarious balance between gratitude and resentment, punishment and reward.

There are plenty of servants or followers who abandon Antony once his fortunes begin to pall. They underscore the rule of the fungibility of both servant and master and the triumph of expediency over ethics. Yet no one benefits or prospers from his switch of allegiance. The clear-eyed Caesar places them in the vanguard of the battle, so "That Antony may seem to spend his fury / Upon himself" (4.6.9–10). Antony wastes himself, his body becoming the synechdochal site of both service and revolt. Caesar thus recognises the continuing affective and symbolic closeness of master and subordinate even when the latter has revolted. Enobarbus is the exemplum of such closeness. As his master's judgement fails, he begins to struggle with his conscience and affection and the conflicting demands of worldly success and fame, in which the loyal servant seeks to "earn a place in the story".

Enobarbus embodies the cognate conceptual relationship between the terms "servant" and "friend" in Shakespeare's England. This conceptual affinity is apparent in two peculiar scenes. In the first, feeling that he has "lost command" (3.11. 23), Antony addresses his personal servants repeatedly as "friends", urging them to make their peace with Caesar and promising them a ship laden with gold and letters of passage. In the second, he embarrasses them and dumbfounds Cleopatra and Enobarbus by thanking his menials individually for their loyal devotion. His queen and right-hand man are outraged and the attendants disconcerted, I suspect, because Antony brings to the surface notions of the dependence of master upon his servant expressed by Vinditius. Yet he utters such thoughts only when his *loss* of power paradoxically prompts him to articulate such ethical aspects of service. Antony acknowledges his servants by recognising the degree to which he is the sum of those who have served him. The discandying of Antony's sense of self is thus not merely the fluctuation of an anticipatory post-modern unfixing of identity but rather the social function of himself as a broader body constituted by his servants' collective devotion, sacrifice, and impending loss:

> (*Enter* SERVITORS)
>   Give me thy hand.
> Thou hast been rightly honest; so hast thou,
> Thou, and thou, and thou; you have served me well,
> And kings have been your fellows.
> [. . .]
> (*to a* SERVITOR) And thou art honest too.
> I wish I could be made so many men,
> And all of you clapped up together in
> An Antony, *that I might do you service*
> *So good as you have done.*
> [. . .]   Tend me tonight.
> Maybe it is the period of your duty.
> Haply you shall not see me more; or if,
> A mangled shadow. Perchance tomorrow
> You'll serve another master. I look on you
> As one that takes his leave. Mine honest friends,
> I turn you not away, but, like a master
> *Married to your good service*, stay till death.
> Tend me tonight two hours. I ask no more;
> And the gods yield you for 't!   (4.210–33)

Here *eros* and *nomos* are combined in a particularly striking way: Antony may sentimentalise the relationship of his servants to his former power by suggesting that his empire was their "fellow", but he also conveys his own sense of waning power as not merely an erotic attachment to their service but also a sacrilised bond.

It is clear from the servants' response and Cleopatra and Enobarbus's comments that this is to some degree a performative exercise in self-pity, especially in his pre-emptive speculation that in the morning they will have turned to Caesar as their master. Servants are thus constrained structurally by the fact that there is no space beyond service: they are structurally fungible because the loss of one master is merely the imposition another. They can bow to this necessity in one of two ways: by remaining loyal to the end, in which case they will either be killed or enslaved, or they can chose to abandon ship before it sinks, but that simply means accepting a new form of servitude. In the first, service is aligned with love and its cognate concepts: loyalty, affect, devotion, and nonfungibility. Antony expresses as few masters do in Shakespeare both a sacrilised sense of being bound, as in marriage, to his servants and also the sense that masters owe an equal service to those who have served him. In doing so he acknowledges, if only obliquely, his failure as a master, unlike Timon, whose signal failure of moral vision lies in his blindness to his bond with his servants.

Antony and Cleopatra draws to a close with a number of further variations on the relationships among service, marriage, loss, and failure. Antony's loving servant, Eros – Philo's alter ego – chooses to sacrifice himself rather than fulfil his promise to kill his master. Decretus carries Antony's sword to Caesar in the hope of a reward from his new master. In contrast, all Cleopatra's women die serving her. Caesar's servants variously fulfil and betray his desires, and Caesar himself reveals the strange conjunction of *eros* and war in his sorrowful response to the news of the death of the delinquent servant of empire. It is possible to trace two conceptions of service in the play, which we might be tempted to dub "Roman" or "Egyptian" if they did not distribute themselves unevenly across the two domains. One is encapsulated by an almost incidental metaphor, when a messenger announces that "Menecrates and Menas, famous pirates, / *Makes the sea serve them, which they ear and wound* / With keels of every kind" (1.4.48–50; emphasis added). The other, contrasted with such instrumentalist violence, is represented by Antony who recognises, even if he does not fully embody, his debt to those who serve him not only as a constituent part of his identity but also a sacred bond to which he tied forever.

Fortune's slaves

These alternatives force us to ask to what extent Antony and Cleopatra manage to transcend the accidents of fortune and the destruction of time.

Does their love elevate them above the force of instrumental reason, even when the latter is being wielded by a man whose Machiavellian aim is to make Fortune (a woman, and therefore, like Cleopatra, to be used) his own?[48] This is what Cleopatra thinks:

> CLEOPATRA My desolation does begin to make
> A better life. 'Tis paltry to be Caesar.
> Not being Fortune, he's but Fortune's knave,
> A minister of her will. And it is great
> To do that thing that ends all other deeds,
> Which shackles accidents and bolts up change,
> Which sleeps and never palates more the dung,
> The beggar's nurse, and Caesar's.   (5.2.1–8)[49]

This speech suggests a way of viewing the contraries of the play in less deterministic, geographical, or racial terms. Instead of seeing Caesar as representative of all Rome, Cleopatra of a racialised and feminised "other" in the form of Egypt, with Antony caught between them, one might apply Grady's analysis of the Henriad to this play by suggesting that it represents the struggle between instrumental reason as encapsulated by the Machiavellian figure of Caesar, and carnivalising tendencies, *in Roman and Egyptian alike*, to undermine, through histrionic pleasure and the devotion of loving service, such instrumentality allied to power.[50] As we have seen, being by definition alien to the fungibility that lies at the heart of instrumental power, service informed by love and love enacted as mutual service are conceptually and ethically, if not politically, the only ways of resisting instrumentalising power.

The question that Cleopatra raises in her meditation on Caesar as "Fortune's knave" is thus whether power encompasses everything. To make this point is not to return to the position, criticised by Dollimore, that Antony and Cleopatra are above the attractions (or even the abuses) of power. It is rather to ask whether power is an absolute value and whether Shakespeare's tragedy finds a "place in the story" for values that are not reducible to relations of power. When Cleopatra opens her scene with the

---

[48] See Niccolo Machiavelli, *The Prince*.

[49] Cf. Cleopatra's mock assumption of the discourse of servile obedience to Dolabella:

> Pray you, tell him
> I am his fortune's vassal, and I send him
> The greatness he has got. I hourly learn
> A doctrine of obedience, and would gladly
> Look him i' th' face.   (5.2.28–32)

[50] The representatives of carnival should not be sentimentalised. Margot Heinemann observes that "if this is carnival it is a rich people's carnival, a scene from Veronese rather than Brueghel" ("Order and Disorder", 171).

general observation, "My desolation does begin to make / A better life", she is making a fresh value judgement both on her own life up to that point and on Caesar's in the future. It is only in the light of that revision that Caesar, who has exemplified the politician as the master of Fortune, may be seen to have become the slave of the strange, theatrical figure of Fortune in the figure of Cleopatra. Here mastery and love combine in unusual ways.

Shakespeare's sonnets, concerned with the preservation of value, offer the constancy of love and the matching durability of poetry as the only forces capable of withstanding "times fell hand" (64.1). In the sonnets, at least, love and reiterative representation go hand in hand: it is not merely the beloved's beauty that will survive; that beauty exists only in relation to the loving poet who dedicates himself to ensuring that it will outlast even the monumental remains of kingdoms and empires. If sonnet 126 is the poet's revenge, by which the servant shifts his allegiance and labour to a new mistress who is revealed to be his master's enemy, sonnet 124 offers a *concept* of love that is pertinent to Cleopatra's deliberations. It suggests that love (rather than beauty) can exist only if it can avoid being reduced to "fortune's bastard". It can transcend time and fortune only if it embodies a courageous refusal to fall under the sway of such things as both make and destroy the "clay" of "kingdoms". Antony makes such a claim from the outset, as we have seen, but nothing up to that point "bears it out" in what he (or Cleopatra) does. Shakespeare offers a concept of love in *Antony and Cleopatra* that is less a kind of emotion or passion than an embodied form of action or performance. Sonnet 124 makes it clear that in addition to its refusal to be "mingled with regards that stands / Aloof from th' entire point" (*King Lear*, F 1.1.239–40)), like "smiling pomp" or "thrilled discontent", love requires courage: it "feares not policy". When Cleopatra proposes to do that "which shackles accidents and bolts up change" (5.2.5) she formulates the only means by which she can make Caesar, rather than herself, "Fortune's knave". She usurps his mastery by making him her servant in the figure of Fortune. By evading, through a determined exercise of her own will, the accident and change to which all policy – even highly successful policy such as Caesar's – is subject, she renders him an "ass / Unpolicied" (5.2.302–3).

She is successful only because she plays a large role in the politician's policy: the importance that he attaches to her as the theatrical foil for his "smiling pomp" puts *him* in *her* power. It is thus only because he values her so highly as an object of powerful display that Cleopatra is given the space to upstage his carefully scripted set in the streets of Rome. Furthermore, we should not forget that Cleopatra requires courage to occupy that new stage of her newly acquired agency. Just as Lucrece reclaims the performantive force of her body, which appears to have been taken from her by Tarquin's possession, so Cleopatra can justly claim the role of Fortune by what she decides to do: by mobilising the performative force of her own actions. Cleopatra represents their collective suicide to her servant-companions as a *Roman* action: "what's brave, what's noble, / Let's do it after the high Roman fashion" (4.16.88–9). She does not simply succumb to or adopt what are termed "Roman values", however. Her declaration to do "what's brave, what's noble" is inflected equally by her peculiar Egyptian situation and by the transformation that her love for Antony has wrought on things both Egyptian and Roman.

"Sweating labour"

First, the intimacy through which she includes her servants, who have acted throughout the play as companions and who sacrifice themselves for her, is decidedly un-Roman, if we measure things Roman by the "boy-Caesar's" relations to his subordinates. Consider her efforts to include her servants in this moment of otherwise personal suffering:

> How do you, women?
> What, what, good cheer! Why, how now, Charmian?
> My noble girls! Ah, women, women! Look,
> *Our lamp* is spent, it's out. *Good sirs, take heart.*
> (4.16.84–7; emphasis added)

Cleopatra echoes Antony's earlier attempt to acknowledge his servants, but whereas her lover was unable to bridge the gap between himself and those who served him, alienating them as much as he included them in his embrace, her speech acts are wholly inclusive, directed outwards at the pain of those who surround her rather than stemming from her own sense of loss. If we take Cleopatra's decision to have occurred at the point of this utterance, when Antony's death means that "All's but naught" (80), then the reason for committing suicide (not to speak of its performative mode) speaks far more strongly of Eros than of Mars. By transcending what may too hastily be called an Egyptian or feminine inclination towards vacillation and flux in the form of erotic devotion to Antony and by staging her death as a kind of sexual consummation, Cleopatra inhabits the form of what is "Roman" in a wholly new way. She transforms its instrumentalising of *eros* as "love that's hired" (5.2.151) into a celebration in which love and sensuality are staged together as things worth dying for.

That her servants accompany her in this death includes their devotion
within the wider ambit of her relationship with Antony. At the very moment
that the play's Egyptian queen appears to transcend the grubby world of
service, the player who embodies her mythical ideal calls attention to his
own real status as the lowliest of servants – dependent, in the words of
one such servant, on "public means which public manners breeds" (sonnet III). This reduction of queen to servant occurs at both levels of theatrical
representation: Cleopatra as character claims that if the "nobleness of life"
is indeed to flaunt the reciprocity of embodied love in a world taken over
by loveless instrumentality, then such nobility is the prerogative of even the
meanest of servants: "No more but e'en a woman, and commanded / By
such poor passion as the maid that milks / And does the meanest chores"
(4.16.75–7).

When Cleopatra "dresses up" for her suicide, for whom is she staging her
display? The performance is directed at multiple audiences, with concomi-
tantly various effects. It is directly contrasted with Antony's dissolution
through his *un*dressing:

> Off, pluck off...
> Apace, Eros, apace.
> No more a soldier. Bruisèd pieces, go;
> You have been nobly borne. – From me a while.
>
>   (4.15.38–43)

There is a peculiarly poignant symmetry in the name of the servant who
helps Antony cast off the costume that seems to constitute his identity as
the "triple pillar of the world" and the lover who takes the place of the
squire called Eros before he goes into battle:

> ANTONY (*calling*) Eros, mine armour, Eros!
> CLEOPATRA   Sleep a little.
> ANTONY No, my chuck. Eros, come, mine armour, Eros!
>   (*Enter* EROS *with armour*)
>   Come, good fellow, put thine iron on.
>   If fortune be not ours today, it is
>   Because we brave her. Come.
> CLEOPATRA Nay, I'll help, too. What's this for?
> ANTONY   Ah, let be, let be! Thou art
>   The armourer of my heart. False, false! This, this!
> CLEOPATRA Sooth, la, I'll help. Thus it must be.
>   (*She helps* ANTONY *to arm*)   (4.4.1–8)

Contrasted with the self-inflated rhetoric that "all kingdoms are clay",
this extraordinarily domestic scene both presages Antony's inevitable military defeat and prepares the ground for the lovers' histrionically embodied

revaluation of instrumental power in its relation to affective reciprocity. It is a moment of exquisitely tender playfulness, whereby reciprocal affection is paradoxically exemplified by the transformation of lovers into mutual servants. Yet it is also ominously prescient of the painful passage that each has to take through the *imagined* betrayal by the other: "Thou art the armourer of my heart. *False, false!*"

Between Antony's impatient response to Cleopatra's well-meaning but inept attempts to protect him from the world and his later acknowledgement that no armour of whatever provenance can save him from the *internal* blows that her loss inflicts upon him ("The seven-fold shield of Ajax cannot keep / The battery from my heart") lies a belated acknowledgement, which he shares with his former servant who himself dies as a result of the "battery" of his own "heart", of the nature of human desire and its difference from love. Antony has been here before. However, whereas the news of Fulvia's death merely gave him pause to reflect on the perversity of what human beings want or think they want, the thought of Cleopatra's loss invokes a curious inversion of Desdemona's puzzle about the betrayal of one's lover for the sake of the whole world. If Othello's wife cannot encompass the thought that betrayal of the one whom one loves may be worth it if one gains the world in exchange, both Antony and Cleopatra experience the sudden and unexpected collapse of the world with the loss of the other. The *intensity* of such realization is theirs alone, although it makes a powerful appeal to our imagination.

We have seen that love's vision is unique, but its investment in the imagination makes it possible for Antony and Cleopatra to embody their vision in public, performative terms. That investment shows itself in the small as much as in the grand gesture. If Antony rages irrationally at Cleopatra's allowing her hand to be kissed by Caesar's messenger, he receives the news that she pretended to be dead with complete equanimity. Even Cleopatra's refusal to descend from her monument for fear of being captured does not upset him, and his well-intentioned advice to trust only Proculeius signals a selfless acceptance that his lover will continue to negotiate a favourable position for herself after his death. He does not have to do this. It would be in keeping with his lack of trust in his lover and with Cleopatra's deadly lie for him to want to reserve some degree of spite – as the servant-poet of the sonnets does – to be exercised after his death. His gift to Cleopatra is the gift of freedom, a kind of erotic manumission, to create her own "place in the story", which may or may not include him.

Cleopatra can show Caesar up as an "ass / Unpolicied", as "Fortune's knave . . . subject to Fortune's will", only by histrionically asserting her own will in the assumed figure of Fortune. It is she who unpolicies the Machiavel by "standing hugely politick", refusing to live only to be used in his elaborate theatre of "smiling pomp". Yet she has to *decide* to do this, to enact this role. She is different in this respect from Antony, for whom the loss of Cleopatra means the immediate diminution of all "labour" and of life itself. Cleopatra's decision is given especial ethical and political weight by the fact that it is always, until the moment it is fulfilled, uncertain. If Cleopatra were to respond without any question of a decision or hesitation, her act would convey little sense of faithfulness or love. It would happen automatically, without the exercise of her will. She would respond, as Octavia would, self-sacrificially, out of *duty*. That is why Enobarbus, who is very close to her here, earns his place in the story: his embodiment of his love for Antony occurs as the very contrary of duty. His betrayal of his master is what gives witness to the labour of idleness that is love and to the consequent "battery of his heart" engendered by idleness as Cleopatra understands it.

Whereas Enobarbus expires in a ditch in enemy territory, Cleopatra kills herself in her own elaborately constructed theatre. Her agency is crucial, even considering the passive mode of her death, and it stages the renewal of the concept of the "idleness" with which service, love, and theatricality are embroiled. The whole play prepares for this moment of decision and action. Shakespeare allows Cleopatra to stage her death for Caesar, to show him up as "Fortune's knave". However, he also stages that death (the obviousness of this should not blind us to its significance) for us, the audience, who have been invited, from the opening line, to "behold and see", to judge for ourselves.

It is a dazzling display of the histrionic capacities of the player-servant. It is simultaneously a show of mastery that, precisely because it is made in the context of uncertainty and vacillation, recrimination and betrayal, lies and anger, asks us to revalue the enticing exigencies of power and love, office and devotion, idleness and labour. In her final scene, which is prepared by Antony's death and would have been impossible without the mode and tone of that preparation, Cleopatra stages what Shakespeare's sonnets repeatedly entertain: the possibility of love's "bear[ing] it out even to the edge of doome" (sonnet 116.12) through its embodiment through poetry and the stage. Contrary to the idealising histrionics of sonnet 116, the love embodied by Cleopatra and Antony belongs to time, even if it would be going too far to declare it "time's fool". It is marked by intensities of feeling that include uncertainty, betrayal, jealousy, hubris, and sensual passion. It is not above power; but it does in its own way put power in its place.

The story in which each of the characters in *Antony and Cleopatra* has a place diverges, depending upon where one is standing in its perspectival theatre. Here is Tacitus on the consequences of the theatre of war represented in the play:

Octavian . . . attracted everybody's goodwill by the enjoyable gifts of peace. Then he gradually pushed ahead and absorbed the functions of the senate, the officials, and even the law. Opposition did not exist. War and judical murder has disposed of all men of spirit. Upper-class survivors found that slavish obedience was the way to succeed, both politically and financially. . . . Political equality was a thing of the past; all eyes watched for imperial commands.[51]

As Augustus, Octavian either bestowed the benefits of his campaign against his "competitor" in the form of "universal peace" (4.6.4) or he exercised his total power in such a way as to obliterate the complex, affective reciprocities of master-servant relationships represented in *Antony and Cleopatra*, in favour of an undifferentiated, "slavish obedience" that also found little place for love. In the embodied "toil of grace" presented by the boy apprentice, the lowliest of servants, representing Egypt's queen – in which the combination of "sweating labour" and "idleness", ensnarement and freedom, and the generosity of love and service alike are brought together – it is Cleopatra as master-servant in love who invites us to see "new heaven, new earth".

[51] Tacitus, *Annals*, 29–31.

CHAPTER 6

"I am your own forever"
King Lear and *Othello*

Othello and *King Lear*, Michael Neill has shown, are united by their mutual investment in the qualities, and uncertainties, of service.[1] Both open with the question of love and the stance of service towards love: to what extent does Othello's service to the state earn him the right to the love of its citizens in general, and one of its daughters in particular; and to what extent does the monarch's demand for a show of love in *King Lear* undermine the bonds of service upon which its very existence depends? Both plays are concerned in very different ways with the *show* of love and service – with an impossible demand in the one instance that love be demonstrated or acted out in the sphere of public life, and in the other with the refusal by the quintessential servant to display anything other than the purely performative dimensions of service.

In a pioneering essay, Jonas Barish and Marshall Waingrow use service as a touchstone for a general reading of *King Lear*.[2] They argue that service, especially *feudal* expectations of reciprocity of rights and obligations, stands at the centre of the play's vision of social and moral order. This enables them to show that social and personal failure, violence, and loss stem from a abrogation of traditional forms of reciprocity.[3] Central to their argument is the division of service into "true" and "false" forms – the former dynamically reciprocal, the latter mechanically self-serving or at least indifferently unresponsive. They might have suggested that another word for "true" service might be "love", as Neill does when he writes that in *King Lear* love is "almost synonymous with" service.[4] Such a conceptual identification provides a fruitful line of enquiry, but that identity should not be assumed without qualification. Reciprocity, which is the essence of good service in its neo-feudal sense, is not conceptually necessary for love, even if it may be desired. The absence of reciprocity marks the difference between loving service and erotic love, and it may explain the strange, troubling scene at the

---

[1] Neill, "*Servile Ministers*".   [2] Barish and Waingrow, "Service".
[3] Burnett argues that such breakdown signals the final ideological failure of service in "*King Lear*".
[4] Neill, *History*, 26.

end of *King Lear* in which Kent remains unrecognised by his master. Here Stanley Cavell's work on the ethics and psychology of acknowledgement (or the blind refusal of acknowledgement) is crucial. However, because Cavell is working within a general framework of philosophical scepticism given its peculiar modern thrust by Descartes some forty years after *King Lear* was written, his conception of acknowledgement may overlook the historical peculiarities of the politics and ethics of service that are essentially feudal in character and derivation. I want to push Cavell's arguments in a different direction by focusing on the *unconditionality* of love and service in the face of failures of recognition and acknowledgement in *King Lear* and on the dark underside of such unconditionality in Iago's refusal to serve under the cloak of perfect service as pure performance in *Othello*.

Despite their essentialising inclinations, the early modern writers whom Neill has called the "propagandists of service" recognise service as a "cluster" or "family resemblance"[5] concept. They invariably conceive service and obedience, for example, as a composite whole or indivisible unit. At first sight, a disobedient servant is a contradiction in terms. To serve is to obey; moreover, such obedience should be shown in "fear and trembling" (Gouge, *Duties*, 163 and 615ff). Plays like *King Lear* complicate such a concept of service, however, by showing that in different circumstances the cluster may change. The concept of service is much less stable than it appears. There may be circumstances in which "perfect service" might take the shape of disobedience, whereas perfect obedience under all circumstances may indicate selfish fear rather than willing duty. Kent's disobedience may thus be not a contradiction of his duty to serve his king but the very embodiment of that duty; Cordelia's failure to declare her love for her father may be the sign of a deeper form of devoted service to him; and both Oswald and Iago's perfect obedience may hide a deep perversion of service.[6]

KING LEAR

On two occasions in the opening scene of *King Lear*, a servant declares his or her bonds of allegiance to a master. Here is Cordelia, speaking to her father:

> CORDELIA Good my lord,
> You have begot me, bred me, loved me.
> I return those duties back as are right fit –
> Obey you, love you, and most honour you.
>   (F, 1.1.93–6)

---

[5] See Wittgenstein, *Books*, 17.
[6] Evett discusses the question of disobedience in relation to proper service in chapter 6 of *Service*. The pioneering essay on servant disobedience is Strier, "Faithful Servants".

And here is Kent, addressing the same man:

> KENT   Royal Lear,
>   Whom I have ever honoured as my King,
>   Loved as my father, as my master followed,
>   As my great patron thought on in my prayers –
>   (F, 1.1.137–40)

Note not only the conceptual but also the structural and syntactical similarities of these declarations. Both preface what the royal master will interpret as attitudes of insubordination and defiance with reminders of their simultaneous allegiance and reciprocity. Daughter and royal courtier conceptualise their relationship to Lear in almost identical terms: through the concepts of honour, obedience, and love.[7] The difference wrought by consanguinity and breeding in the relationship between father and daughter is reduced by the paternal care that, in Kent's eyes at least, marks his relationship to his king and master: "Loved as my father. . . . As my great patron thought on in my prayers". Although both subordinates emphasise their obeisance to the paternal figure, they also remind him of the reciprocity integral to that relationship – of the duty that rests on him as master as much as on them as servants. Neither of them talks openly about service, but service is the cornerstone of each of their declarations. This similarity reduces the political and personal differences – which we tend now to cast in terms of public and private relationships – between aristocratic courtier and family member. Daughter and earl alike are bound to the king as a "father" or "patron": each is obliged to honour him through the equal relations of love and obedience, but both insist in different ways that he acknowledge and honour his reciprocal responsibilities.

We may see from this cluster of terms that the concept of service does not stand alone: it is interwoven with other concepts which together contribute to its meaning. To serve means to love, to obey, to honour, to "think on" (in the sense of "care for"), to follow, and to *recognise*, in the sense of to *acknowledge*, the other. To be a master, equally, means to love, to command, to honour, to think on, to lead, and to recognise or acknowledge. The concepts of service and mastery are not merely antonymic: the duties of each coincide at times, just as service and love do; but they also diverge at the crucial point of inequality of power. Cordelia and Kent catalogue their observance of those duties to remind Lear of this fact. They insist that the

---

[7] This is in keeping with the general conception of the "chain of service" in political and religious tracts, which underscore the patriarchal character of early modern social relations by tracing a common chain of obedience and reciprocal responsibility between monarch and subject, master and servant, husband and wife, and father (and mother) and children. See especially Gouge, *Dvties.*

asymmetry of power relations essential to master-servant relations cannot trump the obligations that masters and servants *share*: those of love, care, and mutual recognition. Lear refuses to recognise either their reminders of his obligations or their declared acknowledgements of their own duties. Because he refuses to acknowledge his daughter and servant in their own acknowledgement of love and duty, he can find no place for them. He can only banish them, removing them from the "paternal care / Propinquity, and property of blood" (111–12) that each, in their own way, has emphasised in the ways in which they have addressed him.[8] I examine this action in due course. For the moment, I draw out the implications of the fact that service is formed by its relations to a cluster of other concepts.

Public and affective concepts of love

My argument reformulates, in terms of the early modern ideology of service, a fairly commonplace reading of the play. The reformulation does serve an original purpose, however, which is to examine the rationality of a political or social institution upon which the society as a whole was based, as opposed to the conventional assumption of the irrationality of love. What does it mean to love *and* serve someone? Why does Lear call upon his daughters to prove their *love* to him before he divides his kingdom among them? What does he understand by love; what do they understand by the concept; and does each of the parties understand the same thing? To ask these questions is to ask what cluster of concepts is brought into contact with the notion of love in each case.

King Lear's opening comment initiates the problematic questions of love, power, and the measure or measurability of each. "I thought the King had more *affected* the Duke of Albany than Cornwall" (1.1.1), Kent says to Gloucester. Liked? Or loved? It could be either, but in a context in which love will be a central concept in the negotiation of public and personal relations alike, it makes sense to take it in the common, early modern sense, of an affect that binds two people together within a broader, public network of mutual obligations and duties.

> GLOUCESTER It did always seem so to us, but now in the
> division of the King it appears not which of the Dukes
> he values most; for qualities are so weighed that
> curiosity in neither can make choice of either's moiety.
>
> (1.1.3–6)

---

[8] Judith Weil is especially perceptive in her account of the absolutely central nature of the dependencies, both affective and material, of master-servant relations and of the devastating consequences of being cast out from the protective presence of a master. See especially chapters 4 and 5 of *Dependency*.

The shift from "affect" to "value", along with the new metaphor of evaluation and calculation in the context of a kingdom that is about to be divided, indicates a double sense of "affect" or "love": the personal, emotional investment in a particular person, which is always to some degree inexplicable, if not irrational, on the one hand, and the publicly available "qualities" that are open to calculation, on the other. Note also the shift from active to passive voice in "qualities are so weighed": the king is thought to love Albany more, but as the context shifts, the evaluation of the dukes' respective merits is robbed of specific agency.

A tension, but not a complete divorce, is thus established within a divided concept of love. We are asked, from the very opening lines, to ponder the political affects of love, especially the question of the degree to which it is amenable to calculation or the product of (over)valuation. This question is going to be pursued with relentless force as the scene (and, indeed, the play) progresses. Within a line or two, Gloucester declares, in a significant intensification of the language of calculation, that neither of his sons is "dearer in [his] account" (1.1.18). Furthermore, the elaborately polite courtier exchange between Edmund and Kent reinforces the links between "love", "deserving", and "service":

> GLOUCESTER (*to* EDMOND) My lord of Kent. Remember
>   him hereafter as my honourable friend.
> EDMOND (*to* KENT) My services to your lordship.
> KENT I must love you, and sue to know you better.
> EDMOND Sir, I shall study deserving.   (1.1.24–8)

Kent presents his love as a publicly acknowledged obligation ("I must love you"), incurred in the reciprocation of Gloucester's friendship and Edmund's service, whereas Edmund declares (hypocritically, as it happens) his duty to subject himself to the injunctions of service that will in turn deserve his superior's love. Note that Kent declares his obligation and intention to love Edmund without knowing him personally, without there being any *affective* relationship between them. Love is felt as a duty incurred by a mixture of personal (Gloucester's friendship) and public (the network of social relations) pressures – it is an inextricable aspect of the bonds of service that hold the society together. They are soon to be catastrophically broken; but we must be clear precisely what they are and how they are destroyed. These declarations of love are public speech acts, affirmations of mutual affinity and recognition that establish social relationships rather than express affective attachment.

The ground thus prepared, we move to the serious amplification of these issues in Lear's division of his kingdom. It should now be clearer why and in what sense Lear demands declarations of love from his daughters before investing them with his political power. He is asking for two different, but related, things, which he confuses, to horrible effect. In the first place, he is asking for a declaration of political allegiance, a statement of their love in the sense that Kent uses the word to Edmund. Such love is conditioned by circumstance, hedged about with carefully balanced, reciprocal obligations that typically mark relations of service. In its most mystified forms, it is invoked to ensure blind loyalty to a superior who may not deserve it. It is also amenable to calculation, scruple, and questions – as Edmund puts it – of "deserving". Lear is obsessive about the latter quality. His momentous, opening declaration of purpose harps incessantly upon love as what we now call a zero-sum game, a space of rivalry, calculation, and potential loss:

> Our son of Cornwall,
> And you, our *no less loving son of Albany*,
> We have this hour a constant will to publish
> Our daughters' several dowers, that future strife
> May be prevented now. The princes France and Burgundy –
> *Great rivals in our youngest daughter's love* –
> Long in our court *have made their amorous sojourn*,
> *And here are to be answered.* Tell me, my daughters –
> Since now we will divest us both of rule,
> Interest of territory, cares of state –
> *Which of you shall we say doth love us most,*
> *That we our largest bounty may extend*
> *Where nature doth with merit challenge?*
>
> (1.1.38–51; emphasis added)

The last line indicates the other sense in which Lear is calling upon his daughters' love: in addition to – or perhaps in confusion with – the ties of political allegiance ("merit"), he is also asking for a declaration of personal devotion to him as father, in accordance with the "natural" bond between parent and child. The ambiguity around "challenge" (51) nicely expresses the fact that these two conceptions of love are in tension rather than mutually exclusive. As the scene progresses, the tensions will be exacerbated.

Goneril and Regan understand equally what is being demanded of them, and they are happy to respond with answers that paradoxically fulfil both challenges by responding only to one. They explicitly reject their father's implication of the social calculability of love by responding entirely as daughters to a father: their carefully calculated rhetoric elevates the quality of their devotion above the calculable vagaries of mere service and duty by declaring their love as something that lies beyond measure, value, and "deserving". Goneril's speech culminates in the conventionally charged declaration of personal devotion – "I love you" – rather than with the indirect formulae of political allegiance:

> GONERIL Sir, I love you more than words can wield the matter;
>   Dearer than eyesight, space, and liberty;
>   Beyond what can be valued, rich or rare,
>   No less than life; with grace, health, beauty, honour;
>   As much as child e'er loved or father found;
>   A love that makes breath poor and speech unable.
>   Beyond all manner of so much I love you.   (1.1.53–8)

Therein is its adroitness. Demanding a declaration of political reciprocity, Lear receives instead an avowal of a "natural" bond that lies beyond rationality, language itself, and the settled calculability of public relationships. He hears these words with the ears of a father rather than with the mind of a king, satisfied that Goneril has indeed "studied deserving". It is as a father, in fact, that he turns to his favourite daughter, expecting her to respond in kind – to exceed her sisters' calculated declaration of the incalculability of their love. Cordelia, however, responds instead to the *public* aspect of Lear's call for love, speaking to him in the civil language of calculable bonds rather than in the affective discourse of personal devotion. Reminded, and warned, that "nothing will come of nothing", she speaks, exactly, of *conditional* reciprocity, literally of "something for something":

>   I love your majesty
>   According to my bond, no more nor less . . .
>   . . . Haply when I shall wed
>   That lord whose hand must take my plight shall carry
>   Half my love with him, half my care and duty . . .
>   (1.1.90–100)

In doing so, she takes him at his word, matching his challenge in kind: bond for bond, measure for measure, calculation for calculation. She does so in part because the language game that her father has asked her to play (to adopt Wittgenstein's terms)[9] – that of personal affection – has been emptied of meaning by its surrounding circumstances.[10] Her sisters have already monopolised the language game of boundless or incalculable personal love: how is she to trump them, other than by offering an increasingly feeble

---

[9] Wittgenstein, *Investigations*.   [10] See Schalkwyk, *Speech*, 111ff.

counter-claim that, whatever inestimable degree of devotion they feel, hers is greater? All she can do is to try to expose the calculated nature of their protestations of incalculability by resolutely returning the language of calculation – which is the language of *reciprocity* – back to the king. She exposes the full import of the suspicion at the opening of the scene of what it might mean if the king were to "affect" one of his subjects more than another, of the reaches of favouritism, provided that the favourite could demonstrate that he or she had "studied deserving".

But she also raises the question as to whether love, like the "shadowy forests ... champaigns riched ... plenteous rivers and wide-skirted meads" (62–3) that Lear divides, may itself be calculated and parcelled out. Is the love one feels for one person halved when one comes to love another? Is it a finite resource amenable to "account"? Does one necessarily love one's father less when one takes a husband, or subtract some of one's love for one child on the birth of another? Love in this sense is not amenable to calculation or division.[11] Goneril is, therefore, correct to imply that "there's beggary in the love that can be reckoned" (*Antony and Cleopatra*, 1.1.15). The question is whether she's sincere. We should take care at this point not to resolve the conceptual issue too hastily, by concluding that we have revealed the "true" nature of love through this analysis of its incalculability. Two concepts of love are at work here: one, now familiar, is personal, not amenable to calculation, and deeply affective; the other, historically distant, is more public, in some ways open to reckoning, and, strange as it may seem, more imbricated with reciprocity – with "deserving" and "study" and therefore more open to calculation.[12] The latter is closest to feudal and early modern conceptions of service in its social rather than literary, erotic form. It is part of the unsettling greatness of Shakespeare's tragedy that in its opening gambit, the two different discourses should be spoken by the wrong characters. Those who live by the calculability of service speak the language of incalculable love. That is precisely what forces those who believe in the latter to adopt the apparently heartless language of public calculability. The language of one kind of love having been expropriated, they are left to merely to adopt a paradoxical, passive action: to "love and be silent".

The opening scene ends with Lear foreswearing the very reciprocity that Cordelia underscores when she declares that she loves him according to her bond, before the king of France enacts the love of which the sisters

---

[11] See the discussion of the indivisibility of a father's love in Guazzo, *Conuersation*, sig. lv[v] ff.
[12] See Derrida, "Passions", 3–31.

merely speak, taking Lear's cast-off daughter without regard for calculation or "price". "Love's not love", France tells Burgundy, in an echo of sonnet 116, "When it is mingled with regards that stands / Aloof from th'entire point" (1.1.236–8).[13] But what is that point? Is Burgundy utterly misguided in insisting upon the exact terms of his bond with the king – Cordelia's dowry and the royal blessing – holding her "dear" only insofar as she is framed by a set of public, political relations? Let us hold that question while we turn to the parallel response of the Earl of Kent to Lear's actions.

Disobedience and the bonds of service

The crucial aspect through which we should view Kent's actions is at first sight not love but service. Just as Cordelia paradoxically speaks the language of love as a public bond to the king out of her deepest affection for her father, so Kent displays his total commitment to the bond of service to his monarch precisely by *defying* him. If unquestioning obedience is commonly coupled to the concept of service by the propagandists of service, that duty is also qualified in the clearest possible terms. Gouge draws a sharp distinction between true servants under God and those whom he terms mere "men-pleasers":

A servant must not wholly give himselfe to sooth and please his master: for so may he in many things displease Almighty God . . . when masters command and forbid any thing against God, they goe beyond their commission, and therein their authoritie ceaseth. (Gouge, 166 and 637–8)

Dod and Cleaver concur, but they cast the net of what must not be obeyed very widely indeed by positing conscience as the final arbiter:

And surely all duty of seruants which is not done of conscience, is but eye seruice . . . Seruants and apprentices therefore . . . must remember, how farre foorth they are bound to obey their maisters, that is, *Usque ad aras*: so farre as Christian religion suffereth, and so far forth as they may do it with an vpright conscience otherwise, if their maisters shall command them to do any thing that is vnhonest, unlawful, wicked, vnjust, or vngodly, then they must in no wise obey it. (Dod and Cleaver, *Government*, A2ᵛ & Aa3ᵛ)

Crucial is the emphasis on *conscience*.[14] Critics who see *King Lear* as the representation of a crisis regarding service itself, or the Protestant ideal

---

13 We are reminded here of Montaigne's comment about loving friendship or *philia*: "This hath no other *Idea* than it selfe, and can have no reference but to it selfe" (149).

14 Cf. Strier's discussion of the ambivalence of both Catholic and Protestant positions in "Faithful Servants". Strier refers to Castiglione and Luther, and the Homily on Obedience, but not to the later Puritan writers such as Gouge.

of service as a sacralised relationship, tend to pay insufficient attention to the fact that an integral part of the Protestant conception of service is that a servant's duty is to disobey his or her secular master or mistress when obedience would mean not only opposing God's will but also the dictates of one's own conscience.[15] God's word is ultimately not mediated institutionally in the Protestant world as it is in the Catholic. Moreover, it is only because secular forms of service derive their authority or "commission" (as Gouge puts it) from God, that service is itself sacralised. This has contrary implications for Neill's otherwise fine treatment of *King Lear* and the sacralisation of service. Neill claims that Kent's disobedience desacralises service: after the earl's initial act of revolt, "neither he, nor the idea of service for which he stands, can ever be 'the same' again" (*"Servile Ministers"*, 36). How we take this depends upon what we believe is the idea of service that Kent embodies. Service may be descralised by disobedience only if the sacred aspect of service lies in absolute obedience to the secular master. But it does not: it lies in absolute obedience to God and one's conscience, which may require disobedience, in this or that case, where a master has required action that is not merely unlawful, but also "vnhonest . . . wicked, unjust, or ungodly".[16] To *preserve* the sacred qualities of service, then, it may be necessary precisely to disobey one's master. The question is how one acts *after* such an act of disobedience. Kent embraces the spirit of service by recommitting himself utterly to his master, under conditions that as one character puts it, are "improper for a slave" (Q, Scene 24, l. 215).

Kent's impassioned opposition to Lear conveys the moral, legal, and theological framework of his resistance. Having declared his honour, devotion, and duty to his king as the prologue to his intervention (1.1.138–40), the earl casts his opposition to Lear's actions precisely in terms of those rehearsed obligations as the king's subject. It is his self-considered duty as servant to the king that prompts him to speak when "power to flattery bows"; it is his honour – derived from the king – that calls for his insubordinate plainness; and it is his fearless devotion to his monarch's safety that allows him to parry Lear's threats of violence upon him. Against these embodied acts of true devotion – exemplified by Kent's servile metaphor of being the "true blank"

---

[15] See especially Burnett, "King Lear". Neill's fine essay on the sacralisation of service gives insufficient weight to the fact that the sacred character of service is derived from the prior duty to serve God above all things and therefore has a certain kind of disobedience as one of its defining characteristics (Neill, *"Servile Ministers"*).

[16] Shuger, *Habits*, 103: "[The] formulation of the contrast between spiritual and temporal in terms of public verses private strongly influences the ecclesiology of the Church of England". Thus Whitgift distinguishes the "visible society and the external government" of the church form "the spiritual government of it by Christ in the heart and conscience of man."

of the king's eye – stands the shocking force of his language, however, which incenses Lear and appals the audience with its brazen familiarity: the initial honorific "Royal Lear" (137) gives way to the near-derisory "old man", and a more subtle but sustained insult of the familiar, second-person pronoun: "thou", "thee", "thine".

It is especially telling that Lear should return the insult by casting his noble servant not merely as a "miscreant" or "recreant", but as a "vassal". This term of absolute servility – only the term "slave" carries greater pejorative weight[17] – deftly indicates the paradox or contradiction in the ideology of service as it is enacted in the conflict between master and servant. It is precisely because Kent is *not* acting as a vassal that Lear applies the insult to him. As an attempt to reduce the Earl of Kent to the position of absolute servility, it reflects a set of rank-inflected values that will in due course be put under pressure. What Lear demands of Kent is precisely to act with the abjection of the "vassal" – with the obliteration of personal subjectivity that we have seen in Shakespeare's sonnets to his master (especially 26, 57, and 58). But Lear's devoted servant takes his obligations of service to his monarch far too seriously to obey the king on this point.

Loving the man

Service could involve disobedience at its core, if pleasing the man means betraying a higher order, of which the hierarchies of service are an inextricable part. It could be argued that Kent is devoted to the office of the king rather than to the "old man" who inhabits it: that when he urges Lear to "reserve thy state",[18] he is reminding the king of his own reciprocal duties as servant to his people.[19] If this is true, it leaves something more to be said about Kent's peculiar devotion (the word hovering between service and love) to the *man* Lear. This suggests another, quite different, language game to account for Kent's behaviour towards Lear, both in his implacable resistance to the king in the opening scene and his subsequent abjection as the minion Caius. It is a discourse that we have seen clearly enough in the sonnets and in the discussion of *Twelfth Night*, in which the obligations of service are transformed (or seek to be transformed) into the related but different devotion of friendship. Tom Bishop has pointed out to me

---

[17] See Neill, "His Master's Ass".
[18] The Quarto text has "reserve thy doom". See The New Variorum *King Lear* for a cogent reason why the Folio makes Kent's outburst primarily concerned about the disastrous political implications of Lear's behaviour rather than an intercession on behalf of Cordelia (1.1.148 note).
[19] See Barish and Wain-grow, "Service".

that whereas Kent's disobedience may be accounted for in the abstract by the Protestant conception of the priority of God's service or personal conscience, Kent does not couch his actions in either term. His devotion to Lear is *profoundly* personal. Such affective attachment is entirely within the bounds of service – especially as we encounter it in the sonnets – but it shifts the concept fully into the realm of friendship, in keeping with the early modern polyvalence of the term. Kent contradicts Lear out of a double sensitivity to the affinities of love and service: first, because he wishes to bring home to Lear in the strongest possible way that he is blindly misrecognising his daughter's love; second, because his own love for Lear will not allow him to let his friend act against his own self-interest. He is prepared, in the best tradition of "loving friendship" to sacrifice himself for his friend and master. Kent as friend *loves* Lear, and his willingness to serve him at all costs reminds those who – like Goneril and Regan – would dismiss the king for slenderly knowing himself that Lear is here betraying his deepest self as well as those closest to him.

When Kent reappears before his old master as the vassal Caius, the notion of servile devotion is thus subtly complicated by a combination of personal devotion and more social disparagement:

> LEAR What wouldst thou?
> KENT Service.
> LEAR Who wouldst thou serve?
> KENT You.
> LEAR Dost thou know me, fellow?
> KENT No, sir, but you have that in your countenance which
> I would fain call master.
> LEAR What's that?
> KENT Authority.
> LEAR What services canst thou? (1.4.19–28)

Both Lear and Kent know at this stage that the king's authority is waning, the latter having foreseen from the beginning the complete eclipse of the monarch's power. But is authority the same thing as power? In his recommitment to Lear's service, Kent underlines the authority that remains even when power has gone. There is a tension in this exchange between the "service" that Kent "professes" (recall Lear's earlier question, "What dost thou profess?" (11)) and Lear's more specific question of utility: "What services canst thou?" It is brought out clearly in Lear's *conditional* acceptance of his former courtier: "Thou shalt serve me, if I like thee no worse after dinner" (35). Barish and Wain-grow point out that the whimsicality of this invitation, like Lear's response to Kent's beating Oswald for insubordination – "I thank thee fellow. Thou serv'st me, and I'll love thee" (77–7) – shows the bond of service as "a document negotiable by a bond salesman, instead of a vital covenant expressive of mutual love and responsibility" (353). Lear's "love" depends upon specific acts of service performed by his new servant – it is tied to Edmund's earlier notion of "deserving". Kent's profession of service, on the other hand, like that professed by one of its most ardent propagandists, is a totality of being, a harmonious state of mutual pleasure in which specific acts are mere epiphenomena of its greater commitment:

> What greater goodwill: What purer loue, or more sincere affection can be found amongst any confort of creatures then this? O happie Seruants, that had your beeing in those goulden dayes, when Maisters would merite such maruels at your hands: and thrise happie Maisters, that past your pilgrimage in those blessed houres, when by your love and liberalitie, you tyed your Seruants with this vndessolueable bonde of assured friendshyp, euen to deserue and merite the full measure of your goodwill towardes them. (I.M., *Health*, sig. C3r)

Kent does not indulge in the effusive sentimentality of the servant-author of this tract, but his overall perspective on service is broadly consonant with I.M.'s sense of the difference between service as a profession that makes a man what he is and services performed as a mere means to compensation. "Goodwill . . . love . . . affection." These are the central affects of service in I.M.'s book. The problem is that, as an integral part of the vocabulary of the ideology of service, they are open to countless instances of obfuscation, mystification, and abuse.

"Eye-pleasing" obedience

Oswald's entry (as "Steward") immediately after Kent's attribution of intrinsic "authority" to Lear broadens the context of that abuse and mystification. For we now enter the world of domestic rather than political service. The two are related but not identical. Oswald is a member of Cornwall's household and therefore, strictly speaking, a member of the family. Barish and Waingrow's claim that "Oswald is Kent turned inside out, the bad servant anatomized" (349) is only half right, for Kent and Oswald are not exactly complementary figures of service. Gloucester is Kent's mirror-image. The two earls are much closer in terms of their conditions and obligations of service, at least at the beginning of the play, than Kent is to Oswald. Kent does, however, reduce the distance between himself and the steward by disguising himself as an attendant of lower degree, thus entering Lear's service precisely as a menial. Again, I am indebted to Tom Bishop for pointing out to me that Kent's banishment as a "recreant" suggests that he is, in effect, no longer Lear's "vassal". This is to say, the *feudal* ties between them have been abrogated. As in *Timon*, Shakespeare shows us the greatest degree of agency (and all that it implies ethically) in the servant when he has been excluded from his master's service and is therefore free to rededicate himself to it out of love.

As a steward, Oswald enjoys much less personal and political autonomy than the king's courtiers, at least before Lear divides and gives away his kingdom. He has no prerogative of counsel, as they do, and his intimacy with his master and mistress is peculiarly restrictive.[20] Propagandists of service make much of the closeness of senior household servants to their masters, but they also underline the subservience that is expected of such servants to the desires of their masters. Stewards are not merely the wards of the household, responsible for its proper order, discipline, and financial management, they are also extensions of their masters' person, committed to further their affairs and keep their secrets against a hostile world:

Such dutifull and submissiue obeysance and curtesie, as beseemeth their sex and place . . . must seruants performe to their masters, as they have occasion to goe to them, to come from them, to receive any charge of them, or to bring any message vnto them. . . . To stande in his masters presence: which testifieth a readinesse to performe any service which his master shall appoint him to doe . . . [nor should they act] on their owne heads without or against consent of their masters, *because while the time of seruice lasteth, they are not their owne, neither ought the things which they doe, to be for themselues: both their persons and their actions are all their masters*: and the will of their master must be their rule and guide (in things which are not against Gods will.) . . . [B]y reason of that neare bond which is betwixt master and seruants, and the neare and continuall abiding together, and the many imploiments which masters have for their seruants, seruants come to know their masters secrets: *faithfulnesse* therefore requireth to keep them close. . . . To this is to be referred a faithfull concealing of masters infirmities . . . if herein seruants be not faithful, masters were better be without seruants in their houses. (Gouge, *Dvties*, 601–28; emphasis added)

Seen within the context of this injunction, Oswald's performance as a household servant is exemplary. It embodies everything that the Protestant cleric enumerates as the ideal form of service, especially the idea that "while the time of seruice lasteth" servants "are not their own". As the steward of Cornwall's household, the good behaviour of all within the house falls directly to his charge, and one suspects that, like his counterpart in *Twelfth Night*, he chafes at the unruliness of Lear's retainers.

---

[20] See Magnusson, *Dialogue*, for a discussion of such constraints in general in early modern England.

The scene introduces the problem of domestic upheaval reminiscent of that comedy (written only some three years earlier than *Lear*). The opening discussion between mistress and steward highlights Lear's abuse of one of Goneril's gentleman servants ("my gentleman" (1.3.1–2)) and a general riotousness that she perceives to be a threat to the general harmony of her household ("that sets us all at odds" (1.3.5)). Oswald's mistress repeatedly instructs him and the servants under his charge to neglect their usual obligations of courtesy to Lear and his knights, emphasising that she will take responsibility for the consequences: "If you come slack of former services / You shall do well; the fault of it I'll answer . . . let his knights have colder looks among you. / What grows of it no matter. Advise your fellows so" (1.3.9–18). She thus overrides one of the traditional responsibilities of the household servant, especially the steward: the maintenance of hospitality and courtesy towards guests.

Is Oswald to blame for carrying out his mistress's instructions, especially when she controls his actions as a mere extension of her own will? With whom, in other words, do his primary duties of faithfulness and obedience lie? Goneril supplies an answer from one perspective when she remarks of her father, "Idle old man, / That still would manage those authorities / That he hath given away" (Q, Scene 3, 16–18). It is precisely as such an old man that her steward treats him. To Lear's imperious, virtually rhetorical question, "Who am I, sir?", he replies not "my King", but "my lady's father" (1.4.67–8). One might say that Oswald is the measure of Lear's actual authority, whatever Kent might say. That is certainly the line that the Fool takes. As a servant himself, he repeatedly underlines Kent's folly "for taking one's part that's out of favour" (1.4.87), in contrast to the canny rationality of "that sir which serves and seek for gain, / And follows but for form" (2.2.244–5). The Fool raises the issue of the contingencies of service, of the (ir)rationality of blind faithfulness and loyalty: "Let go thy hold when a great wheel runs down a hill, lest it break thy neck with following; but the great one that goes upward, let him draw thee after. When a wise man gives thee better counsel, give me mine again" (2.2.238–42). We tend to think of the Fool's vision and wit as an incontestable moral corrective, but this advice could come from the mouths of Iago or Edmund. It is clear-sightedly pragmatic – descriptively accurate rather than idealistically proscriptive – and therefore very different from Kent's own stance, except that what the Fool says and what he does are, owing to the generic requirements of his part, vastly discrepant. Like Kent, he follows Lear selflessly and lovingly, and like his superior, he does not stint from telling his master the truth.

On two occasions Kent indulges in what appears to others to be unprovoked violence against Oswald. This servile steward appears to have rankled
especially, and Kent's hatred and contempt for Oswald have been read as a
sign of his own perspicuity and morality. But why the steward? Why does
Kent not attack Goneril or Cornwall, Regan or Albany, or even Gloucester, for that matter? His violence against the servant is to outside eyes –
especially in Act 2, Scene 2 – unprovoked, hot-headed, and disorderly,
intensifying the feeling among those responsible for housing Lear that the
old king's servants and followers observe no decorum and are a threat to
household and social order. Goneril significantly expresses this idea as an
unnatural *inversion* of the hierarchies of service: "You strike my people, and
your disordered rabble / Make servants of their betters" (1.4.217–18).

In Q Scene 7, 1–28, Oswald greets Kent with exemplary courtesy but is
rebuffed with surprising venom, even taking into account Kent's knowledge of his purpose and past behaviour. Oswald's wary question seeks to
locate Kent (or Caius) both as the provider of expected hospitality and as
a member of the shared community of servants. Certain modes of a supportive community of servants are thus still invoked, even in the household
of Lear's recreant daughters. Kent responds, instead, with a lie (he is *not*
from the house), and then with unexpected, and apparently unwarranted,
invective and violence. In T. S. Eliot's terms, the intensity of his response
seems to exceed its object.[21] The interaction provides Shakespeare with the
opportunity to engage in some malcontent-like, satirical invective, especially in the catalogue of insults that anatomise the worst excesses of the
self-serving servant – precisely the sorts of debased class that I.M. laments
as having corrupted the "gentlemanly profession of serving-man". More
important, Kent's pointed rejection of Oswald's use of the language of love
demystifies that discourse as a general framework for an ideology of social
cohesion. Kent rejects the abstract notion of "love" as a social lubricant – a
loose bond that ties all people who share the same social and political space
(that is to say, the same set of masters) to intersecting lives of general goodwill and courtesy.[22] The other side of such rejection is Kent's own intense
love for Lear as man and king: the depth of Kent's contempt for Oswald is
the inverse of his own devotion to the man whom Oswald has insulted.

---

[21] See Eliot, *Essays*, 145ff.
[22] Such bonds may, of course, give rise to considerable aggression against those who do not belong to
the circle. This is the logic of the retainer band, and its destructiveness is represented with particular
intensity in a play like *Romeo and Juliet*. See Evett, *Discourses*, chapter 5.

Service and love are indistinguishable for Kent – not in the sense of love that Oswald uses so glibly, but in the sense of a total, unconditional devotion: "Now, banished Kent, / If thou canst serve where thou dost stand condemned, / So may it come thy master, whom thou lov'st, / Shall find thee full of labours" (1.4.4–7). As the Fool constantly reminds us, such devotion is fundamentally irrational, impervious to instrumental reason and self-preservation. In that sense, it is related to the irrationality of sexual devotion. Obviously, Kent attacks Oswald because he is able to attack none of the people for whom the steward is little more than an instrument. Yet it is also precisely the steward's palpable *instrumentality* that is his obsessive target.

The instrumentality of service and the unconditionality of love

The instrumentality of service that Oswald exemplifies lies as a paradox or contradiction at the heart of the ideology of service in the early modern period. No matter how much its apologists may stress the reciprocity of the bond of service, their obsessive emphasis on obedience – on the servant as mere extension of the master's will – renders its instrumentality inevitable. Against Barish and Waingrow's claim that Oswald represents the epitome of perverted service, there is reason to suppose that in terms of the conventional reciprocity expected between household servant and master or mistress, he exemplifies not merely the practicalities of service but also its ideal.[23] This ideal, at least as the propagandists describe it, involves an inevitable degree of instrumentality. Such instrumentality is encompassed by Kent's term for the steward, "super-servicable", and Gouge's "parasitical pleasing of masters . . . and . . . bare fear of them".[24] However, seeing service under the sacralised aspect of the overriding duty to serve God above men means that it can no longer be regarded as an abstract ideal without regard for its embodiment in local contexts, where the presence of injustice, dishonesty, unlawfulness, and wickedness confront servants of all kinds with ethical choices regarding their obedience and faithfulness. Here Evett's emphasis on "volitional primacy" is apposite. This or that action by a servant cannot be seen as being exemplary (or not) of the "ideals" of service without taking into account not only a broader ethical and religious context but also the

---

[23] Cf. Strier, "Faithful Servants": "'Serviceableness' – mere instrumentality – is always negative. It is part of Shakespeare's portrayal of what it means, in Johnson's phrase, to be a 'factor of wickedness' that Oswald has so much fidelity. . . . The critique of doglike fidelity is precisely a critique of 'good service' literally conceived" (122).

[24] "Contrary to this restraint is both a parasitical pleasing of masters: and also a bare fear of them. It is the property of a *parasite* to say what a master will haue him say, and deny what he will haue him deny, and so to doe what he will have him to doe" (*Dvties*, 637; emphasis added).

local situation. "Service" can all too easily turn into "super-servicability"; disobedience, on the other hand, may be the purest form of service. Each may involve the *same* action.

No other play subjects service to the demands of local politics and ethics as relentlessly as *King Lear*; no other play, however, simultaneously puts pressure on the very appeal to God's will that serves as the ultimate "bound" of service in the theological literature. In a world that appears to be so relentlessly godless as Britain's heath and castle alike, where do we find access to God's word? In contrast to Jacobean propaganda regarding the status of the monarch as God's absolute representative, Shakespeare's tragedy withholds any sense that Lear is metaphysically anointed.[25] The play bears relentlessly upon the *materiality* of power and authority. Kent may believe that Lear is the incarnation of authority, but given the circumstances, what reason does Oswald have to believe it? His mistress doesn't; nor does the figure who perhaps loves Lear more than anyone else, his Fool. For these reasons, the Protestant qualification of the duty to obey cannot be the final arbiter of the nature of human relationships in *King Lear*, including those of service. Burnett is therefore both correct and misleading to argue that it represents a "decomposition of [the] Protestant logic . . . exploding service . . . what is commended in Protestant polemic is cancelled out even as it is being articulated".[26] It does not "explode service". Rather, it explores the embodiment and enactment of service under particularly severe conditions of political dissolution and human suffering. If the play offered a secure theological framework, then even the Protestant ideology of service would survive its apparent contradictions, because the keystone precept that all service is finally to God allows – nay, demands – individuals to act in terms of their conscience. But it does not offer such consolation – or at least it does not do so absolutely, because "the gods" are either palpably absent from the world of the play or entertained as capriciously cruel beings. How, then, do we reconcile Kent and Oswald as competing paradigmatic embodiments of service? One appears to enact its precepts to the letter; the other to transgress its founding charge.

[25] This point is underlined by the play's pre-Christian setting. See Elton, *'King Lear' and the Gods*. One cannot, however, conclude from this fact that religious or Christian thought is totally irrelevant to the tragedy, even though it is a mistake to take it as a Christian allegory. The concepts of service that the play mobilizes are, even in their pre-Christian context, redolent of deeply Christian modes of thought and belief. The displacement of context from early modern England to ancient Britain may be effective in attenuating certain pressing local concerns – such as the Stuart claim to the divine right of Kings – but the apparently distant British concerns make sense only by relating them to those of Jacobean England.

[26] Burnett, "*Lear*", 71, 73, and 82.

Structure and affect

Historicist and materialist criticism has helped our understanding of the play by shifting attention away from considerations of the nature of individual characters to the structural nature of power in the play. No structures are changed in the transfer of power from Lear to his daughters; both the new and the old holders of power merely inhabit and prosecute modes of politics that are already there. This is exemplified by Edmund's ability to displace his brother by appealing to anxieties and tendencies to abuse power in Gloucester himself. It is fair to assume that when Gloucester orders Edgar to be murdered on sight, he is acting in accordance with customary powers. That is to say, although he calls upon the authority of Cornwall – "the noble Duke my master, / My worthy arch and patron" (2.1.57–9) – to endorse his lawless act, there is no reason to believe that he would not have done so in Lear's name when Lear was still king. Furthermore, service as a structural institution remains unchanged: its hierarchies, bonds, and vagaries are as apparent under Lear as they are under Goneril and Regan. The conditions under which Lear first rejects Kent's service and then accepts it in a different guise are arbitrary and capricious, and the same general politics of service is carried over from one regime to the other. The distinctions between "true" and "false" service are thus much harder to draw when one considers the play in terms of political structure rather than moral character.

A character who understands both such structures and the capriciousness of those who operate them better than most is one who from birth has constantly been forced to bear their burden – the bastard Edmund.[27] He also best exemplifies the absolute instrumentality of service – not, however, like Oswald, who is its object, but rather as its subject: he manipulates the instrumentality of service to his own advantage. Figures such as Edmund provoked the most anxiety in ideologists of service, for they represent a permanent fifth column within its ranks. They could hide behind the purely performative dimension of service discussed in earlier chapters, cloaking their own self-directed ends with the elaborate rhetoric and gestures of servile duty and rationalistic calculation. They do not resent service as an institution as much as use it as an instrument of their own wills. It is therefore not surprising that, in a play in which service is on most characters' lips, Edmund invokes it more than most. He calls upon it repeatedly on being introduced to Kent, and his self-revealing soliloquy opens with a pledge of service: "Thou, nature, art my goddess. To thy law / My services are bound" (1.2.1–2).

---

[27] See Neill, *History*, chapter 5.

Barish and Waingrow argue that despite his rhetoric of servile duty, Edmund represents the abrogation of the reciprocities of service: "What Edmund means by 'Nature' and her 'Law' proves to be nothing but the anarchic principle of his own will and appetite, the absence of obligation to any one or any thing other than himself, the complete denial of reciprocity" (350). In one respect they are right, but they miss the general import of Edmund's address to Nature, namely, that he is expressing a general philosophical principle, a particular view of the universe that goes far beyond the selfishness of any *particular* will. Edmund is the spokesman for a counter-perspective on the view of nature espoused by the ideologists of service. In their eyes, the bond of service is no less than the bond of Nature itself: a framework established by the will of God. Edmund is thus not merely acting as a selfish individual; he is challenging the whole view of nature upon which early modern social theory rested with a Hobbesian counter-theory. Nor is reciprocity as such denied in Edmund's unholy pact with Nature. In return for his dedication to her service, Nature will shower rewards on her servant in the plunder that comes from a ruthlessly self-seeking attitude to the world. The abrogation of Edmund's reciprocal obligations to others is part of his reciprocal contract with "Nature", conceived as a force that acts contrary to the word of God, or simply without it.

Most telling about Edmund's attitude to service is the fact that he fully embodies the instrumentalist conception of love and service for which Lear is chief representative, at least in the early scenes. If Cordelia responds to Lear's demand for quantifiable love – "which of you shall we say doth love us most" (1.1.49) – with a literal insistence on the equal division of her bond of love between husband and father (as does Desdemona, as we shall see), Edmund shows that a certain kind of love (or "service", in the sexual sense) brooks no division. Goneril's growing disenchantment with her "lord", Albany, brings the discourses of love and service, desire and politics, into close contact: "O, the difference of man and man! / To thee a woman's services are due; / My fool usurps my body" (4.2.27–30). Yet such contact also produces friction. The "mistress" in both the erotic and social sense dedicates herself to the man who is, in effect, her servant. She issues "a mistress's command" in a series of staccato orders that implicitly dedicates her "services" to Edmund as lover, in a grotesque embodiment of Malvolio's fantasy:[28]

> I must change names at home, and give the distaff
> Into my husband's hands. This trusty servant
> Shall pass between us. Ere long you are like to hear,

---

[28] "I may command where I adore" (*Twelfth Night*, 2.5.103).

If you dare venture in your own behalf,
A mistress's command. Wear this. Spare speech.
Decline your head. This kiss, if it durst speak,
Would stretch thy spirits up into the air.
(*She kisses him*)
Conceive, and fare thee well.
EDMOND Yours in the ranks of death.   (4.2.18–24)

Edmund's dedication is prophetic: eager to outdo each other as "rivals" to their father's love, the sisters kill each other in their respective efforts to monopolise Edmund's bed.

Beyond reciprocity

The love that Kent and Cordelia bear Lear has deep structural and personal affinities with non-instrumental service. It is unconditional, dependent on no contingency or computation. Paradoxically, it transcends the calculation that is inevitably part of the concept of reciprocity. Cordelia underlines this paradox when she replies "No cause, no cause" to Lear's protestation that she has reason to hate him. She is not being disingenuous. Embodying her earlier determination to "love and be silent", Lear's daughter loves her father without consideration, just as the Earl of Kent loves his king beyond conditions. Yet if Cordelia experiences some degree of consolation in her reconciliation with the man who had earlier "disclaim[ed] all [his] paternal care, / Propinquity, and property of blood", Kent is deprived of the satisfaction of knowing that his services have been acknowledged. As Barish and Waingrow put it, "in the final meeting, the King, numbed by the death of his daughter, scarcely recognizes his vassal and friend" (355). They emphasise Kent's statement to Cordelia that "to be acknowledged . . . is to be o'erpaid" as a sign of his utter eschewal of the usual considerations of contractual reward, whereas Neill's argument about Kent's sacralisation of service suggests a similar degree of disengagement from the real, desacralised world (Neill, *"Servile Ministers"*). We need to ask what such a position means for the concept and the institution of service. It is one thing to posit a notion of service within political theory, where reciprocity – the very *quid pro quoism* that Barish and Waingrow reject – is crucial. It is another to entertain a sacralised concept of service in which even acknowledgement is a gesture too far.

When it reaches the point to which Kent takes it, service shades into love. Whereas a certain kind of erotic desire requires reciprocity – and is consequently open to rivalry and resentment (see Goneril, Regan, and

Edmund – and a thousand other examples) – there is a form of devotion that does not. Unconditional, it is embodied above all in the Earl of Kent. It makes sense to talk of love in this context because sacralised forms of service – the service that Christ demands – are a form of love. The unconditional nature of such devotion resolves the Christian paradox that service of the right kind is perfect freedom. We touch here the absolute point of selfless devotion, in which the conditions under which service is offered – even in the form of recognition by the master – make no mark on the consciousness of the servant. This is the expression of service in sonnet 58 but without the irony and resentment that underlie that poem.

We have seen the degree to which such devotion is incompatible with an everyday political world. The reason that Lear's division of his kingdom is insane lies in the *sentimentality* of his faith in loving devotion and the reciprocity that he believes it entails. If Goneril and Regan loved him as they say they do – that is to say, as Cordelia and Kent do – the division would work. The servant-poet of Shakespeare's sonnets can ultimately find no path between a servile condition of zero subjectivity and a simple mutuality with his well-born patron that "leaues out difference" (105). Kent, on the other hand, is committed to "teaching . . . differences" (Q, Scene 4, 77), especially if they have been forgotten by upstart servants. No structural revolution of social hierarchy occurs after Lear's "deposition". The king may have been displaced, but the structural features of hierarchical relations, including those of service, remain intact. This is the key insight of materialist criticism. Its emphasis on structure above character, politics above ethics, misses a vital point of the tragedy, however, by overlooking the agency of such characters as Kent, who make crucial and consequential moral choices even when they endorse the framing ideologies of early modern political and social life.

This point is important: Kent's absolute dedication to the bonds of service is morally admirable, but as a form of universal social theory, it tends towards mystification. It promises not the absolute freedom that the Book of Common Prayer celebrates but total exploitation in a real world of quasi-feudal hierarchies. Sacralised service is ultimately framed by the *agapē* of Christ as loving master and the *nomos* of the law of total devotion. This is why giving up everything to follow Christ is finally the path to both perfect freedom and absolute riches: it encompasses freedom not merely from want and but also from wanting. Because Kent's embodiment of service is close to selfless love, the earl has no place in the political order at the end of the play. Neill reminds us that "Kent's appeal to the ethos of sacralised service is made in a desacralised world in which no correspondence can be demonstrated between human order and the arbitrary powers that Lear once saw manifested in 'the sacred radiance of the sun'" ("Sacrilization", 37). The crucial thing about Kent's form of service is that it is not an abstract ideal to which he or anyone else appeals: it is something that has to be *lived through*, enacted and embodied, without qualification or condition. This is why talk of the ideal of service in *King Lear* is at least in part misguided. When the object of *nomos* dies, service itself is spent, at least in the secular world that remains. The only place for Kent's service after Lear's death lies elsewhere; it is summoned by a "master" whose demands brook "no denay":

> I have a journey, sir, shortly to go:
> My master calls me; I must not say no.
> (5.3.296–7)

Service has two faces. One is a structural condition of social being in terms of which every member gains his or her sense of social identity in relation to all other members of the society. It can therefore be manipulated, either by characters such as Edmund, to change relations of power and identity, or by those in power, to maintain fixed, hierarchical relations, to the point of exploitation and oppression. The other is an affect, a state of personal devotion that is close to love. In some instances, it can approach the irrationality and abjection of some forms of erotic love. Although the latter might be seen as an antidote to the former, it could also be the very grounds for cynical instrumentalising of personal and social relations in pursuit or exercise of power. The "perfect freedom" of the Book of Common Prayer – like Gouge's notion of "making virtue of necessity" – involves the accommodation of the structural necessity by the affects of individual consciousness, of internalising or being wholly interpolated by the ideology of service. That ideology is all-pervasive; early modern life is unthinkable without it. Even on the heath, where Lear and the audience confront "unaccommodated man" as "a poor, bare, forked animal" (3.4.95–6), the bonds of service persist. The band of people who gather in the hovel during the storm are all either attenuated servants of some kind or a master who has lost his capacity to "command, tend service" (2.2.267). Yet their services to Lear, poor as they may be, persist even under these conditions and gain considerable weight and humanity precisely because they have been stripped of their usual informing power relations.

The remains of service

Lear leaves the protection of his daughters' homes in part because they strip him of the vestigial symbols of the service that are his due, namely, the hundred knights that he reserves for himself. Barish and Waingrow argue that "Lear's impassioned defence of his knights represents his first attempt to grapple seriously with the meaning of service" (353). Contrary to Goneril's claim that his retainers are merely servile instruments easily replaceable by others, Lear's hundred knights are symbols of loyal devotion and (nonexistent) political power:

> GONERIL Why might not you, my lord, receive attendance
> From those that she calls servants, or from mine?
> REGAN Why not, my lord? If then they chanced to slack ye,
> We could control them.   (2.2.408–11)

The issue here is precisely who one is able to "call servants" and who "controls" them. If in Lear's view his retainers enact and embody both a personal and structural sense of power and allegiance, they are regarded as more than a nuisance by the inheritors of that power: they represent both an uncontrollable unruliness at the heart of the household and a broader, political threat to the new rulers: "He may enguard his dotage with their powers / And hold our lives at mercy" (1.4.289–90). In contrast, the band that gathers on the heath is stripped of the power to hold any lives "at mercy": they simultaneously represent a satirical take on the vagaries of service and an extraordinary intensification of ideal service. As Poor Tom, Edgar represents himself as the fallen servant: one who is not rewarded, as Edmund and Oswald are, for their stealthy devotion to themselves but is rather cast beyond law and society as a "masterless man":

> LEAR What hast thou been?
> EDGAR A servingman, proud in heart and mind, that curled my
> hair, wore gloves in my cap, served the lust of my mistress'
> heart, and did the act of darkness with her; swore as many
> oaths as I spake words, and broke them in the sweet face of
> heaven; one that slept in the contriving of lust, and waked to
> do it. Wine loved I deeply, dice dearly, and in woman
> out-paramoured the Turk. False of heart, light of ear, bloody of
> hand; hog in sloth, fox in stealth, wolf in greediness, dog in
> madness, lion in prey.   (3.4.76–84)

Given the perverse way in which service is recompensed in this society, Edgar's vision matches the naïveté that he displays elsewhere. Divorced from its personal source, however, it is a telling caricature of the "profession of servingman" to which I.M. proposes his lengthy (and self-serving) "health".

As Poor Tom, Edgar must have recalled a whole class of people living on the margins of Jacobean society – those who had in fact escaped or been expelled from the secure, if potentially exploitable, "bonds of service" for a plethora of diverging social, economic, and political causes:[29]

> The country gives me proof and precedent
> Of Bedlam beggars who with roaring voices
> Strike in their numbed and mortifièd arms
> Pins, wooden pricks, nails, sprigs of rosemary,
> And with this horrible object from low farms,
> Poor pelting villages, sheep-cotes and mills
> Sometime with lunatic bans, sometime with prayers
> Enforce their charity. "Poor Tuelygod, Poor Tom."
> That's something yet. Edgar I nothing am.
>
>   (2.2.170–8)

As an embodiment of the masterless man, Edgar represents a precarious position beyond service – not as the fearsome renegade or "recreant" (to recall Lear's early banishment of Kent) beyond social control invoked by contemporary propagandists, but as a pitiful wretch deprived of the most basic human necessities – an incarnation of Lear's plea to "reason not the need! Our basest beggars / Are in the poorest thing superfluous" (2.2.430–1).[30] By explicitly taking as his pattern the multitudes who suffered the enforced vagabondage of enclosure and economic hardship, Edgar thus represents a multitude for whom the question of access to land – the "shadowy forests and champaigns riched" (1.1.61–2) that Lear so glibly alienates – was a matter of brute survival.

Kent, on the other hand, who, as an aristocrat of the highest order has reduced himself to "service / Improper for a slave" (Q, Scene 24, 217–18), embodies a peculiarly selfless, unconditional devotion that we might call "true" service if we did not balk at its wider implications for social theory. (It is also important to note that Kent and Edgar are placed on similar paths by the arbitrary powers of Lear's *polis*: had he not returned to his former master's service in disguise, Kent would face the same state of vagabondage and danger as Edgar. There is a price on both their heads.) And then there is the Fool, whose service is akin to that of the dramatist.

---

[29] See Beier, *Masterless Men* and Carroll, *Fat King*.
[30] Weil is especially perceptive in drawing our attention to the precariousness of social existence, whereby the servant was in constant danger of being "cast out" into a life of abject poverty and "unaccommodated" hardship. See especially her sympathetic discussion of the fate of serving-women, who for reasons of pregnancy especially, were confined to a life of penury and helpless suffering (*Dependency*, 116ff). For the most well-known early modern English tract on vagrants and masterless men, see Harman, *Caveat*.

He is an allowed voice of satirical intelligence whose relation to his master is peculiarly intimate, but also precarious.[31] Finally, as the master who has alienated his king and the people who stand in service to him and whom he is in turn responsible for serving, Lear himself castigates the gods for their servile allegiance to his daughters:

> Here I stand your slave,
> A poor, infirm, weak and despised old man,
> But yet I call you servile ministers,
> That will with two pernicious daughters join
> Your high-engendered battles 'gainst a head
> So old and white as this. O, ho, 'tis foul!
>
> (3.2.18–23)

Others have commented upon the peculiar self-deceptions of Lear as a moral consciousness on the heath.[32] I am more interested in the ways in which these forceful scenes reflect upon the attenuation or perseverance of service (and its cognate, love) as a structural feature of social existence even in a condition as stripped of normal social protocols as the bare heath.

Service in deed

From the beginning of the heath scenes (Act 3, Scene 1, in the Folio text; Scene 8 in the Quarto), to the reappearance of Cordelia and the restoration of Lear to his daughter (Q Scene 18), Shakespeare maintains a constant leitmotif of references to the bonds of service – at the very point where those bonds seem to have been irreparably cracked. They continue, however, to be signalled and enacted in a variety of sometimes contradictory ways. Each of the characters in the hovel has a direct and explicit relation to service, including Lear's telling vision of himself as the slave of gods. One of the most striking aspects of the great moments in the storm is the way in which we are asked on the one hand to entertain an egalitarian perspective through the reduction of the king to nothing, while simultaneously witnessing no abatement in the protocols of duty and service expressed by those who remain with him. From the powerful political and metaphysical embodiment of man as no more than a "poor, bare forked animal", through Lear's epiphanous recognition of the plight of the poor under his rule and the farcical mock trial of Goneril and Regan, which demonstrates

---

[31] The "poor fool" disappears. This could be interpreted as either a contingency of the dramatic structure of the play or an indication of social reality, for, like an animal, he creeps off to die somewhere. See Evett, *Service*.

[32] See especially Berger, *Trifles*, chapters 3 and 4, and Cavell, *Knowledge*.

a punitive law pursued in fancy as much as it was under Lear's rule (Poor Tom being the exemplar of that earlier process), characters such as Kent and Gloucester continue to treat the old man as their supreme human master. Kent persists in showing a patient deference to the Lear on the heath that strongly contradicts his sacrilegious epithets in the opening scene. The honorific "gracious my lord" and "good my lord" are repeated no fewer than five times (3.2.60 and 3.4.1, 5, 7, and 23) in his pleas to the king to take shelter. Their illocutionary force reaffirms the king's rank and status.

Kent's deep sense of allegiance and deference is matched by Gloucester in the latter's growing awareness that it is Lear, not Cornwall, who continues to be his "master": "If I die for't . . . the King my old master must be relieved" (3.3.15–16). Cornwall and Goneril's flagrant flouting of the reciprocal bonds of hospitality – in "tak[ing] from [him] the use of [his] own house" (3.3.3) and more – may be what finally wakes Gloucester from his complacent slumbers, but the point remains that once he acknowledges his bond with the king, Gloucester enacts that service in both concrete and symbolic ways, displaying in his actions the double sense of "courtesy" (3.3.18): as a personal act of charity or kindness and as the performance of a social duty. In venturing out himself to bring the king "where both fire and food is ready" (3.4.136), rather than getting a servant to do it, Gloucester echoes Kent's *penitential* level of service. His expression of shock at the quality of Lear's companions – "hath your grace no better company" (3.2.126) – betrays the degree to which he remains blind to the enormity of what has happened. Yet his comment also recalls the crucial symbolical role of a retinue of properly ranked men of service, and it allows Edgar a barbed comment about the relationship between rank and evil: "The Prince of Darkness is a gentleman" (127). The depths of such evil will shortly be experienced by Gloucester himself, when, again, the bonds of service are tested to their limits, but, *pace* Burnett, are not destroyed.

In this harrowing scene, the fabric of social and political life is both torn and repaired at a variety of levels. The desecration of the fundamental allegiance to a king and father that frames the scene is re-echoed in the appalling contravention of the most basic protocols regarding hospitality, age, and, finally, humanity itself. Against these acts, however, stands the courageous humanity of Cornwall's servant, who echoes Kent's earlier act of disobedience:

> CORNWALL (*to* GLOUCESTER) If you see vengeance –
> SERVANT   Hold your hand, my lord.
>   I have served you ever since I was a child,
>   But better service have I never done you

Than now to bid you hold.
REGAN   How now, you dog!
SERVANT If you did wear a beard upon your chin
    I'd shake it on this quarrel.
    (*To* CORNWALL)   What do you mean?
CORNWALL My villein!
SERVANT Nay then, come on, and take the chance of anger.
(*They draw and fight*)   (3.7.69–77)

The questions raised by Kent's disobedience are intensified here: what duty
of disobedience does a servant have in a context in which his master is acting
in an evil way? The Messenger's account of the event underlines both the
intensity of the servant's humanity and the enormity of the revolt:

MESSENGER A servant that he bred, thrilled with remorse,
    Opposed against the act, bending his sword
    To his great master, who thereat enraged
    Flew on him, and amongst them felled him dead,
    But not without that harmful stroke which since
    Hath plucked him after.   (4.2.41–6)

Shakespeare would not recount a scene we have already witnessed on stage
unless he wished to underline its significance: he would want his audience
to feel the thrill of both the servant's extraordinary goodness in the face
of evil and the apparently sacrilegious act of "bending [one's] sword / To
[one's] great master", especially given the intimate relationship of master
and servant established by a deep, familial bond: "a servant that he *bred*".
Neill is right to insist that we miss the complexity of the play if we do not
give full weight to the enormity of the act of disobedience and physical
resistance, even if it is performed for humane reasons. For the notion of
disobedient servants, of "villains" and "peasants" that have been "bred" by
their betters turning against them, threatens to rip the very fabric of a society
founded upon master-servant relations, especially in a society in which
local, feudal loyalties may count for more than more distant, national ones.
The Protestant theology of service includes, as its keystone, the injunction
that, where in the conscience of the individual the master transgresses the
overriding duty of all to obey God's laws, such Godless masters are to be
opposed. What Shakespeare's play displays is the embodied humanity –
both terrible and tender – that such an injunction may adopt in individual
cases.

   The notion of service as the weft that, together with the weave of social
hierarchy, constitutes the fabric of social relations is taken further in the
remarkable scenes that follow Gloucester's mutilation, where the "path

to Dover" converges on a number of minor characters who epitomise in a different key the kindness and humanity exemplified by Cornwall's servant, Kent, and, finally, by Gloucester himself. That kindness is extended in a remarkable passage in the Quarto text, which closes the horrible scene not with a dying Cornwall commanding that the "slave" who opposed him should be thrown "upon the dunghill", as in the Folio, but with the following conversation among the servants who remain:

> SECOND SERVANT I'll never care what wickedness I do
> If this man come to good.
> THIRD SERVANT   If she live long
> And in the end meet the old course of death,
> Women will all turn monsters.
> SECOND SERVANT Let's follow the old Earl and get the bedlam
> To lead him where he would. His roguish madness
> Allows itself to anything.
> THIRD SERVANT Go thou. I'll fetch some flax and whites of eggs
> To apply to his bleeding face. Now heaven help him!
> (*Exeunt severally*)   (Q, 14, 96–104)

This scene looks forward to the morally corrective response of servants in *Timon of Athens*. This direct commentary from the mouths of servants and their immediately humane response is carried over in the next scene, in which the Old Man, like his predecessor Adam in *As You Like It*, reaffirms a tradition of reciprocal relationships at the heart of the ideology of service. There is something unbearably poignant about Edgar addressing his blind father with the conventional, performative greeting of the servant: "Bless thee, master". The speech act re-establishes and reaffirms a status and a relationship that has been abrogated by the play's events, and even if we accept Berger's argument that Edgar's failure to acknowledge his father contributes to the play's tragic outcome, it could be argued that this blessing is an attenuated acknowledgement of a sort. Like Lear in his hovel, the physical figure of Gloucester hardly embodies a "great master", and yet the appellation is not merely an extension of Edgar's disguise. It underscores both the Old Man's sense of deep traditional ties – "O good my lord / I have been your tenant and your father's tenant / These fourscore years" (4.1.12–15) – and Gloucester's own request to the Old Man to help them on the way to Dover "for ancient love" (44). From this point on, the play affirms those ties in the most simple and basic of gestures. It establishes the humane sympathy and support so absent from the denizens of the new regime not merely through the verbal imagery of hands, but concretely through the embodied giving and taking of hands on the stage.

The action at the centre of the play thus represents an ideal form of humane service at the very point at which normal humanity and judicial structures seem to have broken down completely. Characteristically, such service is cognate with love, especially the "ancient love" to which Gloucester appeals in his encounter with the Old Man. Such loving care is most evident when normal relations of power between king and subject, lord and vassal, have collapsed. There is no figure more powerless than "unaccommodated" Lear on the heath, or the mutilated Earl of Gloucester, "thrust...out at the gates" to "smell his way to Dover" (3.7.91). Yet it is precisely under these circumstances of extreme vulnerability that they receive the most devoted service. The scenes on the heath and on the way to Dover do not represent an anarchic or egalitarian levelling of social hierarchy. Shakespeare represents perfect service under conditions in which the normal sanctions that hold the bonds of service in place have disappeared – conditions of almost absolute negation, suffering, and frailty. It is under such conditions that the sanctity of service becomes identical to the holiness of love.

Conclusion

Service is represented in *King Lear* as a dynamic concept: shifting and changing shape from one set of relationships and encounters to the next, at one point approaching love, at another the instrument of pure hatred; in one mode the cloak of self-interest, in another the selfless gift of duty. The play, therefore, is amenable to both modes of critical reading that I have discussed: an emphasises, on the one hand, on structural forms of power, in which the instrumentality of service is an inevitable part of an ideological apparatus that all too easily hides itself behind the rhetoric of social order; and, on the other, a form of agency that is as ethical as it is political and which transforms such ideological instrumentality into the devotional qualities of love in characters such as Kent, the "ancient love" of the Old Man, the devotion of the Fool and the "silent" love of Cordelia. Such devotion is irrational; it cannot give reasons for its actions that will explain them fully, nor can it endure in a world in which its object has been destroyed. There is nothing left for Kent at the end of the play. He has simply done what he has had to do, to a large degree unacknowledged. Here we see that the *nomos* Kent professes as the very core of his being to his master has no need of reciprocating *agapē*. As it most closely approaches love, service has no need of reciprocity. This is, of course, in keeping with the logic of love as *eros*, which seeks but does not necessitate mutuality as the logical condition of its existence, and *philia*, which raises its self beyond the reciprocal economy. *Eros*, however, continues to be driven by a destructive, unquenchable desire for reciprocity in the appetites of Edmund, Goneril, and Regan, whereas Kent's love-in-service is utterly unconditional. It is its own reward, as Evett and Neill both remind us, except that reward itself – however self-reflexive – seems to be an inappropriate word in this context. There is no reward; there is no need for any.

We are thus confronted with a paradox that returns us to the peculiar conceptual relationship between love and service. The source of the king's problems lies in Lear's mistaken faith in the closeness between love and service: in his naïve endorsement of the bonds of reciprocity between father and daughter and king and subject. Yet the resistance to the breaking of those bonds by what Lear constantly refers to as his daughters' "ingratitude" lies precisely in the loving service that is maintained by two representatives of family and political bonds, Cordelia and Kent. Service is therefore not the structural guarantee of social stability and justice; but nor is it a form of false consciousness that mystifies real social relations. Critics who insist upon a purely structural analysis of relations of power are bound to miss the real moral agency of Kent's love for Lear and the difference it makes; those who read the play in terms of the distinctions that it draws between "true" and "false" service miss the fact that such a distinction cannot form the structural basis of a social order: the very selfless, irrational devotion that Kent displays without concern for reciprocal reward would in a different context be the basis for pure mystification and exploitation. Lear plunges his kingdom into crisis precisely because of his own mystification of the notion of loving service. It is important to give full due to the structural continuities of the bonds of service throughout the play, even if it is necessary to recognise the moral differences that specific forms of devotion make to the human world – especially when these may indeed be characterised as love. Far from being the epitome of "false" service, Oswald represents an early modern exemplar of the careful steward. More than any other, Edmund recognises the instrumentality that was an intrinsic part of service as it was characterised by its early propagandists by making it serve himself.

The enigmatic closing lines of the play gesture towards the distinction that I am drawing – that between the structural and the personal – but they do not resolve the tension between them:

> The weight of this sad time we must obey,
> Speak what we feel, not what we ought to say.
> (5.3.298–9)

This is a response to Kent's declaration of a call by a master whom he cannot disobey:

> I have a journey, sir. Shortly to go:
> My master calls me; I must not say no.
> (296–7)

It is also a more general declaration, however. It represents the feelings and positions of all on stage, and perhaps also of those in the audience. Whichever way one reads it, it is framed by an absolutely incontrovertible duty of obedience. Even the need to speak what one feels – to cast off the burdens of convention and expectation in favour of personal expression – is an obligation. It is a form of service to a call beyond oneself.

OTHELLO

Othello, written only about a year earlier than *King Lear*, appears at first sight to represent another world altogether. We move from pre-Christian Britain to early modern Venice; from a polity of kings, nobles, and vagabonds to a proto-capitalist republic pitted against a clash of European and Islamic empires; from the momentous division of a kingdom to the claustrophobic sundering of a marriage bed. Yet the plays have much in common, not least their shared social framework of service and love, warped and self-negating. Neill argues that the representation of service shapes the contours of *Othello* to a much greater degree than anachronistically conceived concerns of race (see Neill's "His Master's Ass").

In *Othello*, Shakespeare shows that master-servant relationships require trust as a human and not merely instrumental need The necessity of trust may be explored in more structural and less ethical or personal terms by returning to Hegel's master-slave dialectic. In his relationship to Othello, Iago exemplifies perfectly the asymmetrical dialectic of dependence of master and servant upon each other: the master is finally more dependent upon the slave or servant because he is unaware that he is a master only through his relation to the servant, whereas the servant's consciousness of that dependence gives him a relative independence which, in Iago's case, he can put to devastating effect. In contrast, however, Emilia reasserts the ethical agency of the servant who chooses to sacrifice herself for her mistress by refusing to obey orders that contradict her conscience.

The unconditionality of resentiment

One of the most shocking and puzzling moments in *Othello* occurs at the very end, when Othello and the representatives of the state who stand appalled at his perverse murder of his wife, demand to know of the servant, Iago, *why* he acted as he did:[33]

> OTHELLO Will you, I pray you, demand that demi-devil
> Why he hath thus ensnared my soul and body.
>
> (5.2.306–7)

This demand for reasons, motivation, a cause, echoes Cassio's statement to his master immediately prior to his discovery of Othello's animus against him: "Dear general, I never gave you cause" (305). Cassio's master acknowledges both the logic and the ethics of his former lieutenant's pained bewilderment: that human beings act for or against each other for some "cause" – that their emotions and actions are not unmotivated or arbitrary.[34] It is precisely because Othello recognises that he had no real or substantial cause against Cassio that he is driven to seek to know why his servant Iago acted as he did against *him*. His capacity to continue to behave as a human being depends upon his own sense of an overarching ethical or rational purpose driving his own actions – however wrongheaded it may have been – "naught I did in hate, but all in honour" (301).

Whatever we may think of Othello's pronouncement as a form of justification, we nevertheless recognise its framing ethical logic in its search for explanation. Iago shakes the very terms in which actions are sought to be understood by refusing the logic of justification – of "cause": "Demand me nothing," he retorts, "What you know, you know. / From this time onward I never will speak word" (309–10). "Demand me nothing" – this is the brazen refusal of the servant to acknowledge his naked subjection to his master, in defiance of the master's traditional and absolute right to demand everything of him. Iago transforms himself via this simple demurral from the servant who resents his obligations to one who denies them altogether – who no longer acts as a servant or accepts the parameters of service as such. In doing so, he casts the ethical imperative back upon his former master: "What you know, you know." This repudiates the common statement "I know you" or "I have found you" as a declaration by a superior who has put a servant in his proper place. Yet it also throws Othello back upon himself in his quest to know the cause of his *own* actions. Moreover, in his subsequent affirmation of silence, Iago ironically reinhabits the position of

---

[33] Both Neill and Evett show decisively that Iago acts as much as Othello's "servingman" or domestic servant as his military subaltern.

[34] Evett's concept of "volitional primacy", which he develops most fully in his discussion of Iago, depends on this logic. See *Service*, chapter 7, "Bad Service and the Primacy of the Will".

the ideal servant, whose silence declares the complete subservience of his own subjectivity before the loquacious will of his lord.[35]

By obliging Othello to seek the explanation for the events of the play within what he himself knows, Iago places the same obligation upon the audience that has witnessed all his master has – and more. Playgoers and critics alike have perennially sought the cause of Iago's evil. The early, Romantic notion of "motiveless malignity"[36] has given way to structural, ideological analysis.[37] Within the context of service, the most explicit reason for Iago's rebellion appears to be his obsessive resentment at the condition of service *as such*. Unlike Edmund, who resents the particular position that his illegitimacy has relegated him to, but is happy to use the structures and rhetoric of service to move from subservient to master, Iago appears to detest service itself. If we take into account the fact that service (of some degree) was a structurally necessary condition of legitimate existence in Elizabethan and Jacobean society, it is easy to understand Edmund's desire to turn himself, through the exercise of his own wit and will, into the Earl of Gloucester proper. It is much harder to fathom Iago's "cause" without turning, as Bernard Spivack does, to the literary and theological roots of the Vice figure and to Marlowe's transformation of that tradition in the form of the devilish servants who attend on Doctor Faustus.

Othello's subaltern is a superbly iconoclastic analyst of the inequities and hypocrisies of service, and it is tempting to credit his sensitivity to the failure of the old bonds of service ("ancient love", as Gloucester puts it in *King Lear*) for his personal jaundice:

> IAGO Why, there's no remedy. 'Tis the curse of service.
> Preferment goes by letter and affection,
> And not by old gradation, where each second
> Stood heir to th' first.   (1.1.34–7)

In the opening lines of the play, before we know anything about him, Othello's disappointed ensign appears to speak on behalf of traditional notions of hierarchy and reciprocity. If Iago is to be taken at his word, he is the victim of a newfangled cult of favouritism and nepotistic connections that have overridden the propriety of "old connections" and "ancient love". This new, self-seeking "affection" gives him cause to abrogate the "love"

---

[35] See Burnett, "Trusty Servant".
[36] The phrase comes from Coleridge, *Shakespearean Criticism*, I, 49.
[37] The classic essay that may be said to have inaugurated materialist readings is Dollimore, "Essential Humanism".

that he would otherwise owe his master. Having conscientiously "studied deserving" he has a right to hate his ungrateful superior:

> Now, sir, be judge yourself
> Whether I in any just term am affined
> To love the Moor.
> RODERIGO I would not follow him then.
>
> (1.1.38–40)

Othello is presented as one of the new breed of masters who, instead of rewarding time-tested loyalty and devotion, has fallen prey to the time-serving machinations of mere "men-pleasers".[38] Under such circumstances the *love* that Iago would normally be expected to have for Othello – based on respect, gratitude, and traditional, hierarchical ties – is no longer owed the master. In a bitter, demystifying jeremiad, Iago justifies his new, self-seeking devotion to the mere *forms* of service by invoking the pervasive abrogation of the duties of reciprocity between master and servant in the society as a whole:

> IAGO O sir, content you.
> I follow him to serve my turn upon him.
> We cannot all be masters, nor all masters
> Cannot be truly followed. You shall mark
> Many a duteous and knee-croo King knave
> That, doting on his own obsequious bondage,
> Wears out his time much like his master's ass
> For naught but provender, and when he's old, cashiered.
> Whip me such honest knaves.

Iago is like Edmund insofar as he presents no egalitarian critique of service, such as that proposed by the Anabaptists, who took literally the words of Corinthians that we are forbidden to be servants of men (1 Cor. 7.23).[39] Within the framing assumption that "we cannot all be masters", however,

---

[38] See especially I.M., *Health*:

The kin kind of vsage and friendly familiaritie, that in former ages did linke the Maister and the Seruant together, is now on the Maisters behalfe held in vtter contempt and disdaine, in regard of their homely, rusticke, and vngentlemenly bringing up, which they regard as it is, and reward onely with bare wages . . . O who would be a Seruant, to hazarde to fall into this detestable daunger, and be driven into these extremeties? euen into all the penurie, beggarie, scarcitie, and meere miserie, that may befall any humane creature: nay when they are in their greatest prosperitie, and had in highest esteeme, yet they are euen then the most contemned and despised companie that lyues in this humane societie. For what doth a Gentleman now adayes care more for his Man, then to serue his present turne? No, no more than he doth for his Dogge or his Horse. (H4ᵛ-Jʳ & J4ʳ)

[39] See Gouge's attack on the Anabaptists in *Dvties*, 593ff.

Iago proposes a selective insubordination which will shape his own, particular form of (dis)service:

> Others there are
> Who, trimmed in forms and visages of duty,
> Keep yet their hearts attending on themselves,
> And, throwing but shows of service on their lords,
> Do well thrive by 'em, and when they have lind their coats,
> Do themselves homage. These fellows have some soul,
> And such a one do I profess myself – for, sir,
> It is as sure as you are Roderigo,
> Were I the Moor I would not be Iago.
> In following him I follow but myself.
> Heaven is my judge, not I for love and duty,
> But seeming so for my peculiar end.   (1.1.34–60)

Iago thus places his own hypocritical attitude to service within a general social critique: first, his failure to be promoted is seen as an instance of a commonplace perversion of traditional bonds of service; then his decision, couched with pointed irony, to "follow [Othello] to serve [his] turn upon him",[40] is presented as part of a general trend amongst servants who respond to the first condition by inverting the obligations of service so that they use their dependency on their masters, and the masters' reciprocal dependency upon them, to their own ends. Iago can use Othello as he does only because the dependency works both ways, and is expected to do so. The old bonds of "love and duty", to which Kent remains so faithful that they constitute his entire sense of self, are in this narrative "cracked" through historical and social change. They are no longer internalised as part of the "social unconscious" because all too apparent now are the contradictions that constitute them, namely, the failure of masters to recognise their reciprocal responsibilities towards their servants.

Despite Iago's broader, social vision and his appeal to an at least implicit ethical framework – the dereliction of duty by masters justifying the rebellion of servants – there is something disturbingly peculiar about the form of his argument. If Edmund uses the forms of service to achieve his father's title – to occupy the position of master – what, we might ask, is Iago's "peculiar end"? What does he mean when he says that he is doing no more than following *himself* in his apparent service to Othello? Unlike Edmund, Iago is divorced from the normal relations of human beings to one another,

---

[40] Compare I.M.'s phrase in the extract quoted in the previous footnote: the *master* abuses the relationship, turning the servant into "his Dogge or his Horse" (J4ʳ). This is echoed in Iago's reference to the servant as "his master's ass".

even relations in which power is pursued and advantage gained. The gnomic enigmas of (dis)identity with which Iago punctuates his otherwise straight-forward social criticism – "I am not what I am" and "Were I the Moor I would not be Iago" (1.1.65 and 1.1.57–8) – render opaque our sense of the position from which he speaks and the place towards which he wishes to move. Besides, all of the ensign's declarations in this exchange are com-plicated by the fact that they are part of a dialogue that is ostentatiously theatrical and unreliable. The carefully presented show to Roderigo is based on a fundamental lie that matches Toby Belch's gulling of Sir Andrew: that Iago will help Roderigo into Desdemona's bed. These statements about the nature of service – made to persuade the suitor of Iago's mere "eye-service" to his master – have a general ring of truth, but they cannot be taken as a straightforward baring of the servant's soul.

This point may be clarified by looking again at Gobbo's representation of his temptation to leave Shylock in *The Merchant of Venice*. Despite its farcical key, Gobbo's monologue echoes issues concerning service and duty central to both the sonnets and *Othello*: the psychomachian temptation or "suggestion" by good and bad angels in sonnet 144 (in which "friend" and "fiend" are barely distinguishable) and the harrowing central acts of the tragedy, the problem of the limits of duty and obedience, and the metaphysical and ideological conjunction of fiendish otherness. Gobbo's decision to leave his master is not utterly self-directed, as Iago's is. He merely wishes to replace a strict master with a more accommodating one. Iago, in contrast, surreptitiously elevates himself into the ultimate master. By serving himself, he is in effect serving the "fiend" that tempts Gobbo from Shylock's side. Iago thus does not occupy the position of the tempted but rather that of the tempter: he is the devil whose very being emerges from his *non serviam* – his complete rejection of the bonds to God which inaugurate all forms of secular service. This is confirmed by the closing scene of the tragedy, in which the racial othering of Othello as devil is paralleled and finally overwhelmed by the perspective which views Iago himself as a figure from hell:

> EMILIA O, the more angel she, and you the blacker devil!
> OTHELLO She turned to folly, and she was a whore.
> EMILIA Thou dost belie her, and thou art a devil.
>
> (5.2.141–3)

Branded a devil by Emilia, Othello himself refers to Iago twice as a "devil" (293) and "demi-devil" (307). Othello's invocations are not mere name-calling, however. By trying to comprehend Iago's nature in satanic terms,

Othello is genuinely trying to come to grips with a figure whose humanity appears to have evaporated:[41] "If thou beest the devil," he declares, "I cannot kill thee", before going on to represent himself as the victim of a genuinely satanic "suggestion":

> Will you, I pray, demand that demi-devil
> Why he hath thus ensnared my soul and body.
> (5.2.307–8)

Lodovico picks up Othello's discourse in the closing lines by referring to Iago as "this hellish villain", but most of the Venetians and Cypriots merely invoke the pejorative word "slave" for the fallen servant. As we have seen in *King Lear*, this is genuine name-calling, a paradoxically transparent attempt to condemn to subjectless abjection the servant who has *not* acted as a slave in the proper sense of the word: who has extended his agency beyond the imposed bonds of subjection.[42]

This analysis of the *fiendish* nature of the subversion of service shows that Iago is not only unlike the servant Gobbo, who gives in to temptation at the devil's suggestion, but also that he is different in kind from perverted or false servants with whom he seems to share much in common, like Edmund and Oswald in *King Lear*. Like his master, Satan, Iago rejects service – the foundation of early modern society – as such, while paradoxically inhabiting all of its performative aspects to the letter. If Edmund might be said to rebel because of the failure of his father (and the society in general) to acknowledge him, Iago is blind to the human necessity of acknowledgement itself. Iago is not simply a Vice-figure, but he carries into his socially realistic role as the discontented servant a peculiarly inhuman quality: a blindness to a responsiveness to others that constitutes human relationships. We should now ask whether such devilishness is purely metaphysical or whether it has roots in the early modern conception of the servant that has not yet been made apparent.

Iago's destruction of the trust necessary for all human relationships by perfectly inhabiting its *forms* is not carried out for the sake of any egalitarian political project, such as those pursued by the Anabaptists and Levellers. His motives, insofar as we can know them, are utterly destructive, and they are so destructive because of his capacity to inhabit the forms of service so perfectly without in turn being inhabited by them.[43] In this decisive respect,

---

[41] In this respect, Iago differs from the perverters of service in *King Lear*, like Edmund, who not only retain their humanity but even seek some kind of redemption.

[42] Neill discusses the relationship between "slave" and "servant" fully in "*Servile Ministers*".

[43] See Evett, who points out that Iago obeys all Othello's commands except the order to kill Desdemona.

he differs from the other servants who are indeed touched and shaped by their different kinds of subordination as servants: Emilia, Desdemona, and, finally, even Othello, who is a servant of the state. Iago's hatred of service and master alike is *unconditional*, unmotivated in the normal sense of personal motives. That is why he refuses to answer to anyone about his motives: "what you know, you know". What Othello and the others know at the end, what they did not before, is the terrifying reaches of their own weakness and blindness. Iago is the catalyst of this tragic knowledge – he brings it to its monstrous birth, but he is not affected by it.

If there is one character in *King Lear* with whom Iago thus has any affinity – albeit a negative one – it is not Edmund, who remains too human in his personal motivation and need for acknowledgement – but rather Kent, whose devotion to service is an inscrutable and unconditional as Iago's determination to destroy it. If Kent reveals the irrational kernel of love at the heart of service, Iago represents not hatred, as one would expect, but a refusal to acknowledge others that is unutterably inhuman. From whence is this inhumanity is derived? Is it a psychological condition? A sort of autism or psychopathology? It has it roots in the furthest reaches of the Protestant concept of the servant. We should distinguish between the observance of forms of acknowledgement, which Iago is especially adept at observing, and the ways in which such acknowledgement fails to impinge upon the core of his identity or being. Recalling the popular emblem of the servant as ass, and its contested expression in sonnets 26, 57, and 58, we might say that Iago's inhuman void is the other, vengeful side of the avoidance, in its other senses, of subjectivity demanded of the servant as mere instrument of the master's will. Othello is sucked into Iago's inhumanity through his all too human fear of losing the acknowledgement of those he loves – first, Cassio, whom he banishes from his side as a punishment for poor service; then Desdemona, whom he turns to stone before he kills her; and finally, even Iago, by whom, as Weil argues, he is mastered and upon whom he develops an inverted dependency (Weil, *Dependency*, 68 ff). This dependency is nowhere more evident than in the parody of the marriage ceremony by which Iago declares himself to be "married to [Othello's] service" and displaces Desdemona in a performative moment of satanic intensity:

> Look here, Iago.
> All my fond love thus do I blow to heaven – 'tis gone.
> [. . .]
> (*He kneels*)
>
> Now, by yon marble heaven,

> In the due reverence of a sacred vow
> I here engage my words.
> IAGO   Do not rise yet.
> (IAGO *kneels*)
> Witness you ever-burning lights above,
> You elements that clip us round about,
> Witness that here Iago doth give up
> The execution of his wit, hands, heart
> To wronged Othello's service. Let him command,
> And to obey shall be in me remorse,
> What bloody business ever.
>   (*They rise*)
> OTHELLO   I greet thy love,
> Not with vain thanks, but with acceptance bounteous,
> And will upon the instant put thee to 't.
> [. . .]
> Now art thou my lieutenant.
> IAGO I am your own for ever.   (449–82)

More than merely histrionic, the scene's power lies in the degree to which it is a parody of the ceremony that for J. L. Austin is the paradigm of the capacity of speech acts to transform the world.[44] In contrast to the unseen, off-stage marriage ceremony through which we assume Othello and Desdemona are wed, this parody is presented centre stage – at the play's core. Its performative force displaces the unseen vows of love and mutual service between husband and wife with a self-authorising declaration of complete dedication by servant to master. Othello initiates that inversion, with his blasphemous vow: "Now, by yon marble heaven, / In the due reverence of a sacred vow / I here engage my words". The horror of this speech act lies in the gap it presents between the effect of the public act and the deluded mind that utters it. Othello invokes "heaven", "reverence", and the "sacred" in the name of a resolute constancy (traditionally associated with married love) that is the very opposite of "sacred" or "heavenly": it is "tyrannous". This invocation of "tyrannous hate" echoes Lady Macbeth's more famous call upon the heavens to "unsex" her. The difference between the two performative utterances lies in Othello's misguided desire to sacralise his resolved course of action, whereas he effectively transforms the sacred into the satanic. Lady Macbeth intends to invoke Satan from the very beginning; Othello is oblivious to the fact that his vow to heaven is in fact an invocation of hell. Faced with a world from which the sacred (in the form of his love for Desdemona and hers for him) has suddenly been drained, Othello

---

[44] Austin, *Words*, 7ff.

attempts to restore its power through an improvised service that proclaims his own constant dedication to revenge. It also institutes his subaltern's instrumentalisation in common pursuit of that action. Homosocial service, based on military solidarity, not only replaces and displaces heterosexual reciprocity, it is elevated and sacrilised in an inverted ritual.

The force of Othello's performative ceremony is intensified by Iago's chilling intervention, in the form of the quiet command, "Do not rise yet". The ensign joins his master on his knees in a dedication through which service and love perform a grotesque dance. The love and dedication that formerly marked man and wife are now obliterated by a similar dedication between master and servant: "Now art thou my lieutenant. / IAGO *I am your own for ever.*" In Othello's declaration, the ensign achieves his preferment at last; Iago reciprocates by displacing not only his master's lieutenant Cassio but also his wife, commonly referred to as "our captain's captain" (2.1.75), in an intensified evocation of the rivalry anxiously entertained between wife and servant for the master's attention. Iago's dedication goes further still: in a grim anticipation of Prospero's ambivalent declaration of Caliban – "this thing of darkness I / Acknowledge mine" (*The Tempest*, 5.1.278–9) – it transforms the dark servant into an ineradicable part of the master's moral and metaphysical being. This recalls one of the central anxieties regarding master-servant relationships, that the intimacy of master and servant would extend to such dependency of superior upon subordinate that the very sense of self or identity of the former would rest upon the former.

The vows performed in this ceremony are clearly parodic. They invert the performatives of the marriage ceremony as a Black Mass inverts those of the Eucharist. We know that at least one of the performers is not sincere. Yet the parodic nature of the ceremony does not mean that its speech acts do not carry their usual force. Iago's dedication *continues* to act, even if only as a shadow or echo. The displacement of Othello's wife by Iago's "love and service" signals on a performative level a broader destruction of marriage as such. I am not suggesting that in his heart of hearts Iago actually wants to be married to Othello. (I am not sure that it is valid to speak of Iago as having a heart.) I am claiming that the public force of the performative utterances here enacts such a displacement. The point, as I have argued elsewhere, is that for speech acts to work – to convey their force – no inner mechanism is necessary, no interiority is essential.[45] We can feel the force of Iago and Othello's performatives without trying to attribute to either of them an interior, motivating "cause".

---

[45] See Schalkwyk, *Speech*, chapter 3. This point is forcefully made by Derrida, *Limited Inc*.

Now imagine the scene in which the imputed interior affect is indeed attributable, but to only *one* of the characters: to Othello only. Whereas Othello's acts are informed by a deeply felt, if warped, intensity, behind Iago's lines lies nothing: the words act, they carry as much force as Othello's, but they signal no feeling, no interior investment, just like those of Hamlet's player. The speech acts can still be understood; they convey the same force: they transform the world and the relationships between the characters in the same ways. However, whereas one of the participants is being affected by them, in the belief that the human dialogue in which he is engaged commits the other a kind of responsiveness and responsibility, this is not true of the other, who is, in effect not a true partner in the dialogue.

John Gibson asks us to entertain the thought experiment of imagining someone who is blind to this aspect of normal language games.[46] The person is able to use words such as "pain" and "suffering" as we do: when confronted by a person writhing in agony after a serious accident, he or she is able to agree that the person is in pain or has been severely injured, or to describe them in those terms himself or herself, but does nothing further. "Yes," he or she agrees, "that person is suffering" or "That is a very serious injury", but makes no move to alleviate the suffering or comfort the person or to call an ambulance. Gibson argues that in the failure to acknowledge the suffering of the person, such figures have failed to understand properly not only the *concepts* of pain and suffering but also of *humanity itself* – such concepts have no place in the weft of their own lives and their relations to others. Such a person may be able to use the full range of human concepts in appropriate situations, but unless that use is accompanied by the acknowledgement of the humanity of others, which necessitates particular kinds of response and behaviour, they are in fact blind to the meaning of such concepts within human forms of life.

Iago may be said to be one of the most finely wrought literary representations of such blindness: as a figure completely adept at playing every language game *as if* he were acknowledging the other, he is in fact incapable of such acknowledgement or unwilling to accede to it. Even Edmund discovers at the end of *King Lear* that he cannot do without the love that is bound up with human acknowledgement. Iago, however, acknowledges neither the other nor his own need for acknowledgement. That is why he is so successful. Critics have blamed Othello in particular for his naïveté, gullibility, or "idiot metaphysics",[47] but they fail to understand this peculiar

---

[46] Gibson, "Between Truth and Triviality".

[47] Gross, "Slander", 827. The extent of Othello's culpability constitutes Leavis's disagreement with Bradley in "Diabolic Intellect".

quality in Iago: his unimaginable and unspeakable capacity to remain completely detached from the usual engagements, commitments, and responses of human intercourse, while playing the games they require to the full. Iago plays the part of the perfect servant – perfectly – but insofar as he remains uninvested in the master-servant relationship, he is the incarnation of the anti-servant, his *non serviam* derived from the Vice or Satan.

The master-servant dialectic

I am arguing that in the broader context of master-servant relations, Shakespeare creates Iago to show what a figure who did indeed lack the subjectivity expected of the "perfect servant" would look like – and how he might behave. Iago's peculiarly performative autism, which allows him to mimic perfectly human modes of behaviour while feeling none of them, may be understood by revisiting the standard assumptions regarding the negation of subjectivity of the servant by the master. I have mentioned Shakespeare's only half-ironical invocation of the irrelevance of subjective interiority to the master in discussions of sonnet 26, and his revengeful payback in sonnet 126. Shakespeare's inversion of servility in the sonnets may be related to Iago's destruction of Othello through Hegel's celebrated analysis of the master-slave dialectic, discussed in Chapter 1 of this text. In that relationship, as Hegel analyses it, the degree of self-consciousness that master and bondsman derive from their respective reflection through the acknowledgement of the other is asymmetrical: both figures need the other to be conscious of themselves as living beings, but whereas the servant is a mirror that reflects the master to himself, the master seems (and only seems) to be an independent mirror to himself: he affirms himself by negating the servant.

As an embodiment of the Hegelian servant (and consequently, a mere simulacrum of the ideal servant of early modern ideology), Iago presents the face of service as pure performance, *refusing* access to an interiority that would, paradoxically, set Othello free from his misrecognised dependence. The "poisonous mineral, [that doth] gnaw my inwards" (2.1.295–6) is thus less sexual jealousy than the paradoxical inner awareness that in the eyes of the master he *has* no innards. His syntactically enigmatic utterance, "To obey shall be in me remorse" (3.3.471), raises the question of what exactly there is that might be considered to be "in" Iago. He has been emptied out by his Hegelian relationship to his master. In consequence, Iago will permit no access to himself as an interior being, which would, in effect, allow Othello to recognise him as another consciousness. His refusal to explain himself at the end, throwing back at his master's demand the enigmatic declaration that could be said of all Hegelian masters, "what you know, you know", is presaged earlier by a similar refusal to allow Othello to acknowledge that he has a heart, an inner being, that may be known and shared:

> OTHELLO   By heaven, I'll know thy thoughts.
> IAGO You cannot, if my heart were in your hand;
>   Nor shall not whilst 'tis in my custody.
>
> (3.3.166–8)

In a strange echo of Hamlet's refusal of his friends' probing, Iago limits the extent to which he can be said to be Othello's man. He presents himself as a parody of the traditional ideal of the servant as *pure* performance in service of the master's needs. In delimiting the extent of his master's writ ("I'll know your thoughts") he makes Othello *his* man, revealing in a way that anticipates the darkest form of the Hegelian dialectic the underside of the total dedication, "I am your own forever". This "forever" is a metaphysical condition, predicated upon the master's unrecognised dependence upon the "thing of darkness" that is the servant. Iago's emptiness, his lack of heart, his inhumanity, may thus be said to be the limit condition of the servant as the Protestant tracts of the time would have him at their most uncompromising: as the pure instrument of the master's desire.

The asymmetry between Othello on the one hand and Iago on the other is what makes their parodic marriage ceremony diabolical – it is what imbues it with horror. We should now be in a position to recognise the social and ideological roots of that horror in the role that is prescribed for the servant. It is diabolical enough in its transformation of the relationship between Othello and Desdemona, but its real horror lies in the fact that Othello believes that he is engaging in human interaction with his servant when the figure that lies behind those speech acts is not human because in its extreme forms, the early modern ideology of service makes no room for the humanity of the servant. The force of such horror is anticipated by Christopher Marlowe, when he cannily represents Faustus as believing that he is Mephistopheles' master, and that the interaction between them follows the usual patterns of human intercourse:

> FAUSTUS *Quin redis, Mephistopheles, fratris imagine!*
>   *Enter* MEPHISTOPHELES *[dressed as a friar]*
> MEPHISTOPHELES Now, Faustus, what wouldst thou have me do?
> FAUSTUS I charge thee wait upon me whilst I live,
>   To do whatever Faustus shall command . . .

MEPHISTOPHELES I am the servant to great Lucifer
　And may not follow thee without his leave.
　No more than he commands must we perform.
FAUSTUS Did he not charge thee to appear before me?
MEPHISTOPHELES No, I came hither of my own accord.
FAUSTUS Did not my conjuring speeches raise thee? Speak.
MEPHISTOPHELES That was the cause, but yet *per accidens*.
　　　　　　　　　　　　　　　(*Doctor Faustus*, 1.3.35–47)[48]

The enigma of Faustus's status as the *cause* of Mephistopheles' appearance is thus the philosophical and theological predecessor of the puzzle of Iago as the cause of Othello's demise. Like those of his satanic counterpart, Iago's declarations on service do not represent the coherent purposes of a person with peculiarly motivated and grounded *human* grievances. They are a composite of different theatrical perspectives: an acute statement of social critique and satire echoed in extra-theatrical tracts; the recognisable expression of personal discontent that is generically valid without being constitutive of a particular character; and the gnomic paradoxes of a metaphysical evil that reveals a horrific otherness at the heart of service. Iago withholds himself from Othello in part so that Othello himself may become the cause of his own demise. He is the catalyst, as Mephistopheles is, for the forces of destruction already working within the master's breast and by extension at the heart of Venetian society.

Emilia's counter-service

The debate between the unconditionality of love expressed most forcefully in sonnet 116, and the conditionality that is best expressed in the scepticism of sonnets such as 93, 138, and 144, is exemplified in the poignant question that Desdemona asks her lady-in-waiting: "Wouldst thou do such a deed for all the world?" (4.3.62). The unconditionality of Kent's dedication to his master is reflected as a mirror-image by a similarly driven imperative in Iago's adaptation of service as mere form. He pursues an equally unconditional *non serviam* that paradoxically achieves its ends by mimicking perfect service perfectly. It reflects to the master pure instrumentality while hiding from him (always a "him") its concealed agency as instrument. Neither of these forms of unconditionality applies to Emilia, who is forced to live three forms of competing service: as Iago's wife, as Desdemona's lady-in-waiting, and, finally, as servant to the head of her household, Othello. If the ideologists

---

[48] Marlowe, *Faustus*.

of service deal directly with the tension between serving men and serving God, they seldom treat the contradictions of loyalty that arise from a society in which service did not work in a linear way but rather across different relationships. Who is Emilia supposed to serve above all? And how are her obligations of service inflected by her various bonds of love and friendship?

In a fine discussion of the relationship between Emilia and Desdemona via a recent Trevor Nunn production, Carol Rutter remarks on the distance that existed in that performance between Emilia and Desdemona. "These women . . . when they come together in the willow scene, were not natural allies, certainly not sisters bonded in common cause. Their business was practical".[49] That practical business is the enterprise of domestic service, in which, at least at first, neither woman had any affective investment in the other. As the scene progresses, their differences are exacerbated, in the gulf between Desdemona's almost unbelievable refusal to believe that there might be any women who would betray their husbands and Emilia's knowing pragmatism. In contrast to Kent and Iago's unconditional stances towards service, Emilia responds expediently to the conflicting demands of love and service as the conditions of a patriarchal world. If it keeps her husband satisfied, she will not scruple about filching something as trivial-seeming as a handkerchief from her mistress.[50] Nor is faithfulness to marriage absolutely binding. She may not be prepared to commit adultery for something as trifling as a handkerchief, or a "joint-ring, nor for measures of lawn, nor for gowns, petticoats, nor caps, nor any petty exhibition". But "the world's a huge thing", she replies to her mistress; "It is a great price for a small vice . . . Ud's pity, who would not make her husband a cuckold to make him a monarch? I should venture purgatory for 't." (4.3.67–76). The catalogue of "petty exhibitions" that Emilia rejects are perhaps unworthy temptations because they represent the very things that keep women sexually subjugated to men. Yet her willingness to entertain the "huge thing" of the world continues to be informed by the discourse of service in ways that the ambitions of a male character like Edmund are not. The service that a wife would be doing her husband in serving herself through adultery would be to make him a "monarch": the world would not be hers; it would belong to the man she is committed to serve.

Precisely because Emilia's attitude towards her obligations of service and loyalty is pragmatic and expedient, her acts of defiance and disobedience towards her male masters, Othello and Iago, and her loyalty to her mistress

---

49 *Enter the Body*, 169.
50 In Rutter's description, Zoe Wannemaker's Emilia procures the handkerchief for Iago in a misguided effort to incur some kind of loving obligation. See *Enter the Body*, 163–5.

in Act 5, Scene 3, are especially powerful and compelling. Like Cornwall's servant in *King Lear* who suddenly finds the courage to stand up to cruelty, Emilia turns a customary habit of accommodation and compromise into a final act of resolute assertion.

> EMILIA I will not charm my tongue. I am bound to speak.
> My mistress here lies murdered in her bed.
> [...]
> EMILIA Villainy, villainy, villainy!
> I think upon 't, I think. I smell 't. O villainy!
> I thought so then. I'll kill myself for grief.
> O villainy, villainy!
> IAGO What, are you mad? I charge you get you home.
> EMILIA Good gentlemen, let me have leave to speak.
> 'Tis proper I obey him, but not now.
> Perchance, Iago, I will ne'er go home. (5.2.191–204)

In her simple statement of defiant disobedience – "I will ne'er go home" – Emilia is not only foretelling her own death but also declaring her independence from the sway of her domestic condition, as wife and servant to her husband, whose place is in the home.[51] Her qualification of her duty of obedience before a crowd of figures of patriarchal authority declares a newly recognised obligation both to truth and to her mistress that is all the more telling for *not* being made from a position of unconditional devotion. Kent's total commitment to Lear's service – which includes defiant disobedience where necessary – may be admirable, but there is something inhuman about it.

Emilia's discovery of her commitment to a mistress from whom she may in fact have been quite detached, to follow Rutter's meditations on Nunn's production, suggests greater reserves of courage in its discovery of the possibilities of ethical choice. The affective loyalty that the apologists expect as a structural condition of service is shown to grow, like love, in strangely irrational ways. In declaring her devotion to her mistress in the teeth of her divided masters, Iago and Othello, Emilia reperforms in her own terms the displacement of married love by service effected between Othello and Iago in their parody of the marriage ceremony. Claiming Othello's place on the marriage bed in which he has murdered his wife, she

---

[51] There is a great deal of literature on the domestic place of women in the English Renaissance. Rutter offers a good, short discussion which refers to some of the conduct books on service that I have used in this study in *Enter the Body*, 155ff. The classic texts are Dusinberre, *Women*, and Jardine, *Daughters*. Two recent texts informed by considerable scholarship are Wall, *Domesticity*, and Korda, *Economies*. Wall especially breaks the mould of received ideas about women's agency.

looks forward to "bliss" even as Othello relegates his own divided soul to the devil:

> EMILIA Ay, ay. O, lay me by my mistress' side!
> ... What did thy song bode, lady?
> Hark, canst thou hear me? I will play the swan,
> And die in music.
> (*Sings*)   "Willow, willow, willow." –
> Moor, she was chaste. She loved thee, cruel Moor.
> So come my soul to bliss as I speak true.
> So, speaking as I think, alas, I die.   (244–58)

Emilia's "speaking as I think" echoes Edgar's declaration at the end of the tragic events of *King Lear* that they should "speak what we feel, not what we ought to say" (5.3.299). It affirms an independent subjectivity by a servant who finds ethical freedom in such agency. It is also a declaration of affective loyalty through which service becomes indistinguishable from love. In this act and sacrifice, Emilia marks the greatest distance between herself and her husband in their capacity as servants. In the next chapter, we see in the figure of *The Winter's Tale*'s Paulina the degree to which *critical* service is exemplified in women.

Iago and the players

A final comment remains on the inscrutability of Iago as the embodiment of the fiendish friend with which I introduced this section. Iago can play the role that I have indicated because he embodies the nature of the player on the stage. As an agency in human form able to play every language game without being committed to the normal ethical constraints of any, Iago exemplifies the monstrosity of the player in the imagination of anti-theatrical ideologists.[52] He is adept at playing every language game without the commitment to others that acknowledgement entails. He it is who, as Hamlet puts it, can display a "monstrous" passion without any palpable "cause" – for Hecuba! I discussed earlier the double embodiment of the player as servant with regard to Shakespeare's comedies, but in the figure of Iago such service takes on much more sinister aspects. We can feel the genuine concerns of the anti-theatrical ideologues when we watch Iago at work, and the more general ethical anxieties are exacerbated by the specific context of service. For it is the essence of playing that the player embodies the (in)humanity of a performance that is monstrous in its metaphysical,

---

[52] For a selection of anti-theatrical tracts, see *Sourcebook*, ed. Pollard.

necessary disengagement from the commitments and reciprocities that inform normal social relations. In that sense, like Iago, playing itself may be considered fiendish. Yet the fact that players are also servants makes their metaphysical monstrosity even more monstrous, for they are the pattern of the false servant whose perfect words and gestures show everything except his surreptitious emancipation from the acknowledgement that is the essence of all service.[53] The player is the exemplar of Iago's gnomic declarations, "You cannot [know my thoughts], if my heart were in your hand" and "I am not what I am".

As the professional, commercial theatre began to emancipate the servant-player from feudal forms of service and acknowledgement, it imposed upon him the bond(age) of the commercial transaction, through which the servant becomes the slave of the audience, ever seeking – indeed, begging for – the acknowledgement, and the indulgence, that would set him free – at least until the next performance. Yet we can also glimpse the vulnerability of the player through another of Iago's utterances: if the absence of interiority is a source of Protestant anxiety, his exposure to the new conditions of service on the professional stage is encapsulated by the histrionic displacement of the heart in performance, by his literally "wear[ing his] heart upon his sleeve / For daws to peck at" (1.1.64–5).

[53] For a discussion of the monstrosity of the servant, see Burnett, *Monster* and "*King Lear*".

CHAPTER 7

"Something more than man"
The Winter's Tale

The Winter's Tale is densely populated by servants. They carry messages, offer comfort, retreat into despair, act loyally and disloyally; they even engage in the poetry of praise. The brunt of Shakespeare's fascination with the inwardness of service and its material restraints and opportunities is carried by Leontes' noble attendant, Camillo; the sacrificial Antigonus; and, in a different, pastoral key, the mercurial Autolycus. Yet nowhere is Shakespeare's distinctive conception of service as apparent as in Paulina, wife of a councillor, companion to the queen, and, finally, critical (in every respect) servant and advisor to Leontes himself. She is obviously the chief agent of resistance, healing, and restoration in the play's transformation from erotic deathliness to pastoral life. It is perhaps less apparent that the combination of these three forms of ethical action constitute the epitome of service in the Shakespearean canon. The royal brothers, given to tyranny in their own distinctive ways, are taught the virtues of service where they least expect it: in the hands and tongues of women, who were always meant, they believe, to serve and obey them.

Shakespeare's late romance represents to an even greater degree than *King Lear* the crisis of service in the face of tyranny. The play shows that service in its fullest sense is impossible under tyrannical masters, except insofar as servants are prepared to oppose magisterial intransigence. Disobedience, critical opposition, and judicious counsel are thus shown to be of the essence of service. This perspective runs counter to any idea that service is inherently conservative, but Shakespeare's concern with the affective ethics of *continued* service even in the face of tragic obduracy, represents a dimension that cannot be encompassed by the mere politics of resistance.

THE RESISTANCE OF SERVICE I: CAMILLO

Three servants of considerable status are confronted with the choice between abject obedience and various forms of resistance or self-sacrificial choice: Camillo, Antigonus, and Paulina. Camillo occupies a position similar to Kent's at the opening of *King Lear*. He is required to choose between loyal service to his king and abandoning that service altogether. Kent chooses to risk the displeasure of his master but then rededicates himself to the king under a different, socially denigrated guise. Camillo finds himself in more a difficult predicament, although to the apologists of service his course of action upon being ordered to murder Polixenes would have been beyond reproach. His duty is to God when God's law clashes with earthly service.[1] Camillo's decision to disobey his master is clear enough: he lives up to his obligation to serve his master when he refuses the order to murder Polixines. Whether Camillo is entitled to leave Leontes' service is a different question. A further question, absent from contemporary tracts but central to this play's concern with affective relationships of service, is the influence that his master's order has on Camillo's *love* for his king. The situation puts him in a peculiar bind: he is compelled to warn Polixenes to leave Sicilia, but his subsequent reticence is barely sustainable in the face of the king of Bohemia's demand for an explanation for his strange warning. Once he has provided that and made it good by assisting Polixenes in his flight, his treachery is sealed: he cannot remain in Leontes' service, at least in his ordinary persona.

The transition from Leontes to Polixines is not easy for Camillo. Shakespeare gives a great deal of weight to his affective investment and attachment to his former country and king, even after the passage of sixteen years. The noble servant is overcome by an intense desire to return to his homeland, but his new master refuses to brook that loss of service. Polixenes' attachment to his servant is represented as an unusually deep form of dependence. His efforts to dissuade Camillo from returning to his former master involve a manipulative form of emotional blackmail that calls upon the affective dimensions of the master-servant relationship which shade, as we have seen, into friendship and love:

> POLIXENES I pray thee, good Camillo, be no more importunate.
> 'Tis a sickness denying thee anything, a death to grant this.
> CAMILLO It is sixteen years since I saw my country. Though I have
> for the most part been aired abroad, I desire to lay my bones
> there. Besides, the penitent King, my master, hath sent for me,
> to whose feeling sorrows I might be some allay – or I o'erween
> to think so – which is another spur to my departure.

---

[1] See the discussion of this issue in Chapter 6.

POLIXENES As thou lov'st me, Camillo, wipe not out the rest of thy
services by leaving me now. *The need I have of thee thine own*
goodness hath made. Better not to have had thee than thus to want
thee. Thou, having made me businesses which none without
thee can sufficiently manage, must either stay to execute them
thyself or take away with thee the very services thou hast done;
which if I have not enough considered – as too much I cannot –
to be more thankful to thee shall be my study, and my profit
therein, the heaping friendships.   (4.2.1–20; emphasis added)

The mode of this exchange approximates that of two lovers or friends. The
master tries to instil a feeling of guilt in the servant through a devious
form of passive aggression. He appeals to love, especially in his refusal of
substitute or competitive loyalty and his claim that nothing but complete
dedication will suffice. In accordance with his powerful position, Polixines
takes back what he gives by harping on his own supposed lack of power: he
conveys his incapacity to deny his servant's request while simultaneously
trumping that move by shifting the ethical responsibility onto the person
making the request to be granted leave. He acknowledges the services that
Camillo has performed but at the same time negates his kindness and devotion by suggesting that Camillo's return to Sicily would obliterate all his
accumulated bonds and debts. Above all, he appeals not to his servant's
sense of obedience but rather to his love, engendering a sense of responsibility and indebtedness based on his achieved dependency. Once he has
ensnared him with that appeal, he tries to secure the hook by alternating
an appeal to his own dependence upon Camillo with the promise of future
reward. Perhaps the most devastating of his devices is the transformation of
"profit" into "friendship". This final, decisive move trumps a commodified
concept of service with an appeal to an affective one. Camillo responds
at the end of the exchange not, however, with the language of love, but
pointedly (following Cordelia) with the servile discourse of willing but
dutiful obedience – "I willingly obey your command" (46). What should
linger in our ears (and in those of Polixenes) is the fact that, after sixteen
years, and in the presence of his king, Camillo still refers to *Leontes* as his
"master". The old lines of command are unbroken, the original affective
bonds remain, especially in the light of his old king's penitence and need for
comforting. Camillo responds to the demands of affective comfort and support, but his awakened longing is allayed only temporarily. If erotic service
cannot endure the splitting of allegiances, can Camillo serve two masters?

Although Camillo allows Polixenes to overrule the call of his earlier
master, his attachment to his new king will soon be subjected to a number of

pressures. He is unique amongst Shakespeare's devoted servants in engaging in a further, double betrayal for what he regards as a noble end. Perhaps prompted by his uneasiness at the excessive violence of Polixenes' response to his son's impudent marriage, Camillo first commits himself to helping Florizel escape with his betrothed, but he then betrays the prince by telling his father of their escape. This double treachery is in fact a compensation for his initial betrayal of Perdita's father. He uses it as a device to return to his old country and master without outwardly breaking his trust with his new master, Polixenes. What neither Polixines nor Florizel recognize (and this is an occupational hazard of Shakespeare's masters) are the aspects of service that preoccupy Shakespeare throughout his work – the deep, often inexplicable, emotional attachments that servants incur to particular masters, or to the particularity of such masters, so that substitution or displacement becomes unthinkable or unbearable. Here service is close to erotic devotion. Yet we have also seen, in Polixenes' response to Camillo's possible loss, that such dependency belongs to the master's part as much as to the servant's. Polixenes cannot bear Camillo's loss because he has become dependent upon him – not merely practically or instrumentally but also emotionally. The intensity and tone of his protestations at Camillo's desired departure exceed their object, but they do so only if we assume that servants are fungible: instruments that can be replaced merely because they function in practical and exploitable ways. Polixenes' claim that no one else will be able to manage the affairs that Ploxines presently administers is disingenuous – management skills are fungible, but friendships are not. Affective bonds also incur their own, unique forms of exploitation and extortion.

THE RESISTANCE OF SERVICE II: ANTIGONUS

Camillo finally finds a way back to his old master by *repeating* his initial betrayal. Back in Sicilia we encounter a different modulation of the question of fungibility and loss in the presence and absence of Paulina and her dead husband, Antigonus. Like Camillo, the king's irrational betrayal of the bonds that tie him to the welfare of his subjects and his wife force upon Antigonus a choice that will end in his death. Antigonus appears only briefly in the play, but his role is decisive for the intensity of its focus. With Camillo gone, he bears the burden of responsibility as the most senior of the king's servants to ensure the welfare not only of his monarch but also of the state as a whole. "Be certain what you do, sir", he cautions Leontes, "lest your justice / Prove violence" (2.1.129–30). Having affirmed his royal

responsibility to act justly rather than merely legally, Antigonus speaks in
his capacity as master of a household. He addresses the king intimately, as
a fellow husband and father. In doing so, however, he betrays a frightening
conception of patriarchal authority that puts the relationship of justice to
violence in the realm of gender even more starkly than even the jealous
king has expressed it:

> ANTIGONUS (*to* LEONTES)   If it prove
>   She's otherwise, I'll keep my stables where
>   I lodge my wife, I'll go in couples with her;
>   Than when I feel and see her, no farther trust her.
>   For every inch of woman in the world,
>   Ay, every dram of woman's flesh is false
>   If she be.
> LEONTES   Hold your peaces.
> A LORD   Good my lord –
> ANTIGONUS (*to* LEONTES) It is for you we speak, not for ourselves.
>   You are abused, and by some putter-on
>   That will be damned for 't. Would I knew the villain –
>   I would land-damn him. Be she honour-flawed –
>   I have three daughters: the eldest is eleven;
>   The second and the third nine and some five;
>   If this prove true, they'll pay for 't. By mine honour,
>   I'll geld 'em all. Fourteen they shall not see,
>   To bring false generations. They are co-heirs,
>   And I had rather glib myself than they
>   Should not produce fair issue.   (2.1.135–52)

Like his predecessor, the Earl of Kent, Antigonus's fearless refusal to be
cowed into silence is signalled by his deliberate failure to use the master's
customary honorific titles and his signal reminder of the altruistic displacement of the servant's subjectivity for the sake of or on behalf of the best
interests of the monarch: "It is for you we speak, not for ourselves". That
displacement will be tested to the utmost when he is called upon to sacrifice
himself for Hermione and Leontes' daughter. Despite his sacrificial devotion to Hermione and the infant and his robust insistence on the integrity
of his service across all other voices, including his king's, his conception
of himself as master of his household is much more disturbing, and not
far from the king's. It reveals a notion of power that goes beyond personal
aberration to the heart of the social order itself: it speaks of structure rather
than mere character. If scepticism does indeed lie at the heart of this play,
as Stanley Cavell, argues, then it is not the attribute or weakness of a single

human being, but the collective and exclusively gendered lot of a whole society and complete manner of speaking.[2]

THE RESISTANCE OF SERVICE III: PAULINA

We have not yet encountered the wife whom Antigonus so rashly imagines confining to his stables. When we do meet her, she turns out to be one of Shakespeare's most remarkable embodiments of those aspects of service that the rest of his texts endorse. Paulina is fearless – less daunted than her husband – dedicated to truth and justice, shameless in the most positive way, and the kind of servant who, through the very toughness of her dedication and clarity of vision, inverts magisterial hierarchy at crucial moments. It is all the more significant that she is a woman. From the beginning, she marks her difference from her husband by refusing the high-handed and self-serving interpretation of the royal prerogative with which Leontes silences his protesting court:

> LEONTES   Why, what need we
> Commune with you of this, but rather follow
> Our forceful instigation? Our prerogative
> Calls not your counsels, but our natural goodness
> Imparts this; which, if you – or stupefied
> Or seeming so in skill – cannot or will not
> Relish a truth like us, inform yourselves
> We need no more of your advice. The matter,
> The loss, the gain, the ord'ring on 't, is all
> Properly ours.   (2.2.163–72)

Paulina reminds the king that the "matter" and the "ord'ring on't" is *not* his sole prerogative. She fearlessly holds his daughter up to him and insists, against his impotent protestations, that Hermione's child is also his. She bears the brunt of his hysterical protestations that she is a shrew and her husband a weakling who cannot properly master his wife (so much for the "stabling" and "gelding"!) without flinching. Although she clearly shares a deep, affective bond with Hermione, her dedication in service to Leontes is total: she brings him back from the brink of his madness, nurtures and guides him during the sixteen years that Perdita is lost, and then, in a final coup that combines theatre and grace, restores his wife to him. This makes her one of the most extraordinary embodiments of service in the canon – more complex than Kent, more dedicated than Enobarbus, and close to that strange master, Prospero, in her supernatural command, although not in temperament or motive.

---

[2] Cavell, *Knowledge*.

THE RESISTANCE OF SERVICE IV: HERMIONE

The Winter's Tale as a whole follows Shakespeare's other plays in representing the relationships of service and mastery between women in supportive terms. David Evett remarks on the fact that there are very few relationships between mistress and female servant that show treachery or reluctance on the part of the servant or neglect on the part of the mistress. There are instances of gentle rivalry and teasing, as in *Much Ado about Nothing*, *The Two Gentlemen of Verona*, *Antony and Cleopatra*, and *The Merchant of Venice*, but on no occasions do female servants express bitter resentment towards their mistresses. "Once committed", Evett observes,

> Shakespearean women are almost without exception faithful, as wives, as lovers, as servants, regardless of changes in circumstance. Shakespearean men may well, as we know, waver and change, forsaking parents, siblings, wives, lovers, and masters. But the women are almost always ready to take risks, leave home, put on a new and dangerous identity, to serve those to whom they have pledged themselves. (*Discourses*, 180)

This tendency is especially apparent in *The Winter's Tale*, which carefully creates a space of warmth, support, and gentleness within the queen's circle of gentlewomen in waiting. As many have observed, Mamilius is ripped from this nurturing environment by his death-giving father, who furthermore, as Hermione herself puts it, cruelly refuses her the sustaining comforts of childbirth: "with immodest hatred / The childbed privilege denied which 'longs / To women of all fashion" (3.2.100–2). Allowed the supportive services of her women only in a prison cell, Hermione is emotionally trapped by the peculiar combination of service and love that was expected of royal wives. She reminds Leontes in her poignant, dignified trial speech that the love she showed to Polixines was a form of obedience to her husband, a form of *service* that she was obliged to undertake as his wife and queen:

> For Polixenes,
> With whom I am accused, I do confess
> I loved him as in honour he required;
> With such a kind of love as might become
> A lady like me; with a love, even such,
> So, and no other, as yourself commanded;
> Which not to have done I think had been in me
> Both disobedience and ingratitude
> To you and toward your friend, whose love had spoke
> Even since it could speak, from an infant, freely
> That it was yours.   (3.2.60–70)

Hermione uses the word "love" four times in a single sentence. In all instances except the last, it is a concept hedged about with duty, obligation, and subordination, reflected in phrases such as "he required", "become . . . me", "yourself commanded", "disobedience and ingratitude". Against her constrained love – arising from conditions such as honour, gratitude, duty, and obedience – Hermione contrasts the love given freely between the now estranged male friends. In doing so, she recalls her own exclusion from the circle of love in the opening scene, when Polixenes and her husband celebrate their mutual, childhood innocence, untainted by the evil desire of women. We see that circle of exclusion inverted at the end of the play, when the three women embrace and turn their backs on the men.

In the poignant dignity of her response to her husband's charge, then, Hermione speaks the language of service: of obedience and gratitude, duty and subordination. But like the best of servants, she also speaks her mind. She refuses to be cowed by tyranny. "Sir, spare your threats", she counters her raving husband. She reminds both the king and his court of the failure of reciprocity and duty that her accusation and treatment embody, and, like Antigonus before her, she insists upon the distinction between "rigor" and "law". Like Cordelia, she is attentive to the social bonds of love while she withholds from public scrutiny the pain of her personal investment and betrayal. I return to Hermione and Paulina in due course.

THE RESISTANCE OF SERVICE V: AUTOLYCUS

In the play's second half, service is embodied in a different mode. The device that effects the passage from Bohemia to Sicilia, from the tale of winter to a new season of redemption, draws our attention most acutely from the neo-feudal bonds of aristocratic service to those of Shakespeare's commodified profession: to the actor as a liminal figure between the bonds of neo-feudal service and the different play of freedom and restraint in the new service industry of the theatre. The chorus figure of Time evokes the tension between the representation of authority and the authority of that which represents, which, as Weimann puts it, is evidenced in "the unique capacity of the Shakespearean stage for simultaneously widening and closing the gaps between role and actor, between the site of dramatic illusion and the real place of the stage".[3] Although the use of the chorus in the later romance is neither as dramatically nor politically momentous as the opening chorus of *Henry V*, the structures or modes of representation

---

[3] Weimann, "Bifold Authority", 411.

are used to similar effect, namely, to oscillate between an affirmation of the power of that which is being represented and the frailty of the actor who represents it. The actor unmasks himself, drawing attention to his theatrical position of dependency, paradoxically to ensure the smooth passage of his presumptuous mimesis:

> I that please some, try all: both joy and terror
> Of good and bad; that makes and unfolds error,
> Now take upon me, in the name of Time,
> To use my wings. Impute it not a crime
> To me, or my swift passage, that I slide
> O'er sixteen years, and leave the ground untried
> Of that wide gap, since it is in my power
> To o'erthrow law, and in one self-born hour
> To plant and o'erwhelm custom. Let me pass
> The same I am ere ancient'st order was
> Or what is now received.   (4.1.1–11)

The opening phrase conveys the double identity of the actor-character, splitting the first person "I" across two personae embodied by a single figure: the actor who seeks always to "please", on the one hand, and the incorrigible omnipotence of Time which "tries all", on the other. This structure of "bifold authority" is extended and complicated as the speech progresses. The enactment of what Weimann calls "unsanctioned uses of a self-authorised, indecorous mimesis" or "self-propelled modes of theatrical signification" (401 and 402) is evident in the player's brazen appropriation of "the name of Time". The assumption of the power to "o'erthrow law" and "plant and o'erwhelm custom" (which resonates beyond the mere breaking of the artistic rules of dramatic unity and includes the place of the stage in contemporary disputes about licence and misrule) is invoked in the self-empowered autonomy of the "self-born hour" of theatrical representation. Part of that power to change law and custom comes from the gradual transformation of the player's status from servant to independent, professional man. As a condition of possibility of the actor's appropriation of authority and independence, however, the mimetic presumption (the "glass" of the "growing scene" (16)) is unmasked as an *allowed* convention, a "crime" but for the "allowing patience" (15) of the "gentle spectators" (20). "Let me pass / The same I am." The split "I" of the first line is repeated here. It attests to a bifold vision that plays off the necessary assent of all that is beyond the stage against the self-proclaiming integrity of those upon it.

The chorus's opening speech invokes complexities of representation that are put into play in the last two acts of *The Winter's Tale*. Specifically, they may be seen in the multiple instances of the adoption and stripping away of roles, masks, and costumes, especially by servants or former servants, and they are informed by the self-conscious reflexivity of such mimetic processes. A prime example is Autolycus, whose brazen rejection of service and celebration of his masterless, vagabond state and mimetic transformations are signal instances of the self-authorisation that Weimann discerns in the tradition of ritual mimesis and which, I have been arguing, are residual elements of even the professional theatre. Delivered in a *platea* mode, Autolycus's criminal self-expression corresponds to the historical origins of the popular English Renaissance player:

> I have served Prince Florizel, and in my time wore three-pile,
>   but now I am out of service.
> But shall I go mourn for that, my dear?
> The pale moon shines by night:
> And when I wander here and there,
> I then do most go right.   (4.3.13–22)

The appropriation of autonomous authority of the chorus's speech is re-expressed here, but without qualification and with a social thrust that is absent from the more abstract, metaphysical appropriation of the power of Father Time. These are the appropriations of the thief, the snitch, the vagabond, son of Mercury, "snapper-up of unconsidered trifles", liminal itinerant whose "impertinency" in the underscored lines constitutes, as Weimann nicely puts it, precisely the pertinence of the self-expressive mode. It makes possible "the appropriation of cultural power and communicative action by unsanctioned social groups" through its double mode of representation ("Shakespeare (De)Canonized", 79).

Most striking is Autolycus's obsessive concern with service, or its loss, and its relation to apparel. The first word he addresses directly to the audience about himself is that he was once a servant of some standing: like Poor Tom in *King Lear* he once wore "three-pile". Furthermore, when he describes the "manner of fellow" that is supposed to have robbed him to the hapless Clown, he focuses on his fallen or unmoored position as an ex-servant: "I knew him once as a servant of the prince." Far from being an object of social fear, however, Autolycus as the self-proclaimed "masterless man" – "out of service" either through free choice or because he was "whipped out" of the court – is a source of delight. His songs, topsy-turvy misplacing, and the sheer mimetic bravura characteristic of Shakespeare's comic servants, provoke not only the laughter of the audience *with* rather than at the actor but also moments of insight into real social conditions.[4] He represents in

---

[4] For a discussion of this distinction, see Weimann, *Traditions*, Appendix.

a peculiarly beguiling way both the comic impertinence of the real actor and anxieties about the player as an *essentially* masterless figure: on the margins of service, able to transform himself into any shape, embodying the combined pleasures of entertainment, sex, and crime. This is the other side of Iago as the embodiment of the player as an irresponsible, affective emptiness. The peculiarly obsessive appeal by the Chorus to be excused of the "crime" of theatrical embodiment and representation (4.1.4) is taken up and complicated by Autolycus's combination of the roles of balladeer and pick-pocket, which in turn anticipates Paulina's more profound demand that her powerfully transformative (feminine) magic at the end of the play should be considered "lawful" (5.3.96).

COMMODIFICATION AND SERVICE IN PLAY

Despite the festival promise of the play's pastoral scenes, its rural celebrations are infused with a sense of the instability (and, let it be said, the freedom) of the commodified circulation goods and money. The sheep-shearing feast, introduced as a problem of counting money and calculating prices, is situated in a world in which agricultural production and entertainment are equally commercial enterprises. Autolycus's cony-catching trick on the Clown, preoccupied with his shopping list and reckonings, calls to attention the early modern political semiotics of apparel, equally embodied and voided by the shape-shifting skills of common player and criminal. The amenability of clothing to being appropriated to unauthorised ends – to the "graft", to allude both to work of Jacques Derrida and the conversation between Perdita and Polixenes at the centre of the feast[5] – is exemplified by the fact that Autolycus does not even need the apparel of a gentleman to represent himself as a member of that rank. All that it takes is a certain native cunning and, crucially, the histrionic capacities of a good actor:

> AUTOLYCUS O help me, help me! Pluck but off these rags, and then death, death!
> CLOWN Alack, poor soul, thou hast need of more rags to lay on thee rather than have these off.
> AUTOLYCUS O sir, the loathsomeness of them offend me more than the stripes I have received, which are mighty ones and millions.
> CLOWN Alas, poor man, a million of beating may come to a great matter.
> AUTOLYCUS I am robbed, sir, and beaten; my money and apparel ta'en from me, and these detestable things put upon me.
> (4.3.48–58)

---

5 See Schalkwyk, *Literature*, chapter 4, for a discussion of the graft and the role of clothing in the play.

The presence of Autolycus at the sheep-shearing feast does not, however, strip the world of agricultural festival of all its traditional associations. At the festival itself two forms of service, both imbued with the spirit of topsy-turvy, rural festival, play themselves out in productive tension. Both are intimately related to dressing up, to pretending to be what you are not, and to the transformative powers of the theatre as communal ritual rather than mimetic representation.

The first of these involves Perdita's transformation, through the licence of play and the symbolic force of her "unusual weeds", from "shepherdess" into "Flora / Peering in April's front" (4.4.1–3). The scene's pastoral mode deftly allows Perdita to be transformed from a *real* shepherdess (although there are further ironies behind this) into a rustic goddess, while it reduces her lover's actual social status to a more commensurate, festival role: "Your high self, / The gracious mark o' th' land, you have obscured / With a swain's wearing" (7–8). Thus disguised in "borrowed flaunts", she is able to engage freely in the erotic game of reciprocating desire with a man who would otherwise be beyond her reach. The pastoral mode thus allows her to renegotiate what Paul Alpers calls her "strength relative to the world" through sexual and social play, just as Rosalind's role as a young shepherd in *As You Like It* allows her to engage erotically with the lesser-born Orlando.[6] Perdita's transformation is not without its abiding anxieties, however. She remains constantly aware of the fragile nature of their respective sumptuary transformations, fearing, presumably like many a real player, the stern audience of the king, who would recoil from the erotic and political inversion of his son "so noble, / Vilely bound up" and his beloved a "poor lowly maid / Most goddess-like pranked up" (9–10). Her fears are confirmed when Florizel's father disrupts the carnivalising disguises of the festival to prevent his son's supposedly denigrating marriage.

Before that happens, Perdita is brought back to a more gentle reality by her father, who reminds her of her double role of "both dame and servant":

> Fie, daughter, when my old wife lived, upon
> This day she was both pantler, butler, cook,
> Both dame and servant, welcomed all, served all.
> [. . .]   You are retired
> As if you were a feasted one and not
> The hostess of the meeting . . .
> Come, quench your blushes, and present yourself

---

[6] Alpers, *Pastoral*, 40 passim.

> That which you are, mistress o' th' feast. Come on,
> And bid us welcome to your sheep-shearing,
> As your good flock shall prosper. (55–70)

In contrast to Timon's approach to feasting, the Old Shepherd offers a lively conception of the complexity of the demands of service that we have seen throughout this study, and particularly in this play. Service cannot be confined to a single social position or status: it involves a manifold set of roles or performances that encompass both menial and creative tasks – "both pantler, butler, cook" – and the expansive responsibility for the welfare of others that is encompassed by the notion of hospitality – "welcomed all, served all". The pastoral mode of the play is precisely what allows this paradoxical idealisation of service, just as it permits the eradication of social difference and the free play of erotic desire between Perdita and Florizel.

Pastoral and the commodity

What is remarkable about its staging in *The Winter's Tale*, however, is the sharp sense of realism, the full-blooded life and its quotidian demands, with which Shakespeare imbues his pastoral scene. It allows us to hold in a convincing whole a number of otherwise contradictory elements. This differentiates the play sharply from *The Tempest*, which splits the elements in tension into their constituent parts, dominated by the contradictory efforts of Prospero's will to mastery and his reluctant decision to relinquish power once his dynastic ambitions have been satisfied. *The Winter's Tale*'s pastoral realism is further embodied in the masterless man in the form of Autolycus' playful criminality. The commodities (including those involving entertainment) that Autolycus brings to the sheep-shearing festival are sharply contrasted to the scene of "Flora / Peering in April's front", especially given that the eroticism represented by his "knacks" (335) and his ballads is an earthy counterpoint to the aristocratic couple's chaste desires. Yet if the shepherds' tendency to fetishise Autolycus's commodities is a form of slavery – see the Clown's canny pronouncement, "being enthralled as I am, it will also be the bondage of certain ribbons and gloves" (227–8) – the circulation of goods and money affords mobility to the snapper-up of unconsidered trifles and releases him from traditional bonds: "Come to the peddler / Money's a meddler, / That doth utter all men's ware-a" (308–10).

The relationship between what Evett has characterised as the "relationship of commodity" and the "relationship of ordination" (*Discourses*,

168–9) in master-servant relations is thus given a considerable degree
of flexibility and nuance through Shakespeare's canny intermingling of
commodification, the pastoral mode, and erotic desire. With characteristically aristocratic hauteur, Florizel declares himself above the commonplace
erotic commodifications upon which his former servant thrives and which
offer the eager shepherds the traffic of desire.:

> POLIXINES Sooth, when I was young
> And handed love as you do, I was wont
> To load my she with knacks. I would have ransacked
> The pedlar's silken treasury, and have poured it
> To her acceptance. You have let him go,
> And nothing marted with him. If your lass
> Interpretation should abuse, and call this
> Your lack of love or bounty, you were straited
> For a reply, at least if you make a care
> Of happy holding her.
> FLORIZEL   Old sir, I know
> She prizes not such trifles as these are.
> The gifts she looks from me are packed and locked
> Up in my heart, which I have given already,
> But not delivered.   (4.4.345–58)

Florizel speaks as if love transcended ordinary traffic: as if the gifts "packed
and locked up in [his] heart" bore no relation to, and were thus untouched
by, such common, external things as clothing, the commodity that is
Autolycus's chief means of change and exchange. In the ex-servant's hands
and words, clothing becomes infused with an erotic intensity; it is informed
by a satirical mode that parodies the transcendent idealism of disembodied
love:

> SERVANT He hath ribbons of all the colours i' th' rainbow; points
> more than all the lawyers in Bohemia can learnedly handle,
> though they come to him by th' gross; inkles, caddises,
> cambrics, lawns – why, he sings 'em over as they were gods
> or goddesses. You would think a smock were a she-angel, he so
> chants to the sleeve-hand and the work about the square on 't.
>   (4.4.205–11)

As "pranked-up" queen of the feast, Perdita is an echo of Autolycus's
"smock" transformed into a "she-angel", whereas Florizel will soon discover
that the naked reciprocity which he likes to think of as the full condition
of his love is hedged about by the impositions of difference over which he
has little control.

The bounds of service and the bonds of love revisited

From the sudden irruption of the unmasked king into the festival, which forestalls the kind of marriage ceremony that Rosalind stages in the Forest of Arden, the remainder of Act 4 interweaves the instabilities of service, love, and attire before they are transformed completely in the final act. Such instability is embodied in the handy exchange of clothing between Florizel, who needs a disguise that will obscure his noble birth, and Autolycus who, following the stunning success of his guise as an itinerant peddler at the festival, receives a further windfall in the form of the prince's garb and a bonus cash payment for the exchange. In his new aristocratic attire, our vagabond-peddler-thief revels in the opportunistic improvisation that is the mark of the theatrical player, playing his part and embodying it in the same breath:

> I see this is the
> time that the unjust man doth thrive. What an
> exchange had this been without boot! What a boot is
> here with this exchange! Sure the gods do this year
> connive at us, and we may do anything extempore.
>
> (4.4.656–60)

The ex-servant Autolycus's extemporising is an ironical counterpoint to the servant Camillo's intervention. The old retainer quickly improvises a script and a set of roles for Florizal and Perdita, who ruefully acknowledges the performative constraints of her new situation: "I see the play so lies / That I must bear a part" (4.4.638–9). The aristocratic servant further underlines his role as dramaturg when he reassures the prince of his personal investment in the new plot:

> CAMILLO My lord,
>   Fear none of this. I think you know my fortunes
>   Do all lie there. It shall be so my care
>   To have you royally appointed *as if*
>   *The scene you play were mine*. For instance, sir,
>   That you may know you shall not want – one word.
> (*They speak apart.*)
> (*Enter* AUTOLYCUS)
> AUTOLYCUS Ha, ha! What a fool honesty is, and trust –
>   his sworn brother – a very simple gentleman!
>
> (4.4.578–85; emphasis added)

But Autolycus's theatrical entrance puts into ironical question the exact nature of the royal servant's investment. For, as we have seen, Camillo's hidden motive is in fact to break free of his new master and return to his old king:

> Now were I happy if
> His going I could frame to serve my turn,
> Save him from danger, do him love and honour,
> Purchase the sight again of dear Sicilia
> And that unhappy king, my master, whom
> I so much thirst to see.   (496–501)

Once again, Camillo refers to *Leontes* – not Polixenes – as his "master". Consequently, his dialogue with Florizel is filled with an anxious emphasis on his loyalty to the king, Florizel's father: "Sir, I think / You have heard of my poor services i'th' love / That I have borne your father" (502–4). The prince replies reassuringly, but not without some anxiety of his own, about the reciprocal love, care, and recompense due to the dedicated servant:

> Very nobly
> Have you deserved. It is my father's music
> To speak your deeds, not little of his care
> To have them recompensed as thought on.
> CAMILLO   Well, my lord,
> If you may please to think I love the King,
> And through him what's nearest to him, which is
> Your gracious self, embrace but my direction,
> If your more ponderous and settled project
> May suffer alteration.   (505–13)

It is to Camillo's response that Autolycus's subsequent remark about honesty will ironically echo. For in reassuring the prince that his service to him under these strained circumstances will be patterned on his record of loyalty to the prince's father, Camillo elides his triply divided loyalties: in serving the prince, he must necessarily betray his father; and in doing so he is, as he says, most unservant-like, "serving his own turn" (compare Iago), although this self-directedness is complicated by his sense of a higher duty to his former master.

In his excitement at the prospect of being saved from his predicament, Florizel presumptuously suggests a bond between himself and the old nobleman that is more deeply affective than that of mere master and servant:

> How, Camillo,
> May this, almost a miracle, be done? –
> That I may call thee *something more than man*,
> And after that trust to thee.
> (522; emphasis added)

As the scene develops, a growing dependency of the young royal master upon the older servant becomes apparent. It promises a transformation of the servile relationship into one of love and friendship ("something more than man"). That dependency is expressed most forcefully in Florizel's recognition of a new, ethical bond with the senior servant – "I am bound to you" (552) – through the preserving support of the latter's service: "Camillo, / Preserver of my father, now of me, / The medicine of our house" (574–6).

The question of gratitude and recompense that so occupies Florizel in his immature eagerness – which presumes that his personal desires are identical to that of "our house" – is central to this scene. Why is Camillo behaving in this way? What are the wellsprings of his service, and where do its limits lie? What forms of recompense does he require? These questions do not occur to Florizel, because he is preoccupied with his own condition, and in his babbling of trust, he forgets the degree to which he is suborning his *father's* man. The questions are, however, powerfully raised in the dramatic construction of the scene, especially in the counterpoint figure of Autolycus. Having initially flaunted his free movement beyond the bonds of service, the vagabond now gradually moves back within those bounds in his encounter and exchange with his old master, just as Camillo and Florizel loosen the bonds that tie them to Polixines.

The recovery of service

Autolycus and Camillo trace different paths to the recovery of their respective bonds of service. Their ironic juxtaposition begins with their conflicting views of their respective duties to inform the king of his son's flight. "If I thought it were a piece of honesty to acquaint the King withal", the son of Mercury confesses, "I would not do't. I hold it the more knavery to conceal it, and therein am I constant to my profession" (4.4.661–4). Camillo, on the other hand, does tell Polixenes of Florizel's elopement. His motives for doing so, however, are arguably as much a piece of knavery as Autolycus's decision to remain silent, especially considering the fact that Camillo is the one who, under the cover of long-trusted service, instigated the plan:

> CAMILLO (*aside*) What I do next shall be to tell the King
> Of this escape, and whither they are bound;
> Wherein my hope is I shall so prevail
> To force him after, in whose company
> I shall re-view Sicilia, for whose sight
> I have a woman's longing.   (645–50)

Camillo's treachery towards the prince is counter-balanced by the at least formal fulfilment of his obligations to his adopted king, but this tension is itself conditioned by a prior attachment that stems from his prior, servile devotion to an earlier master. The royal servant is happily the beneficiary of what Isaiah Berlin calls "moral luck", because everything turns out well, and his betrayal is hardly commented upon or noticed.[7] Camillo is not motivated by the conventional things that preoccupy Florizel when the latter considers service: recompense, personal advantage, preferment. His longing is deeply affective, significantly and ironically gendered as an irrational, female desire.

Turning to Autolycus, we are entertained by his bravura improvisation upon his own thoroughly immoral luck. He makes use of his "borrowed flaunts" to lord it over the cowed Old Shepherd and his son, who are urgently seeking to put as much distance between their blood and Perdita's as they can. His motivation for doing so is striking. "I know not what impediment this complaint may be to the flight of my master" (689–900), he confides to the audience, suddenly reclaiming Florizel as master, and reinstating himself, at least implicitly, as his servant: "I am courted now with a double occasion: gold, and a means to do the Prince my master good, which who knows how that may turn back to my advancement?" (803–5). Unlike Camillo, Autolycus resumes the role of servant ostensibly to do his master good and to secure his own material and social profit. His plan does not quite work out, however, and he is transformed, almost in an instant, into a figure like Paroles in *All's Well That Ends Well*. Confronted by the now elevated rustics, who comically boast of being "gentlemen born . . . any time these four hours" (like Shakespeare himself), Autolycus is driven to beg the country bumpkins whom he had cheated and duped in the play's pastoral mode for their gentlemanly testimonial of his good character at the Sicilian court: "I humbly beseech you, sir, to pardon me all the faults I have committed to your worship, and to give me your good report to the Prince my master" (5.2.133–5). In *All's Well that Ends Well* Paroles gratefully accepts service under the mastership of a real gentleman. It is a sign of the diminution of Autolycus as a figure of free improvisation that he readily prostrates himself before the two bumbling figures who had earlier been the victims of his protean cunning. "Come, follow us", they airily command, assuming the unfamiliar carriage of gentlemen, as he had earlier, "We'll be thy good masters" (157). And no doubt they will.

[7] See Engle, *Pragmatism*, 98ff.

Autolycus reminds us of Caliban prostrating himself before Stephano and Trinculo, but he does so in a different key. Unlike Caliban, Autolycus ingratiates himself knowingly, well aware of the precariousness of his situation. In his return to service, Autolycus appears to confirm Michael Neill's claim that to the early modern mind the condition of being truly without a master would have been unthinkable. Yet it perhaps also marks the new distance, a decade or so into the reign of James, and three decades after the Vagabond Act, between the "sharer" in the professional theatre and the ideological position of vagabond – a recuperation by a master of a formerly liminal position within the master-servant relations of the new theatre itself.

WOMAN AS CORRECTIVE, LOVING SERVANT

The final act of *The Winter's Tale* is one of the most skilful and singular in all Shakespeare. The theatrical challenges are formidable: first, we need to be taken back, across sixteen years, to Sicilia, where contact with Leontes and the members of his court needs to be re-established quickly and concisely. This is followed by a series of events that occur in rapid succession: the arrival of Florizal and Perdita, followed by the precipitous and unexpected interruption of Camillo and Polixenes, hot in pursuit of the delinquent prince. The resolution of that conflict, through the revelation of Perdita's real identity, demands a series of reconciliations of peculiarly affective intensity, made all the more difficult because of the sudden transformation of already heightened feeling: disappointment is turned into satisfaction; anger into love; loss into discovery; fear into relief; sorrow into joy; service into friendship; desire into resolution. All this has to happen in preparation for the climactic scene of Hermione's restoration, where the emotional charge of the preceding events is intensified even further.

Shakespeare solves the problem of having to represent *two* scenes of intense wonder and reconciliation by having one of them narrated rather than presented on stage. This allows him to hold back the intensity of the first so that the second may be properly climactic. It also allows him to establish verbal patterns in the first which, although not quite as deeply emotional, are cumulative in effect. The descriptions of the three gentlemen are a kind of musical prologue to the awakening of Hermione. They restore personal and social bonds through the reiterative effects of narrative via the embodied narrators who, sharing the experience among themselves and with the audience, enact a new, communal space that had been twice destroyed by the "pair of kings". Such reconciliation is conveyed by a repeated pattern of represented emotion, exemplified in typically Shake-spearean fashion by tears shed undecidably between overwhelming joy and intense sorrow.

The reunion between master and servant is as passionate in affect as the reconciliation of the royal friends:

> FIRST GENTLEMAN I make a broken delivery of the business, but
> the changes I perceived in the King and Camillo were very
> notes of admiration. They seemed almost, with staring on one
> another, to tear the cases of their eyes. There was speech in
> their dumbness, language in their very gesture. They looked
> as they had heard of a world ransomed, or one destroyed. A
> notable passion of wonder appeared in them, but the wisest
> beholder, that knew no more but seeing, could not say if th'
> importance were joy or sorrow. But in the extremity of the
> one, it must needs be. (5.1.8–17)

This is as intense an expression of the closeness of service and friendship or love as anything else in Shakespeare, and it calls for admiration and wonder precisely because, like the other relationships in the play, it is recovered from what appears at first to be complete alienation and loss. The affirmation of love described here is a product of earlier carelessness. It is a mutual dependency rediscovered anew precisely because it was unheeded before. That pattern is repeated in Leontes' relationship with Paulina and height-ened in the miraculous recovery, through Paulina's unbounded service, of Hermione herself.

Act Five opens with Leontes being offered contradictory counsel by a variety of aristocratic servants. Shakespeare recalls both the events of the previous sixteen years and Leontes' changed disposition in their efforts to console the king, who continues to suffer the loss of his wife, accepting his own responsibility for that loss. The servants are not at one about the way forward for their master. Cleomenes and Dion on the one hand, and Paulina on the other, take distinctive positions on what is best for both the king and the kingdom. Cleomenes argues that Leontes has "done enough". He should "forgive himself" (5.1.1 and 6). Paulina, on the other hand, continues to act as the spur that, over a period of sixteen years, has ensured that neither Hermione's memory nor his acknowledgement of his own "blemishes" fades through the naturally dimming process of time. Both sets of servants believe that they are serving the king best. The men take a pragmatic and resolutely political view of the situation. To Paulina's

indignant charge that he "is one of those / That would have him wed again"
(23–4), Dion replies:

> If you would not so
> You pity not the state, nor the remembrance
> Of his most sovereign name, consider little
> What dangers, by his highness' fail of issue,
> May drop upon his kingdom and devour
> Incertain lookers-on. What were more holy
> Than to rejoice the former queen is well?
> What holier, than for royalty's repair,
> For present comfort and for future good,
> To bless the bed of majesty again
> With a sweet fellow to 't?   (5.1.24–34)

Dion's sharp retort reminds Paulina of their collective duty to the well-being
of the state, the major burden of which is borne by the king. Although *The
Winter's Tale* was written a decade after the death of Elizabeth, many in the
audience would have recalled the crisis occasioned by the absence of a royal
heir. Dion's concept of service is spread more widely and impersonally. It
includes the king, and it offers a concept of service in relation to the state
recalled from *Othello*: "I have done the state some service, and they know 't"
(*Othello*, 5.2.348). A queen may serve by providing her king with "present
comfort", but her chief role is the more instrumental one of ensuring
"royalty's repair" and "future good" through the provision of an heir: she
is primarily a "bedfellow". That role was exemplified by the actions of
Elizabeth's father, who treated his successive queens as fungible instruments
of the state, and it lies at the centre of the discomfiting reduction of wife
to "uneared womb" (sonnet 3) in Shakespeare's first seventeen sonnets.

   In insisting that Hermione cannot be replaced by any other substitute,
Paulina underlines both her own singularity as the king's servant and the
uniqueness of her queen – the fact that she is neither fungible nor a mere
political instrument: "There's none worthy / Respecting her that's gone"
(34–5). It is the person herself that matters – she cannot be replaced, or
reduced to a set of attributes or roles:

> LEONTES   Good Paulina,
> Who hast the memory of Hermione,
> I know, in honour – O, that ever I
> Had squared me to thy counsel! Then even now
> I might have looked upon my queen's full eyes,
> Have taken treasure from her lips.

PAULINA   And left them
More rich for what they yielded.
LEONTES   Thou speak'st truth.
No more such wives, therefore no wife.

                                              (5.1.49–56)

By reminding Leontes of the paradoxically replete economy of sexual
reciprocity, Paulina underscores the fact that it does *not* work, as most
economies do, on circulation, substitution, and consumption. It is precisely the singularity of the one-to-one relationship that constitutes the
paradoxical economy of sexual love: each person should come away "more
rich for what they yield". This singularity, above all, is what makes the
queen more than an instrument of royal succession.

In offering her singular counsel to her king, Paulina again sets herself
against the other royal servants. She follows the pattern of her earlier, fearless
service when she refused to indulge the king's fantastic jealousy and abuse
of power. In this respect, only Kent matches her in dedicated resolution,
but Kent's lack of the regenerative power that Paulina commands raises the
question of the interaction of gender and service. There are few substantial
servants in Shakespeare who are also women. Evett remarks on the peculiarly
supportive and loyal nature of almost all female servants in the plays and
poems, but they are all relatively minor characters, who make little major
mark upon the events or action of their respective play worlds. Paulina, who
is excoriated by the angry king for being a "mankind witch", approaches the
mage Prospero both to the extent that her power is supernatural – "graves
at my command / Have waked their sleepers, oped and let 'em forth / By
my so potent art" (*The Tempest* 5.1.49–51) – and in the enormity of her
resurrectionary intervention.

Dion's references to what might be considered "holy" with regard to the
restoration of a queen to Leontes' bed look forward to the anxiety that
accompanies the miraculous awakening of Hermione. In her response to
those who would have the king wed again Paulina is in fact the one who
recalls the will of the gods. It is her appropriation of the royal prerogative
to decide whom the king will wed that is most remarkable:

LEONTES   Stars, stars,
And all eyes else, dead coals! Fear thou no wife.
I'll have no wife, Paulina.
PAULINA   Will you swear
Never to marry but by my free leave?
LEONTES Never, Paulina, so be blest my spirit.

PAULINA Then, good my lords, bear witness to his oath.
CLEOMENES You tempt him over-much.
PAULINA   Unless another
   As like Hermione as is her picture
   Affront his eye –
CLEOMENES   Good madam, I have done.
PAULINA Yet if my lord will marry – if you will, sir;
   No remedy but you will – give me the office
   To choose your queen. She shall not be so young
   As was your former, but she shall be such
   As, walked your first queen's ghost, it should take joy
   To see her in your arms.
LEONTES   My true Paulina,
   We shall not marry till thou bidd'st us.
PAULINA   That
   Shall be when your first queen's again in breath.
   Never till then.   (5.1.67–84)

Paulina demands the transfer of power from a patriarchal nexus to a female matrix. In doing so, she inverts a number of conventional truisms about the nature of service, obedience, freedom, and subordination. For the king to give up his power to choose somebody as crucial, personally and politically, as his marriage partner to a servant is unconventional enough; for him to give a woman such power is extraordinary. Moreover, he gives her unconditional authority, transferring a prerogative that in its freedom and scope is actually, as we have seen in the failed attempt by Polixenes to determine his son's marriage partner, beyond even that of a king. Leontes agrees to marry only by Paulina's "free leave"; he allows her to choose his queen, and he subjugates his own will and choice to her command: "My true Paulina, / We shall not marry till thou bidd'st us."

Leontes can move from viewing Paulina as a "mankind witch . . . gross hag! . . . a callet / Of boundless tongue . . . And lozel . . . worthy to be hanged" (2.3.68, 91–2, 108–9) to addressing her repeatedly as "good Paulina" and "my true Paulina" (5.1.49 and 81) because he acknowledges, as Lear never does of Kent, the depth of her service to him, and especially that such service is most dedicated when she sets her face against him. By transferring as much power to Paulina as he does, Leontes subscribes wholly to the paradox that service is freedom. If we have encountered many servants who not only accept but actively encourage such a state, *The Winter's Tale* is unique in embodying it in the person of a king. Leontes thus engages in a speech act of unusual performative politics: he gives his servant the freedom to choose a wife for him, binding himself through that performative to her will. Like some of Shakespeare's other males who have lived in fear and suspicion of the female as such, Leontes responds to the demand for *unconditional* trust – the birth of faith in herself as loyal female servant and in the ghost of his wife. "It is required / You do awake your faith" (5.3.94–5), she says at the brink of Hermione's restoration. She nonetheless feels the need to forestall a general, patriarchal anxiety about the feminine power as witchcraft: "those that think it is unlawful business / I am about, let them depart" (96–7). Leontes' act of faith – so conspicuously absent from his earlier behaviour – makes it possible for Paulina to perform her greatest act of service by releasing him from the emotional and psychological prison in which he has kept himself during the previous sixteen years.

Eros, nomos, *and* agapé: *transforming desire*

How complete is that release? I opened this study with the claim that it is desirable, as the great theoretical movement of the late twentieth century begins to fade, or, perhaps more accurately, to become the uncritical foundation of English studies, to resist the hegemony of the theorised concepts of power and desire by inflecting them with those of service and love. As we reach the final scene of one of Shakespeare's most complex late treatments of the relationship between love and service, power and desire insist upon their due. My discussion of the relationship between Paulina and Leontes has necessarily been conducted in terms of power – the transfer of power from patriarchal king to matriarchal servant. Although it is clear that Camillo and Leontes love each other, and that Polixenes and the king of Sicilia recover the long-standing *philia* that was interrupted, but not destroyed, by the latter's jealousy, it is less clear whether Paulina devotes herself to her king because she loves him, or even that he loves her in any kind of personal sense. In other words, we return to the dialectic of *nomos* and *agapē*.

In the narrated reconciliation in Act Five, Paulina is a somewhat grotesque figure, torn between the joy of Perdita's recovery and her sorrow at the confirmation of her husband's death:

> But O, the noble combat that 'twixt joy and sorrow was fought in
> Paulina! She had one eye declined for the loss of her husband,
>   another elevated that the oracle was fulfilled.   (5.2.66–9)

Her eye is upon the oracle, not the king, and she stands, in a sense, "for sacrifice", for she and her husband are the two servants who have suffered irrecoverable loss through their dedication to preserve the king's daughter.[8] She has every reason to hate Leontes, but she doesn't. What she does instead is to take upon herself the impossible task of forestalling the return of *eros* as a destructive, all-consuming male desire and replacing it with a different kind of love. It is the corrosive scepticism of such desire that led to the loss of Mamilius, Hermione, her husband Antigonus, and, for a time, Perdita, in the first place. Male desire in *The Winter's Tale* not only suffers from, but is founded upon, an intense anxiety that its object is essentially unknowable, and therefore beyond possession.[9]

Joel Davis argues that male desire is encapsulated by Pygmalion, who creates an object of desire that can have no secrets:

The classical form can be properly the object of the gaze, because the gaze takes in nothing other than the opaque surface. But the desire to touch the statue, and the experience of feeling it yield as would flesh, evoke the Bakhtinian grotesque. By creating the statue as an object to be seen but not touched, and by then bringing readers into Pygmalion's imaginary tactile experiences, Ovid evokes desire.[10]

Desire, not love – for love demands a reciprocity that arises from a will not controlled or created by the desiring person. The play of surface beauty evokes desire, but that is not where desire stops. It wishes to move beyond mere surface, which, however alluring, resists the penetrative efforts of the gaze. It wishes to know, comprehend, and possess what lies beyond its capacity – that which it thinks is hidden beneath the surface of its gaze. Cavell has shown that the movement of such desire involves the *avoidance* of love through the incapacity to acknowledge, on the one hand, that someone one loves is capable of giving birth, of being something other than one's complete possession, and, on the other, that one *needs* the love of such another. Cavell's argument is exemplified by the other side of Leontes' desire for Hermione – his horror at what he takes to be the monstrous birth of her daughter.

There is a considerable amount of anxiety about "breeding" in the play: it runs from the obvious revulsion of Leontes from his wife's pregnancy and the sexuality that it represents, to the fraught exchange between Polixenes and Perdita about the naturalness of "grafting". Following his brother king,

---

[8] See the arguments, by Hunt and Bristol, that in being consumed by the bear, Antigonus is in fact consumed by his master, the tyrant Leontes, in Hunt, "Bearing Hence", and Bristol, "In Search of the Bear".

[9] This is the burden of Cavell's argument in *Disowning Knowledge*, chapter 6.

[10] Davis, "Paulina's Paint", 121–2.

Polixenes shows violent anger and horrified revulsion at the simultaneously open and ensnaring female body:

> (*To* PERDITA)   And you, enchantment,
> Worthy enough a herdsman – yea, him too,
> That makes himself, but for our honour therein,
> Unworthy thee – if ever henceforth thou
> These rural latches to his entrance open,
> Or hoop his body more with thy embraces,
> I will devise a death as cruel for thee
> As thou art tender to 't.   (4.4.412–19)

Such revulsion is the converse of the desire that Perdita evokes in the first place, especially in her shamelessly free talk of her own and her lover's wish to "breed":

> No more than, were I painted, I would wish
> This youth should say 'twere well, and only therefore
> Desire to breed by me . . .
> [. . .]
> . . . like a bank, for love to lie and play on,
> Not like a corpse – or if, not to be buried,
> But quick and in mine arms.   (4.4.102–4 and 130–3)

Perdita's unselfconscious expression of sexuality, not only as reciprocal desire but also as a paradoxical intertwining of life and death, freedom and captivity, recalls the expression, in a completely different key, of Leontes' pathological imagination of his wife being "sluiced" in his absence and of his own spiritual death through the "breeding" that that imagined event brings forth. Something of the same pathology is evident in Polixenes who, like his brother king, finds the desire that female sexuality breeds so horrifying that he seeks to expel it in the form of his own blood:

> (*To* FLORIZEL)   For thee, fond boy,
> If I may ever know thou dost but sigh
> That thou no more shalt see this knack, as never
> I mean thou shalt, we'll bar thee from succession,
> Not hold thee of our blood, no, not our kin,
> Farre than Deucalion off.   (414–19)

It is Paulina's task – it is the epitome of her service – to exorcise the simultaneous entrapment in this desire and the revulsion from its effects in the body and mind of her master. Initially the focus of the monstrosity of female sexuality, Perdita as epitome of loss and absence becomes the repeated object of male desire, provoking in turn the erotic attentions of

Florizel, Camillo, Polixenes, and, finally, her own father. The "desire to breed by her" is thus distributed across almost all the males in the play, but it is framed in a different key by Leontes' and then Polixenes' revulsion from such "breeding" as the very condition of the female.

Paulina's self-imposed task of forestalling Leontes' desire by keeping him in a state of penitence and sorrow, and by ensuring that he is forever haunted by the memory of Hermione, is thus dangerously challenged by his erotic response to his daughter:

> LEONTES Would he do so, I'd beg your precious mistress,
>   Which he counts but a trifle.
> PAULINA   Sir, my liege,
>   Your eye hath too much youth in 't. Not a month
>   Fore your queen died she was more worth such gazes
>   Than what you look on now.   (5.1.222–6)

This arousal is the first sign of Leontes' escape from the endlessly reiterated "gelid theatre of remorse" that Tom Bishop characterises so acutely.[11] Yet Paulina, who keeps Leontes to the script of that cold theatre and who has prepared the text for a new stage of release, is deeply aware that Leontes' "eye", awakening to youthful desire and filled with Perdita's youthful desirability, threatens to repeat the cycle that began with his perception of Hermione's pregnancy sixteen years earlier. Within the structure of repeated remorse, desire, memory and death engage in an endless dance; if desire is death, as Shakespeare suggests elsewhere (sonnet 147.8), in this context marriage is murder:

> LEONTES   Thou speak'st the truth.
>   No more such wives, therefore no wife. One worse,
>   And better used, would make her sainted spirit
>   Again possess her corpse, and on this stage,
>   Where we offenders mourn, appear soul-vexed,
>   And begin, "Why to me?"
> PAULINA   Had she such power
>   She had just cause.
> LEONTES   She had, and would incense me
>   To murder her I married.
> PAULINA   I should so.
>   Were I the ghost that walked I'd bid you mark
>   Her eye, and tell me for what dull part in 't
>   You chose her. Then I'd shriek that even your ears

---

[11] Bishop, *Wonder*, 148.

> Should rift to hear me, and the words that followed
> Should be, "Remember mine".
> LEONTES   Stars, stars,
> And all eyes else, dead coals! Fear thou no wife.
> I'll have no wife, Paulina.   (5.1.55–69)

Hermione needs to be transformed from haunting spirit into present stone, and then from stone to flesh. For it is only on being confronted by her as an object of silent wonder – as art embodied in theatre – and then through appropriate *human* interaction, that Leontes can be released from the coldness of desire and the bitterness of remorse, and in turn release his wife from the grave to which he has driven her. The problem, as Paulina perceives all too well, is to allow desire and love to accommodate each other. Desire is not sufficient, as its theorists from Plato to Lacan have shown, for it feeds upon absence and lack. Without desire, however, love loses touch with *eros*. But desire remains fraught with peril, a peril that it is Paulina's task to exorcise through the play of her commanding interventions.

The grace of service

The scene opens with the king's frank acknowledgement of the debt that he owes Paulina for her services and her acknowledgement of reciprocal reward:

> LEONTES O grave and good Paulina, the great comfort
>   That I have had of thee!
> PAULINA   What, sovereign sir,
>   I did not well, I meant well. All my services
>   You have paid home, but that you have vouchsafed
>   With your crowned brother and these young contracted
>   Heirs of your kingdoms my poor house to visit,
>   It is a surplus of your grace which never
>   My life may last to answer.
> LEONTES   O Paulina,
>   We honour you with trouble.   (5.3.1–9)

Paulina's response, however, goes far beyond the calculable concepts of justly weighed service and recompense. By adopting the language of grace, she introduces the idea of the incalculable or unconditional that is central to the tragedies. She is incapable of repaying the king for gracing her house. Although valued and appreciated, her own presence lacks the substance or form of royalty that Polixenes was so anxious to preserve by keeping his son from impure grafting in Act 4. As the scene unfolds, however, we begin to see that Paulina is in fact the one with the power to bestow a much greater gift upon her royal master; she it is who, with Hermione, has the gift of grace. That gift has to be more than accepted – it needs to be *called for* by its recipient, in an act of double acknowledgement and vulnerable exposure, to the wife that has been killed and the servant spurned.

It is significant that the reawakening of the queen should take place within the *private* space of Paulina's home, and that Paulina should insist repeatedly on the statue as her possession. Although Leontes speaks of the "statue of our queen", he acknowledges that it is situated and belongs in "your [Paulina's] gallery". And Paulina underlines that concession by reminding him that she "keep[s] it / Lonely, apart" (17–18). In recalling for Leontes the fact that it was always in her power to keep Hermione's statue to herself or share it, she pointedly iterates the claim that it *belongs* to her:

> PAULINA [*to* LEONTES]   Indeed, my lord,
>   If I had thought the sight of my poor image
>   Would thus have wrought you – *for the stone is mine* –
>   I'd not have showed it.
>   [*She makes to draw the curtain*]
> LEONTES   Do not draw the curtain.
> PAULINA No longer shall you gaze on 't, lest your fancy
>   May think anon it moves.   (5.3.57–61; emphasis added)

At the same time, in the act of sharing the statue, Paulina emphasises the public nature of art and the necessary intersubjectivity of human beings who create and respond to it.

Paulina now occupies the position that has been the domain of the servant-player throughout this study, as the "impertinent" discloser of ruling blindness. Yet she transforms that domain entirely through her own individual piece of theatre. First, even the *virtual* positions of the *platea* and *locus* are relocated, because Paulina and Hermione, wife and servant, take up both positions at once, and they shift the kings into a position in which their customary centrality is subtly decentred. They occupy female, *domestic* space, at once marginalised and transformed through its theatricality into the central locus for the transformation of the "pair of kings". They draw those kings into *their* space, requiring of them that they both watch patiently and act ethically. Leontes becomes simultaneous spectator and protagonist, watched and watching, actor and acted upon. Just as Helen allows the impetus of male desire to trap her husband into redirecting the impetus of his aspirations towards her, so Paulina invites Leontes to displace himself by taking upon himself the responsibility of an ethical action that is both internally motivated and judged from outside. It is as if the player were to be held accountable for the actions of his part.

The statue as representation of Leontes' queen represents her alienation from him – one could say her freedom from him – as she passes from his possession to that of a servant and friend – Paulina. (Here we see a deepening of the notion of girlish female friendships that recur throughout Shakespeare into the possibility of female *philia* that even Montaigne acknowledges in his meditation on his adopted daughter.)[12] The law of property, which Leontes had earlier attempted to apply to human relationships, comes back to haunt him. It can be broken or suspended only through the free action of the gift. "The stone is mine": this speech act, which acts as a claim, a reminder, and a crucial qualification, looks back at the unsolicited gifts of servants to their often undeserving masters: to old Adam's gift of his pension to Orlando in *As You Like It*, to Flavius's to Timon in *Timon of Athens*, and to the inversion of such gifts in the treasure that Antony sends after Enobarbus. Nevertheless, it little prepares us for the extraordinary nature of Paulina's grace in the gift of her shaped stone to Leontes: unlike the other cases, for Leontes to put himself in the position in which he is capable of *receiving* the gift from his servant, he has to do something else: he has to transform performatively the conditions of possibility, so that the gift can be both given and accepted as a gift. We tend to forget that the performative act of the gift is entirely mutual or reciprocal: it involves both giving and acceptance. While Hermione is stone, she is Paulina's, but yet not Paulina's gift: belonging to Paulina, she may be briefly shared, shown, displayed. As an object of remarkable art, she induces wonder, admiration, and desire. Yet to receive her, Leontes has to call for her and to call upon her.

In his rich insight into the wonder of this scene, Bishop shows how Hermione's stoniness is a form of protection from the hardness of male desire (or what Cavell calls scepticism, the incapacity for acknowledgement; Bishop, *Wonder*, 162–3, and Cavell, *Knowledge*, chapter 6). One of the gifts of service that Paulina gives Leontes is the opportunity to dissolve that hardness. Her husband is the only one who can restore warmth and softness to Hermione, but such restoration bears the indelible lines of time and suffering that the sonnets vainly attempt to erase or prevent. An opportunity is all that his servant can give Leontes, along with some apposite caveats and directions. She cannot herself unfreeze Hermione. Leontes has to perform that unrepayable service for himself, and he has

---

[12] *Essays*, 599. See also Chapter 3 of this text, and Shannon, *Amity*, chapters 2 and 3.

to do it unconsciously, without knowing that he is performing it. He very nearly fails. The moment of near failure, which induces something close to panic in Paulina, comes when he moves from awed admiration of the statue as art to the wish-fulfilling belief that it is an object not merely of contemplation and wonder but also of desire and possession.

The scene of this near failure, or heart-stopping success, is organised as a series of liminal moments, in which we pass, along with the characters between emotional, spiritual, and ethical states: from expectation, to silent wonder, to interrogation bordering on disappointment ("But yet . . . Hermione was not so much wrinkled, nothing / So aged as this seems" (27–8)), to end, decisively in Leontes' case, in a renewed vision of the woman he once loved:

> So much to my good comfort as it is
> Now piercing to my soul. O, thus she stood,
> Even with such life of majesty – warm life,
> As now it coldly stands – when first I wooed her.
> I am ashamed. Does not the stone rebuke me
> For being more stone than it? O royal piece!
> There's magic in thy majesty, which has
> My evils conjured to remembrance, and
> From thy admiring daughter took the spirits,
> Standing like stone with thee.   (33–42)

The speech hovers between death and life, coldness and warmth, love and shame, returning each moment of promised release back to the second of these antitheses. Comfort turns to piercing; warm life to cold immobility; wooing to shame; the magic of majesty to remembered evil; and admiration to stone. The wintry tenor of admiring desire recalls Camillo's response to Perdita along with her just riposte:

> CAMILLO I should leave grazing were I of your flock,
>   And only live by gazing.
> PERDITA   Out, alas,
>   You'd be so lean that blasts of January
>   Would blow you through and through.
>   (4.4.108–12)

Camillo's substitution of gazing for grazing looks forward to Leontes' astonished cry that Hermione's revival should be "an art / Lawful as eating" (5.3.110–11), but before he is able to lose himself in the overwhelming fact of his wife's warmth ("O, she's warm"), he comes close to reliving the old impulse to possess what is desired, an impulse encapsulated, as Kenneth

Gross points out, in his speaking of the quickening figure in the third person.[13] Paulina's urgent warnings that he will soil himself on the freshly painted statue and spoil its features are more than an impromptu device: they invoke the contaminating violence of male desire that resides in Shakespeare's Ovidian sources.

Leontes' impulse to possess the statue is in stark contrast to his daughter's willingness to remain in a position of unpossessive, but possessed, admiration:

> LEONTES   Let no man mock me,
> For I will kiss her.
> PAULINA   Good my lord, forbear.
> The ruddiness upon her lip is wet.
> You'll mar it if you kiss it, stain your own
> With oily painting. Shall I draw the curtain?
> LEONTES No, not these twenty years.
> PERDITA   So long could I
> Stand by, a looker-on.   (79–84)

This impulse to erotic possession also stands in contrasted relief with another description of peculiarly erotic intensity earlier in the play:

> When you speak, sweet,
> I'd have you do it ever; when you sing,
> I'd have you buy and sell so, so give alms,
> Pray so; and for the ord'ring your affairs,
> To sing them too. When you do dance, I wish you
> A wave o' th' sea, that you might ever do
> Nothing but that, move still, still so,
> And own no other function. Each your doing,
> So singular in each particular,
> Crowns what you are doing in the present deeds,
> That all your acts are queens.   (4.4.136–46)

Bishop offers the key to this passage, both in its context and for the rest of the play, when he remarks that "it is the crowning moment of the scene, and will be answered itself in turn in the final animation of Hermione's statue, also a greatly stilled and moving moment" (156). He focuses on the way in which Florizel's praise of Perdita figures the relationship between desire and fiction. I wish to shift the emphasis slightly, bringing out what is implicit in Bishop's analysis concerning the relationship in tension, so difficult to sustain, between desire and love. There is no doubting the

---

[13] Gross, *Statue*, 105.

intensity of desire in the speech; but desire is turned irresistibly into love – just as Hermione is turned from what is wonderful as stone into breathing and responding warmth, itself just as wonderful – at every moment of Florizel's rapture. How he transforms the Petrarchan blazon, giving voice, movement, fluidity, singularity, and agency to the stony deadness of that genre! His is a more youthful, less knowing form of Enobarbus' praise of Cleopatra, which also focuses on the enrapturing singularity of action. It is a transformation of the stock Shakespearean thought of waves, as the signifiers of devouring time or deathly stagnation, into a movement that contains time in continuous beauty while neither arresting it nor being overcome by it. Hermione is released from frozen time into wondrous movement, into the reciprocal embrace of flesh that touches back as it is touched, unconditionally, without consideration. As Gross reminds us, however, that release into movement and flesh is not without its dangers and uncertainties, especially in its potential for loss and death.

Hermione has to be released. This requires effort, activity, and discipline. Leontes is required to make that gift happen not only by accepting it at the hands of the "mankind witch" (and *all* women, who will "say anything"), but also by living up to it. He lives up to it by doing what Florizel seems to do naturally: continuously turning the statis that desire wants into the movement that love requires, for it is upon movement or action that reciprocity depends, an endlessly transforming wave that dances. Yet the statis of the stone is itself a necessary condition of pause and silence, of reawakening attention that is the precondition for acknowledgement. As Gross puts it, "the scene is a testing of the terms of wish and the gestures of mourning. It is a testing of the idea of the theatre, of the conventions of dramatic unconcealment, of the ethical and epistemological burdens of recognition" (104).

That testing is the epitome of service in Shakespeare: of the gift of service and its demands, of its resistance and its acquiescence, and of its readiness to command and its acceptance of obedience. Both king and queen come alive under the spell of obedience to their common servant: Leontes succeeds because his obedience to Paulina is unconditional – like faith – and Hermione comes alive not of her own accord but in obedience to Paulina's insistent, obsessive commands:

PAULINA   Music; awake her; strike!
    (*Music*)
    (*To* HERMIONE)
    'Tis time. Descend. Be stone no more. Approach.
    Strike all that look upon with marvel. Come,

> I'll fill your grave up. Stir. Nay, come away.
> Bequeath to death your numbness, for from him
> Dear life redeems you. (*To* LEONTES) You perceive she stirs.
> (*Hermione slowly descends*)
> Start not. Her actions shall be holy as
> You hear my spell is lawful. Do not shun her
> Until you see her die again, for then
> You kill her double. Nay, present your hand.
> When she was young, you wooed her. Now, in age,
> Is she become the suitor?   (5.3.98–109)

ENDING

After the miraculous wonder of Hermione's gift, the play threatens to disappoint by returning to a mundane world of loss and exclusion, recompense and storytelling. Paulina, shepherding her party from her house as "precious winners all", threatens to withdraw into her own emptiness and abandon the extraordinary fiction of command that she epitomised in her control over the life-given statue and its lookers-on. She returns, like the player-dramatist after the miracle of the play is done, to the position of mere servant. She differs from the figure of Rosalind/Ganymede who, having directed a theatrical performance chiefly (but not solely) to her own advantage, refuses to forgo that advantage even in the position of the epilogue, when she continues to manipulate the audience, as she did everyone else on the stage, into showing their approval for her performance.

It is difficult to receive the return of the royal, male prerogative after Paulina's magical direction with anything other than some irritation and disappointment. In an earlier reading of the play, I suggested that the reconciliation of husband and wife, male and female, does not actually take place but is destroyed by the remorseless return of the authority of male desire and the repression, once again, of the female voice.[14] I now think that reading was too harsh. The wave breaks and moves towards the shore. We return to a world in which mastery and service resume a recognisable but radically transformed shape. What we witness through the inversion of master and servant in Act Five are the transformations of desire into love and of power into service. Leontes could well have attempted to reabsorb Hermione into the pit of his desire, but that would have confirmed her death, returned her to stone. Paulina might well have kept the king in a state of gelid remorse once he had become her servant, but instead she

---

[14] Schalkwyk, "Woman's 'Verily'".

uses that power to serve him, freeing him from himself. Once again her king and master, Leontes, uses his prerogative to give Paulina what she had resolutely, through her implacable service, refused to allow him: a substitute companion, a way out of the withered and withering state of lamentation. His gift of Camillo to Paulina is a kind of compensation. It is a payment for services rendered, an acknowledgement of debts incurred and reciprocal obligations met that, unlike the miraculous restoration of Hermione, are to be taken for what they are: part of the real world; aspects of the quotidian, imbricated relationships of service, duty, and love; and an acknowledgement that, given time, love may well be comforted through substitution. That substitution is dynamic, however: what Camillo and Paulina make of it, in the autonomous movement of their own desires and love, is what counts. This return to the ordinary means that we can take the wonder that we have just visited only provisionally, or uncertainly, as a "rebirth", in Gross's words, "in which possibly everything, possibly nothing, has changed" (109).

PLAYER-SERVANTS, FINALLY

The reality of the quotidian world to which the play returns us is reinforced by the strange hurrying of the actors from the stage, characteristically drawing attention to themselves as the servants that they actually are. This action is not as obviously self-reflexive as Shakespeare's epilogues, but it does call attention to the burden that rests on the creation of the miraculous fiction that has conjoined player, poet, and audience. The gap of time created by the "two-houred traffic of [their] stage" has passed. The players, in communal service to each other and to their profession, for once bypass the audience. Instead they look forward to the demands that they will make *upon each other* in the space of their *own* dressing-room, reciprocally requiring "each one [to] demand and answer to his part" (153–4). There is no freedom beyond the demands and the gift of reciprocal community.

Bibliography

Adelman, Janet, *The Common Liar* (New Haven and London: Yale University Press, 1973).

Alpers, Paul, *What Is Pastoral?* (Chicago and London: University of Chicago Press, 1996).

Althusser, Louis, "Ideological State Apparatuses", in *Reading Capital*, edited by Ben Brewster (London: New Left Books, 1970).

Amussen, Susan Dyer, *An Ordered Society: Gender and Class in Early Modern Society* (New York: Columbia University Press, 1988).

Anonymous, *The Taming of a Shrew*, facsimile by C. Praetorius (London, 1886).

Ariès, Phillippe and Georges Duby, *A History of Private Life, Volume II, Revelations of the Medieval World*, translated by Arthur Goldhammer (Cambridge: Belknap, 1988).

Austin, J. L., *How to Do Things with Words* (Oxford: Oxford University Press, 1975).

Austin, William, *Haec Homo. Wherein the Excellency of the Creation of Woman is Described. By Way of an Essay* (London, 1637).

Bacon, Francis, "Of Love", in *Essays, Civil and Moral and The New Atlantis*, edited by Charles W. Eliot (New York: P. F. Collier and Son, 1937), pp. 26–7.

Barish, John, and Marshal Waingrow, "'Service' in *King Lear*", *Shakespeare Quarterly* 9 (1958), 347–55.

Barker, Francis, and Peter Hulme, "Nymphs and Reapers Heavily Vanish: The Discursive Con-Texts of *The Tempest*", in *Alternative Shakespeares*, edited by John Drakakis (London: Methuen, 1985), pp. 191–205.

Barry, Jonathan and Christopher Brooks, *The Middling Sort of People: Culture, Society and Politics in England, 1550–1800* (London: Macmillan, 1994).

Beier, A. L., *Masterless Men: The Vagrancy Problem in England 1560–1640* (London: Methuen, 1985).

Belsey, Catherine, "Love in Venice", in *Shakespeare and Gender*, edited by Deborah Barker and Ivo Kamps (London and New York: Verso, 1995), pp. 196–213.

Belsey, Catherine, *Desire: Love Stories in Western Culture* (Oxford: Blackwell, 1994).

Berger, Harry Jr., *Making Trifles of Terrors: Redistributing Complicities in Shakespeare* (Stanford: Stanford University Press, 1997).

Bernard, John, and D. F. McKenzie (eds.), *The Cambridge History of the Book in Britain, Volume IV: 1557–1695* (Cambridge: Cambridge University Press, 2002).

Bishop, T. G., *Shakespeare and the Theatre of Wonder* (Cambridge: Cambridge University Press, 1996).

Bloom, Alan, *Shakespeare on Love and Friendship* (Chicago: University of Chicago Press, 2000).

Brathwait, Richard, *The English Gentleman* (London, 1630).

Bristol, Michael, *Carnival and Theater: Plebeian Culture and the Structure of Authority in Renaissance England* (London and New York: Methuen, 1985).

Michael D. Bristol, "In Search of the Bear: Spatiotemporal Form and the Heterogeneity of Economies in *The Winter's Tale*," *Shakespeare Quarterly* 42 (1991), 145–67.

Brown, J. R., *Shakespeare and His Comedies* (London: Methuen, 1957).

Brown, Paul, "'This Thing of Darkness I Acknowledge Mine': *The Tempest* and the Discourse of Colonialism", in *Political Shakespeare: Essays in Cultural Materialism*, 2nd ed., edited by Jonathan Dollimore and Alan Sinfield (Ithaca and London: Cornell University Press, 1994), pp. 48–71.

Burnett, Mark Thornton, "'The Trusty Servant': A Sixteenth-Century English Emblem", *Emblematica* 6 (1992), 237–54.

Burnett, Mark Thornton, *Masters and Servants in English Renaissance Drama and Culture* (Basingstoke and New York: Palgrave Macmillan, 1997).

Burnett, Mark Thornton, *Constructing 'Monsters' in Shakespearean Drama and Early Modern Culture* (Basingstoke: Palgrave, 2002).

Burnett, Mark Thornton, "*King Lear*, Service and the Deconstruction of Protestant Idealism", in *International Shakespeare Yearbook 5*, edited by Greham Bradshaw and Tom Bishop (Aldershot: Ashgate, 2005), pp. 66–85.

Callaghan, Dympna, "The Ideology of Romantic Love: The Case of *Romeo and Juliet*", in *The Weyward Sisters: Shakespeare and Feminist Politics*, edited by Dympna Callaghan, Loraine Helms and Jyotsna Singh (Oxford: Blackwell, 1994), pp. 59–101.

Cavell, Stanley, *Disowning Knowledge in Seven Plays by Shakespeare*, updated ed. (Cambridge: Cambridge University Press, 2003).

Charney, Maurice, *Shakespeare on Love and Lust* (New York: Columbia University Press, 2001).

Chartier, Roger (ed.), *A History of Private Life, Volume III, Passions of the Renaissance*, translated by Arthur Goldhammer (Cambridge: Belknap, 2003).

Coefetteau, Nicholas, *A Table of the Passions. With Their Causes and Effects*, translated by Edward Grimerton (London, 1621).

Cognatus, Gilbertus, *Of the Office of Servavnts*, translated by Thomas Chaloner (London, 1534).

Coleridge, S. T. *Coleridge's Shakespearean Criticism*, 2 Vols., edited by T. M. Raysor (1930).

Cook, Carol, "'The Sign and Semblance of Her Honour': Reading Gender Difference in *Much Ado*", *PMLA* 101 (1986), 186–202.

Danby, John, *Elizabethan and Jacobean Poets* (London: Faber and Faber, 1952).

Darrell, Walter, *A Short Discourse of the Life of Servingmen* (London, 1578).

Davis, Lloyd, "Desire and Presence in *Romeo and Juliet*", *Shakespeare Survey* 49 (1996), 57–67.

Deakin, Simon and Frank Wilkinson, *The Law of the Labour Market: Industrialization, Employment, and Legal Evolution* (Oxford: Oxfoed University Press, 2005).

Derrida, Jacques, *Speech and Phenomena and Other Essays on Husserl's Theory of Signs*, translated by David B. Allison (Evanston: Northwestern University Press, 1973).

Derrida, Jacques, *Limited Inc.* (Evanston: Northwestern University Press, 1988).

Derrida, Jacques, "Aphorism Countertime", in *Acts of Literature*, edited by Derek Attridge (London and New York: Routledge, 1992), pp. 414–34.

Derrida, Jacques, *Given Time: I. Counterfeit Money*, translated by Peggy Kamuf (Chicago and London: Chicago University Press, 1992).

Derrida, Jacques, "Passions: 'An Oblique Offering'", in *On the Name*, edited by Thomas du Toit (Stanford: Stanford University Press, 1995), pp. 3–31.

Derrida, Jacques, *Politics of Friendship*, translated by George Collins (London and New York: Verso, 1997).

DiGangi, Mario, "Asses and Wits: The Homoerotics of Mastery in Satiric Comedy," *English Literary Renaissance* 25 (1995), 179–208.

Dod, John, and Robert Cleaver, *A Godly Forme of Household Gouernment* (London: R. Field, 1630).

Dusinberre, Juliet, *Shakespeare and the Nature of Women* (London: Methuen, 1975).

Elam, Keir, "The Fertile Eunuch: *Twelfth Night*, Early Modern Discourse, and the Fruits of Castration," *Shakespeare Quarterly* 47 (1996), 1–36.

Ebreo, Leone, *The Philosophy of Love*, translated by F. Friedeberg-Seeley and Jean H. Barnes (London: The Soncino Press, 1937).

Eliot, T. S., *Selected Essays* (London: Faber and Faber, 1934).

Elton, G. R., *England under the Tudors* (London: Methuen, 1974).

Elton, William, *'King Lear' and the Gods* (San Marino, CA: Huntington Library, 1966).

Engle, Lars, *Shakespearean Pragmatism: Market of His Time* (Chicago: University of Chicago Press, 1993).

Engle, Lars, "'I Am That I Am': Shakespeare's Sonnets and the Economy of Shame", in *Shakespeare's Sonnets: Critical Essays*, edited by James Schiffer (New York and London: Garland, 1999), pp. 185–98.

Everet, Barbara, "Romeo and Juliet: The Nurse's Story", *Critical Quarterly* 14 (1972), 129–39.

Evett, David, "'Surprising Confrontations': Ideologies of Service in Shakespeare's England", *Renaissance Papers 1990* (1990), 67–78.

Evett, David, *Discourses of Service in Shakespeare's England* (Basingstoke and New York: Palgrave Macmillan, 2005).

Fernie, Ewan, "Shakespeare and the Prospect of Presentism", *Shakespeare Survey* 58 (2005), 169–84.

Fernie, Ewan, *Shame in Shakspeare* (London and New York: Routledge, 2002).

Fernie, Ewan (ed.), *Spiritual Shakespeares* (London and New York: Routledge, 2005).

Ferrand, James, *Erotomania, or A Treatise Discoursing of the Essence, Causes, and Syptoms, Prognosticks, and Cure of Love, or Erotique Melancholy*, 2nd ed. (London, 1645).

Ficino, Marsilio, *Marsilio Ficino's Commantary on Plato's Symposium*, translated by Reynold Jayne Sears (Columbia: University of Missouri Press, 1944).

Fineman, Joel, *Shakespeare's Perjured Eye: The Invention of Poetic Subjectivity in the Sonnets* (Berkeley, Los Angeles and London: University of California Press, 1986).

Fitz, Linda T., "Egyptian Queens and Male Reviewers: Sexist Attitudes in Antony and Cleopatra Criticism", *Shakespeare Quarterly* 28 (Summer 1977), 297–316.

Fletcher, John, and Anthony Stevenson (eds.), *Order and Disorder in Early Modern England* (Cambridge: Cambridge University Press, 1985).

Fosset, Thomas, *The Seruants Dutie or the Calling and Condition of Seruants* (London: G. Eld, 1613).

Fraser, Antonia, *The Weaker Vessel: Women's Lot in Seventeenth-Century England* (London: Phoenix Press, 2002).

French, Marilyn, *Shakespeare's Division of Experience* (London, 1982).

French, Marilyn, "Antony and Cleopatra", in *Antony and Cleopatra: Contemporary Critical Essays*, edited by John Drakakis (London: Macmillan, 1994), pp. 262–76.

Freud, Sigmund, "The Uncanny", in *Collected Papers*, IV, translated by Joan Riviere (London: Hogarth Press, 1948).

Freud, Sigmund, *Civilization and Its Discontents*, edited by James Strachey, translated by Joan Riviere (London: The Hogarth Press, 1973).

Friedman, Alice T., *House and Household in Elizabethan England: Wollaton Hall and the Willoughby Family* (Chicago: University of Chicago Press, 1989).

Fuchs, Barbara, "Conquering Islands: Contextualizing *The Tempest*", *Shakespeare Quarterly* 48 (1997), 45–62.

Garber, Marjorie, *Shakespeare after All* (New York: Pantheon, 2005).

Gibson, John, "Between Truth and Triviality", *British Journal of Aesthetics* 43 (2003), 224–237.

Girouard, Mark, *Life in the English Country House: A Social and Architechtural History* (New Haven: Yale University Press, 1978).

Goldberg, Jonathan, "Romeo and Juliet's Open Rs", in *Romeo and Juliet: Contemporary Essays*, edited by R. S. White (Basingstoke: Palgrave, 2001), pp. 194–211.

Goldberg, P. J. P., *Women, Work, and Life Cycle in a Medieval Economy: Women in York and Yorkshire c. 1300–1520* (Oxford: Clarendon Press, 1992).

Gouge, William, *Of Domesticall Dvties: Eight Treatises* (London, 1622).

Gournay, Marie le Jars de, *Preface to the "Essays" of Michel de Montaigne by his Adoptive Daughter*, translated and edited by Richard Hillman and Colette Quesnel (Tempe, Arizona: Medieval and Renaissance Texts and Studies, 1998).

Grady, Hugh, *Shakespeare, Machiavelli, and Montaigne: Power and Subjectivity from Richard II to Hamlet* (Oxford: Oxford University Press, 2002).

Grady, Hugh, and Terence Hawkes, *Presentist Shakespeares* (London and New York: Routledge, 2007).

Greenblatt, Stephen, "Friction and Fiction", in *Shakespearean Negotiations: The Circulation of Social Energy in Renaissance England* (Berkeley and Los Angeles: University of California Press, 1988), pp. 66–93.

Greenblatt, Stephen, "Resonance and Wonder", in *Learning to Curse* (London: Routledge, 1990), pp. 161–83.

Greenblatt, Stephen, *Will in the World: How Shakespeare Became Shakespeare* (London: Jonathan Cape, 2005).

Greene, John, *A Refutation of the Apology for Actors* (London, 1615).

Greene, Thomas M., "Pitiful Thrivers: Failed Husbandry in the Sonnets", in *Shakespeare and the Question of Theory*, edited by Patricia Parker and Geoffrey Hartmann (London and New York: Methuen, 1985), pp. 230–44.

Gross, Kenneth, *The Dream of the Moving Statue* (Ithaca: Cornell University Press, 1992).

Gross, Kenneth, "Slander and Scepticism in *Othello*", *English Literary History* 56 (Winter 1989), 819–52.

Guazzo, Stefano, *The Ciuile Conuersation of M. Stephen Guazzo, Translated Out of French by M. Pettie* (London, 1586).

Gurr, Andrew, *The Shakespearean Stage 1574–1642*, 3rd ed. (Cambridge: Cambridge University Press, 1992).

Harman, T., *A Caveat or Warening for Common Cvrsetors, Vulgarly Called Beggars* (London, 1567).

Harrison, William, *The Description of England*, edited by George Edelen (Ithaca: Cornell University Press for the Folger Shakespeare Library, 1968).

Hawkes, Terence, *Shakespeare's Talking Animals: Language and Drama in Society* (London: Edward Arnold, 1975).

Hawkes, Terence, *Shakespeare in the Present* (London: Routledge, 2002).

Hay, Douglas, "Master and Servant in England: Using the Law in the Eighteenth and Nineteenth Centuries", in *Private Law and Social Inequality in the Industrial Age: Comparing Legal Cultures in Britain, France, Germany, and the United States*, edited by Willibald Steinmetz (Oxford: Oxford University Press, 2000), pp. 227–64.

Hay, Douglas, and Paul Craven, *Masters, Servants, and Magistrates in Britain and the Empire, 1562–1955* (Chapel Hill and London: University of North Carolina Press, 2004).

Hegel, G. W. F., *The Phenomenology of Mind*, translated by J. B. Baillie (New York: Harper Torchbooks, 1967).

Hegel, Georg W. F., *Phenomenology of Spirit*, translated by A. V. Miller (Oxford: Oxford University Press, 1977).

Heinemann, Margot, "'Let Rome in Tiber Melt': Order and Disorder in *Antony and Cleopatra*", in *Antony and Cleopatra: Contemporary Critical Essays*, edited by John Drakakis (London: Macmillan, 1994), pp. 166–81.

Hobsbawm, Eric, *Industry and Empire* (Harmondsworth: Penguin, 1968).

Honan, Park, *Shakespeare: A Life* (Oxford: Oxford University Press, 1998).

Houlbrooke, Ralph, *The English Family: 1450–1700* (London: Longman, 1984).

Horowitz, Maryanne Cline, "Marie de Gournay, Editor of the Essais of Michel de Montaigne: A Case-Study in Mentor-Protegee Friendship", *Sixteenth Century Journal*, 17 (1986), 271–84.

Howard, Jean, "Renaissance Antitheatricality and the Politics of Gender and Rank in *Much Ado about Nothing*", in *Shakespeare Reproduced*, edited by Jean E. Howard and Marion F. O'Connor (New York: Routledge, 1987), pp. 163–87.

Hulme, Peter, *Colonial Encounters: Europe and the Native Caribbean, 1492–1796* (London: Methuen, 1986).

Hunt, Maurice, "Slavery, English Servitude, and *The Comedy of Errors*", *ELR* 27 (1997), 31–56.

Hunt, Maurice, "'Bearing Hence': Shakespeare's *The Winter's Tale*", *SEL* 44 (2004), 333–346

Hunt, Maurice, *Shakespeare's Religious Allusiveness: Its Play and Tolerance* (Alderhsot: Ashgate, 2004).

Hutton, Ronald, *The Rise and Fall of Merry England* (Oxford: Oxford University Press, 1994).

Ingram, William, *The Business of Playing: The Beginnings of the Adult Professional Theater in Elizabethan London* (Ithaca: Cornell University Press, 1992).

Ingram, William, "The Economics of Playing", in *A Companion to Shakespeare*, edited by David Scott Kastan (Oxford: Blackwell, 1999), pp. 313–27.

International Shakespearean Yearbook, edited by Graham Bradshaw, Tom Bishop, and Michael Neill (Aldershot: Ashgate, 2005).

I. M., *A Health to the Gentlemanly Profession of Seruingmen* (London, 1598).

Jackson, Ken, "'One Wish' or the Possibility of the Impossible: Derrida, the Gift, and *Timon of Athens*", *Shakespeare Quarterly* 52 (2001), 34–66.

Jardine, Lisa, *Still Harping on Daughters: Women and Drama in the Age of Shakespeare* (Brighton: Harvester, 1983).

Jardine, Lisa, *Reading Shakespeare Historically* (London and New York: Routledge, 1996).

Jonathan Dollimore, "*King Lear* (c. 1605–6) and Essential Humanism", in *Radical Tragedy: Religion, Ideology and Power in the Drama of Shakespeare and His Contemporaries* (Brighton: Harvester, 1984), pp. 189–203.

Joubert, Elsa, *The Long Journey of Poppie Nongena* (Johannesburg: Jonathan Ball, 1980).

Kantorowicz, Ernst, *The King's Two Bodies: A Study in Medieval Political Theology* (Princeton: Princeton University Press, 1957).

Kermode, Frank, "Introduction", in *The Tempest*, edited by Frank Kermode (London: Methuen, 1954), pp. xxiv–lix.

Kernan, Alvin, *Shakespeare, the King's Playwright: Theater in the Stuart Court, 1603–1613* (New Haven: Yale University Press, 1995).

Korda, Natasha, *Shakespeare's Domestic Economies: Gender and Property in Early Modern England* (Philadelphia: University of Pennsylvania Press, 2002).

Korda, Natasha, "Labours Lost: Women's Work and Early Modern Theatrical Commerce", in *From Script to Stage in Early Modern England*, edited by Peter

Holland and Stephen Orgel (Basingstoke: Macmillan Palgrave, 2004), pp. 195–230.

Krieger, Eliot, *A Marxist Study of Shakespeare's Comedies* (Totown: Barnes and Noble, 1979)

Kristeva, Julia, "'*Romeo and Juliet*: Love-Hatred in the Couple'", in *Shakespearean Tragedy*, edited by John Drakakis (Harlow, Essex: Longman, 1992), pp. 296–315.

Kussmaul, Ann, *Servants and Husbandry in Early Modern England* (Cambridge: Cambridge University Press, 1981).

Lamb, Mary Ellen, "Tracing a Heterosexual Erotics of Service in *Twelfth Night* and the Autobiographical Writings of Thomas Whythorne and Anne Clifford", *Criticism* 40 (1998), 1–25.

Lamming, George, *The Pleasures of Exile* (London: Allison & Busby, 1984).

Laslett, Peter, *The World We Have Lost*, 3rd ed. (New York: Charles Scribner's Sons, 1984).

Laslett, Peter, and Richard Wall (eds.), *Household and Family in Past Time*, (Cambridge: Cambridge University Press, 1972).

Legatt, Alexander, *Shakespeare's Comedy of Love* (London: Methuen, 1974).

Leavis, F. R., "Diabolic Intellect and the Noble Hero . . . or The Sentimentalist's Othello", in *The Common Pursuit* (Harmondsworth: Penguin, 1976).

Leinwand, Theodore, *Theatre, Finance and Society in Early Modern England* (Cambridge: Cambridge University Press, 1999).

Lindley, David, *Shakespeare and Music* (London: Arden, 2006).

Loomba, Ania, *Gender, Race, Renaissance Drama* (Manchester: Manchester University Press, 1989).

Lopez, Jeremy, *Theatrical Convention and Audience Response in Early Modern Drama* (Cambridge: Cambridge University Press, 2003).

Macfarlane, Alan, *Marriage and Love in England: Modes of Reproduction 1300–1840* (Oxford: Blackwell, 1986).

Machiavelli, Niccolo, *The Prince*, translated by Peter Bondanell (New York: Oxford University Press, 2005).

Magnusson, Lynne, *Shakespeare and Social Dialogue* (Cambridge: Cambridge University Press, 1999).

Malcomson, Christina, "'What You Will': Social Mobility and Gender in *Twelfth Night*", in *The Matter of Difference*, edited by Valerie Wayne (Ithaca: Cornell University Press, 1991).

Marlowe, Christopher, *Doctor Faustus*, in *English Renaissance Drama*, edited by Lars Engle, David Bevington, and Katherine Eisaman Maus (New York and London: W.W. Norton, 2002).

Marotti, Arthur F., "'Love is not Love': Elizabethan Sonnet Sequences and the Social Order", *English Literary History* 49 (1982), 396–428.

Marx, Karl, and Friedrich Engels, *Manifesto of the Communist Party* (Moscow: Foreign Languages Publishing House, 1951).

Maus, Katherine Eisamen, *Inwardness and Theater in the English Renaissance* (Chicago and London: University of Chicago Press, 1995).

Mauss, Marcel, *The Gift: The Form and Reason for Exchange in Archaic Societies*, translated by W. D. Halls (New York: W.W. Norton, 2000).

McMillin, Scott, "The Sharer and his Boy: Rehearsing Shakespeare's Women", in *From Script to Stage in Early Modern England*, edited by Peter Holland and Stephen Orgel (Basingstoke: Palgrave Macmillan, 2004), pp. 231–45.

Mertes, Kate, *The English Noble Household 1250–1600* (Oxford: Blackwell, 1988).

Montaigne, Michel de, *The Essays of Montaigne*, edited by J. I. M. Stewart, translated by John Florio (New York: The Modern Library, n.d.).

Milton, John, *The Doctrine and Discipline of Divorce* (London, 1644).

Moisan, Thomas, "'Knock Me Here Soundly': Comic Misprision and Class Consciousness in Shakespeare", *Shakespeare Quarterly* 42 (1991), 276–90.

Montrose, Louis Adrian, "'The Place of a Brother' in *As You Like It*: Social Process and Comic Form", *Shakespeare Quarterly* 32 (1981), 28–54.

Neill, Michael, *Putting History to the Question: Power, Politics and Society in English Renaissance Drama* (New York: Columbia University Press, 2000).

Michael Neill, "'He that thou knowest thine': Friendship and Service in *Hamlet*," in *A Companion to Shakespeare's Works: Volume 1, The Tragedies*, edited by Richard Dutton and Jean Howard (Malden and Oxford: Blackwell, 2003), 319–38.

Neill, Michael, "'His Master's Ass': Slavery, Service, and Subordination in *Othello*", in *Shakespeare in the Mediterranean*, edited by Stanley Wells and Tom Clayton (Newark: University of Delaware Press, 2003).

Neill, Michael, *"Servile Ministers": Othello, King Lear and the Sacralization of Service* (Vancouver: Lonsdale Press, 2004).

Neill, Michael, "'A Woman's Service': Gender, Subordination, and the Erotics of Rank in the Drama of Shakespeare and His Contemporaries", *The Shakespearean International Yearbook* 5 (2005), 127–46.

Newman, Karin, *Fashioning Femininity and English Renaissance Drama* (Chicago and London: University of Chicago Press, 1991).

Orgel, Stephen, *Impersonations: The Performance of Gender in Shakespeare's England* (Cambridge: Cambridge University Press, 1996).

Paster, Gail Kern, *Humoring the Body* (Chicago and London: University of Chicago Press, 2005).

Perkins, William, *Christian Oeconomy* (London, 1590).

Petrarch, Francis, *Petrach's Secret or the Soul's Conflict with Passion: Three Dialogues between Himself and S. Augustine*, translated by William H. Draper (London: Chaotto and Windus, 1911).

Pollard, Tanya, (ed.) *Shakespeare's Theatre: A Sourcebook* (Oxford: Blackwell, 2004).

Pugliatti, Paola, *Beggary and Theatre in Early Modern England* (Aldershot: Ashgate, 2003).

Rackin, Phyllis, "Shakespeare's Boy Cleopatra, the Decorum of Nature, and the Golden World of Poetry", *PMLA* (March 1972), 201–12.

Rackin, Phyllis, *Staging History: Shakespeare's English Chronicles* (Ithaca: Cornell University Press, 1990).

Reynolds, Edward, *A Treatise of the Passions and Faculties of the Soul of Man* (London, 1640).

Richardson, R. C., "Social Engineering in Early Modern England: Masters, Servants, and the Godly Discipline", *Clio* 33 (Winter 2004), 163–87.

Robbins, Bruce, *The Servant's Hand* (New York: Columbia University Press, 1986).

Roberts, Sasha, "Reading Shakespeare's Tragedies of Love: *Romeo and Juliet, Othello,* and *Antony and Cleopatra* in Early Modern England", in *A Companion to Shakespeare's Works: Vol. 1 The Tragedies,* edited by Richard Dutton and Jean E. Howard (Oxford: Blackwell, 2003), pp. 108–33.

Rose, M. B., *The Expense of Spirit: Love and Sexuality in English Renaissance Drama* (Ithaca, N.J.: Cornell University Press, 1988).

Roe, John, *Shakespeare and Machiavelli* (Cambridge: D. S. Brewer, 2002).

Rowe, Katherine, Gail Kern Paster, and Mary Floyd-Watson (eds.), *Reading the Early Modern Passions: Essays in the Cultural History of Emotion* (Philadelphia: University of Pennsylvania Press, 2005).

Rubin, Miri, *The Hollow Crown: A History of Britain in the Late Middle Ages* (Harmondsworth: Penguin, 2005).

Rutter, Carol Chillington, *Enter the Body: Women and Representation on Shakespeare's Stage* (London and New York: Methuen, 2001).

Ryan, Kiernan, "*Romeo and Juliet*: The Language of Tragedy", in *The Taming of the Text: Exploration in Language, Literature and Culture,* edited by Willie van Peer (The Hague: Ministry of Housing and Physical Planning, Information Department, 1988), pp. 106–21.

Schalkwyk, David, "'A Woman's "Verily" Is as Potent as a Lord's': Woman, Word, and Witchcraft in *The Winter's Tale*", *English Literary Renaissance* 22 (Spring 1992), 242–72.

Schalkwyk, David, *Speech and Performance in Shakespeare's Sonnets and Plays* (Cambridge: Cambridge University Press, 2002).

Schalkwyk, David, *Literature and the Touch of the Real* (Newark: University of Delaware Press, 2004).

Schalkwyk, David, "Love and Service in *The Taming of the Shrew* and *All's Well That Ends Well*", in *International Shakespearean Yearbook,* edited by Graham Bradshaw, Tom Bishop, and Michael Neill (Aldershot, Hants: Ashgate, 2005).

Schoenbaum, Samuel, *William Shakespeare: A Compact Documentary Life* (Oxford: Clarendon Press, 1977).

Searle, John R., *Speech Acts: An Essay in the Philosophy of Language* (Cambridge: Cambridge University Press, 1969).

Sedgewick, Eve Kosofsy, *Between Men: English Literature and Male Homosexual Desire* (New York: Columbia University Press, 1985).

Shakespeare, William, "Introduction", in *The Two Gentlemen of Verona,* edited by Clifford Leech (London: Methuen, 1972), pp. xiii–lxxv.

Shakespeare, William, *Shakespeare's Sonnets,* edited by Stephen Booth (New Haven and London: Yale University Press, 1978).

Shakespeare, William, "Introduction", in *The Taming of the Shrew,* edited by Ann Thompson (Cambridge: Cambridge University Press, 1984).

Shannon, Laurie, *Sovereign Amity: Figures of Friendship in Shakespearean Contexts* (Chicago: University of Chicago Press, 2002).

Shaw, George Bernard, *Three Plays for Puritans* (London: Faber and Faber, 1930).

Shklovsky, V., "'Art as Technique'", in *Russian Formalist Criticism: Four Essays*, edited by Lee T. Lemon (Lincoln: University of Nebraska Press, 1965), pp. 3–98.

Shuger, Deborah Kuller, *Habits of Thought in the English Renaissance: Religion, Politics, and the Dominant Culture* (Toronto: University of Toronto Press, 1997).

Sinfield, Alan, "How to Read *The Merchant of Venice* without Being Heterosexist", in *Alternative Shakespeares 2*, edited by Terence Hawkes (London and New York: Routledge, 1996), pp. 122–39.

Singer, Irving, *The Nature of Love 1: Plato to Luther*, 2nd ed. (Chicago and London: Chicago University Press, 1984).

Singer, Irving, *The Nature of Love 2: Courtly and Romantic*, 2nd ed. (Chicago: Chicago University Press, 1984).

Singh, Jyotsna, "Renaissance Anti-Theatricality, Anti-Feminsim, and Shakespeare's *Antony and Cleopatra*", *Renaissance Drama* 20 (1989), 99–119.

Skura, Meredith Anne, "Discourse and the Individual: The Case of Colonialism in *The Tempest*", *Shakespeare Quarterly* 40 (1989), 42–69.

Skura, Meredith Anne, *Shakespeare the Actor and the Purpose of Playing* (Chicago and London: University of Chicago Press, 1993).

Smith, Bruce R., *Homosexual Desire in Shakespeare's England: A Cultural Poetics* (Chicago and London: University of Chicago Press, 1991).

Southern, R. W., *The Making of the Middle Ages* (London: Hutchinson, 1953).

Spivack, Bernard, *Shakespeare and the Allegory of Evil* (New York: Columbia University Press, 1958).

Starkey, David, *The English Court: From the Wars of the Roses to the Civil War* (London: Longman, 1987).

Stone, Lawrence, *The Crisis of the Aristocracy 1558–1641* (Oxford: Clarendon Press, 1965).

Stone, Lawrence, *The Family, Sex and Marriage in England, 1500–1800* (London: Weidenfeld and Nicolson, 1977).

Strachey, William, "A True Repertory of the Wreck and Redemption of Sir Thomas Gates, Knight, Upon and from the Islands of the Bermudas", in *Haklytus Posthumus or Purchas His Pilgrimes (1625)* (Glasgow: James MacLehose and Sons, 1906), XIX pp. 5–72.

Strier, Richard, "Faithful Servants: Shakespeare's Praise of Disobedience", in *The Historical Renaissance: New Essays in Tudor Literature and Culture*, edited by Heather Dubrow and Richard Strier (Chicago and London: University of Chicago Press, 1988), pp. 104–33.

Tacitus, *The Annals of Imperial Rome*, translated by M. Grant (Harmondsworth: Penguin, 1964).

Tasso, Torquato, *The Householders Philosophie* (London: Thomas Hacket, 1588).

Thompson, E. P., *The Poverty of Theory and Other Essays* (London: Merlin, 1978).

Tillyard, E. M. W., *The Elizabethan World Picture* (London: Chatto and Windus, 1943).

Todorov, Tzvetan, *The Imperfect Garden: The Legacy of Humanism*, translated by Carol Cosman (Princeton and Oxford: Princeton University Press, 2002).

Traub, Valerie, "The Homoerotics of Shakespearean Comedy", in *Shakespeare: An Anthology of Criticism and Theory 1945–2000*, edited by Russ McDonald (Oxford: Blackwell, 2004), pp. 704–26.

Turner, Henry S., "The Problem of the More-Than-One: Friendship, Calculation, and Political Association in *The Merchant of Venice*", *Shakespeare Quarterly* 57 (2006), 412–42.

Vendler, Helen, *The Art of Shakespeare's Sonnets* (Cambridge and London: Harvard University Press, 1997).

Vickers, Brian, *Shakespeare, Co-Author* (Oxford: Oxford University Press, 2002).

Vickers, Nancy, "Diana Described: Scattered Woman and Scattered Rhyme", *Critical Inquiry* VIII (1981), 265–79.

Vitkus, Daniel, "'Meaner Minsiters': Mastery, Bondage, and Theatrical Labour in *The Tempest*", in *A Companion to Shakespeare's Works, Vol. 4: The Poems, Problem Comedies, Late Plays*, edited by Richard Dutten and Jean E. Howard (Oxford: Blackwell, 2003), pp. 408–26.

Wall, Wendy, *Staging Domesticity: Household Work and English Identity in Early Modern Drama* (Cambridge: Cambridge University Press, 2002).

Webster, John, *The Duchess of Malfi*, in *English Renaissance Drama: A Norton Anthology*, edited by Lars Engle, David Bevington, and Katherine Eisamen Maus (London and New York: W.W. Norton, 2002).

Weil, Judith, *Service and Dependency in Shakespeare's Plays* (Cambridge: Cambridge University Press, 2005).

Weimann, Robert, *Shakespeare and the Popular Tradition in the Theater: Studies in the Social Dimension of Dramatic Form and Function*, edited by Robert Schwartz (Baltimore: Johns Hopkins University Press, 1987).

Weimann, Robert, "Bifold Authority in Shakespeare's Theater", *Shakespeare Quarterly* 39 (1988), 401–17.

Weimann, Robert, "Shakespeare (De)Canonized: Conflicting Uses of 'Authority' and 'Representation,'" *New Literary History*, 20 (1988), 65–81.

Weimann, Robert, "Textual Authority and Performative Agency: The Uses of Disguise in Shakespeare's Theater", *New Literary History* 25 (1994), 789–808.

Weimann, Robert, "Performance-Game and Representation in *Richard III*", in *Textual and Theatrical Shakespeare: Questions of Evidence*, edited by Edward Pechter (Iowa City: University of Iowa Press, 1996).

Weimann, Robert, *Author's Pen and Actor's Voice* (Cambridge: Cambridge University Press, 2000).

Whittier, Gayle, "The Sonnet's Body and the Body Sonnetized in *Romeo and Juliet*", *Shakespeare Quarterly* 40 (Spring 1989), 27–41.

Whythorne, Thomas, *The Autobiography of Thomas Whythorne*, edited by James M. Osborne (Oxford: Oxford University Press, 1962).

William Carroll, *Fat King and Lean Beggar. The Representation of Poverty in Early Modern England* (Ithaca: Cornell University Press, 1994).

Williams, Raymond, *Marxism and Literature* (Oxford: Oxford University Press, 1977).

Williams, Raymond, *The Country and the City* (London: Hogarth Press, 1985).

Wilson, Richard, "Like the Old Robin Hood; *As You Like It* and the Enclosure Riots", in *Will Power* (Hemel Hempstead: Harverster Wheatsheaf, 1993), pp. 63–82.

Wilson, Richard, *Will Power: Essays on Shakespearean Authority* (Detroit: Wayne State University Press, 1993).

Wittgenstein, Ludwig, *Philosophical Investigations*, edited and translated by G. E. M. Anscombe (Oxford: Blackwell, 1953).

Wittgenstein, Ludwig, *Lectures and Conversation on Aesthetics, Psychology, and Religious Belief*, edited by C. Barrett (Oxford: Blackwell, 1966).

Wittgenstein, Ludwig, *The Blue and Brown Books* (Oxford: Blackwell, 1969).

Wittgenstein, Ludwig, *On Certainty*, edited by G. E. M. Anscombe and G. H. von Wright, translated by Denis Paul and G. E. M. Anscombe (Oxford: Blackwell, 1979).

Wittgenstein, Ludwig, *Remarks on the Philosophy of Psychology Vol. 2*, edited by G. H. von Wright and H. Nyman, translated by C. J. Luckhardt and M. A. E. Aue (Oxford: Blackwell, 1980).

Wofford, Susanne, "'To You I Give Myself for I Am Yours': Erotic Performance and Theatrical Performatives in *As You Like It*", in *Shakespeare Reread: The Texts in New Contexts*, edited by Russ McDonald (Ithaca: Cornell University Press, 1994), pp. 147–69.

Wright, Thomas, *The Passions of the Minde in General* (London, 1640).

Wrightson, Keith, "'Sorts of People' in Tudor and Stuart England", in *The Middling Sort of People: Culture, Society and Politics in England, 1550–1800*, edited by Jonathan Barry and Christopher Brooks (London: Macmillan, 1994), pp. 28–51.

Wrightson, Keith, "The Politics of the Parish in Early Modern England," in *The Experience of Authority in Early Modern England*, edited by Paul Griffiths, Adam Fox and Steve Hindle (London: Macmillan, 1996), pp. 10–46.

Wrightson, Keith, *Earthly Necessities: Economic Lives in Early Modern Britain, 1470–1750* (Harmondsworth: Penguin, 2002).

Wrightson, Keith, *English Society 1580–1680* (London and New York: Routledge, 2003).

Index